"THE HIGHER CHRISTIAN LIFE"

SOURCES FOR THE STUDY OF THE HOLINESS, PENTECOSTAL, AND KESWICK MOVEMENTS

*A forty-eight-volume
facsimile series reprinting
extremely rare documents for the study of
nineteenth-century religious and social history,
the rise of feminism, and the history of the
Pentecostal and Charismatic movements*

Edited by
Donald W. Dayton
Northern Baptist Theological Seminary

Advisory Editors
D. William Faupel, *Asbury Theological Seminary*
Cecil M. Robeck, Jr., *Fuller Theological Seminary*
Gerald T. Sheppard, *Union Theological Seminary*

A GARLAND SERIES

SEVEN
"JESUS ONLY"
TRACTS

with a Preface by
Donald W. Dayton
Northern Baptist
Theological Seminary

Garland Publishing, Inc.
New York & London
1985

BT
101
.S53
1985

For a complete list of the titles in this series
see the final pages of this volume.

Library of Congress Cataloging in Publication Data
Main entry under title:

SEVEN "JESUS ONLY" TRACTS.

("The Higher Christian life")
Reprint of 7 works; 2 originally published
in 1919 and 1921.
Contents: The doctrine of the new birth, or, The
perfect way to eternal life / Andrew D. Urshan—The
Almighty God in the Lord Jesus Christ / Andrew D. Urshan
—The revelation of Jesus Christ / Frank J. Ewart—[etc.]
1. God—Addresses, essays, lectures.   2. Jesus Christ
—Person and offices—Addresses, essays, lectures.
I. Urshan, Andrew D.   II. Ewart, Frank J. Revelation of
Jesus Christ. 1985.   III. Haywood, G. T. (Garfield
Thomas). Selections. 1985.   IV. Series.
BT101.S53 1985   231'.044   84-25856
ISBN 0-8240-6414-3 (alk. paper)

The volumes in this series are printed on
acid-free, 250-year-life paper.

Printed in the United States of America

CONTENTS

PREFACE

One of the most intriguing and at the same time least well studied and understood branches of the Pentecostal movement is popularly called "Jesus Only" or perhaps better "Oneness" Pentecostalism. This wing of Pentecostalism emerged in a controversy over the proper formula to be used in water baptism of new converts. The question emerged casually in a sermon in April 1913 at the World Wide Pentecostal Camp Meeting in Los Angeles when Canadian Robert E. McAlister (1880–1953; originally a Presbyterian who became prominent in the founding of the Pentecostal Assemblies of Canada) commented before a baptismal service that the New Testament book of Acts seemed to indicate that the early church baptized "in the name of Jesus" rather than in the name of the trinity: Father, Son, and Holy Spirit.

This troubled a John G. Scheppe who in an all-night prayer vigil that night claimed to have received a revelation that all true believers should be rebaptized "in the name of Jesus" only. This suggestion gradually became the conviction of a sizable group of Pentecostal leaders with the result that this "new issue" split the emerging Assemblies of God. As the logic of this new position was worked out, it led to a rejection of the classically Christian doctrine of the Trinity in favor of what has been called a "unitarianism of the second person" in which the whole Godhead was understood to have found expression in Jesus. The movement has largely adopted the label "apostolic" to express its claim to have rediscovered the genuine apostolic Christianity that predates the "apostasy" of mainstream Christianity and its "fall" into a form of polytheism.

The emphasis on the baptismal formula lifted the importance

vii

of baptism in this wing of Pentecostalism in such a way as to lead to a very high-powered initiatory experience that included not only conversion but also "water baptism" and "spirit baptism" with speaking in tongues as essential elements. The movement also caused friction by adopting wine for use in communion services, a violation of typical Pentecostal taboos on alcohol, and by strict adherence to mores of dress and behavior. As a result Oneness Pentecostalism was largely repudiated by the rest of the movement as a heresy and has lived in isolation not only from the rest of the Christian tradition but even from the rest of Pentecostalism. In spite of this isolation, the movement has grown, penetrating in many places in the United States the black community and in Colombia becoming the largest Protestant body in that South American country.

This volume reprints seven tracts illustrating the teachings and diversity of Oneness Pentecostalism. Andrew bar David Urshan (1884–1967) was born in Persia and attended a Presbyterian training college there before immigrating to the United States to settle in Chicago to work at odd jobs. In these years of menial labor and spiritual struggle he fell under the influence of the holiness movement and in 1908 was led by an acquaintance into the Pentecostal experience. When they refused to renounce their new-found Pentecostalism, Urshan and the Persian group he led were forced out of Moody Church in Chicago into association with emerging Pentecostal groups, especially the Durham Mission (where he was ordained in 1910) and the Stone Church. Urshan was present at the World Wide Pentecostal Camp Meeting in 1913 and began to rebaptize in the name of Jesus during missionary work in Russia about 1916. Upon his return to the United States his Oneness convictions gradually became more explicit and he was eventually forced out of the Assemblies of God into various antecedents of the United Pentecostal Church, International, the largest of the Oneness Pentecostal groups in the United States, which he served as pastor and international evangelist until his death. Urshan is represented in this volume by two tracts, *The Doctrine of the New Birth* (1921), illustrating Oneness teachings on Christian initiation, and *The Almighty God in the Lord Jesus Christ* (1919), illustrating Oneness doctrines and opposition to trinitarian teaching.

Preface

Frank J. Ewart (1876–?) was an Australian Baptist who immigrated to Canada in 1903 and fell under the influence of Pentecostalism in Portland, Oregon. Forced to resign his pastorate, he moved to Los Angeles to assist William Durham and to take over that church after Durham's death in 1912. Ewart was in attendance at the 1913 camp meeting that saw the emergence of the "new issue" and soon became a major leader, historian and theologian of the new movement, editing as well *Meat in Due Season*, its major journal. Ewart is represented in this volume by an early undated tract, *The Revelation of Jesus Christ*, reprinting articles that first appeared in *The Pentecostal Defender*.

Oneness Pentecostalism took root especially in the black community in the United States, and this aspect of the movement is represented in this volume through the writings of Bishop Garfield Thomas Haywood (1880–1931). Haywood was born in Greencastle, Indiana, and active as a youth in both black Methodist and Baptist churches. After coming into contact with Pentecostalism in 1909 he opened a mission in Indianapolis, which became, after he accepted Oneness teachings in 1915, the major center of the Pentecostal Assemblies of the World. Haywood was known as pastor, evangelist, gospel-song writer, editor, and author. He is represented in this volume by four undated pamphlets that collected his writings and sermons on topics related to the Oneness tradition. Much of the material is reprinted from his monthly paper, *Voice in the Wilderness*.

Donald W. Dayton
Northern Baptist
Theological Seminary

... The ...

Doctrine of the New Birth

.... or ....

The Perfect Way to Eternal Life

As taught by our Lord Himself, proclaimed by
His Apostles, confirmed by the Holy
Spirit and foreshadowed
by the Law and the Prophets.

BY ANDREW D. URSHAN
Cochrane, Wis., U. S. A.

Printed by Witness of God, Publishers
Cochrane, Wis., U. S. A.
1921

Contents

INTRODUCTION.

The need of a book LIKE THIS, on the infallible and unchangeable.doctrine of our Lord is most important; especially in these days of world-wide Apostasy. Just as the worldly commercialists and politicians are continually busy making inventions and machinery to make money and satisfy their mad selfish desires, even so are the modern nominal Christians doing, busy inventing new man-made ways of salvation; they are not only revolutionizing the traditions of their mistaken Elders, but are making many new and strange doctrines under pretense of the Name of Christ. The truth in this book on "The New Birth" is so plain and strictly scriptural no one need to fear, but believe it and we know God's spirit is in the truth of the following pages. Therefore, there will be conviction and stirring of minds in reading it and there will also be joy to those who are sincerely true and earnestly searching for the truth as the blessed Christ and His Apostles taught.

We prayerfully send this book forth in the Name of Him who said, "Verily, verily I say unto thee, except a man be born (come forth) of WATER and of the SPIRIT, he cannot enter into the kingdom of God" "Heaven and Earth shall pass away; but my words shall not pass away." John 3:3-5. with Mark 13:3. Amen.

A. D. URSHAN.

Preface.

Is it necessary to preach the doctrine of the new birth?

Ans. Yes! indeed, because it is the doctrine of our Lord and John the Apostle said, "He that abideth not in the doctrine of Jesus Christ hath not God." In other words, he is an infidel. It is therefore not only necessary to preach that doctrine; but also to be received and to be permanent in it. Apostle Paul wrote to Timothy, "I charge thee therefore before God, and the Lord Jesus—preach the word—exhort with all long suffering and doctrine." Again, "Take heed unto thyself and unto the doctrine, contnue in them: (Why?) for in doing this thou shalt both save thyself, and them that hear thee ." 2 Tim. 4:1-2. 1 Tim. 4:16 etc. Of the early church it is said, "They (the saints) continued steadfastly in the Apostle's doctrine." See Acts 2:42,5:28. The doctrine is the meat which makes us strong men and women of God. To get saved and yet be ignorant of the sound doctrne; it is to be in a place of danger and liable to deception. The reason why the false prophets succeed among God's children is, because God's children are kept ignorant of the doctrine of their Lord. To this and we are sending forth the foregoing pages in Jesus Precious Name on the docrine of he new birth as taught by our own Lord and His Holy Apostles. Blessed is every one who will do His will that he may know of His doctrine. Amen.   A. D. URSHAN.

CHAPTER I

Seeing and Entering the Kingdom of God.

HERE has always been much of religious disputation among Christians regarding the "New Birth" doctrine in all ages and we have it now everywhere. Natural wisdom trying to explain the divine mysteries, and the sectarian spirit of man, with much speculation, are the cause of such unnecessary disputes.　c

But the hungry souls and honest seekers after Christian reality have also been involved in these disputes, they entering into them not for religious discussion, but for more light on this most important subject. This is the very reason why we wish to take up the subject in the name of the Lord Jesus , appeal to all the honest readers to see for themselves if we are proclaiming "the truth as it is in Christ Jesus."

THE KINGDOM

Our blessed Lord, in explaining the mysteries of His kingdom, took the natural to explain the divine, and it is by listeniing to and accepting His explanations of the eternal facts that we shall receive eternal good. Let us therefore hush before Him and let Him tell us all about it.

"Jesus answered and said unto him (Nicodemus), Verily, verily, I say unto thee, except a man be born again he cannot see the kingdom of God. Except a man be born of water and of the Spirit, he cannot enter into the kingdom of God." Jno. 3:3-5.

To get into the heart of the subject before us, we must prayfully consider and meditate upon the following words of our Lord, viz., "born" "into", "the kingdom", "of God." The biggest word of all these six words is "God." Therefore the first question is, "Who is this God of which Christ is speaking?" The exact answer is in the inspired text. God is the only personal owner and ruler of that divine kingdom: that is why it is called "The Kingdom of God." The next question is, "What is a kingdom?" Logically speaking, a kingdom is a large realm of land, occupied by multitudes of citizens, over which a King reigns with his majestic per-

3

son and forcible laws. But the divine kingdom is a Spiritual Realm which is occupied by he myriads of Spiritual Beings, such as the angels and "spirits of just men" and God's children in this world, through which God Himself rules and reigns in and through His Spiritual Word.

Our Lord, speaking of this blessed kingdom, said, "My Kingdom is not of this world;" in other words, The Kingdom of which I speak and into which men must be born, is not earthly, but it is from above and is heavenly. The mysterious part of this subject is that which puzzled the old ruler of the Jews, Nicodemus; Jesus, saying as He did, that Kingdom is Spiritual, invisible, and from above, yet rational and natural man could see and enter into it. "How can these things be?" naturally is man's puzzled question, but the answer is, "With God all things are possible." Yea, all things are possible also to him that believes God." Hence the way to that eternal kingdom is God Himself with man's undisputed faith in His wonder-working power.

When the Almighty came in the flesh and actually lived in this visible world as a real, perfect, visible man, then He made it also possible for all men who dare to believe to see and to enter into this invisible, yet tangible and real realm of God's reigning place. Hallelujah! Who is the explanation and solution of all these mysterious problems? Jesus Christ Himself, the King of Kings and the Lord if Lords. Amen and Amen

What is the Kingdom of God?

1st. The Kingdom of God is a kingdom of a life eternal. Jesus claimed to be that very life when He said, "I am the life." The Apostle John calls that eternal life the true God Himself, when he said, "This is the true God and eternal life." See 1 John 5:20-21.

2nd. The Kingdom of God is a kingdom of light. Jesus claimed also to be that very light when He said, "I am the light." The Apostle Paul affirmed this fact when He said, "Giving thanks unto the Father, which hath made us to be partakers of the inheritance of the saints in light, who hath delivered us from the power of darkness and hath translated us into the kingdom of His dear Son. Col. 1:13. See also 1 Peter 2:9, 2 Peter 1:11, Rev. 1:9.

3rd. Jesus actually claimed not only to be the king of this kingdom, but also that He Himself was that very kingdom. He therefore said to the Jews, "The Kingdom of God is at hand." That means right here within your reach. He said again, "The kingdom of God is come nigh unto you,"

4

referring to His own personality. Again, "No doubt the kingdom of God is come unto you." Again, "Behold (or look on me and see), the kingdom of God is in the midst of you," or "I am among you now". Our Lord, reproving the Pharisees said unto them, "Woe unto you, scribes and Pharisees, hypocrites, for ye shut up the kingodm of Heaven against men" "Ye neither go in yourselves, neither suffer ye them that are entering to go in." See Matt. 23:13 with Luke 11:52. The Pharisees were preaching continually against Jesus Christ and warning the people to keep away from Him and not accept His claims.

When our great Lord spake of the kingdom of God in parables, His disciples asked Him why He was talking to the people in parables. He said unto them, "Unto you it is given to know the mystery of the kingdom of God, but nnto them that are without, all these things are done in parables. See Mark 4:11 Our blessed Lord said to His disciples that they were more blessed than all the prophets and the righteous men of old, because they actually saw and heard the things concerning the kingdom of God. See Matt. 13:10-19. The question is, what did they see? They saw the King and the Kingdom of God in the face and the words of Jesus.

All these scriptures and many more prove that in the person of Jesus are all the glories and the mysteries of the Kingdom. Hence, to get into Him is to get into the Kingdom.

Since the person, the life and the fulness of our Lord is the Kindom of God, then it remains that, to get into Him is to get into the Kingdom of God, or to be in Him is to become a new creature, just as the Apostle said, "If any man be in Christ, he is a new creature," or he is born again. Blessed be the name of our Christ, the LORD, who is our all. Yea, He is not only all the mysteries of the eternal Divine kingdom, but also the solution of the mystery of the Godhead, because "in Him dwelleth all the fulness of the Godhead (the Father, the Son and the Holy Spirit) bodily and we are complete in Him." Col. 1:9. Remember! "It is all in Him." Amen! Hallelujah!   A. D U.

5

CHAPTER II

Seeing the Kingdom.

HERE is some difference between seeing and entering. There are hundreds who come from the old countries as far as Ellis Island, and see America, but they can not eenter into it. So it is with many people, whosee the Kingdom of God from afar off, but they must enter into it in order to share its glory and enjoy the King's reigning power. The Old Testament saints saw the coming King Jehovah, their Lord Messiah, from afar off, who was to bring that kingdom down; but they could not enter into it then, and they died in the faith of entering. And they are waiting for that great day when they shall actually hear the voice of their God, the King, and by the power of His voice they will receive the power of that kingdom, even the Spirit, which will raise them up out of the graves, to see Him who has the keys of Hades. THen shall they enter into the eternal life, light, power and glory of His majestic presence, which is the Everlasting Kingdom of God.

The disciples saw the Kingdom, or the Kingship, of their Lord. They saw "the life", the power and the love of that Kingdom in the person of Christ Jesus; but that Kingdom was not in them, nor were they in it until the day of Pentecost. It was of this mighty truth that our Saviour spake to them, when He said, "At thatday ye shall know that I am in my Father and ye in me (in the kingdom) and I in you," (or the King of the Spiritual Kigndom in you). What was that day to which our Lord referred, It was the day of receiveeing "the Spirit of the Truth' or the Holy Spirit. It is an infallible fact and that according to all the Scriptures, that we do not really enter into the kingdom of God until we enter into the Spirit of Christ, or until Christ the living and glorified One, enters into our hearts by His Spirit, which is called "the Spirit of the Truth." This may be strong meat to some abnormal Christians of our day, nevertheless it is the eternal truth. Hence, to be actually born of the Spirit is to enter into the Spiritual Christ; or it is to be baptized by the Spirit of the Truth into the mystical and spiritual Body of Christ. "The Spirit bloweth where He listeth and thou hearest His voice; but canst not tell whence He cometh or whither He goeth. So it is with every one that is born of the Spirit." Jno. 3:6-9. (The above translation is the nearest to the original words of our Lord.)

THE APOSTLE TEACHING CONCERNING THE KINGDOM OF GOD.

The inspired apostles did not say, the kingdom of God is a mere touch of conviction, or a shallow conversion, such as we hear of in these days, neither did they say it is the beginning of a little change in our lives, or a declaration, "I am born again and I know it." But they said, "The Kingdom of God is not in word, but in power." 1 Cor. 4:20. If the kingdom of God is in power, it remains that you and I are not in it until we actually enter into the power, or are clothed upon with the power of God. What is the power of God but the Holy Spirit? Yea, it is Christ in us in the power and the demonstration of the Holy Ghost

Again, the Apostle Paul, exhorting the Church of Rome, says, "The kngdom of God is righteousness, peace, and joy in the Holy Ghost." See Rom. 14:17. Mind you, please, that that kingdom's righteousness, peace and joy are in the Holy Ghost and not apart from Him. Then the question is, who is all the righteousness? Who is all the peace? Where is the fulness of the divine joy? All must admit that the risen Lord is our righteousness. He is also our peace, and in Him is the fulness of joy. Here again, Christ's person and fulness is proved to be that Kingdom. But the apostle says these blessings and characters of God are in the Holy Ghost. Yes, they are in Christ, or in the Holy Ghost which is in Christ. Then it is clear that if the glorified Christ is in us and we are in Him, we are clothed upon with the righteousness, peace and joy of that kingdom in the Holy Ghost. Reader! Have you entered into the power of God? Have you entered into all righteousness and peace? Have you entered into the joy of your Lord? If not, then you have not entered into the kingdom of God, because the kingdom of God is in power! It is righteousness! is peace! is joy in the Holy Spirit!

So dear ones, the truth is plain that all the Spirit, the power, the righteousness, the peace, the joy and the fulness of eternal life are in the risen Lord, and if you are really and normally born again you have really, actually entered into, not a crucified and buried Christ, but into the crucified, buried and RISEN LORD. Henceforth you know no more Christ after the flesh, but you know Him in the power of the Holy Spirit. Therefore, if any man be in (spiritual) Christ, He is a new creature. Old things are passed away; behold, all things are become new."

We have quoted the above scripture so many times, applying it to our own experiences with a little consideration but, it must be remembered that if there are some of the old things yet remaining in you, you cannot say "all are become new." You should say, "Some have become new and some of the old things are passed away, and I am daily asking God to let me enter into the fulness of His Kingdom, and for His kingdom to fill me completely, so much more until there shall be nothing in me but the fulness of power, righteousness, and peace, yea, till I be filled with the joy of my Lord, and that in the fulness of the Spirit." Amen.   A. D. U

CHAPTER III

The Way and the Entrance Into the Kingdom of God.

BEFORE we proceed to show forth the literal way of the new birth, or the entrance nito the kingdom of God, we wish first briefly to show the necessity of the new birth.

We must be born of the Spirit, because we are all born once of the flesh, and "the flesh lusteth against the Spirit." "The mind of the flesh is enmity with God." There is nothing good that dwelleth in our flesh." "They that are in the flesh cannot please God." "For the works of the flesh are these, adultery, fornication, uncleanness, lasciviousness, idoltry, witchcraft, hatred, variance, emulations, wrath, strife, seditions, heresies, envying, murders, drunkenness, revellings and such like." Just stop and think what a wretched condition it is for us to be in, being filled with all these terrible works of the flesh! That is why we must be born of God anew.

When our first parents died spiritually, in Eden, they at once became selfish and devilish; but God in His own great mercy promised us "the power of an endless life," and that promise of the new life was to be in the seed of woman, and in the seed of Abraham, Isaac, Jacob and David. Centuries later, that seed was found lodging in the virgin Mary, a daughter of Abraham from the tribe of Judah. In the fulness of time, when the shadow of the Almighty rested upon Mary, the Holy Spirit filled her, and as soon as the eternal Spirit touched that word of the promise in Mary, the miraculous conception of a new creation began, and in the period of the ninth month, the Holy Child, even "The Word", which became flesh, was born, "created after God in righteousness and true holness."

This new man, a Unique One, was to be known as ,and called "The Lord," "The King," "The God with us," "The Jehovah Saviour" (Jesus), yea, "The promised Messiah," who is in the truth "The endless life of God," the Kingdom of God, the fulness of God, the glory of God, the power of God, yea, the righteousness, peace and joy of God, the Spirit. All these were promised to fallen humanity, not in woman

9

or in Abraham, not in David or the Virgin Mary, but "in the Seed." Gal. 3:16. Even to them and to us all, who believe. Here again, we come face to face with the new birth in the person of Christ, the Son. Yea, we come in contact with the Father, who's alone is the Kingdom. And we see Him in His Son, Christ our Lord.

When we see this heavenly Kingdom entering into us, or when we really enter into it, then we see more clearly the Father, the Spirit, and the power, with al the right-eousness, peace, and joy in the Name of Christ. Hence, "As many as received Him (in the Spirit, of course), to them gave He power to become the Sons of God, even to them that believed in His Name, which were born of God." Why born of God?

1st. Because they accept Christ as their Creator and as their light of life. See John 1:10.

2nd. Because in believeing in His Name they actually receive from Him the power which makes them the Sons of God.

Reader ! Do you believe in Christ the Word of God? Do you believe in God who is in Christ? Have you received the Christ and God in Him, in you? If? you have, you are "born not of blood, nor of the will of the flesh, nor of the will of man, but of God."

Now we will come more closely to the way of the new birth, or to the entrance into the Kingdom of God.

THE WAY OF THE NEW BIRTH OR THE TRUE ENTRANC INTO LIFE ETERNAL

We learned from the foregoing pages that eternal life is the true God Himself; that the Kingdom of God is in pow-er and in the Holy Ghost, a realm of a life of righteousness, peace and joy,—yea, a realm of the light and glory of God in the person or Face of Jesus Christ. Now we must know the way into all these blessed mysteries. According to the claims of Jesus, He seems not only to be the King, in whom is that great spiritual realm of life out that He is also the way. This proves our Saviour to be still more mysterious and greater. He said, "I am the Way" to the person and mystery of the Father. See Matt. 11:2. with Jno. 14:6. He said also, "I am the Dor; by me if any man enter in, he shall be saved." Jno. 10:9. How can Jesus be the door, or the only entrance into eternal life, and yet the eternal life it-self? Again, the life-giving shepherd, and the owner of all these things? It remains a mystery beyond explan-ation, but to be believed and humbly accepted.

But some may say, Christ is invisible now, He is away up i . Heaven How can I go there and get into Christ, "the Way"? This is a logical question and must be answered logically and scripturally. It is true that the real glorified Christ, who died and was buried and arose and entered into heaven itself, is far above us all, and that it is impossible for Him to be seen now as He is; but it is true also that His great Name is given under Heaven by which all men can be saved. What Christ is in glory, His Name is down here. What His matchless Name is down here, His majestic person is in Heaven. This is the greatest gift of all gifts that God has given to the church down here, even the highlyexalted name of Christ. See Eph. 1:18-22 with Phil. 2:5-11. It is all in His name, and His name should be in His Church to make it a powerful organism, through which the world should believe and be saved. So the factor of all the hidden mysteries should be the church of God, which is the fulness of Him that fills all. In the church His Name should be exalted. This is the very reason why all the apostles went everywhere preaching the Kingdom of God and the name of Jesus Christ. See Acts 8:12, 19:5-8, 28:23-31. It is an evident fact that the apostles' doctrine was nothing more than the name of Jesus Christ. See Acts 2:41-42 with Acts 5:42.

They preached repentance, forgiveness, and the remission of sins in His name. They proclaimed that the power to save, to heal, to keep, were all in Jesus' name. They declared that God Himself with all His fulness dwelt bodily in Christ's wonderful name. Whatsoever they did, in word or deed, they did it all in the name of Jesus Christ the Lord. They baptized all who repented and believed God into the gracious name, Jesus Christ, and they laid hands on the converts to receive the Holy Spirit, and that also in Jesus' name.

They strongly affirmed that, though God is invisible and Christ is in that very God in glory, yet man can get into God's power, God's life, God's light and God's fulness if they only believe on the name of the Lord Jesus. As soon as people heartily believed this message in those olden times, they were immediately baptized into the name of Jesus Christ and they received the Holy Spirit and were born into the kingdom of God and the kingdom of God was establised in their hearts. Then Christ was the King and the Lord of their lives for time and eternity. They confessed Christ in the Holy Ghost as their Messiah and their risen Lord, they suffered and died as martyrs for His name.

11

This was the way that the apostles preached; the way to eternal life and the way into the kingdom of God. They were so loyal and radical for it that they lost their lives for it. This was the way that was then "spoken evil of everywhere." This was the narrow way which only few find, as our Lord said. Yea, this is the eternal and unchangeable way to the Kingdom of God. Therefore let all repent and be baptized into the name of Jesus Christ and receive the Holy Spirit and enter into the Kingdom of God. A hundred years after the apostolic martyrdom, false prophets entered the church of Christ and proclaimed their own ways instead of the way of God. The outcome was the long period of the dark ages.

During the Reformation, which began through different reformers at different ages, we received the truth by slices, by degrees, in small portions, "here a line and there a line." Every slice is called The Salvation; every portion is called the New Birth. So every reformer called his message the full message of the Gospel, hence the birth of so many denominations, bringing a portion of the Gospel in each revival. God had to raise others to proclaim more of it, until in these last days the Holy Spirit has fallen upon the believing souls and the outcome is a primitive gospel message. The full and perfect way of the new birth is again proclaimed, the name and the Deity of the Son of God properly and fully set forth. Dismay has broken out in the midst of the denominational preachers and laity. Once more the old good and narrow way is being spoken evil of everywhere. The definite prophecy of our Lord is actually being fulfiilled, namely, "Ye shall be hated of all men for my name's sake." Why for His name? Because His name is again benig made the subject of all subjects. Because His Name is being proclaimed to be the name of the Deity which contains the kingdom of God and the Father of the kingdom. Because the faith and the baptism in His name is again emphasized as the only way into the Kingdom of God. Because He is called not only "he child born and the Son given unto us," but also "the Mighty God, the Everlasting Father and the Prince of Peace." "Of the increase of His kingdom and of peace there shall be no end," etc. etc. See Isa. 9:6-7 with Rev. 15:1-4.

Now in the closing of this article, let me say, please, that we do not magnify merely the water and the spirit of man, and say that they are the way nito the kngdom, but the water and the Spirit of God in the name of Jesus are the way into the Kingdom. The material water we use in

12

baptism into the name of God is only an emblem of the Word which became flesh, the real humanity of Christ which consisted of the water and the blood by the Spirit of God. So when we preach His name, we do not magnify **water,** but the **atonement** through Christ's perfect humanity, of which the material water at the baptistry, and the bread and wine at the communion table are visible elements to represent the real broken body of our Lord and His red hot blood and the holy water of life which come forth from His broken heart on the cross. The power of baptism is not in the water or in what we say, but in the faith of obedience in the name of the Lord Jesus, who is our all and in all. Amen. Amen.   A. D. URSHAN.

CHAPTER IV

The Two Aspects of God's Kingdom.

I T must always be remembered that God's plan of redemption contained both Spirit and matter, or spiritually and materiality. We find that, from the very beginning, this is proved all the way through the Bible from the creation of man to the end of the Millenial Kingodm. Adam was created both spiritual and material. The people of God, Israel, were earthly and yet in them and through them was God, the Spirit, known, and Christ was in their loins, to be revealed in due time. He was to be born of them, therefore "salvation is of the Jews." For this very reason, and to confirm this blessed divine plan of ages past; to fulfill all those material types and shadows, our Lord and God took upon Him, not the nature of angels but the seed of Abraham. Hence Christ, though being "the lifegiving Spirit" and "the Lord from glory," and "the Everlasting Father" according to His Deity, yet was to be manifested as the real Son of Man and the Son of God. Therefore to spiritualize Christ and His gospel and deny the real materiality of His gospel, is to deny His real blood and water which came out of His wounded side, which proved Him to be the real Son of God,—to deny this revealed fact is to deny that Jesus Christ came into the flesh, which the Anti-Christ's spirit does. Yet to make the gospel all material and deny the God in the gospel which makes it "the power of God," is Unitarianism, and it is the denial of the Absolute Deity of our Saviour, who was and is today, "God manifested in the flesh." God's earthly people are the saved Jews and Gentiles which are calld the Church; for in Christ there is neither Jew nor Gentile, but all together a new creation. Without the real earthly people of God there could have been no Christ, no salvation, and without the spiritual Christ (GOD) and a spriutal people of God, chosen in Christ before the world was, the Jews could not be lost nor restored to their earthly kingdom. But Israeel will yet be restored to their land and to their God and Messiah. Their kingdom will be yet restored, but when? After God

14

gets "a people for His name" from among all the nations," a people born into the Heavenly Kingdom by being baptized in water and the Spirit and that into His name, then after this He will return to raise the ruins of David. Please read Acts 15:13-18. When the new Jerusalem comes down from Heaven, then the earthly Jerusalem will be cleaned up from all the enemies of God, and the earthly kingdom of David will be restored over all the earth by the Kingdom of God from above, or by the great King of Heaven, even Jehovah Messiah, who shall come down with His great glory to cause the restitution of all things. See Zech. 14: 1-5 with Psalm 45:13-17.

It was of this earthly kingdom being brought into existence by Jehovah Himself that the Jews' minds were always occupied. That is why Nicodemus could not understand the new birth doctrine of Christ, nor did the Disciples of Christ understand it until after the day of Pentecost, for we see them asking their Master even after His resurrection, saying, "Lord, wilt thou at this time restore again the Kingdom to Israel?" See Acts 1:6-8.

Jesus was talking to His disciples about the power of God and their entering into that power by being clothed upon in the spiritual baptism, which we proved before to be the new birth; but their minds were on the earthly kingdom. See Luke 24:49. Yet one thing is sure, those disciples believed with all their hearts that Jesus was that very Jehovah God of Israel, who would again restore the Davidic kingdom. That is why they eagerly asked Him that important question.   A. D. U.

15

CHAPTER V

The Water and the Spirit Insep-
arable in the Old Testament
Types of the New Birth
Dootrine.

HE first thing we see showing forth the power
of the Godhead through the visible things
(Rom. 1:20) is in the birth of the earth. This
earth was begotten by the Word of God and
born of the water and of the Spirit. "And the
earth was without form and void: and darkness
was upon the face of the deep. And the Spirit
of God moved upon the face of the waters." "And God said,
Let the waters under the heaven be gathered together unto
one place, and let the dry land appear; and it was so. And
God called the dry land Earth; and the gathering together
of the waters called He Seas: and God saw that it was
good." Gen. 1:2-9-10.

The second marvellous thing we see is the birth, or
the creation, of man. He was formed of water and dust,
and made alive by the Spirit of God, so God made the first
man by water and Spirit That is why we are called "clay",
which means dust molded or made a chunk, by water;
there can be no clay by mere dust, it is the liquid or water
in the dust, on it and all over it, which makes clay. See
Gen. 2:7 with 3:19 and Isa. 64:8.

The third type of the water and Spirit together we see
in Noah's case. He was saved by the water and by the
Spirit of God in the ark just as much as Noah; that is
why he could live 40 days without any air whatever, for
the ark was continually under floods of rain from above
and beneath. It was God Himself being with them, after
they all entered into the ark, "The Lord shut him in."
No modern ship could have stood those terrible winds,
storms and floods for that forty days that Noah's ark stood,
thoughnot being equipped with an engine, etc., etc., if it
had not been kept by the power of God, it would have been
smashed in a few days. See Gen. 7:15-24 with 1 Peter
3:20-21.

The fourth type of the water and the Spirit together is

16

found in Gen.24, where Eliezer, the servant of Abraham, represents the Holy Spirit's work while Rebecca represents the Bride of Christ. Here w see Eliezer (the Holy Spirit) asks God for the sign of water and the obedience of the damsel going into the well and coming out of it, would make him sure of the right and the God-given Bride to Isaac. Read the whole chapter and see the birth of the water and the Spirit typified' in Rebecca's profound obedience in regard to the water, according to the plan of the Holy Spirit or Eliezer, who represented the work and plan of the Spirit.

The fifth wonderful type of the birth of water and Spirit is found in Gen. 30:25-43, where Jacob is being led by God to put piles of rods of green popular in the watering troughs where the flock was to drink and see Jacob's white strakes in the rods in the water. What happened? All the she-goats, by looking into the water and drinking the same, conceived before the rods and brought forth cattle ring-straked, speckled, and spotted, just as Jacob needed to have. No. one will dare to deny that this was a mighty miracle of God, and that the Spirit of God teaches us that this was not only the plan of prosperity to Jacob, but it was the Spirit of God in the water brooding upon the rods that caused that miraculous conception and the birth of many lambs in and through the water. What a profound type of Jesus, the Son of Israel, who was stripped by His own relations, like Jacob, stripped naked of all his rights, by his father-in-law yet through Christ's death, burial, and resurrection He put the plan of the new birth in the hearts of His servants, through baptism in water and the Spirit to bring forth many lambs unto Him. Oh, praise Him for this plan, and come to the watery grave and see the white strakes of the cross, and the atonement of the green rod, "the tender plant," the Son of Jacob, and be filled with His life by the Spirit brooding upon the water through which you should go into His great Name and be baptized.

The sixth type of water and Spirit is shown in the saving of Moses by the water and the Spirit. It was on the water of the river Nile that Moses' little ark was floating. It was the water that drew Pharoah's daughter to the voice of the little Moses when she came to wash herself. It was the echo of the water that made the child's crying aloud to pierce the heart of the King's daughter. If there had been no water, she would never have come there and we would have had no Moses left. We, of course, know that that water alone was not the cause of Moses' deliverance, but the Spirit of God suggested that to Moses' mother to do what she

17

did. It was the same Spirit created pity in Pharaoh's daughter's heart to take the boy from the watery grave of death and adopt him for her son. See Exo. 2. Moses' deliverance was a typpical salvation of all God's chosen people, who shall be saved for His Name's sake through being baptized into that wonderful name and be filled with the Holy Spirit. Through such a process they become the children of the Kingdom of God, a greater kingdom than that which Moses entered.

Seventh, the Israelites were saved through the water and the Spirit. Read 14th chapter of Exodus and see what Moses said to the frightened people, "Stand still and see the salvation of the Lord." Did they see it? Yes! How? Whenthey entered the Red Sea through the water and the Spirit brooding over them. Therefore they were baptized unto Moses. What a beautiful type of our salvation from the old life, the old enemy; even through the baptism of water and the Spirit, by which we are baptized unto Jesus Christ, our great spiritual Moses.

8th The Israelites again were delivered from the serpents by looking upon the brass serpent. The question is, how was that brass serpent made? No one will doubt that it was made by going through the process of water and fire and shaped by hammer beating it on the anvil. The type of our Lord, the new man Christ Jesus, who came not only by the water, but by the blood also which flowed from His hands and feet being hammered with nails, and that through the power of the Spirit. Being lifted upon the cross, He proved to be a perfect man; when His side was pierced the water and the blood came forth, and His resurrection by the Spirit of God proved Him to be the firstborn among His brethren, who are to be born of the water and of the Spirit. See John 19:34-35 with John 5:8.

9th. Another remarkable type of the water and the Spirit baptism is found with Elias' challenge to the prophets of Baal, as recorded in 1 Kings 18. There we see, after the bullock was killed, Baal's prophets called on the name of their gods, but the fire did not come; but when Elijah built an alter of stones in the name of the Lord, he poured water on the dead bullock until it was sopping wet all over, and filled the trench with water; then Elijah called upon the name of the Lord God of Abraham, thefire came and the victory was won, and Israel was restored to their true God. The water connected with the name of the Lord poured upon the dead animal, with th faith of the prophet, brought the Holy fire from Heaven; so does the real faith in the

18

death, burial and resurrection of Christ, being baptized into His name with a real repentance and faith in that great name brings down the Holy Spirit upon the the crucified flesh, and consumes its lusts thereof and makes the soul alive forevermore.

10th. Th cleansing of the Captain Naaman, the Syrian, is another typee of the power of the Spirit working in and through the water. Read 2nd Kings 5th chapter and see that when Naaman humbled himself and obeyed the word of God perfectly, by going into the water and dipping himself seven times, (one perfect immersion) he was thoroughly cleansed from his leprosy. Leprosy signfies sin in the Bible, and obedience to God's command and that in and through the water immersion, caused the Holy Spirit to so cleanse the man that he had to turn to the man of God and give glory to the name of God and the Lord of Israel.

11th. The children of Israel who were born in the wilderness and who were not older than twenty years, had to go through the water of Jordan, being driven in heaps around them by the rushing wind of God's Spirit before entering the Promised Land, which typifies the spiritual life of Christ. Why? Because they had not entered through the water and the Spirit of the Red Sea, and the type had to be performed before they could enter into the new Kingdom given to them by God. See Joshua 3rd chapter. Lo! another beautiful type of the entering into the Spiritual kingdom and that by water and the Spirit.

12th. Gideon's victorious band is another type of a band of God's people who shall conquer their enimies in the name of their Lord. How was that army 300 strong tried? By the water and on the water. Who put or ordered that plan of testing the worthy men for God's battle? The Spirit of God. Read Judges 7th chapter and see how the water and the Spirit again are inseparable and are working together to perform God's will. Amen.

The other types of the water and the Spirit to the new birth of the New Testament, you will find in many washings of the old people of God. For instance, they used to be baptized for their dead relatives. Why? That God may count them worthy of the resurrection of the righteous; so it is with our baptism in water into the name of Him who was dead, buried and arose for our justification, likewise we are baptized into His death with hope of resurrection from the liquid grave to receive that very Spirit which raised our Lord from the grave.

You will find also the holy water in the temples of

19

Israel and the sacrifices washed in water, and with the water before putting on the fire to be burned as an acceptable sacrifice to God in order to cope with His good will to please Him. So, dear Reader, all these types and shadows were to prove that what our Lord said to the Jewish Rabbi was not something accidental, but a truth settled in Heaven before the world was, and proclaimed and foreshadowed through the whole Old Testament and proclaimed in due time and confirmed by the Lord Almighty in the flesh; obeyed and practised by the real early church of Christ. Therefore, if any man is not born (baptized) of the water and of the Spirit, he cannot enter the kingdom of God. Heaven and earth will pass away, but the Word of the Lord shall abide forever. Therefore, O man, give up your ideas and try not to climb the walls to enter into the safe fold of God, but be baptized (put in) into the name of Him, who is the only door and the way to eternal life. Amen. A. D. U.

CHAPTER VI

The New Testament Teaching on the New Birth.

NOW we will come to the teaching of our Saviour and His comissioned Apostles concerning "the Water and the Spirit" Birth.

We have already seen the wise way of God through His Holy Law, mastering His people, leading them to His Gospel ("theGospel of God,") and how our Lord comes forthwith the truth of Salvation, proclaiming it as in a nut-shell, being broken to pour out its precious kernel to the leader of Israel, named Nicodemus, when He said: "Verily, Verily, I say unto thee, Except a man be born (come forth) of WATER and of the SPIRIT, he cannot enter into the Kingdom of God;" and to His own disciples when commissioning them He said unto them, "Go ye into all the world, and preach the Gospel (of he Kingdom) to every creature (every Person). He that believeth, AND IS BAPTIZED, shall be saved, but he that believeth not (of course needs not to be baptised) shall be damned; and these signs (the wonderful operations of the Holy Spirit) shall follow them that believe (of course being baptised also) IN MY NAME, etc."

Here again, the Water of Baptism and the Holy Spirit's Power casting out Devils, causing believers to speak with other Tongues, healing the sick, etc., etc., are in connection, and that in the Name of the Lord Jesus.

After His triumphant resurrection our Lord once appeared to His Disciples, and found them fishing. He had previously said to Peter, "Fear not; from henceforth thou shalt catch men", (Luke 5:4:10,) and now to encourage His weary Apostle who worked in vain all night to catch fish, He said, "Cast the net on the right side of the ship, and ye shall find." They cast, therefore, and now they were not able to draw it for the multitude of fishes." Here our Lord demonstrates His Power which was to be given to them to catch men, by obeying His word, and that man-fish which they would catch had to come forth (be born) out of water, even as they pulled the mulitude of fish from the sea.

But you will say, "Where is the symbol of the Spirit here?" Well, if you look up the next two verses (John

21

21:7-9) you will see that the fish caught cut of the water were laid on the Fire and roasted, not by them, but by Jesus, for them to enjoy with the Master.

Why did He not let them make the fire and bake the fish° Because that would have spoiled the reality which that oc asion typified. It was for the Disciple t the word of our Lord with obedience to the last jot, and the converts (the men-fish) were to be put in the water and pulled out of the water (the baptism) by them, Peter first, then being helped by the other disciples, to bring forth the multitudes out of the water: which represents the baptism ceremony given to them. But Jesus was and is today THE BAPTISER with the Holy Ghost and the fire. For this very reason Hehad to make the fire and put the fish on the same fire for the enjoyment of them all.

Reader, are you one of these men-fish, caught by the net of the gospel? If you are, you must have been brought out of the water, or born of water. Have you given yourself to Jesus so pliably that He could put you on the fire. If you have, then the sweet savour of your consecrated life, having been washed by the holy water in His Name, is ascending like the smoke of those fish on the fire, and it not only gives a spiritual appetite to hungry souls, but it makes your great Lord enjoy the delicious odor of the same by the fire of the Holy Spirit.

Now we will come to the Apostolic preaching and practice regrding the water and Spirit. Who were the first multitude of men caught in the gospel net by Peter and the other Apostles who helped him? You must admit, the 3,000 souls on the day of Pentecost. What happened to those convicted people before they were added to the Assembly (Church) of God? You must say. they were all immersed. Into whose Name were they baptised? You must again agree with me, "Into the Name of Jesus Christ." What happened to them next? We read, Peter told them that they "shall receive the gift of the Holy Spirit. For the promise was unto them, etc., etc." Did they receive the Holy Spirit? No doubt they did; otherwise it would not have been written, "The Lord added to the church daily such as should be saved." Here we actually see Peter on the job doing his part by preaching the gospel, and bap tsng those who believe the gospel—with others helping him; and the Lord Jesus also working with them His part, which was putting the converts on the fire, or. baptising them with the Holy Spirit and setting them on the fire for a sweet savour for His Name.

"The Lord added" means the LORD baptised them into His Body, which is the church, by, or in, or with the Holy Spirit. For Verification of these questions and answers please read Acts, second Chapter verse one.

Before going any further regarding the Apostolic teaching, we wish to call the attention of our readers to John 2:1-12. Why did our Lord take water as a means of showing forth the first glimpse of His glory in Cana? Why did He say to His disciples to fill to the brim the six water-pots of stone there? Why did He turn water into wine? Why did He command His disciples to handle the water part? The proper answer to these questions will explain why in the following chapter of the same book He said to Nicodmus, "Except a man be born of water and the Spirit he cannot enter into the kingdom of God."

Now we will answer the questions. The reason He chose water and filling the water-pots to the brim was to show His disciples symbolically "the washing of regeneration" which comes by being baptised (immersed) into His Name for the remission of sins. Those pots were put there for washing purposes and Jesus wanted His disciples to know of a better washing, and a complete washing of the whole body by the holy water, representing the forgiveness of all sins of him who believes and is baptised, going through the watery grave into His Mighty Name. See 1 John 2:12.

The water turning to the best wine was another symbolic lesson of the Holy Spirit being given to them that obey His word fully: that is, to repent, and to be baptized into His Name, and to receive the Holy Spirit. As Apostle said, "He giveth the Holy Spirit to them that obey Him." Notice, please, that the water did not turn to wine until the word was fully obeyed. He said, "Fill the water-pots with water;" they did exactly so. Then He said, "Draw out now." And as they obeyed again, they had the Heaven-born wine to "bear unto the governor of the feast." He tells us, His ministers, now, "Baptise them that repent and believe." when we do, they receive the Holy Spirit if they really have repented, and believe. Here again we see that in order to show forth the glory of the Lord in the land of the living, we must employ water, according to His eternal command, and God will turn our action and faith in His Name, with the obedience to His word, into a spiritual blessing. Amen.

Now coming to the Apostolic teaching on the subject, we would like to ask, why Peter is the first one to receive the promise of the fishing of men; why not the other disciples first? Because Peter was the holder of the keys of the unopened kingdom, and the Lord, according to His own pleasure had given the opening of the fifirst entrance into the hands of Peter. But one may say, "Was the kingdom of God locked until Peter opened it?" Yes, indeed! No one ever had entered into the kingdom of God until the day of Pentecost, for no one ever was baptised into the Name of the crucified, buried, risen, and ascended Lord, until then. Neither had any man yet received the "promise of the Father" (or been baptised into the Holy Spirit) until the day of Pentecost. Therefore from that memorial day until this very day the gates of the glorious kingdom of God were opened by Peter, for the Jews, first, yea, also for all who really will be born of water and the Spirit to enter in.

At times we have wondered why the evangelist Philip was not able to get his Samaritan converts through the baptism of the Holy Spirit, having such tremendous power to cast out the devils, heal the lame and blind, turning the whole town toward the Lord and baptising hundreds into the Name of Christ Jesus. We have finally found that out; and it is because the keys of the kngdom to enter in were in the hands of Peter. That is why the church at Jerusalem had to send Peter and John to lay hands on the Samaritins to receve the Holy Spirit, which they did. Here again we see not only that water and the Spirit in the Name of Jesus Christ are the divine means of entrance, but that the holder of the keys, with others cooperating, had to do just what our Lord demonstrated in His symbolic action in Cana wedding feast and at the shores of the sea where He gave them the fish on the fire to eat. read eighth chapter of Acts, please.

Now the other class of human race to be dealt with is the Gentiles. We see in that case also Peter, helped by six Jewish brethren, opening the gates of the kingdom for the first Gentile family at the house of Cornelius. As soon as Peter came to the sentence, "the remission of sins in the Name of the man Christ Jesus," the Heavens opened and sent forth the spiritual rain on all them that heard the word gladly. In this case we see the Spirit birth ahead of the water birth. God allowed this to happen that way that we may know He knows the hearts of men better than we do, and that He is God alone who has power to revise the things according to His mysterious plan; but even at this case, the water question is not neglected, and it had to be

24

performed right on the spot. So we read Peter challenged his audience and said, "Can any man forbid water?" Again we read, "He commanded them to be baptised in the Name of the Lord Jesus, or Jesus Christ," and they did obey the word of God and went through the plan of the Second Birth as taught by our Lord, and were born of the Spirit and water while the key holder unlocked the gates of Salvation to the Gentiles. Read tenth chapter of Acts, please.

THE KEYS OF THE KINGDOM

Why did our Lord give His apostles the keys, and not just one key? How many keys were given to Peter and others to unlock the Kingdom of God? We answer, **Three keys only.** Why three? First. Because the human family consists of three classes, namely, Jews, Samaritans, and Gentiles or Heathen. That is why Peter had to be the present and principal propagator in the beginning of the gospel revival among each class of these three classes. Second. Becau· every individual is three-fold being and salvation of God is not for the spirit of man only, but also for his soul and body. Third. Because the means of entrance into the kingdom are three—faith in the Name, obedience to the word, and receiving the Holy Spirit; in other words,—the WORD which contains the blood of the atonement through the crucifixion; the WATER baptism which symbolises the grave; and the SPIRIT which is the resurrection and brings us into the Kingdom of God, and God as the King into our lives. Hence—"This is He that came by **water** and **blood,** EVEN Jesus Christ; not by water only but by water and blood And it is the SPIRIT that beareth witness, because **the Spirit is TRUTH.** (1 John 5:6). Well, glory! Jesus said He is the Truth, He also said, "Thy word is Truth, and His Apostle says, "The Spirit is Truth." A three-fold Truth that everyone may know and thereby be made free from sin and Hell, as our Lord said in John 8:34-35.

Oh! dear ones, let us not emphasize just "Spirit" and neglect the Blood, as the Spiritualists do. Neither let us emphasize the "blood" only and neglect the water in the Bible, of which the perfect humanity of our Lord consisted, thus becoming like modern non-immersed Christians of our day. Neither let us emphasize the "water" and blood, and neglect the baptism of the Holy Spirit, becoming humanitarians only. But let us preach emphatically "the Word" which became flesh, namely, the Son of God, who died for us to atone for our sins; from whose riven side came forth, not only blood, but also water; and that He was buried and arose by

25

the power of the Spirit of Holiness; and that repentance toward God, and the faith of obedience in His Name for the remission of sins through obedience to the commandment regarding water baptism into His Name; and the reception of the Holy Spirit. Yea, let us preach the three-fold gospel of One God who has revealed Himself to us as the Father—the Son—and the Holy Spirit—in the Name of Jesus Christ, in whom dwells all the fulness of the Godhead bodily, and in whom we also are not only saved, but are to grow and be made complete. See Col. 2:1-9.

Fourth. Because the Kingdom is of GOD, who has been manifested or revealed in three principal Dispensations (of Promise, of Law, and of Grace) as the Father—Son—and Spirit, in and through His three-fold Name—Jesus, Christ, and Lord. Fulfilling the law and the prophecy all in "JESUS", the Jehovah-Saviour, which is the Name of the Father. "CHRIST", the Word which became flesh by the conception of the Spirit in the Virgin's womb, filled and annointed by the Holy Spirit, was offered to God on the Cross by the same eternal Spirit, and was raised for our justification by the Spirit. The "LORD", the eternal and rightful title of the Deity. Elohim—the—Lord, El Shaddai the Lord, Jehovah—the—Lord. All the Apostles preached. (See Acts 5:41-42; Acts 2:41-43 with 2 Cor. 4:1-5) and Jews with Samaritans and Gentiles believed, and were born again by "water and the Spirit", and were delivered from the Kindom of darkness and were brought into the Kingdom of God's dear Son—even the Kingdom of God which our Lord preached to Nicodemus as in John Three.   A. D. U.

CHAPTER VII

Are There Two Gospels?

OW three-fold entrance into the Kingdom is opened and Peter's specific ministry to all the nations is fulfilled. Therefore God could now use His chosen Apostle to the Gentiles, even Apostle Paul—the Saul of Tarsus. The Lord now can use Ananias, just a common saint of God, to baptise Saul of Tarsus and lay hands on him to receive the Holy Spirit "**while calling upon the Name of the Lord**". Read Acts, chapters 9 and 22. Yes, Paul also had to go through the water in the Name of Jesus Christ before he could receive the washing away of his sins and receive the Holy Spirit. See Acts 9:1-18 and Acts 22:11-16. Yes, the threefold means of God had to be applied in Paul's life and experience before he could preach the Kingdom of God and the Name of Jesus Christ to the Gentile world.

What???!!! Did Paul preach the gospel of the Kingdom? He most certainly did. How can you prove this? His own words prove it. Where? In Acts 20th and 28th chapters. See, please, first, Acts 20:17-27, particularly verse 25. Compare with Acts 28:23-31, particularly verses 23 and 31. Compare with Rom. 14:16-17. But some teach, "Paul preached the gospel of Grace to the Gentiles and Peter preached the Gospel of the Kingdom to the Jews. The gospel of the Kingdom belongs to the Jews only, and that is why they had to be baptised into the Name of Jesus Christ for the **remission** of their sins."

We wish to say first that this theory has no Scriptural ground at all and it is an invention of men who attempt to prove it by twisting the Word of God all around. If Paul's gospel is "the gospel of God," the "gospel of Jesus Christ," we ask "Whose gospel is Peter's gospel? Of the flesh? Of the Pharisees? Of the Devil?" Again, if the gospel of Grace is the good news of the crucified, buried, and risen Christ, which Paul preached to the Jews and Gentiles according to 1 Cor. 15:1-11, we ask, "What did Peter preach on the day of Pentecost to the Jews, if not the crucified, buried, risen and glorified Christ?" Please read Acts 2 and see for yourself. Please read Acts 8: and see if Philip did not preach to the eunuch the crucified, buried, risen Christ from the book of Isaiah, 53. Let us ask again please, "If the gospel of Paul was the only gospel of Grace, was the gospel

27

of Peter the gospel of Law?" Can you find such a thing in the New Testament as "the Gospel of Law"? Well then, Paul puts a curse upon every man or even an angel if they should preach any other gospel than that which he preached. According to that theory of the two gospels, poor Peter and the eleven Apostles with him, who went to India, Hindustan, and Persia, and many other countries of the Gentiles to preach their gospel, are all under that divine curse and all those thousands of Indian, African, and Medo-persian Christians were saved by the gospel of the flesh and law.

Furthermore, allow us please to say that if Peter preached repentance and remission of sins in the Name of Jesus Christ, what did Paul preach if not the same thing? See, please, Acts 20:21; Acts 17:30.

If Paul was not preaching the gospel of the Kingdom how could the words of our Lord, which we quote here, come to pass?—"And the gospel of the Kingdom shall be preached in all the world (beginning from Jerusalem) for a witness unto all nations, and then shall the end come". Then opened He their understanding, that they might understand the Scriptures and said unto them, "Thus it is written, and thus it behooved Christ to suffer, and to rise from the dead the third day, and that repentance and remission of sins should be preached in His Name" among the Jews only? No, indeed! "Among ALL NATIONS, beginning from Jerusalem. And ye are my witnesses of these things". "And being assembled together with them, He said unto them, "But ye shall receive power after that the Holy Spirit is come upon you: and ye shall be witnesses unto me, both in Jerusalem, (Jews), and in all Samaria (proselytes), and unto the uttermost part of the earth" (to all the Gentiles) Matt. 24:14. Luke 24:43-52. Acts 1:4-9. Did the Twelve Apostles preach what the Scriptures had said? Did they preach what Christ commanded them? Did they preach to all the three classes of the human race the same gospel everywhere? Well then, what did Paul preach if not the same gospel which was promised by God and prophesied by His Holy Prophets and literally fulfilled by the death and resurrection of Jesus Christ?

Paul said to the Gentiles that he was not ashamed of the Gospel of Jesus Christ, for it is the power of God unto salvation—to the Gentiles only? No Thank God! "To the Jews first, and also to the Greeks who believe". See Rom. 1:14-17. Was Paul's gospel "the power of God unto salvation" and Peter's gospel the power of Law to Jews?

But one may say, Paul got his gospel by Revelation.

28

Yes, indeed, but we ask if his revelation was contrary to the Scriptures from which Peter preached the gospel? Furthermore, do you think the Twelve preached from their head and the dead letter only? Oh, no. They preached the gospel **"with the Holy Spirit sent down from Heaven."**

O, dear ones, let no man deceive you with vain words upon which the wrath of God will come, even on the children of disobedience. But repent, and be baptised into the Name of Jesus Christ for the remission of your sins, and you shall receive the gift of the Holy Spirit. For this is the only way of entering into the Kingdom for all races of humanity. And never forget that "Except a man be born of water and of the Spirit, he cannot enter into the Kingdom of God. Marvel not that I say unto thee, YE MUST BE BORN AGAIN.' Amen and Amen.

But some may say "Didn't Paul speak of the Gospel of uncircumcision and the Gospel of the Circumcision?" Yes, he did not say there were two different Gospels one of Grace to the Gentiles another one of Kingdom to the Jews but he taught the one Gospel both to Jews and Gentiles. So Gospel of uncircumcision means the Gospel for Gentiles and it does not mean at all another Gospel. Of course it is evident that the Jew Christians went through some of their Old Testament ceremonies; observing Saturday and the first day too etc, etc, but they were taught by Apostles; that their salvation depended absolutely on the finished work of Christ and the means of their salvation were faith in the name of Jesus Christ The Saviour only, please see Acts 15:6-18 and also observe Peter and James saying that the Gospel of Grace was the Gospel by which they were all saved, see also Acts 4:10-12.

Gospel of Grace is the Gospel of the Kingdom; for it was the Grace of God that gave us the promise of the Saviour through the mouth of the Prophets. It was the Spirit of Grace that gave us a Saviour full of Grace and Truth and it was God of all Grace who was willing to give the Kingdom for His little Flock. Yes it is the Gracious Father that hides the mysteries of the Kingdom from the wise of this world and He reveals them to us in Christ. It is by His Grace we are privileged to be baptised with both water and the Spirit in the name of the Lord. Praise God! The Gospel of the Kingdom is not another, but the gospel of Grace; so that men may not glory in the presence of God for are not all saved by Grace through Faith of the obedience, and that not of ourselves, but IT IS ALL A GIFT OF GOD.

CHAPTER VIII

Obeying The Gospel.

OU will find twice Apostle Paul using the word obeying in connection with the Gospel of God; also Peter mentions it. See Rom. 10:16. "But they have not all obeyed the Gospel." Again in 2 Thes. 1:8, "In flaming fire taking Vengenace on them that obey not the Gospel of OUR Lord Jesus Christ". 1 Peter 4:17. "For the time that judgement must begin at the House of God: and if it first begin at us, what shall be the end of them that Obey Not the Gospel of God?" etc. etc.

The two Apostles are plainly teaching that there is something in the Gospel that must be obeyed, otherwise the great danger awaits the dis-obedient ones. The question is; What is that which ought to be Obeyed in the Gospel that whereby the Believers May Be Saved? The answer is plainly given in every narrative of the many Apostolic conversions. On the day of Pentecost they were commanded to Repent and be baptised in the name of Christ and they obeyed. See Acts 2:37-41. So did the Samaritans. see Acts 8:5-17. So did the Ethiopian Acts 8:26-38. So did Saul of Tarsus, see Acts 9:17-18, so did the Cornetias see Acts 10:47-48. So did the Jail Keeper, see Acts 16:31-34. So did the Ephsians see Acts 19:1-7. In fact all churches were not recognized Churches of Christ until they Believed the Gospel and were Baptised both with Water and with the Spirit. See Rom. 6:1-5. 1 Cor. 1:11-15, Gal. 3:26-27, etc, etc.

That teaching of some namely "we have nothing to obey, nothing to do to be Saved", is not Apostolic; for in all the above cases in the book of Acts there was first a cry, which came out of the hearts of the convicted souls and that was, "What Shall We Do", "What Shall We Do" and again, "What Shall I Do To Be Saved?" etc. etc. Apostles did not say, "there is nothing for you to do", but they said, "Repent", "Be lieve! Be Baptised", etc. etc. And as soon as the sinners obeyed the Gospel, they were blessed both by God and His servants; therefore they rejoiced together. Amen.

So dear ones, by obeying the gospel of the Kingdom, we do not make salvation of our own souls, but we simply yield our will and life to God of Grace and He graciously saves us for His Name Sake, and blesses our Water baptism and pours upon it The Holy Spirit, sealing us for the day of redemption.

It is an evident fact that Paul preached to both Jews and the Gentiles the Gospel of the Kingdom of God; otherwise he would not have so much emphazied the New Birth, or the New Creation. He was taught by His Lord that the Kingdom of God was not only an earthly affair but also Heavenly, and that the only way to enter into that Kingdom of Heaven; was The New Birth; that is why he said to the Galician Christians "For in Christ Jesus neither circumcision, availeth anything, nor uncircumcision, but a new creature" or, The New Creation. To the Corinthans said; "If any man be in Christ. HE IS A NEW Creature." etc. etc. He strived to present every believer Perfect in Christ, or in the Name of Christ because all the mysteries of the Kingdom of God are in Him, who alone is the King of the Saints. Rev. 15:3. It is the same Spirit of Isms that crept once among God's pe ple; now working amongst us so much until some boldly are saying they are "Paulens" just as the Roman Catholics are supposed to be "Peterens". These are the two extremes; one emphazis the dead works of man as means of Salvation (Romonists). The other emphazises a faith without works; which is called by God's servant "A Dead Faith" O Brethren! let us be temperance in all things and preach the principles of the doctiine of Christ, Heb. 6:1-2, to the unbelieveing world, and to the nominal Christians; but preach Perfection to those who have been already born of Water and of the Spirit.

But one may ask what are the principles of the doctrine of Christ? They are following:

      FIRST—REPENTANCE.
      SECOND—FAITH.
      THIRD—BAPTISM.
      FOURTH—LAYING ON HANDS.
      FIFTH—RESURRECTION.
      SIXTH—ETERNAL JUDGEMENT.
      SEVENTH—PERFECTION.

This is the Divine arranged order, that a sinner first of all must repent, or turn toward God, and second, he must believe on the name of the Lord Jesus, third, believeing he should obey the ordinance of the baptism; forth, after being Baptised hands should be layed on him in the Name of the Lord that he may receive the baptism of the Holy Spirit, fifth, after being born of Water and The Spirit he must count all things but loss and go on to know Christ and to suffer with Him for the hope of a better resurrection, from among the dead, sixth, doing all these things he must rejoice that he has passed from the eternal judgement to Life Everlasting, seventh, continue to grow perfect in love, perfect in Holiness, perfect in Peace and in the full statue of the man Christ Jesus. This is the only God's eternal settled way and the order for salvation through the new covenant. Let us therefore follow Christ's foot-steps as did His holy Apostles, making our calling and election sure. "He that hath ears, let him hear". Amen.   A. D. U.

CHAPTER IX

The Essentiality of Water Baptism.

S the water Baptism essential to salvation? This is a familar question Among the Believers, over its various answers there has been much comment and discussin for centuries; but to avoid any unnecessary debate over it, we will beg our readers to decide for them selves, but we do ask the honest and fai... of all toward our indirect answer.

Yes! We are compelled to think that the water baptism when performed with a real faith in the Name of Jesus Christ and coupled with genuine Repentance IS ESSENTIAL TO OUR SALVATION, but baptism without repentance and a real Faith is useless and is false. Simon the sorcerer had that kind of baptism as we read in Acts 8:13-22 and Peter told him he was going to perish if he didn't repent. You see, he received water baptism with a false pretense and with an unrepented heart. So mere baptism alone is essential to nothing, but being baptised Into the Name of Deity, theFather—The Son—The Holy Spirit which is The-Lord-Jesus-Christ for this dispensation; is essential, for it is a Part of the New Birth and an important part of it too, since our Lord said "Ye must be born of water". etc. etc.

There is still another kind of water baptism preformed in these days which has nothing to do whatever with the real salvation, and that is to be baptised into a denominational church; to be baptised into the baptist, and Cambelists denominational churches does not save us at all; or being sprinkled and then confirmed into Lutheran, Episcopalian and Catholic churches dosen't do us good at all as far as our soul salvation is concerned, only it brings us into society of these modern Religious folks. Our Lord never commanded us to be baptised into any church but he emphatically commanded His Apostles to baptize the disciples into the Name of God of the church, and He Himself is that very God of that church, see Matt. 18:16 and Rom.16:16 and Acts 20:28, etc. etc.

The essence of the water baptism is not in what we are doing, nor in water alone but in the great name of our

Saviour into which we should be baptised both by water and the Spirit, and since His Name is the only way of our salvation the baptism of water when being done properly and solemnly does save us. If the water baptism was not essential to our salvation, why did God labor so hard to make so many types for it, all the way through the Old Testament.

If it was not so much necessary why He ordained John The Baptist just for that service alone. Why Jesus Himself went into it and said, it was to fulfill all righteousness, why Our Lrd so emphatically said "He that believeth And is Baptised shall be saved. Mark 16:15-16. Why He commanded His Apostles to perform it. Why the Apostles were so particular about it so that they never let a believing sinner get out of it, why God confirmed it by pouring out His Holy Spirit upon it. Why Jews and Heathens began to kill a believer, as soon as they learned he was baptized into the name of Christ. And why God made it one of the principles of His unchangeable doctrine. Surely it must be essential to something!! What could that thing be but salvation? But some may say "We believe it is essential to obedience and not to salvation, well, we ask is obedience of Faith essential to salvation? You must admit that it is. Well then, is your obedience any good except it is proved by your action? Obedience without action is false and will not save; but obedience and action according to the commandments of God, is the way of the eternal blessing; therefore Baptism and the real obedience go together and it takes both with Faith in the Name of Jesus Christ to save the repented sinner.

THE WATER TEST

The water test proved the real people of God and saved them during the flood but destroyed the wicked ones. In the red sea near Egypt the real people of God were seperated from the wicked ones by the water. While it saved Israel from the land of slavery, yet it destroyed the cruel Heathens. The Gidions army were also tested by water, the half hearted and fearful soldiers of Israel were turned away, but the real soldiers of Jehovah proved their genuineness by water test and were sent forth to conquer.

So it was in the days of John the Baptist; the true sons of Israel received John's baptism with repentance and confession of their sins, but the supposed leaders among God's people were proved that after all they were sons of serpents and the generation of vipers, because they were the very ones who thought it was not necessary to be baptised and rejected the council of God. It is said

34

that the water test is also a scientific test. If you wish to know the real diamond stone, they say throw it in clear water, if it continued shining it is the real thing, but if it gets white loses its real color, it is false. Reader, have you gone through the water test? After being baptised, do you continually show forth the friuts of your repentance, if you haven't you had better repent, and be baptised that you may be saved, but be sure to be baptised not into modern churchanity but into the Name of our Lord.

THE FOLLOWING IS SELECTED

A bird is perfectly safe sitting on a high-voltage wire so long as no connection is made or circuit made. The wire is connected with sufficient energy to instantly kill a horse, but this energy is unmanifested until a circuit of resistance Is formed . When the air is filled with dampness of water the position of this bird would become dangerous. An arc is liable to form through this damp air as water i s a conductor of electrical energy. You can see in this the position of water in the place of regenertion. Water alone has no power to transform or impart life or Divine energy. When properly applied, at the opportune time, it becomes the channel through which eternal or Divine life is imparted.

It means death to the material or old creation, and the bringing forth of the new. Now you can see why Jesus told Nichodemus that he must be born again, of the water and of the spirit, in order to see and enter into the Kingdom of God, or eternal state.

                                                                    Selected.

MODE OR ESSENCE WHICH?

It is an evident fact that the most of us who were immersed, saw our need of immersion instead of Sprinkling and as soon as we discovered that the real mode of baptism was not sprinkling but immersion, we hastened into water: all we saw then was the true mode of baptism and we were willing to lose even friends for it, and were immersed for which God blessed us. But we had not seen yet the essence of the baptism and the stress upon that part which Our Lord put; in fact our Leaders did not know themselves that most essential part of baptism; so we were blind to the essential part though our eyes were opened to the mode—part; hence imperfect baptism. The Lord who searches the hearts saw that we were faithful worthy of more light in His blessed word, so He baptised us with the Holy Spirit that we may know more of the truth. The result was that we had to be baptised again, this time not into the mode but into the essence of the baptism which is the Name of God.

Our Lord speaking of baptism He did not put stress upon the mode though He taught His disciples the right way of baptism; but He put all the stress upon the Name of the Father The Son and of The Spirit. When He said "Go ye therefore and teach all nations, Baptising them

INTO THE NAME OF."

The essentiality is "The Name" not names, but The Only One Name of the Godhead,we did not stop in those days to think and search for the one name of Our God into which we are commanded to be immersed, we only wished to be buried with Christ in Baptism. We did not ask our pastor to tell us what is that one Name into which you are to baptise us, all we saw was water and immersion, satisfied with mere quotation of the commandments upon us instead of actually and inteligently obeying it up to the last letter. The Apostles preached the gospel in the Name. Yea, The Name of Jesus was their powerful doetrine by which they filled Jerusalem, They preached—

REPENTANCE IN THE NAME.
FORGIVENESS IN THE NAME.
REMISSION OF SINS IN THE NAME.
THE FAITH IN THE NAME.
AND SALVATION IN THE NAME.
ACTS—5:29-31; 3:38; 16:4-16.

They healed the sick, They Preached, They Baptised, and they suffered all for that One Name of God, if you wish to know exactly what that one name is, search these items in the Bible and you will find out that it was no other Name but JESUS CHRIST THE LORD. Many are baptised into the water but not very many INTO THE NAME, and to do so it means Persecution. Luke 21:16-17.

HISTORICAL FACTS

Note "THE TEACHING OF THE TWELVE," a compilation of the Apostolic teaching, it is claimed written down about 10 years after the death of Apostle John. In speaking of the Lord's Supper it says no one was to be admitted to His table, unless he had been baptised "into the name of the Lord," 9:5.

And Caiphas's report to the Sanhedren is as following:

36

The two charges of the high priest of Jews against Jesus our Lord are taken from "The Archko Volume", a book translated from the Authorized Ancient Manuscripts found in The Great Vatican Library in the City of Rome.

"Caiphas, Priest of the Most High God, to The Masters of Israel, Greetings: in obedience to your demands for a reason for my action in the case of Jesus of Nazareth, and in defense of my conduct, I beg leave to submit the following for your consideration:—

"He (Jesus of Nazareth) taught the people that there was but one living and true God, but he taught them that He was that God, and that His Father was merged into Himself, and could not manifest only Himself through him."

"He teaches (of water) as the seal of God, instead of circumcision, which was established by the decrees of God with Abraham as a seal of the Jews."

We do not believe all the report of the old high Priest being the real truth, but we believe his two reported charges against our Great Saviour as stated above, because to the first one John the Apostle bore witness. See John 14: 5-10 and John 8:56-59. As to His teaching of baptism being the real God given separating sign of His people from the sinners; is another truth confirming what Mark wrote about the essenciality of the baptism taught by our Lord. See Mark 16:15-16.

You see dear reader, the profane history bears witness with church history written by the Christian fathers to the truth as being recorded in the Bible in regard of the absolute Deity of our Lord and His teaching on baptism being so very important to cu· Christian faith. Amen.   A. D. U.

WHAT THE COMMENTATORS SAY ABOUT WATER AND THE SPIRIT IN REGARDS OF THE NEW BIRTH.

Concerning John III. 5.

From Adam Clarke's comment on this verse, the following is given, as showing that, in Clarke's view, the birth and baptism of the Spirit are one:

"When John came baptising with water ,he gave the Jews the plainest intimations that this would not suffice; that it was only typical of that baptism of the Holy Ghost, under the similitude of fire, which they must all receive from Jesus Christ: see Matt. 3:11. Therefore, our Lord asserts that a man must be born of water and the Spirit, i.e., of the Holy Ghost, which, represented under the similitude of water, cleanses, refreshes and purifies the soul. He who receives

not this baptism, has neither right nor title to the Kingdom
of God; nor can he with any propriety be termed a Christian, because that which essentially distinguished the Christian dispensation from that of the Jews was, that its Author
baptized all His follows with the Holy Ghost."

On this text, Rev. F. W. Robertson (Anglican) wrote a
sermon; in which he observes concerning WATER:

"A large number of Protestant commentators have endeavored to explain this passage away, as if it did not apply
to baptism at all. But, by all the laws of correct interpretation, we are compelled to admit that 'born of water' has
here a reference to baptism."

———oo———

WHAT PROFESSORS SAY ABOUT NEW BIRTH.

The following article by Prof. W. H. T. Dau; appeared
in "the Christian Herald", meditation page; which bears
witness to the truth of the new birth, containing **Water and
The Spirit.** It appeared under head **"THE ONE WAY."**

**"Verily, verily, I say unto thee, Except a man be born
again, he cannot see the kingdom of God."** Just from what
motive Nicodemus sought his faint-hearted interview with
the Lord, we cannot tell. It is likely however that the great
events which were transpiring in Judea at that time had some
connection with this coming of Jews. Without relying directly to the reverent greeting of his learned visitor, the Lord
refers at once to the baptism of John, which was at that
time and for many years after a mootedquestion among the
Jews. For the expression "water and Spirit," which the
Lord uses during his conversation with Nicodemus, is an
unmistakable reference to baptism. Now John had in strong
terms denounced the ruling church party among the Jews,
going even so far as to call them generation of vipers.
Luke tel s us that the Pharisees showed contempt for the
baptism of John. It is possible that Nicodemus also dis-
dained the terms which John laid down for admission to
the kingdom of God. It seemed almost an insult to these
men from the upper classes of Jewish society to be treated
on a level with soldiers, publicans, and the lowest classes
of Jewry. Their pride revolted from the idea. Accordinly
the Lord finds it necessary to reinforce the teaching of his
faithful forerunner with the solemn assertion in our text.
This assertion discounts heavily against all natural fitness
for the kingdom of God supposed to exist in men. Nicodemus was outwardly an upright man and even occupied a
high rank in the Jewish Church. Perhaps he was silently

38

appealing to the law and traditions which he had kept. The Lord tells him in effect: You have not even begun to be fit for the kingdom. Do not think that the religion which I have come to proclaim merely wishes to give you a little supplementary advice regarding spiritual matters, or to recommend to you a few more works which are still lacking to your perfection. No, I am come to begin the good work in you. There is not so much as a seed or rootlet of spiritual worth in you. Your former works must be renounced, and you must enter upon a new phase of living. You must be made all over again, not physically but spiritually, because you are dead in trespasses and sins.

W. H. T. D.

———oo———

NEWSPAPPERS PREACHING THE TRUTH.

The Montreal Star of Montreal, Quebec, Canada is one of the largest daily papers in the Dominion has about 100,000 daily readers. The following article on baptism of water appeared in one of its issues. It was written as a challenge to all the bible scholars, but no one dared to answer it though the subject was for sometime being discussed by different preachers. This article was the final one which closed the discussion and we wish to let our readers read it.

A. D. U.

———oo———

FOR THE REMISSION OFSINS.

The Editor, Montreal Daily Star.

Sir,—Like Mr. J. W. Crighton, I, too, have wondered if your correspondents who are contending for baptism by immersion really are aware that the atonement of Jesus for the sin of the whole world is only made applicable individually by the "washing of awter" (Eph. 5:26). If your correspondents will take time to look this matter up they will find the following.

1st. That it is expressly taught in thirteen of the books of the New Testament that baptism is for "the" remission of sins," and only those who need salvation are eligable for baptism.

2nd. That in the Acts alone the conversion of twelve different groups of people is related, stating in every case that they were baptized, making in all eighteen references to this subject in these twelve cases alone.

3rd. That the Apostles always administered baptism

39

in Jesus ' Name only, which is the only name of God for this age. That in one instance on record the Apostle Paul ordered re-baptism because it had not been administered in the Name of Jesus.

4th. That baptism is valueless, unless followed immediately by the outpouring of the Spirit, and that in nineteen passages of Scripture the water and the splrlt are expressly coupled, and clearly implied in many more.

5th. That the baptism of the Spirit was always accompanied by the sign of "speaking in other tongues as the Spirit gave utterance." Of this, Chrysostom (A. D. 357) says: "Whoever was baptized in Apostlic days, he straightway spake with tongues; for the Spirit being invisible, God bestowed some sensible proof of his energy; for one spake in the Indian language, another in the Persian, and so on, it being clearly manifest to the onlookers that it was the very Spirit Himself in the person speaking." Now there may be individuals in the various churches who preach this truth, but it is a startling fact that, as a body, the Pentecostal Assemblies of the world are unique in this matter. May we hope that scholarly men will honestly examine these maters?

John Patterson.

CHAPTER X

The One Christian Baptism.

Ephsians 5:5.

HE real Christian baptism is twofold and it contains the two elements, Namely: water and The Spirit. Therefore, the water baptism without the Holy Spirit baptism is not full Christian baptism; seeing this truth clearly, we will understand why Peter and John rushed to Samaria to lay hands and pray over the Samaritan baptised believers that they might receive the Holy Spirit; for He had yet fallen upon none of them. Acts 8:14-17.

The Spirit baptism alone without water baptism is not full Christian baptism, either, seeing this divine fact, you will understand why Peter was so stern about baptising the Household of Cornilius with water after they had received the Holy Spirit. See Acts 10:44-48. Yet in the face of these divinely and eternally settled facts, people go in their ways and teach all that Christian baptism is when you are baptised with water; others say, all you need is the Holy Spirit baptism and you don't need to be baptized in water, for the water does'nt save. Etc, etc. If these kinds of teachings are not the tradition of men, we ask what are they? Yes, it was such a kind of Spirit the old Pharasies had that caused them to deceive men and women of their time and made them to keep the tradition of elders more than God's commandments, making God's commandment without effect through their traditions. Matt. 15: 3-7-8. Oh, people of God "beware of the leaven of the Pharasies", and keep the commandments of our Saviour, who said, "If ye love me keep my commandments." Be not satisfied until you have a real full Christian baptism before you dare to call yourself a bible born Christian.

O! Sons of men, remember, just as a body is one being and one Person, yet contains three parts and that body cannot live and is not body without each part together, so it is with the Christian baptism, though it is one baptism, yet it contains Repentance, Faith, and going in water and the Spirit also, and that in the Name of the Lord. So, baptism without reepntance and faith in the Name of Christ will not stand in the presence of God, nor will repentance and faith without the real obedience to the infallible commandments of God; neither Spirit baptism will stand the test if it is not completed with water baptism of renptance and faith in Christ. Such partcial baptism is false, it is man-made, though apparently wonderful; God's real twofold baptism will only stand the test of the fire. Oh, let us flee from the falsehood of the modern times and build our foundation upon the rock. Matt. 7:24:27. May the Lord open your understanding whoever you are that contends for something which is not fully according to all God's Word, and change your mind and turn from your man-made ways to God's narrow and perfect way which leads unto life eternal.

SANCTIFICATIION AND THE NEW BIRTH.

Is the new birth sanctification. The new birth is not the complete sanctification but it is the beginning not only of the sanctification but of all the other Christian traits. The bible teaches there is a beginning of the sanctification, and there is a perfect holiness. This we see in the Apostolic exhortations to "The holy brethren." Though they being holy yet they needed to be sanctified wholly yet. See 2 Thess. 5:23-27 with Heb. 3:1 and Heb. 12:12-15. Etc, etc.

We are also taught by God's Spirit to trust and believe on Christ not only as our "God the Saviour", but also as being made unto us "wisdom and righteousness, and sanctification," etc. When we are born, we get Christ's Spirit into us and that Spirit of the truth is "the Spirit of holiness" which comes into our lives to change us from day to day into the perfect image and the full statue of the man Christ Jesus. Let us therefore never forget that there is awaiting us a more perfect sanctification yet, and let us see that we are not only keeping clean daily, but that if we are also growing into the perfect holiness. There is a sanctification of the soul and there is a sanctification of the body also. This threefold sanctification for the threefold being of man begins at the new birth experience and we find its traces all over us; but God means for us not only to have the traces of His Holiness, but be filled with all His fulness and become Holy as He is Holy. Eph. 3:13-20. Etc, etc. Amen.

THE SECOND RESURRECTION.

Thank God! there is another birth (coming forth) ahead of us yet. This will be our final birth into a life of Glory, Perfection, Power and eternal bliss. Our Lord had this birth from among the dead and that blessed birth made

Him to be "The First begotten among His brethren." He was born once of a woman as a new creature miraculously and He was born (begotten) triumphantly of the dead also. So it must be with us, we must not only be bobrn of the water and the Spirit, but also we must be born of the dead or come forth from among the dead ones. Some day; if we should happen not to be in grave, yet we must be born out of our body which "is dead because of Sin; a tabernacle liable to corruption in which we groan and travail with pangs of birth that we may be delivered from this body of the death and be clothed upon with that glorious eternal tabernacle which God has promised to all His water—Spirit —born children. See the folloiwng references for the scriptural light on the second resurrection, or our next miraculous birth. Rom. 7:24; 8:10. Phil. 3:21. 2 Cor. 5:2-4. Rom. 8:23; 6:7. Phil. 3:11. Heb. 11:35. Rev. 20:5-6.

A. D. U.

CHAPTER XI

Baptism.

Reprinted from "Eusebia" of August 1898.

In the performance of Baptism into the Name of Yah-sous, the subject is inducted into the death of Christ by a similtude of His death, together with Him," (Rom. 6:5) by which, the thing symblized, viz., the death of Christ, becomes ours. We thus, by symbol, pass through the death state, and rise with Christ. In so doing, the death sentence has been executed upon us, and if we abide in Him, we shall be made immortal when He comes. The old rites of circumcision was but a fore-shadowing of flesh cut off for sin —death for sin—which if suffered in Christ satisfies the sentence. If we are not in Christ when the day of doom— the judgement day—comes, the penalty will take hold of us with an eternal grasp.

But Baptism, without a knowledge of the Gospel, or how we get remission of sins by the death process in Christ, is of not the least avail. Those who imagine they get remission of sins before baptism can have no correct knowledge of its significance. If we receive remission of sins before baptism, there would be no use for baptism, which is the "birth of water," or "the washing of regeneration," "the cleansing of water in Word."(Eph. 5:26) The "word" of the gospel understood, accompained by the water, completes the regeneration. The facts concerning the method of redeeming us and giving us eternal life are, by a similitude, exhibited in the process of baptism. It is the "FORM OF DOCTRINE." delivered first to us, and "into which we are delivered,"—and to "obey it from the heart"we have first to comprehend it.,(Rom. 6:17.) The foolisness of the practise of rhantizing or pouring water on a person in three names, and calling it baptism, is too obvious to need comment. A person ignorant of the gospel is no subject for baptism. Those who practise sprinkling or pouring can certainly have no proper knowledge of the gospel. Their irregular use of water is in keeping with their irregular faith, and the whole accompaniment of swarm of errors. The man who comprehends the glorious gospel, needs not be told that he must be buried in the water to represent his faith. To pretend to symbolize the death, burial, and resurrection process by the use of a teaspoonful of water would be as appropriate as to scatter a handful of earth upon a dead man and pronounce him properly buried.

CHAPTER XII

Editorial Pen Points on the New Birth.

A. D. Urshan

ET not him that is independent from the Lordship of Christ in his daily life, pretend to know what the new birth doctrine is. You are not entered into the Kingdom of God, or "born again" until Jesus Christ actually is the King of your heart and the owner of your character For to be born of the Spirit or to enter into the Kingdom of God, is nothing less than a life being not only filled with the living Christ, but also being led by the Spirit of God, they are the Sons of God." And "Unto as many actually received Him, to them gave He the **power** to become the sons of God." Are you a son of God? Do you belong to Christ the Lord? Is Jesus really your Lord? If so, then you are born of God.

To be born again is to be **born from above.** There are many who claim the second birth but their lives are a worldly life, they are seeking and longing and indulging in the things that all the worldly people run after. But the truth is tnat he that is born from above seeks the thingss which are from above. (Col. 3:1.). This is not only the scriptural test of a new creation, but even the law of gravitation confirms it. Throw a stone in the air, it will at once rush down to the earth. Why? For it is all earthly, but get one who is really born from above, no matter how much earthly people and temptation try to drag him down, yet they will not prosper; that pérson will arise and run after God and the things of God, because he. is born of God and he is a pilgram here, for his sweet home is where the angels chant, Holy, Holy, Holy, the Lord God Almighty.

To argue elaborately on the new birth doctrine will save none but to have the Spirit in us that makes us "Christ's." "For he that hath not the Spirit of Christ, he is none of His." The most important question is Christ in you and if you are in Him. You may get angry if someone tells you that unless you speak in other tongues as the Spirit gives utterance you lack the Heavenly sign of youra oneness with Christ or the Spiritual Christ's presence within you, but what the Scripture say! And if your life and experiences are really magnifying the Word of God. Our Lord said to His Disciples, in the day they receive the Holy Spirit baptism they will know then that He was in the Father and they were in Him and He was in them, and not until then they counld actually say "The Spirit of God bears witness with our Spirit that we are the children of God." If that was the way they received Christ in them; no doubt that was the way they preached the truth. Then, how, anyone dares to fix another way? The truth is, that whoesover is possessed with the Spirit of Christ of the Spirit of the Truth, He is normally Christ's, and those who are Christ's "They have crucified their flesh with the lusts thereof."

To be Christ's in the real sense is to be His, and only His. Not of the world, not of the flesh, not of blood, but of God, born of God, a child of God and owned by God. Amen.

He that is not clothed upon with the righteousness of God;let him not boast of the Thealogical knowledge of the new birth doctrine, for it is settled in Heaven that "The Kingdom of God is Righteousness." If you have entered into the Kingdom by your second birth you should prove it by your inward and outward life of righteousness. Do you act right before your loved ones? Are you right in your public life? Are you right in your motives, thoughts and all actions? Are you right in the sight of God and man? If not; you have not entered into Righteousness yet which is the Kingdom of God.

He that is not in a passionate love with the Person, Name, and fulness of Jesus Christ, let him not claim the New Birth experience. For Jesus said to the deceived Jews, "If God were your father, you owuld love me; for I proceeded from God." Amen. Reader, do you love Jesus with all your heart, strengeth, soul and mind? Ycu may say you love God, but this is not the proof; the available proof is your loyal and sincere love to Him who loved you and gave His life for you. If you really love the Lord you will depart from all iniquity, you will keep all His commandments and you will not love the world, no! you will not love fame, money, fashion, easiness of this life, and shun the cross. No! You will not love your own self, but you will love to

47

see Christ exalted as the Lord God Almighty and you will love to worship Him as such.

He that entertains sin in his daily life, let not him deceive himself by imagining that he is born again; because it is written, "Whosoever is born of God doeth not commit sin. He that committeth sin is of the devil." Again, "For whosoever is born of God overcometh the world." Again, "He that is begotten of God keepeth himself, and that wicked one toucheth him not."

He that is born of God hath that seed of women in him which hath great enimity against the works of iniquity. God hath ordained from the beginning of sin in the Human race that divine hatery. (Gen. 3:14-15). Reader! Do you hate sin as you would hate poisin to drink? The religion that denies the existance of the real personal David and says all is lovely and that God does not hate; it is a deception aldredy. But he that is bobrn of water and the Spirit, hates the very "'government spotted by the flesh." Amen.

The Almighty God
in
The Lord Jesus Christ

By Andrew D. Urshan

1121 S. MOTT STREET,
LOS ANGELES, CALIFORNIA
1919

APOSTOLIC BOOK CORNER

u.p.c. of portland

CONTENTS.

PREFACE.

May the mercy and grace of the Almighty God in Christ Jesus, our glorious Lord, cause the mind of the reader of this book to grasp the divine motive in its contents and fill his heart with a true worship and adoration toward God, our Heavenly Father, who dwelleth and manifesteth Himself in His only begotten Son. Amen.

It is to satisfy the desire of the lovers of the Lord that we are putting these blessed messages on the Infinite NAME of God and His Majestic Fulness into book form. It is to magnify the matchless NAME of God, our Saviour, that we are sending this book into the world.

We have already proved God's rich blessings upon the seekers of His knowledge and fulness, through these messages, which were sent to thousands in the form of open letters, and this encourages us to publish them again.

We therefore commit prayerfully the truth in the chapters of this little book to you, reader, and beg your prayerful study of the same, with your open Bible. Be sure, therefore, that you look up every reference; otherwise you will miss the best of the feast.

In order to confirm the truth of God in this book, we have taken the writings and testimonies of many eminent Christian men on the great theme, that the Scripture might be fulfilled, "In the mouth of two or three witnesses every word shall stand." Reader, you will find more than three witnesses in this book proclaiming God in Christ. Yea, you will find a great cloud of witnesses speaking the same thing, exalting and lifting up Jesus Christ, the God-Man.

May the abundant grace, through the thanksgiving of many, redound to the glory of God. Amen.

ANDREW D. URSHAN.

INTRODUCTION.

To know the **Name** of God is to know **Him**, for He reveals His great power and majestic Person with His fathomless love and grace and all His infinite attributes, **by and through His great and holy Name.**

God has revealed Himself at different times in past ages by His excellent Names given to His people, but "Yah-weh" (Jehovah), the Name of God, is the fullest explanation and manifestation of His great and infinite Being. "Yah-weh" therefore is the memorial Name of the T-h-r-e-e—O-n-e God, which literally means the **present** and **future** one self-existing, unchangeable **God, the LORD"** which is, which was, and which is to come," or the "I AM THAT I AM."

The "I AM" Name of God, which He gave to Moses, applies to His then present revelation and active purpose revealed to His people Israel, that they might believe in **their one true God, the Saviour,** who had come to deliver them from their long-continued Egyptian bondage by the power of His mighty **Name.** But the Lord gave Moses and Israel at the same time another great promise for another great deliverance, and that deliverance was to take place in the future. This promise is included also in His blessed revealed Name, viz., "THAT I AM." ("I AM THAT I AM" means a present and future God.)

The word "THAT" points to His other or future manifestation, when He should appear again, not through a mist of darkness on a high mountain, nor through clouds in the air, neither through angelic beings, as if appeared at the first to His people, on Mount Sinai, but in the promised seed of Abraham, as David's Son and the Lion of the Tribe of Judah, yea, through the Seed of the woman, as **"God manifest in the flesh,"** making His tabernacle with man, thus becoming IMMANUEL, which is, being interpreted, **"God with us."**

The Lord graciously revealed this final manifestation to the prophet Isaiah, also, saying:

"Ye are my witnesses, saith the Lord, and my servant whom I have chosen, that ye may know and believe me and understand that I am He: before me there was no God formed, neither shall there be after me.

I, even I am the Lord; and beside me there is no saviour. . . . I, even I, am He that blotteth out thy transgressions for mine own sake, and will not remember thy sins." Is, 43:10, 11, 25.

Here we see the blessed message of the great salvation promised, through His anointed Son to be accomplished, that that future day He would appear again, to save not only Jews, but all them that call and believe on his NAME, delivering them this time, not from Egypt but from the world, the flesh, sin, and the devil, bringing them not only to the promised land, but unto Himself, lifting them up to His own glorious habitation. So we read that "in the fulness of time" the holy child was conceived in the virgin Mary by the power of the Holy Ghost, through the shadow of the Almighty; and the angel of the Lord appeared to Joseph and said to him, "Joseph, thou son of David, fear not to take unto thee Mary, thy wife: for that which is conceived in her is of the Holy Ghost, and she shall bring forth a son, and thou shalt call His name JESUS: for He shall save His people from their sins." Here is that memorial Name of Jehovah revealed to Moses in three words, viz., "THAT I AM," which expressed His future manifestation, being literally fulfilled. The God of Abraham, the God of Isaac, and the God of Jacob, who said unto Moses, "I AM THAT I AM" was coming with His word and Spirit into human form. That "holy thing" which was to be called "Jesus" was "YAH-OSHUA" or "Jehovah the Saviour," coming to His own people in the flesh (Jno. 1:8-12), to fulfill for fallen man the law which he had broken, to take away the sin of the human race, to destroy the power of the devil,—yea, to reconcile the world unto Himself, as the Apostle Paul affirms. **"God was in Christ, reconciling the world unto Himself."** Hallelujah.

The God who created the old world, things visible and invisible, by His WORD, now comes down in His incarnate WORD to create a new generation, making manifest "the mystery hid for ages," even **"the great mystery of godliness."** God the Father, by the power of His Spirit, comes with and in His Son, into the world, to give everlasting life unto all them that should believe on His NAME; the Name which is above every name, in heaven, in the earth, and under the earth, the lofty Name of the Father given to His Son, the Name at which every knee shall · bow and which every tongue shall confess, JESUS, the Lord. Phil. 2:9, Eph. 1:21, Acts 1:21.

So all the revelation of the Names of God and His great promises in the Old Testament were pointing to the great Sin-Bearer, who in the last days came forth from the bosom of the Deity, to bring life and immortality to light, and to save the poor, benighted, sinful race, and after accomplishing the redemption through His precious blood, He arose triumphant from the dead and entered into Heaven, and sat down at the right hand of majesty, receiving back unto Himself all the fulness of the Deity (Godhead). He sent His Holy Spirit on the earth to prepare His people by the power of the Spirit for His second coming. This is the Apostolic message of salvation, and the Apostle Peter proclaimed it boldly before the leading men of Israel, when he was brought forcibly, with the other apostles, before their council. "Peter, filled with the Holy Ghost, said unto them, Ye rulers of the people, and elders of Israel, . . . be it known unto you all, and to all the people of Israel, . . . this is the stone which was set at naught by you builders, which is become the head of the corner. Neither is there salvation in any other; for there is none other NAME under heaven given among men, **whereby we must be saved.**" Acts 4:12. These leading men of Israel knew that their salvation could come only through the great Name of their Jehovah God, and when Peter said that the Name of Jesus was the Name by which alone all can be saved, He proclaimed Him to be both Christ and the Lord Jehovah. Acts 2:36. Praise God! The God of Israel actually came upon this old earth, to take out a people for His holy Name, as we read in Acts 15.

"And after they had held their peace, James answered, saying, Men and brethren, hearken unto me:

Simeon hath declared how God at the first did visit the Gentiles, to take out of them a people for his name,

And to this agree the words of the prophets; as it is written,

After this **I will return,** and will build again the taberacle of David, which is fallen down; and I will build again the ruins thereof, and I will set it up;

That the residue of men might seek after the Lord, and all the Gentiles, **upon whom my name is called,** saith the Lord, who doeth all these things.

Known unto God are all His works from the beginning of the world." Acts 15:13-18.

Please, reader, notice the three prophetic words mentioned in the 16th verse, "I will return." The word "return" signifies that He had come once to His people, and He was to come yet again. Here is again the explanation and the fulfillment of the prophetic name of the Almighty God, "E'YEH ASHER E'YEH." (Some Jewish scholar tells us "E'yeh Asher E'yeh" does not mean "I AM THAT I AM," but "I WILL BE THAT I WILL BE.") However, in both translations we see that the God of Israel gives Himself a name to Moses in which His people may not only enjoy His different deliverances at different times, but His great and final revelation and salvation through His beloved Son, Jesus Christ our Lord, who is the fulfillment of the "ASHER E'YER."

"O, Hark the voice of love and grace,
Sounding in the names of God,
Down the blessed God incarnate
Comes to shed for men His blood.
Hallelujah| It is finished,
Christ has triumphed by His Name 'JAH!' "

ANDREW D. URSHAN.

CHAPTER I

The Deity of Jesus Christ.

as spoken of by

John Bunyan, Martin Luther, Charles Spurgeon, F. C. Jennings, Samuel Greene, Isaac Watts, Thoro Harvie, Samuel Stennett, Edward Perronet, I. O. Brown, the Apostles, the Church Fathers, Martyrs, Bishops, German Protestant Fathers, Reformers, Poets, Philosophers, Historians, with the Deity of Christ in Epistle to the Hebrews, and Seven Strong Reasons for Preaching It .

By A. D. Urshan.

IT IS very inspiring to read the testimonies of these pious men who lived and died for Christ our Lord; sparing not their voice they cried aloud, saying, **Jesus is God.** It certainly encourages us to join them and speak the same thing knowing the day is fast approaching when He shall appear with His great glory, to fill the earth with the knowledge of the One true God, and cause all the nations of the earth, high and low, great and small, kings and citizens, to fall at His feet and acknowledge Him, worship and fear Him as the Jehovah of hosts and the King eternal and as God over all (Zech. 14:5; 1 Tim. 6:14, 15; Rom. 9:5) we also hesitate not to proclaim His soon coming, and exhort you all to get ready for that greatest of all events.

The kings and the rulers of the earth have ignored His eternal authority, the Mohammedans have rejected His divine Sonship and the redeeming blood of His cross, the Jews have refused His Messiahship and His great salvation, many of the evangelized heathen have disobeyed His glorious gospel, and the apostate Christians, with modern theologians, are denying His absolute Deity. What about you, dear reader What do you think of Christ, and what are you doing with Him?

As for me, I have personally accepted Him as my Saviour and the only LORD. and believe in Him as my God and my All in All His matchless NAME is my refuge and stay. Therefore I glory in nothing less than in the blood of His cross and in His powerful resurrection, ascension, glorification, and His absolute Deity.

It is a matter of great joy to me to preach not only Jesus Christ as the Lamb of God slain before the foundation of the earth for our blessed redemption, but to declare His eternal Godhead also. To this end I join the great cloud of His faithful witnesses and mingle my glad testimony with theirs concerning **"God manifested in the flesh,** justified in the Spirit, seen of angels, preached unto the Gentiles, believed on in the world, received up into glory." (1 Tim. 3: 16).

The Latter Rain outpouring of the Spirit caused the Christian world to go to the Bible as never before, searching diligently to see if these things were so,—the things which they saw happening to those who were receiving the baptism of the Holy Ghost, with shakings and speaking in other tongues, etc. This has been the case in every advance movement of God's people, when they have been graciously crowned with the revelations and illuminations of the hidden truths of the good old Bible. So it is with this wonderful present-day truth. God is revealing to and energizing His people to proclaim, as never before, a full and glorified Saviour, who is God-man. This divine movement is also causing the people of God everywhere to go to their Bibles again, and it has caused me to do the same. Therefore, I will endeavor, in His blessed NAME, to give you a brief exposition of the Deity or Jesus Christ as it is recorded in the Epistle to the Hebrews.

The Deity of Jesus Christ in the Epistle to the Hebrews

There are four books in the New Testament which especially and more specifically reveal the deity of our Lord and Saviour, or **Jesus'** being the very God; viz., the Gospel of St. John, the epistles to the Colossians and the Hebrews, and the book of Revelation. At this time we will only meditate a little on the Deity of Christ as in the book of Hebrews. (Read carefully Hebrews, first chapter.)

"The key word of the book of Hebrews is 'Better.' Hebrews is a serious of contrasts between the good of Judaism and the 'better' things of Christ."—Scofield.

Christ is being proved in this epistle better and much higher than the angels, than Moses, than Joshua, than Aaron. The Apostle in this book not only exalts the perfect humanity and sacrifice of the Saviour with His divine Sonship, but He calls Him **God, the Creator and Upholder** of all things by the power of **HIS WORD.** To prove his teaching to the wavering Christians (Jews), he quotes to them a part of the forty-fifth Psalm, a prophecy which is most wonderful and beyond comprehension, about the eternal God, the King, with His glorious Bride, who is the Son of God and yet the image and shining-forth God, our Creator.

In these days of ours, not only are thousands of so-called Christians denying the absolute Deity of our Lord, but those who believe it are trying to preach Him feebly as God the Son, and by so doing they think they have gone to the limit in exalting "the Lord of Glory." But the Apostle in the above Epistle exalts Him above all human and angelic dignitaries and proclaims Him as God, in addition to proclaiming Him as the Son. And still he appears not to have finished his great discourse; for with a seemingly disappointed exclamation he says: **"Of whom we have many things to say, and hard to be uttered, seeing ye are dull of hearing."** (Hebrews 5:11.)

The Apostle saw that all that those doubting Christians could comprehend then was what he preached to them through his letter, and that they could not stand 'any deeper and higher—yea, more mysterious—Holy-Ghost-given utterances on the person of our **Blessed Creator and Redeemer.** Evidently Jesus Christ was beyond and much higher, in the mind of the Apostle, than what we read of Him in the Epistle to the Hebrews. This confirms the saying of our Lord: "No man knows the Son but the Father; neither knoweth any man the Father save the Son, and He to whomsoever the Son will reveal Him." In this Scripture our Lord limits the revelation and the manifestation of the Father to that which is made **in and through Himself.** Therefore the Son is a great mystery, as is the Father. (Matt. 11:27). So many of us, with our narrow minds, are apt to think that we know all about the person and the glory of Jesus Christ, and that He is the second person in the Trinity, or the Son of man and the Son of God, inferior to God the Father. If that is all there is to it, the Apostle Paul would not have said in humble confession, "But what things were gain to me, those I counted loss for Christ. Yea, doubtless, and I count all things but loss for the excellency of the knowledge of Christ Jesus, my Lord; for whom I have suffered the loss of all things, and do count them but dung, that I may win Christ . . . . that I may know Him," etc. (Phil. 3:7-10.) If the great Apostle did not know Him as he ought to know Him, how dare we, who are far less spiritual than those leaders of the ancient Christians, come to such man-made, feeble conclusions concerning the glorified One? Our very traditions and so-called Bible fundamentals prove that we are so proud and so limited in our knowledge that we are not even able to listen to the doctrine of Jesus Christ as our God, the Creator (John 1:10; Col. 1:15-19), and as God, our Saviour (Jude. 25; Tit. 2:13), and the God who bought us (Acts 20:28), much less believe it. We shrink from falling on our faces before Him and crying out, "My Lord and my God!" as Thomas did (John 20:28). If one dares to utter such remarks, the people of God, so-called, get troubled, thinking that such a man is deluded, that he has a new and strange teaching, and that something is wrong with his belief.

I praise God for finding a great host of witnesses who lived in the ages past, who were loyal to their Lord and God, Jesus, the Christ, and who spared not their lofty utterances, but cried aloud and gave the following testimonies about our God, the Saviour:

John Bunyan seemed to have a clear-cut understanding of the mysterious Christ of the Bible. The following is copied from Bunyan's Works, Vol. III, pp. 84 to 86:

The Mysterious and Marvelous Christ.
By John Bunyan.

"The Scripture saith that all the fullness of the Godhead dwells in him (Christ) bodily. It also saith that He is the mercy-seat, that is, the Throne of God; and yet again, that He sits on the right hand of the throne.

These things are so far from being comprehended by the weakest, that they strain the wits and parts of the strongest; yet there is a heavenly truth in all. Heavenly things are not easily believed, no not of believers themselves, while here on earth; and when they are, they are so but weakly and infirmly.

I believe that the very appearing of Christ before God, is an intercession as a priest, as well as a plea for an advocate; and I believe again, that His very life there is an intercession, a continual intercession.

But there is yet something further to be said. Christ the humanity of Christ, if in it dwells all the fullness of the Godhead bodily, how then appears He before Him to make intercession? Or if Christ is the throne of grace, and mercy-seat, how doth He appear before God as sitting there, to sprinkle that now with His blood? Again, if Christ be the altar of incense, how stands He as a priest by that altar, to offer the prayers of all saints thereon, before the Throne?

That all this is written, is true; and that it is all truth, is as true: but that it is all understood by every one that is saved, I do not believe is true. I mean, so understood, as that they could all reconcile the seeming contradictions that are in the Scripture.

There are, therefore, three lessons that God has set us, to the perfecting of our understanding in the mysteries of God: 1. Letters. 2. Words. 3. Meanings.

1. Letters. I call the ceremonial law so; for there all is set forth distinctly, everything by itself, as letters are to children. There you have a priest, a sacrifice, an altar, a holy place, a mercy-seat; and all distinct.

2. Now in the gospel, these letters are put all in a word, and Christ is that Word, that Word of God's mind; and therefore the Gospel makes Christ that priest, Christ that sacrifice, Christ that altar, Christ that holy place, Christ that throne of grace, and all; **for Christ is all.** All these meet in Him, as several letters meet in one word.

3. Next to the word, you have the meaning; and the meaning is more difficult to be learned than either the letters or the word; and therefore the perfect understanding of that is reserved till we arrive at a higher form, till we arrive at a perfect man. "And when that which is perfect is come, that knowledge which is in part shall be done away." Meantime our business is to learn to bring the letters into a word—to bring the ceremonies to Christ, and to make them terminate in Him; I mean, to find the priesthood in Christ, the sacrifice in Christ, the altar in Christ, the throne of grace in Christ, **and also God in Christ, reconciling the world unto Himself by Him.** And if we can learn this well, while here, we shall not at all be blamed; for this is the utmost lesson set us, namely, to learn Christ, as we find Him revealed in the gospel. "I determined," saith Paul, "Not to know anything among you, save Jesus Christ, and Him crucified." And Christians, after some time, I mean those that pray, and look into the word well, do attain to some good measure of knowledge of Him. **It is life eternal to know Him,** as He is to be known here, as He is to be known by the Holy Scriptures. Keep then close to the Scriptures, and let thy faith obey the authority of them, and thou wilt be sure to increase in faith, for therein is the righteousness of God revealed from faith to faith, as it is written, "The just shall live by faith."

Comments of Prominent and Godly Men on the Deity of Jesus Christ.

So prominent and so constant was the worship paid Christ by the primitive Christians, that it did not escape the observation even of the heathen. Says Pliny, in writing to Trojan. "They, Christians, sing in social worship a hymn to Christ as God." (Lib. 10. Ep. 97.)

Justin Martyr, born A. D. 103, and beheaded at Rome, A. D. 167, has the following sentence: "That ye might also know God, who came from above, and became man among men and who is again to return, when they who pierced Him shall see and bewail Him."

Theophilus was ordained bishop of the Church at Antioch about the middle of the second century, and says, "The Word was God, and sprung from God."

Irenaeus who suffered martyrdom under Severus, A. D. 202, was a disciple of Polycarp, a disciple of John, and says, "The Ebionites are vain, not receiving the union of God and man, by faith, into their souls."

Clemans Alexandrinus, the friend of Ireneus, says, "Believe, O man, in Him who is both man and God; believe, O man, in Him who suffered death, and yet is adored as the living God." This father flourished about the close of the second century.

Epiphanius, one of the Church Fathers, who lived 310 to 407 A. D., says: "My Christ and God was exceedingly beautiful in countenance."

A Swedish philosopher (1688-1772) says: "He is the Lord Jesus Christ, who is Jehovah the Lord, Creator from eternity, Saviour in time, and Reformer to eternity."

Thomas Chatterton, an English poet, (1752-1770) says:

A humble form the Godhead wore,
The pains of poverty He bore,
To gaudy pomp unknown:
Tho' in a human walk He trod,
Still was the Man Almighty God,
In glory all His own.

Lord Byron, the English poet, (1778-1824) says: "If ever man was God or God man, Jesus Christ was both."

Thomas B. Macauly, English essayist and historian, (1800-1859) says: "It was before Deity embodied in human form walking among men, partaking of their infirmities, leaning on their bosoms, weeping over their graves, slumbering in the manger, bleeding on the cross; that the prejudices of the synagogue and the doubts of the academy, the faces of the victor and the swords of thirsty legions were humbled in dust."

Cyrus D. Foss, Bishop of the Methodist Episcopal Church (1834-1910), says: "'But whom do men say that I am? If my tongue did not cling to the roof of my mouth, I would say, 'Some say that Thou art a myth, a fancy portrait, and that a myth has changed the face of the world.' And then suppose He should demand of us, 'But whom say ye that I am?' O, if again I might be your happy spokesman, on bended knees and with streaming eyes I would cry, 'Thou art Christ, the Son of the Living God, Thyself very man and very God'."

Luther Tracy Tounsend, an American Clergyman, born 1838, says: "This true soul, the ruler of nations, sinless and infinite, a God and a man, is an established fact."

Francis E. Willard, American Temperance reformer (1839-1898) said (her last words): "I am safe with Him. He has other worlds and I want to go. I have always believed in Christ. He is the incarnate God . . . How beautiful it is to be with God."

Richard Watson Gilder, American poet and Editor (1844-1909), says:

"If Jesus Christ is a man,
And only man I say
That of all mankind I cleave to Him,
And to Him I will cleave alway.

"If Jesus Christ is a God,
And the only God, I swear
I will follow Him through heaven and hell,
The earth, the sea, and the air."

Spurgeon, in "The Exaltation of Christ," says: "In heaven, in earth, in hell, all knees bend before Him, and every tongue confesses that He is God. If not now, yet in time that is to come, this shall be carried out, that every creature of God's making shall acknowledge His Son to be God over all, blessed forever. Amen."

The following attributes are given by the nineteenth century Christians to our Lord and Saviour concerning His Deity. You will notice that frequently they declare Him to be the Lord Jehovah. Some may be puzzled over such attributes given to Him, and question within themselves how Jesus Christ can be the Son of Jehovah, and yet Jehovah Himself; or how He can be the Son of God and yet the Almighty God. Such a question cannot be fully answered with a satisfactory explanation, because therein lies "the great mystery of Godliness," but believe it we must. Yet the Scriptures give us some explanation, as for instance: Jesus Christ, being of the same substance as that of the Father, and being His only begotten Son, who sprang forth from the bosom of the Deity, and by right inherits the Name of His Father, and the Father being pleased that in Him should all His fulness dwell,—all these scriptural facts give Him the rightful title of Jehovah, just as He calls Himself the Almighty. There are not three Almighties, there is but one Almighty God. Jesus Christ being the Word, the Son, the expression, the image, the Heir, the embodiment, and the revelation of the trione God, makes Him the Almighty. So in Christ our Lord we have the Almighty God, the Father, the Son, and the Holy Ghost; for "in Him dwelleth all the fulness of the Godhead bodily." Praise His Holy Name.

The following testimonies, comments, and arguments of eminent Christian men of our day will make this subject more clear to the reader, if he wishes to grow in the knowledge of Christ our Redeemer.

NOTE.—The following facts of the absolute *Deity* of our Lord, are the remarks of Mr. F. C. Jennings, who preached eleven years ago in the great Fulton Street prayer meeting of New York City:

THE PERSON OF THE LORD JESUS, THE CLEAREST EVIDENCE OF THE DIVINITY OF THE GOSPEL.

Christ's Supernatural Birth and Witnesses Prove Him to Be God.

What child amid the myriads of earth had ever been divinely named Jesus? Not one. When God gives a name it invariably expresses fully the one who is named. Could He have called any Jesus or Saviour? Eve thought she had gotten the promised Seed in Cain, but God does not tell her to call him Jesus—no indeed, nor Abel, nor any infant that ever slept in human breast, for not one is a Saviour, all need one. At last the coming of One is foretold and God says: Call Him Jesus. Here is a Saviour at last, one who can save. But who is it who said "Beside me there is no Saviour?" (Isaiah 43). God Himself so speaks. Then if that child can be, with divine truth, called Jesus or Saviour, what follows? He is none other or less than God. But see, He is a human Babe—yes, it is God with us,—Immanuel as Matthew 1:23 carefully tells us. Do you not see how beautifully, how profoundly the prophecy is fulfilled? Oh the joy, the bliss to see in that dear Babe in human weakness, God, our God come down so very close to us guilty, sinful rebels. Not blasting, not damning, not cursing, not striking, but in this lovely infant form, appealing as it were to the creature that has wandered from Him, yea "reconciling the world to Himself."

His Sinlessness Proves That He Is God.

The very best men have always, without any single exception, confessed to sin. Any man who claims sinlessness is esteemed, and rightly, a crazy fanatic, and provokes ridicule rather than confidence.

The good of the earth as Abraham, Isaac, Jacob, Isaiah, Job, David, and Daniel either confessed with their own lips, or it is told of them, that they sinned. Never once is there the slightest suggestion of the possibility of the Lord Jesus Christ sinning. He never confesses to the slightest moral lapse, or heedless slip. You may possibly say "But see Mark 10, does He not there disavow goodness?" "Why callest thou me good? There is none good but one, that is God?" Far from disavowing goodness, he here really enforces His higher claims. The young man had addressed Him as "Good Master, what must I do to inherit eternal life " His first word answers his question, in a veiled way it is true, but answers it. "You call me good," He says: "For that to be true, you must see and confess in me far more than a man, for none is good but God. So that first, there is no hope for any man on the basis of which you are speaking, 'Doing good;' but see in me, what you have called me, 'Good,' and then you have **God before you**—the giver of the Eternal Life you seek." It is a marvelous answer—none like it in all history.

His Speech Proves Him To Be God.

Did ever man—mere man—in all the myriads who had preceded, or followed Him, speak as He? Let the keenest of all human intellects take counsel together, and with satanic ingenuity so frame a question that any answer, apparently, must involve Him in the destruction of all His claims. Does He plead for a little time to take counsel with His friends? Would it not have been perfectly reasonable? If He had said to those who asked Him as to giving tribute to Caesar: "Just give me half an hour to talk this over with Peter, and James, and John. You have had time to consult. Now give me a few minutes." Not a word like it, but instantly He gives such an answer as makes even His enemies marvel, for it is far beyond all mere human capacity. **He is God manifest in the flesh.** What good man in all the history of the world ever did, ever could use such words as did He? Can you even think of Paul saying, "Come unto me all ye that labor and are heavy laden, and I will give you rest?" What would you think of any Apostle, prophet, or martytr who would say "Before Abraham was, I am," or "If any man thirst, let him come unto me and drink?" Again I say it is simply unthinkable unless **the Speaker is God.**

NOTE.—The following are some of the remarks of Samuel Greene, a prominent minister of Boston, and are taken from a booklet entitled, "One Hundred Incontrovertible Arguments for Believing in the Deity of Christ," published in Glasgow:

A Word About the Humanity of Christ.

"Jesus was made a little lower than the angels for the suffering of death." He was made lower for the accomplishment of a specific object—what was he originally? This is perfectly consistent with His oeing God, and "all the angels" being commanded "to worship Him." Ungrateful mortals, because you behold your Lord in the form of a servant, and suffering death for your redemption, will you take occasion from this very expression of His condescending love, to rob Him of His divine glories?

He is pronounced in so many words to be God over all. "Of whom," (the Jewish nation) "as concerning the flesh, Christ came. who is over all, God blessed for ever." Rom. 9:5. Is anything above Him who is God over all? Note, also, the antithesis between His two natures: of the seed of Abraham according to the flesh. What was He according to His divine nature? "God over all."

Concerning His Absolute Deity.

He is the Jehovah whom Isaiah saw in vision. "I saw, also, the LORD sitting upon a throne, high and lifted up. Above it stood the seraphim. And one cried unto another, and said, Holy, holy is the Lord of hosts. And He said, Go, make the heart of this people fat, and make their ears heavy, and shut their eyes." Isa. 6:1, 2, 3, 9, 10.

It is written, "All things were created by Him and for Him" (Col. 1:16). Not only, then, is Jesus Christ the Creator of all things, but likewise the ultimate end for which all things were made. But the Scripture saith, "The Lord hath made all things for Himself" (Prov. 16:4). Then is Jesus Christ this Lord, or Jehovah. If being the Creator and the end of all creation does not designate the Supreme God, what does?

We again hear Christ Himself declare, "The Son of man shall come, and then He shall reward every man according to His works" (Matt. 16:27). But is not the Judge of all the earth God? See Gen. 18:25. Then is our Lord Jesus Christ God, for in more than thirty different passages is He represented as the final Judge of the world. Are there two final Judges? It is very evident we must stand before the throne of God and the throne of Christ; and render an account to God and to Christ. The Judge is God alone; but Jesus is the Judge. Therefore Jesus is God.

He is absolutely declared to be "the head of all Power" (Col. 2:10). The head of all power must be He who originates and wields all power; and who is this but the Almighty God?

He is represented as the great fountain from which Christians of all ages and countries receive their supplies. "Of His fullness have all we received, and grace for grace" (John 1:16). Just as God is represented: "With Thee. O God. is the fountain of life" (Psalm 36:9).

He not only healed all manner of diseases and raised the dead in His own name; but with the same air of divine authority, said to the paralytic, "Son, thy sins be forgiven thee" (Mark 2:5). Would not this be blasphemy, were He not Himself the great Lawgiver, the Supreme Judge, even God? "Who can forgive sins but God only?" The language of Jehovah is "I, even I am He that blotteth out thy transgressions" (Isaiah 43:25). Jesus Christ authoritively pronounced the forgiveness of sins: He is therefore God.

He declared Himself to be in heaven at the same time He was on earth, thereby showing that He was omnipresent. In conversation with Nicodemus He says, "No man hath ascended up to heaven but He that came down from heaven, even the Son of man which is in heaven" (John 3:13). Paul to the Ephesians, chapter 1:23, speaks of "The fullness of Him, Christ, that filleth all in all." This accords with the language of Jehovah: "Do not I fill heaven and earth? said the Lord" (Jer. 23:24).

We find it required, in so many words, "That all men should honour the Son, even as they honour the Father" (John 5:23). Would the Father thus speak, were not the Son truly divine? His language is, "I am the Lord, that is my name; and my glory I will not give to another" (Isa. 42:8). Now to ascribe to the Son any thing short of real Deity, is to degrade Him infinitely below the Father; for between God and the most exalted creature there must be an infinite distance. This requirement is absolutely and necessarily broken by all men who do not believe in the real Deity of Jesus Christ. They rob God our Saviour. Weigh the solemn thought!

Said a Unitarian to a venerable clergyman, "If the doctrine of Christ's Deity were true, I am sure so important a doctrine must have been revealed with a clearness no one could have mistaken." "And what language would you have chosen?" said the clergyman. "I would have had him called the true God." replied the man. "Right," said the venerable clergyman—"the very language of the Apostle" (1 John 5:20).

Now reader, what thinkest thou of Christ? A question of great moment, more vital to your eternal well being, cannot be asked you. Answer it with His own solemn warning before you. "If ye believe not that I am He, ye shall die in your sins." Will you incur the guilt, and run the hazard of robbing your Saviour of His divine glories? Will you not this moment imitate the angels and all the redeemed, and cast yourself at His feet, and with adoring gratitude ascribe all glory to His NAME? As His personal dignity is exalted or debased in your estimation, so will be your confidence in Him, and expectations from Him. • A creature as your Saviour, however exalted, cannot satisfy your soul, cannot pardon your sins. Rise, then to loftier views; let a heaven-born faith present Him before you as that Being in whom dwelleth all the fullness of the Godhead bodily. Then, great indeed will be your expectations; and they will forever rise and swell, as you gaze on the glories of His person, and the unsearchable riches of His grace. And, I beseech you, remember whatever your views of Christ, in a few days you must stand before His judgment seat. He that came in swaddling bands shall come in clouds, and every eye shall see Him, even they who have pierced and dishonored Him.

Therefore in the Holy Scriptures we learn of Christ, that His name is Jehovah; the Lord of Hosts; the Lord God; the Lord of Glory; the Lord of all; He is the true God; the Great God; and God over all; The First and the Last; the self-existent I AM.

We see that all the attributes and incommunicable perfections of Jehovah belong to Christ. He is Eternal, Immutable, Omnicient, Omnipotent and Omnipresent God.

We see that the works which can be done by none but Jehovah Himself, are done by Christ. He created all worlds; upholdeth all things by the word of His power; governs the whole universe, and provides for all creation; the power of His voice will call forth all the millions of the dead at the resurrection; He will judge them all in the great day. Although the company before His awful tribunal will be innumerable as the sand upon the seashore, yet will He perfectly recollect all their actions, words, and thoughts, from the birth of creation to the end of time; too much for man, easy for the Christ!

He is also to His Church what none but God can be. He hath chosen His people before the world was; the church is His own property; He redeemed a lost world; He is the source of all grace and eternal salvation to His people; and it is He that sends the Holy Ghost down to prepare the church for glory, which He presents unto Himself at last, and gives Her the Kingdom.

And we are to act towards Christ exactly in the same manner as we are to act towards God the Father; to believe in Him; to be baptized in His name; to pray unto Him; and to serve and worship Him, even as we serve and worship the Father.

These are the things which irresistibly prove the Godhead of Immanuel. What stronger proofs than these have we of the existence of Jehovah?

NOTE.—The German Protestant fathers seem to have had a greater faith in the deity of our Saviour in their day than present-day Protestants. The following verses in their hymns prove this fact.

SOME QUOTATIONS COPIED FROM A GERMAN ALMANAC

No. 483. *"Ein' feste burg ist unser Gott."*—by Martin Luther.

Fragst du, wer er ist?　Er heisst Jesus Christ.

Der Herr Zebaoth!　Und ist kein ander Gott."

Do you ask who He is?　He is Jesus Christ! The Lord of Hosts!　And there is no other God.

From a German Almanac:

"Hast du solche Glaubensaugen, dass du ein stimmen kannst: Es ist der Herr Christ, unser Gott, der uns will helfen aus aller Not?"

Have you such an eye of faith that you can say (consent, agree, accept). it is the Lord Christ, our God, that will help us out of all trouble or need?

"Was dunket euch um Chirtsus?　Wes Sohn ist er?"—Matt. 22:42.

An dieser wichtigsten Fraga sind Jesu Feinde zu schanden geworden.　Auch heute ist's der Fels, an dem die eistesstrome sich scheiden. We dunket dich um Christus?　Ist er dir nur mensch, zwar alles uberragend, was Mench heisst, aber doch verflochten in Menschenwesen, Ringen und Schuld?　Oder ist er dir gottmensch, der sich aus Menschentum durch Treue und Gehorsam zur Gotteshohe emporgearbeitet? *Oder ist er dir der ewige Gott, der* in unser Fleisch sich einsenkte, an unserm Elend telnahm, aber sich in dem Riss stellte, unsere Schuld ubernahm, die Strafe trug, das Leben aus dem Grab brachte, beim Vater eintritt, also *der* wahrhaftige, einzigartige Gottmensch im Sinn der Schrift?　Ist er dir das letztere geworden, so bekenne ihn, bezeuge mit deinem Leben, was dir dein Heiland ist, was seine Gnade aus dir gemacht.

O Vater, zieh uns kraftiglich, das wir im Sohn erkennen dich,
Und werden deine Kinder.
O Jesu, deine Gnad' uns gib, der du mit ewig treuer Lieb
Aufsuchst verlorne Sunder.

"What think ye of Christ?　Whose son is he?"—Matt. 22:42.

On this most important question were Jesus' enemies put to shame.　So today it is the rock on which the Spirit's stream separates.　What think you of Christ?　Is he only a man to you, though indeed a superior among mankind, yet restricted with mankind in failure and fault?　Or is He to you a Godman. *that through virtue and obedience has worked His way up to God's favor (merit or character)?*
Or is He to you the everlasting God, that sank (buried) Himself in our flesh, took part in our misery (distress. want), but placed Himself in the breach, took on Him our guilt, car- ried our punishment, brought life out of the grave, entered in to the Father, the true, only one of His kind, God-man, in the sense of the Scriptures?　If He is become to you this last, so *acknowledge Him (as such), witness in your life what your Saviour is to you,* and what His grace has made of you.

O Father, draw us mightily, *that we may know you in the Son,* and be your children, etc.

From German Allegemeines Gesangbuch (Common Song Book):—

No. 409.—"Gott sei gelobet und gebenedeist, Der uns selber hat gespeiset mit seinem fleische und mit seinem blute."

God be praised and magnified, who Himself has fed us with His flesh and blood.

No. 478.—"Bleibt noch der grosste theil von seinem reiche fern,
Und ehrt den Heiland nicht als seinen Gott und Herrn."

There remains yet the greater part far from His kingdom, and honor not the Savior as their God and Lord.

No. 484.—"Fragst du, wer er ist?　Er heisst Jesus Christ!　Unser Herr und Gott."

Do you ask who He is?　He is Jesus Christ! *Our Lord and God.*

No. 529.—"Vergossen ist dein heilig's blut, das gnug fur die sunde thut.
Heiliger! Schopfer! Gott! Heiliger! Mittler! Gott!
Heiliger! barmherziger Troster!　Du ewiger Gott!"

Your holy blood is shed, that satisfies for sin. *Holy One! Creator! God! Holy One! Mediator! God! Holy One! Merciful Comforter! Thou everlasting God!*

No. 531.—"O Jesu, du mein Herr und Gott, litt'st willig angst und schmach und spott.
Als du fur mich am kreuze starbst, und mir ein ewig heil erwarbst."

O Jesus, thou *my Lord and God,* suffered willingly anguish and shame and mocking, as you for me on the cross died, and won an eternal salvation for me.

No. 630.—"Derr Herr ist Gott!　Der uns die Sterbliche gebar,
Der Gottmensch ist, wird sein, und war!
Du Liebe! Mensch! und Gott! Du unerforschte Liebe! Gott!
Uns, uns hast du bis in den Tod, am Kreuz geliebt,
Sei, Heil der Welt, auch unser Gott."

The Lord is God, born of humanity for us, He that Godman is, will be, and was.
Thou Love! Man! God! Thou unfathomable Love! God!
As hast thou loved to the death on the cross, Be salvation to the world, also our God.

THE DEITY OF JESUS CHRIST IN SONG BY ENGLISH HYMN-WRITERS

Hymn by Isaac Watts

"When I survey the wondrous cross
On which the Prince of glory died,
My richest gain I count but loss,
And pour contempt on all my pride.

"Forbid it, Lord, that I should boast,
Save in the death of Christ, *my God;*
All the vain things that charm me most,
I sacrifice them to His blood."

Hymn by Thoro Harvie

"This sacred truth means more to me
Than aught on earth could ever be,
That now, and thru eternity,
God lives within my soul.

"God manifest in form of man,
Once wrought redemption's wondrous plan;
Completing what He then began,
God lives within my soul."

"Within my soul, within my soul,
His Spirit guides, for He abides
Within my soul."   II Cor. 4:5, 6.

"MAJESTIC SWEETNESS"
By Samuel Stennett

"Majestic sweetness sits enthroned
Upon the Saviour's brow;
His head with radiant glories crowned,
His lips with grace o'erflow.

"To Him I owe my life and breath,
And all the joys I have;
He makes me triumph over death,
And saves me from the grave."
—II. Cor. 5:14, 15.

"ALL HAIL THE POWER OF JESUS' NAME"
By Edward Perronet

"All hail the power of Jesus' name,
Let angels prostrate fall;
Bring forth the royal diadem
And crown Him Lord of all.

"Crown Him, ye morning stars of Light,
Who fixed this earthly ball;
Now hail the strength of *Israel's might,*
And crown Him Lord of all.

"Sinners, whose love can ne'er forget
The wormwood and the gall,
Go, spread your trophies at His feet,
And crown Him Lord of all."

SING HIS PRAISE
By I. O. Brown.

"Forward move, ye soldiers of the living God,
Sing His praise, Sing His praise;
Lift the blood stained banner where the saints
have trod,
Sing His praise, Sing His praise.

"Be a valiant soldier, routing every sin,
Sing His praise, Sing His praise,
Christ, the great Jehovah, will be sure to win,
Sing His praise, Sing His praise.

"Sing His praise, sing His praise,
Let the glory in your soul sing His praise;
Sing His praise, sing His praise,
While the endless ages roll, sing His praise."

THE NECESSITY OF PREACHING JESUS CHRIST AS GOD.
By A. D. Urshan.

Reader, do you believe the truth in the above songs? Can you heartily sing them day and night before men and angels with a joyful heart? If you can, then you are a true Christian and free from the spirit of Unitarianism and Christian Science. Consider these questions, please.

Some people think it is not necessary to preach the absolute deity of our Saviour, as these men of God declared Him, because they think it is unprofitable and confusing; therefore, it causes division and trouble. To such we answer, If the Holy Scriptures proclaim Jesus Christ as the Son of God and yet God, manifested in the flesh, and the fullness of the Godhead bodily dwelleth in Him, how then, can a minister of the Gospel, who is commanded by the Holy Spirit to preach the "Word," ignore so many chapters and Bible texts on this great theme if he be a faithful steward of the household of God?

Again, we read of the specific office of the Holy Spirit, which is to reveal and glorify not the Father, not Himself, but the Lord Jesus Christ. How then can a Spirit-filled and Spirit-led man of God dare to grieve Him who came to teach and lead us into all the truth? No, he that is a faithful and obedient servant of the Lord Jesus, will have fresh revelations from heaven through the illumination of the Scriptures by the Holy Ghost, and he will declare the eternal truth concerning the "God-man" (Matt. 13:52).

Some may ask "Would the Holy Spirit move a man to preach something which is hard to comprehend?" We answer, Yes! First, because the Holy Spirit's office is to reveal the things of Christ—yea, the things that the mind of natural man has not imagined and that his ears have not heard. He is sent to reveal these things to them that have the mind of Christ and walk in the Spirit (1 Cor. 2:11, 16). Second, because the Blessed Holy Spirit knows more definitely than we do the fact, that men in these days have advanced in their inventions and knowledge, and the whole of humanity in unbelief is eagerly seeking something which is not less than the very **Almighty God.**

People nowadays have proved that heathenism is but an empty and senseless worship; they have in general also found out that the wealth and pleasures of this world are nothing more than vanity, that education and increase of knowledge are only vexation of spirit. They have also lost confidence in the present-day civilization, man-made religions and nominal Christianity. Although millions of such people are indulging themselves in these things, yet there is an appalling dissatisfaction in their hearts and minds. Therefore, they are unconsciously waiting and working toward the manifestation **of a Great ONE.**

Knowing this and knowing our Lord and Saviour is the only satisfying portion of all the human race (for not only has He provided the great deliverance from sin, and eternal life for all those that believe, but He is also **"The Almighty,"** as He said Himself) (Rev. 1:8), will the Holy Spirit let the thousands upon thousands of hungry and thirsty souls be deceived and filled with the influence and power of the coming Anti-Christ who soon will appear as a Great One, exalting himself above all that which is God, sitting in the Temple of God and being worshiped by such people? No, we must perform our solemn duty toward many who would not otherwise be saved. O brethren! let us preach a full Christ, not only the Son of God and the Son of Man, but the very God Almighty who fills all things.

Third: We must proclaim the Lord of Glory as the Jehovah God now, because the so-called Christian countries have heard and read much of the man Christ and of His humiliation, His suffering and death. It is become like a common story to them, and therefore, in general they make light of it; but concerning the absolute deity of our Lord they hardly know anything, although some say with dark and doubting hearts that Jesus is divine. However, when false prophets and human philosophy confront them, they are so weak and ignorant about this important Bible theme, they soon are deceived, and they have, therefore become the victims of Russellism, Unitarianism, Christian Science, so called, Higher Criticism and the New Theology.

The startling fact is evident that, if these people, being members of the Christian churches, had been taught and trained regarding the deity of Jesus, as much as in other Bible themes, they would not have been so easily mislead. Therefore the backsliding and the great loss of life of these precious souls concerning this great divine truth lies in the lack of preaching the glorious deity of our Saviour. This subject has been touched upon very little by only a few ministers—and that but once in a great while. But what is that compared with the great importance and the need of the blessed message? So our Saviour has been veiled from the eyes of His people behind His humanity, and that because the Gospel has been preached only in part. If this were not the case, the people of God would have been prepared long ago against the wicked devices of the deceivers of our day, and they would have conquered all the doubt and would have become a people that knew their God, and they would now be strong in Him and do exploits (Dan. 11:32).

Fourth: We must, preach this blessed message, because it is a message that tests the faith of believers and like the two-edged sword of the Spirit, reveals and separates the true from the false.   There are people who have hidden themselves behind a false profession, claiming they believed in the deity of the Lord, but now, since the glorious light of this message shines forth, these very people are stirred with indignation and they are finghting this timely message of God and using all their influence to make it without effect, proving unto themselves and to others their falsity.   God knew about this kind of people and He graciously let the true light of His Deity shine forth, and He is making His messengers also to be known to all those who are earnestly seeking His fulness.   His true messengers are proving to be the light of the world and the salt of the earth now, through the glorious reflection of Christ's Godhead in their lives and testimony.

Fifth: We must declare this wonderful truth, because Satan is arrayed and is attacking the Christian Faith in the believers on this point of the Bible fundamentals more than all other Christian principles.   It is a common thing in these days among thousands of the church members to deny the deity of the Lord God who bought us (Acts 20:28).   They sneeringly and boldly are saying, "We believe in Jesus as a great man, nearest to God's heart, and as a great prophet who is the best teacher and the perfect example for us; but we do not believe He is God.   We don't understand why some people say Jesus Christ is God and preach such stuff," etc., etc.

Brethren, if there is no other reason for us to declare this truth, this one thing alone is sufficient to make us burn with a holy zeal for our blessed LORD, and taking the sword of the Spirit, smash the enemy right on the head and deliver many honest souls from his captivity and bring them face to face with Him who is above all principalities, powers and dominions both in Heaven and on earh—Jesus Christ, the Blessed INMANUEL.

The Bible Salvation.

If these people knew that the Bible teaches that salvation is so great, because it is wrought by God Himself, they would be thinking and saying differently.   Compare, please, Hebrews 1:8, 14 and 2:1, 4. These people do not know that Jehovah Himself has become our Salvation.   (Compare, please, Luke 2:25, 29 with Isaiah 12:2.)   Simeon, a man of God, filled with the Holy Ghost, had revealed unto him by the Holy Ghost that before his death he would see the "Lord's Christ." and he came by the Spirit into the temple; and when the parents brought in the child Jesus, to do for Him after the custom of the Law, then took he Him up in his arms and blessed God and said, "Lord, now lettest Thou Thy servant depart. in peace, according to Thy word: **for mine eyes have seen Thy Salvation.**"   Simeon says here. he had seen God's salvation.   The question is. What did Simeon see? It is clear that he saw the Child Jesus.   He calls this holy child "Salvation of God."   Thus, Jesus Himself is our salvation.   Isaiah also saw this great salvation in the Spirit, centuries before His revelation. so he says, "Behold God is my Salvation; I will trust and not be afraid: for the Lord JEHOVAH is my strength and my song: He also is become my Salvation." God showed this great salvation to Abraham; so we read in Genesis 15:1, "After these things the word of the LORD came unto Abraham in a vision, saying, 'Fear not, Abram: I am thy shield and thy exceeding great reward.' " Here the Almighty God not only gives promise of many blessings to Abram, but He offers HIMSELF unto Abram as a reward to his faith. Here is one of all the promises of God which are in Jesus Christ yea and Amen for us (2 Cor. 1:20).

It is so little known that the sure foundation of "The New Birth" or the birth by the Spirit is the accepting and believing in the Lord Jesus as God, the Creator! As such the Jews received Him not, because He came in the humble form of a servant to minister unto them the promises given unto their fathers concerning eternal life. The record proves this; so we read, "He was in the world and the world was made by Him and the world knew Him not." Ask any Sunday school boy, who created this world, he will say God—the Bible says Jesus of Nazareth is that God. He came unto his own—His chosen people (His creatures) and His own received Him not, but as many as received Him (as what? as God the Creator) to them gave He power to become the sons of God, even to them that believed on His NAME: which were born, not of blood, nor of the will of the flesh, nor of the will of man, but of God" (John 1:10-13). Here is the great Christian fundamental and the real beginning of eternal life The day is coming, thank God, that all those who are truly born of God will realize sooner or later see that Jesus Christ is God, their Creator, as well as the Saviour, and that their miraculous new birth took place because of the Godhead, life and power in His NAME. How can the new converts understand this wonderful foundation of their great salvation, except they are taught this blessed truth? But the sad fact is, many preachers do not know, nor do they preach this powerful and full Gospel of our Lord.

Our Lord said plainly that the way of being loosed from our sins is to believe that He is God, Jehovah; so He declared, "Except ye believe that I am He, ye shall die in your sins" (John 8:24). Compare with Isaiah 43: 10-25. Why, the very name J-E-S-U-S in Hebrew means Jehovah saves. Please look up the best commentaries.

All those who are shutting their eyes to the preaching of the Jehovah Christ and thinking it is something foreign to the Gospel of God are ignorant of the nature and the fulness of the Apostolic Gospel. "My people perish because of the lack of knowledge." If I ever preached the full Gospel, I am doing it now and expect to continue until the return of the Great Author of eternal life through the Everlasting Gospel of God.

Sixth. We speak of the Lord's deity, because it is a timely message.

There is no doubt that, if ever the Bride of Jesus should make herself ready, it is now; if she should ever know her Bridegroom in this life, it is now. The more she discovers the glory and the excellent majesty of her future Husband, the more she will accordingly prepare herself to suit Him. There is still another phase of this truth, and that is, that the glorious change of the Church of God "going from glory to glory" depends solely upon our spiritual vision of Christ's glory. The Apostle Paul declares that, by beholding Him, we are changed into the same image, from glory to glory (see 2 Cor 3:18).

Apostle John says, "When we shall see Him as He is we shall be like Him" (1 John 3:2): before we can be more worthy to look upon His glorious, shining, sun-shine-like face, we must see Him now in the revelations of the Holy Spirit, that we may become more like Him and be ready to win Him for our eternal Bridegroom. Thus, to have true visions of our glorified Lord in the Spirit, we must search for Him and seek His face in the written word; for the Spirit of God has come to reveal Christ unto us in and through the Word which is the Truth. Therefore, it is most important for us to "Preach the Word."

Seventh. We ought to proclaim the deity of our Saviour, because it is the dispensational message. We often speak of the present Dispensation, which is called the Dispensation of the Spirit; but little we know about there being another dispensation which is right in the present one—even "The dispensation of the fulness of times" (see Eph. 1:10). The Apostle tells us the purpose of God for this last dispensation of the Gospel is gathering "together in one all things in Christ."

Between the Old and the New Testament dispensations there was an overlay dispensation which began from the preaching of John the Baptist and lasted up to the memorable day of Pentecost. John's message was "To Make ready a People prepared for the Lord. (Luke 1:17). Even so in this last dispensation God is raising His chosen messengers not to make a people ready but to make "The People" ready and prepared for the soon-coming Lord and the Millennium reign during the coming "Dispensation."

The Bible speaks of the coming One and says that He is the Lord God Almighty. "And the four beasts had each of them six wings about him; and they were full of eyes within: and they rest not day and night, saying, Holy, holy, holy, Lord God Almighty, which was, and is, and is to come."—Rev. 4:8.

The question is, "Who is the Lord God Almighty which is to come?" The last verse of the same chapter says He is the One who created all things for His pleasure. The old prophets of the Old Testament saw this coming One, also, and they acclaimed with astonishment this great event (see Zech. 14:5. Compare with Jude 14). Since the Lord God is coming, and He is coming to be seen by all eyes, then what can we preach in these days but 'Prepare to meet thy God?" John preached the Lamb of God and the Baptizer in the Holy Ghost and fire and that the Lord was coming after Him to take away the sins of the world and to baptize His people with the Holy Spirit.

But now we should preach the One who died on the cross, who rose from the dead and who is interceding now in our behalf. He is soon to come the second time, not as a babe and a servant, but as the King of Kings, the Lord of Lords—yea, as the Almighty with the great glory of the Father. "Behold, He cometh with clouds; and every eye shall see Him, and they also which pierced Him: and all kindreds of the earth shall wail because of Him. Even so, Amen."

CHAPTER II.

The Name of God and the Name of His Son.

Reprinted from "Eusebia," August 1898.

O DEFINE the great name of God, would be to cite all the testimony given pertaining to Him concerning His character and attributes. The Scriptures reveal God to us as ever living and eternal; all powerful, all knowing, everywhere present, unchangeable and unconditioned. Man can but feebly conceive the immensity of all these attributes; and were it not for **revelation,** mankind would be in utter darkness concerning God's existence or His purpose in the universe. The holy men of old speaking as they were moved by the Holy Spirit discussed in sundry portions and various manners the attributes of Deity. The crude conception of our first parents in Eden that they could hide themselves from the presence of God, (Gen. 3:10) did not obtain with Abraham, Isaac, and the fathers in Israel."

The Name.

"**All nations whom Thou hast made shall come and worship before Thee, O Lord; and shall glorify Thy Name. Teach me Thy way, O Yahweh; I will walk in Thy truth; unite my heart to fear Thy Name.**"—Psalm 86. 9, 11.

"The word YAHWEH is as nearly as possible a transliteration of the sacred Hebrew name of the Creator. It represents the Diety as an ever-living and acting person, who enters into personal relations with His people and would have them address Him by a proper Name in their personal approaches unto Him in prayer and worship. The later Jews, influenced by feelings of profound reverence, which soon passed over into superstition, abstained from pronouncing this Name, and substituted for it usually **Adonay,** "**Lord;**" or, where **Yahweh Adonay** occurred, "Lord God," **Elohim** God." Hence, the Massoretes pointed **Yahweh** with the vowel-points which belong to **Adonay** and these other names of God to be used in place of **Yahweh,** and so the original pronunciation of **Yahweh** became lost. The word **Jehovah** is sometimes used in English for this word, but it is a linguistic monstrosity. The Old Testament revelation in its use of **Yahweh** emphasized the activity of the ever-lasting personal God of revelation. The doctrine of God needs to be enriched at the present time by the enthronement of the idea of the living God to its supreme place in Biblical theology, and the dethronement of the idea of divine sovereignty from the usurped position in dogmatic theology. Yahweh is the NAME that God himself gave to HIS people; and if any name should be correctly pronounced and written, it would seem that it should be this one above all others."—**Messianic Prophecy.**

The Great Reason For God's New Revealed Name Unto Moses.

"It was through him (Moses) that Israel disengaged itself completely from those elements of polytheism which still clung to it among the children and descendants of Abraham himself. It was through him that the name, already known but not generally used YAHWEH, was substituted for the ancient name EL SHADDAI, the Almighty, by which they had before addressed the God who revealed Himself to the father of the race,— the name by which God had most frequently designed Himself in addressing the patriarchs. This substitution was nothing less than the starting-point of a great religious revolution. The name El Shaddai, the Almighty, left room for the existence of other powers by the side of God, subject, indeed, to His supremacy, but still able in some sort to compete with Him. The name signifies nearly the same as that which a certain class of religious persons still like to use; the Being of beings, the Supreme Being. But YAHWEH signifies He Who is and shall be. YAHWEH, therefore, does not only mean the most Powerful of beings, but the One only self-existent Being; the absolute Being, absorbing in Himself the idea of existence; the Being existing by His own power; the Being as subject, noun and attribute in one. By the side of El Shaddai there is room for others interior to Him; outside of Yahweh there is but non-entity. If anything does exist outside of Him it is only through His power, and in consequence of His 'creative will. The worship of El Shaddai did not then expressly exclude polytheism. But the adoration of Yahweh is, in its principles, what it has become more and more in fact, the absolute divorce of the conscience from all forms of paganism actual or conceivable. We have in Exodus 3 and 6, the simple and solemn narrative of the Vision granted to Moses, in which God for the first time revealed Himself in the character of Yahweh. At that moment was laid the foundation of the Jewish monotheism, and of the definitive religion of mankind.

The Name of God Became the Strong Foundation of The Divine Faith For Israel.

"This name Yahweh, inscribed by Moses in letters of fire on the Jewish consciousness—it is this which has worked this prodigy. It dissipated for Israel the seductive charm of a sensual life, and secured the proponderance of spirit over matter. If God alone exists, and matter only through Him, it must be entirely subject to Him. Man is no more a slave to it than God Himself. While spelling out the name Yahweh, man has recovered the knowledge of his own greatness. Made in the image of this absolute Being, of this pure Spirit, he can and he must become like Him; and henceforth, the royal road is opened which leads from Moses up to Jesus Christ. Holiness is no longer an unattainable ideal; the Kingdom of God, instead of being an empty sound, becomes the one true word of history. God's plan is revealed together with His name YAHWEH.

"We see, then, how inevitably the preparation of the salvation of the world by Israel required as its starting-point the revelation of this fundamental verity, 'I am that I am,' to which the natural intelligence of mankind could not of itself attain. Accordingly God, after having revealed to Moses this sublime idea, inscribed it on Mount Sinai at the head of the national law: 'I, Yahweh, am thy God.' (Ex. 3: 14.) The fulfilment of the ancient promises made to Abraham by El Shaddai, the present work entrusted to the ministry of

Moses, the future salvation of mankind to be effected by Christ, all rested definitely upon the doctrine, as the entire building, from the lowest to the highest story, rests upon the foundation laid once for all."—GODET.

The Old Testament quotations, previously cited, show that a great deal of material bearing upon the NAME of Deity was given to ancient Israel. To understand the signification of the name of Israel's God was synonymous with the proper understanding of the true worship as opposed to idolatry. It was from idolatry that God called Abraham, and constituted him the father of all the faithful adown the ages. Abraham was a man of faith, as was Isaac, also Jacob, but in the fourth generation, idolatry began again to assert itself. When Israel went into Egypt and perceived the wonderful development there, and their civilization, they fell away, and by the time Moses appeared as a leader they had quite forgotten the knowledge of the Lord, that had been handed down by Abraham, Isaac, and Jacob, and they followed the Egyptians, having virtually become their slaves.

Moses had a tedious task to arouse them, but succeeded partially by dint of patience, and God's specially manifested wonder working power. They crossed the Red Sea, to wander in the wilderness forty years,—for discipline to fit them to serve God. After their miraculous redemption from Egypt, they were so perverse and obdurate that they could not maintain their good behavior forty days, but lapsed into idolatry and worshipped the golden calf. They perished in the wilderness because of unbelief. Yet it cannot be said they did not hear something of the Great Creator and His NAME,—and the difference between life and death. (Deut. 30:15.) Only two of that great company, of over a million souls, that left Egypt, passed into the promised land. Hardness of heart and unbelief did the mischief. With leaders appointed directly by God Himself, they failed to apprehend the vital lessons. Joshua, the courageous captain, was obliged to punish disobedience summarily, and to impress their minds with what true devotion meant. Achan perished with his goodly Babylonish garment, and others met like fate. The history of the people of Israel after their establishment in Canaan, with their God-inspired leaders, priests, judges and prophets, to the time of the carrying away into captivity is one of successive lapses into gross and dark idolatry, from the worship of the Living God to the worship of idols.

The Significance Of The Name Yahweh Was a Starting Point To The Gospel Dispensation.

"God spoke to the fathers by the prophets," "here a little and there a little,—line upon line, precept upon precept,"—but only they of faith were blessed with faithful Abraham,—the larger portion of the nation failed to bring forth good fruit, and perished because of unbelief. The test of faith was the same in that time as it was when the writer to the Hebrews said:

"He who cometh to God must believe that He is (i. e. Yahweh,—the living God, the Self-Existing God), and that He is a rewarder of them who diligently seek Him."—Heb. 11:6.

The man of faith "endured, as seeing Him who is unseen," and apprehends the message God caused to be preached from the beginning, for the gospel was preached to those who have died. (1 Pet. 4.

6.)—"God preached aforetime through His prophets." In the divine plan the development and discipline of a divine family was to be brought about by knowledge concerning the nature and name of the Deity Himself. Over three thousand years ago, the Psalmist exclaimed in ecstasy: "I shall be satisfied when I awake in Thy likeness." With all our latter day civilization and erudition no more fit and exalted aspiration than this is possible. One's fondest and best wish is to be like God,—but the Psalmist foresaw the accomplishment, in the resurrection awakening. In those far off days when the prophets were the teachers and with the law as a schoolmaster pointing to the great NAME bearer, men learned the characteristics of God—"The eyes of YAHWEH are in every place, beholding the evil and the good." "He that keepeth Israel neither slumbers nor sleeps."—That God existed "before the mountains were brought forth," that He was all powerful and mighty, inhabiting eternity, before Whom the inhabitants of the earth were as grasshoppers.

With the unequal disparity between the Deity and the family of earth-borns, the expectation that the ultimate day would bestow Deity's likeness upon the chosen and redeemed, appears entirely impossible, and in the means of the accomplishment, lies the secret of the gospel.—God's Own Son, called after Him, bearing relation both to the Great God and Father, and also to the earth-born family,—by inheritance having a more excellent NAME than the angels, and yet bearing a relationship to flesh, (2 Cor. 5. 16.) "born of a woman, born under law," (Gal. 4. 4.) was exactly fit and competent to succeed where all others had failed. After Christ had fulfilled the law perfectly, and yielded up His life to satisfy its demands, there remained nothing against Him, and God with perfect justice might raise Him from the dead,—no more related to the "flesh of sin."

"I came in My Father's Name." "As the Father hath Life in Himself, so has He given the Son to have Life in Himself."—John 5. 43, 26.

"As the Living Father (Yahweh) hath sent Me, and I live by the father; so he that eateth Me (takes into his understanding) shall Live because of Me."—John 6. 57.

JESUS, or more properly, YAH-OSHUA, is Deity's name with an affix, and means YAH'S deliverer, or savior.

Worshipping Jesus as Yahweh.

We are often met with the assertion that, if Jesus is not God, it is idolatry to worship Him. I wish all such persons were not so often guilty of idolatry. My reply is: To say Jesus Christ is the Eternal Supreme Deity, is idolatry. The homage that belongs to Him recognizes His true relation to God as His Father, Who was in Him working out our salvation. The testimony of the prophets, apostles, and Christ Himself enlightens us on this subject. The enlightened worshipper knows how to worship. Under the former dispensation the angels were worshipped as the representatives of Yahweh. The Elohim, or Mighty Ones, had charge of the world's affairs, and spoke and wrought as Yahweh. Yahweh said to Abraham:

"I am El Shaddai," i. e., the strength of the Mighty Ones, or Elohic messengers.— Gen. 17. 1. By this appellation YAH was known to the patriarchs, but Deity revealed His memorial NAME to Moses in the bush through one of the Elohim or angels, who said:

"When I come to the children of Isreal, and say unto them, The Elohim of your fathers hath sent me unto you; and they shall say unto me, What is His NAME? What shall I say unto them? And Elohim said unto Moses, EYAH ESHER EYAH. Thus shalt thou say unto the children of Israel, EYAH hath sent me unto you."—Ex. 3, 13, 14.

And Elohim said further to Moses:

"Thus shalt thou say unto the children of Israel, YAHWEH (Elohim) of your fathers; the Elohim of Abraham, of Isaac, and of Jacob, hath sent me unto you; this is My Name forever, and this is My memorial to all generations."—Ex. 3. 15.

The Elohim were the representatives of the Deity, and spoke in His NAME. God promises Moses that He would go with Israel by him in the person of one of the Elohic messengers:

"Behold, I send an angel before thee, to keep thee in the way, and to bring thee into the place which I have prepared; beware of him, and obey his voice; provoke him not, for he will not pardon your transgressions; for MY NAME is in him. But if thou shalt indeed hearken unto his voice, and do all that I speak; then I will be an enemy unto thine enemies, and an adversary unto thine adversaries." —Ex. 23. 20-22.

Israel worshipped this Angel as God's Elohim all the way to the promised land. He delivered the law to them in company with other Elohim by Moses and the elders of Israel.

"And they saw the Elohim of Israel; and there was under his feet as it were a paved work of sapphire stone, and as it were the very heaven for clearness. And upon the nobles of the children of Israel he laid not his hand: and they saw Elohim, and did eat and drink."—Ex. 24:10, 11. This fact of God's administering His affairs through the angels was well understood by the Jews, as is seen by reading Stephen's discourse: (Acts 7:30-53.)

"Who received the law as it was ordained by angels, and kept it not."—Acts 7:53.

The Sinaitic covenant is also called by Paul, "The word spoken by angels."—Heb. 2:2, in contrast with the "words of the Lord Jesus," then recently spoken. The old "house of Israel" under the old covenant subject to angels; but Paul says:

"For not unto angels did He subject that habit-ble (hokoumenen) which was about coming, whereof we speak."—Verse 5.

Paul was not talking of a world altogether in his future, but the house (hoikas) that had already been made subject to Christ, in contrast to the former, which had been subject to angels. These Elohim as well as the patriarchs and prophets) were all waiting anxiously for the new dispensation, and praised God, and worshipped Christ when He was born. Christ was made so much superior to the angels—though they had spoken in Deity's Name, they had never inherited it by birth and divine sonship, as Jesus had,—that

"When He (God) bringeth His first-born into the world, He saith, Let all the angels of God worship Him,"—Heb. 1:6; and they did not commit idolatry in doing so. May we not do the same?

Jesus' Question Confirms Such A Worship.

Jesus once asked the Pharisees:

" 'What think ye of Christ? whose Son is He?' " They answered, "the Son of David." He said to them "How then doth David in spirit call Him Lord, saying, the Lord said unto my Lord, sit Thou on My right hand until (while) I make Thine enemies Thy footstool. If

David then call Him Lord, how is He his Son?' "—Matt. 22:41-45; Ps. 110.

To have answered correctly they would have had to admit that Christ was both David's son and Son of God. By being paternally related to David by His mother, He was David's son. Being paternally related to God as His Father, made Him David's Lord. Here are two Lords alluded to: "The Lord" and "My Lord." The Lord said to My Lord." "My Lord' is invited to sit on the right hand of "The Lord,' while the latter puts the former's enemies under His feet. But the translation fails to give the complete sense. The Common Version follows the Septuagint which confounds the two words, "Yahweh" and "Adonai," by rendering both by Kurios—Lord. The true reading is—"Yahweh said unto my Sovereign," etc. YAHWEH puts all things under the feet of Yah-sous. "Thou hast put all things under his feet," (Ps. 8:6) said the Psalmist, speaking of "the Son of man" prophetically. Yah-sous' death and resurrection redeemed men from the death sentence. The race thus became His property by purchase. This made Him Lord of the living and dead—giving Him the keys of death and Hades.—the grave. So He becomes "Lord of all;" (Acts 10:36-42) henceforth, "the Father judgeth no man, but having committed all judgment to the Son," commanded men to do honor to the Son as to Himself. (John 5:21-23). Christ is thus God's representative among men, the "mediator between God and men," so that all negotiations must be through Him, and in His NAME. He bears the father's name "YAH," as "the angel of His presence" did to Israel under Moses. (Ex. 23: 20, 21). He is now supreme "Head over all things, to the ecclesia, His body." We now occupy the "habitable (hoikumenen)· which was "about coming," that is. the one which was to succeed the old house under the angels and the mediatorship of Moses, spoken of in Hebrews 2:5.

Christ YAH-SOUS having "purged our sins sat down at the right hand of God—angels, authorities, and powers being subjected to Him," (Heb. 1:3-3) being "above every name that is named, both in this and the world to come." (Eph. 1:20, 21.) Here "He must reign until He hath put all enemies under His feet," up to "the last one—death." When this is accomplished, all the work of Christ in subduing all things to Himself by the power put into His hands by the Father will terminate. The exception of the "all things" put under Christ, is the Father—the Power that did it. (1 Cor. 15:25-28.) At the end of this epoch, the supremacy of the Father will be reannunciated. In this great gospel theme we see the signifiance of the name YAHSOUS Christ, or Anointed. He is God's name-sake, in and through whom He reconciles a world to Himself. He is the Anointed Sovereign of living and dead—heaven and earth. When, therefore, the apostles affirmed that He was Christ, they affirmed His sovereignty. When the Jews denied that He was Christ, they denied His Lordship.

"If thou shalt confess with thy mouth that Jesus is Lord, and shalt believe in thy heart that God raised Him from the dead, thou shalt be saved."—Rom. 10:9.

All things are at His disposal. He possesses unlimited power in the heavens and on earth.

"And Jesus came to them and spake unto them, saying: All authority hath been given unto Me in heaven and on earth."—Matt. 28:18.

Being the Son of David He inherited the kingdom and throne of David according to the ´oath and covenant of God, to which Peter alludes. (Acts 2:22-36.) David's lordship extended over the twelve tribes only, and not over the nations. Nor did it extend to the inhabitants of Sheol. Christ inherited from His Father's side supremacy over the living and dead, Jew, and Gentile. When "at the right hand of God exalted," above angels and men, living and dead, "Head over all things," "both Lord and Christ," the proclamation was sent first to Jew and then to Gentile—"He is Lord of all," With all in His power, friends and foes, the work of "subduing all things unto Himself" was inaugurated, and "He must reign until He hath put all enemies under His feet." (1 Cor. 15:25, 26.) When the holy ones are immortalized, and the sinners blotted out, "death, the last enemy," will cease to be.

The Name Of The Father In The Name Of The Son.

We can understand the significance of the apostle's "preaching peace through YAH-sous Christ: (He is Lord of all:) testifying that it is He who was ordained of God to be the Judge of living and dead." (Acts 10:36-43.) We doubtless have but a summary of this, Peter's first discourse to the Gentiles, but it was Redemption, Life eternal through the Christ, backed up by all the prophets,—by an eye witness of the death and resurrection. Peter gave his audience a summary of the facts from the baptism of John until the consummation,—recalling the last commission to the apostles; and when he arrived at the conclusion that YAH-sous was Lord universal of living and dead, the Lord confirmed the Word by the descent of the Holy Spirit upon the receivers of the testimony, who were commanded to be baptized **"Into (eis) the NAME of the Lord YAH-sous, "One Name"** which was the Father's given to the Son, and as the Father was in the Son by the Holy Spirit,—His own divine substance through whom all the testimony came—so it was all of YAH.

The substance of the gospel proclamation is, that YAH-sous died and rose to redeem the race, and bring them into the relation of sons and daughters to YAHWEH, and that He had become Master of all things, of the living and dead. "God has given Him the NAME that is above every name, that at the NAME of YAH-sous every knee shall bow, and every tongue confess that YAH-sous Christ is Lord, to the glory of God the Father." (Phil. 2:9-11.) The glory and wisdom of God shines out in the whole arrangement.

From the different construction of the commission to the apostles by the four evangelists, it will be seen that **"into (eis) the NAME of the Father, Son, and Holy Spirit," is equivalent to "His (Christ's) NAME"** according to Luke. The **NAME is one**—the NAME of the Father, YAH—which is above every name, and which He gave to His Son—Yah-sous. (Phil. 2:9,10.)

This NAME is, by tradition and the Common translation, entirely obscured. It is "the NAME into which the righteous run and are safe." (Prov. 18:10.) In this passage, as in nearly all others, the NAME of YAHWEH is suppressed. It is the NAME "from whom the whole family in the heavens (the angels) and on earth are named." (Eph. 3:15.) It is only by becoming a constituent element of what this NAME covers, that we can receive remission of sins.

After the Lord took His departure to the "right hand of the Majesty in the heavens," the promised Holy Spirit came upon the expecting ones, who began in the NAME of YAH-sous (that is the Name of the Father, Son, and Holy Spirit) to announce the "good message" or gospel (euangellion—from eu, good, and engellion, a message) to the Jews first, on the day of Pentecost, or fiftieth day after the Passover, when Christ was slain, as the antitypical lamb."

As YAH-sous who bore the Father's NAME, had been seated on the throne of universal empire—"having all power in the heavens and on earth." (Matt. 28:18.)—His commissioned servants began to announce the fact, and show to the good people what had been accomplished in the tragedy of fifty days previous, and what followed. (Acts 2.) This being at the time of the yearly "festival of weeks," beginning with the Passover and ending with the Pentecost—answering to the accomplishment of the antitype—the Jews from the parts of Proconsular Asia were assembled at Jerusalem, and their speech was in the different tongues of the people among whom thy sojourned, twelve to fifteen different languages. The multitude of people were confounded by the strange phenomena.

This very crowd had but fifty days before, cried, "crucify Him," and were witnesses of the tragedy. When Peter had rehearsed the circumstances, and showed its significance in the light of the prophets, "they were pricked in their hearts, and said unto Peter and the rest of the apostles, 'Men—brethren—what shall we do?' Then Peter replied, 'Repent, and be baptized every one of you in the NAME of YAH-sous the Anointed, for the remission of sins, and ye shall receive the gift of the Holy Spirit.' " (Acts 2 38.)

Observe, that it was but one NAME, that of YAH-sous. It is thus seen that the Popish and Protestant practise of using three appellatives, "Father," Son," and "Holy Ghost," is but a piece of ecclesiastical sorcery—in ignorance of the thing to be accomplished, and the way to accomplish it. They say to the candidate for baptism, that they do something which they do not do. They do not mention the Father's Name, YAH, nor the Son's Name, YAH-sous. The Father's name is not "Father," nor the Son's name "Son;" but the Name belonging to both is YAH. So it will be seen that all the apostles did, whether preaching, baptizing, or working miracles, was all in or into the NAME of YAH-sous. "In the Name of YAH-sous Anointed of Nazareth, rise up and walk," (Acts 3:6)—"YAH-sous Anointed maketh thee whole." (Acts 9:34.) Not always by a set form of words, but the NAME of YAH-sous was mentioned in the discourse as He Who was the Doer, or by Whose authority the thing was done. The tri-form of words in the Catholic formula is entirely foreign to any primitive Christian practice. The Greek and Latin fathers were bewitched with the trinitarian fiction as early as Justin's time, and entirely misunderstanding the words in Matthew 28:19, instituted the senseless ceremony. When we witness a Catholic or Protestant divine drawling out his triune formula, it reminds us of the "hocus-pocus" of the jugglers. Indeed, it is all off the same piece. The Lord of heaven and earth has much less respect for the former than the latter, which only pretends to trickery. Why do men take so kindly to humbuggery, and why are they so slow to learn the truth?

"And it shall come to pass, that whosoever shall call on the Name of the Lord —(Yah-weh—the Living God), shall be saved."—Acts 2:21.

"The Lord said . . . he—Paul—is a chosen vessel unto Me, to bear My Name before the Gentiles, and kings, and the children of Israel."—Acts 9:15.

"Neither is there salvation in any other; for there is none other

Name—(Yah-oshua)—under heaven given among men, whereby we must be saved."—Acts 4:12.

Comparing scripture with scripture, the unity of the everlasting gospel is disclosed. The Old and New Testaments are in perfect accord. That the great Life NAME of God, was understood and made known by Moses, and the holy men of old, had been referred to, but it will be profitable to follow the New Testament somewhat and observe the emphasis placed upon Deity's Name, especially the prominence given it in the gospel discourses. The gospel "brought life and incorruptibility to light." The unfolding and development of God's purpose is expressed in the text:

"The earth shall be full of the knowledge of the Lord—(Yahweh —the Self-Existent One), as the waters cover the sea."—Is. 40:9.

This knowledge would pertain "to YAHWEH," and become a source of security and sure refuge.

The Old Prophets Speaking Of The New Covenant In The Name Of The Messiah.

The prophets raised up at opportune periods, heralded the tidings that the knowledge of YAHWEH would ultimately abound and prevail, and associated with this abundance of knowledge there was always something pertaining to the life NAME. "My people shall know my NAME:" "they that know MY NAME; shall put their trust in ME."

"Behold the days come, saith Yahweh, that I shall make a new covenant with the house of Israel, and with the house of Judah; not according to the covenant that I made with their fathers, in the day that I took them by the hand, to bring them out of the land of Egypt;—I will put My law in their inward parts, and write it in their hearts; and will be their God, and they shall be My people. And they shall teach no more every man his neighbor, (as was the case in the old covenant), and every man his brother saying, Know Yahweh; for they shall all know Me, from the least unto the greatest of them."—Jer. 31:31-34; Heb. 8; Cor. 3:6.

How circumstantially, concisely, and completely these prophecies were realized in the gospel message,—the new and eternal covenant!

"Go ye therefore, and make disciples of all nations, baptizing them into the Name of the Father, and of the Son, and of the Holy Spirit."—Matt. 28:19.

"Repent and be baptized every one of you into the Name of Yah-oshua, the Anointed One, for the remission of sins."—Acts 2:38.

The Savior said:

"I came in My Father's Name."

The oneness or unity of the Great Father with His only begotten Son is thus perceived, and the necessity for induction into that life-giving name is obvious if one desires to become related to something higher than one's natural inheritance of dust and ashes.

"And that repentance and remission of sins should be preached in His Name unto all nations, beginning from Jerusalem."—Luke 24:47.

"Now when He was in Jerusalem at the passover, during the feast, many believed on His NAME, beholding His signs whicn He did."—John 2:23.

"He that believeth not hath been judged already, because he hath not believed on the Name of the only begotten Son of God."—John 3:18.

"I manifested Thy Name unto the men who Thou gavest Me out of the world." . . . . "Holy Father, keep them in Thy Name which Thou hast given Me, that they may be one, even as we are. While I was with them, I kept them in Thy NAME which Thou hast given Me." . . . . "I made known unto them Thy Name, and will make it known." John 17:6, 11, 12, 26.

"Simeon hath rehearsed how first God did visit the Gentiles, to take out of them a people for His Name."—Acts 15:14.

"And I saw, and behold, the lamb standing on the mount Zion, and with Him a hundred and forty and four thousand, having His Name, and the Name of His Father, written on their foreheads."— Rev. 14:1.

"Far above all rule, and authority, and power, and dominion, and every name that is named, not only in this world, but also in that which is to come." "The Father, from whom every family in heaven and on earth is named."—Eph. 1:21; 3:15.

Baptism.

In the performance of Baptism into the Name of Yah-sous, the subject is inducted into the death of Christ by a similitude—"planted in the similitude of His death, together with Him," (Rom. 6:5) by which, the thing symbolized, viz., the death of Christ, becomes ours. We thus, by symbol, pass through the death state, and rise with Christ. In so doing, the death sentence has been executed upon us, and if we abide in Him, we shall be made immortal when He comes. The old rite of circumcision was but a fore-shadowing of flesh cut off for sin—death for sin—which if suffered in Christ satisfies the sentence. If we are not in Christ when the day of doom—the judgment day—comes, the penalty will take hold of us with an eternal grasp.

But baptism, without a knowledge of the gospel, or how we get remission of sins by the death process in Christ, is of not the least avail. Those who imagine they get remission of sins before baptism can have no correct knowledge of its significance. If we receive remission of sins before baptism, there would be no use for baptism, which is the "birth of water," or "the washing of regeneration," "the cleansing of water in the Word." (Eph. 5:26.) The "word" of the gospel understood, accompanied by the water, completes the regeneration. The facts concerning the method of redeeming us and giving us eternal life are, by a similitude, exhibited in the process of baptism. It is the **"form of doctrine"** delivered first to us, and "into which we are delivered,"—and to "obey it from the heart" we have first to comprehend it. (Rom. 6:17.) The foolishness of the practice of rhantizing or pouring water on a person in three names, and calling it baptism, is too obvious to need comment. A person ignorant of the gospel is no subject for baptism. Those who practise sprinkling or pouring can certainly have no proper knowledge of the gospel. Their irregular use of water is in keeping with their irregular faith, and the whole accompaniment of a swarm of errors. The man who comprehends the glorious gospel, needs not be told that he must be buried in the water to represent his faith. To pretend to symbolize the death, burial, and resurrection process by the use of a teaspoonful of water would be as appropriate as to scatter a handful of earth upon a dead man and pronounce him properly buried.

The Form of Baptism.

The Greek lexicographers do not differ in defining the word baptizo, "to dip, to plunge, to immerse, to submerge, to wash, to sink, to soak." Words meaning "to pour" or "sprinkle" are never applied to baptism. Philip preached redemption to the Ethiopian eunuch who, when they had arrived at a certain water, wished to be baptized. (Acts 8:26-39.) Just as soon as a man comprehends the gospel, in the love of it, he will never rest until he is baptized. Our fellow membership and identity with Him Who died and rose again is the basis of all hope of an incorruptible life.

"If we have been planted together in the similitude of His death, we shall be also sharers in His resurrection, ... If we died with Christ, we shall also live with Him'—(as literally as He re-lived.)—Rom. 6:3-11.

"He died to sin," or was freed from His relation to sin by His death, and as soon as His death becomes ours; "our old man was crucified with Him," and the old body of sin is superseded. If we have thus, in Christ, ceased to live in the old sin relation and in our rising live related to God, as a new creation, death can have no more dominion over us than it could over Christ. Though we may die, it is not under condemnation but simply because our physical constitution is not yet changed. That change will pass upon us when YAH-sous comes to claim us as His own. "We sleep in YAH-sous," and therefore awake in Him. If He had not died under the sentence as our representative, we could never have escaped final and eternal death. If He had not risen to lead us out of the dismal charnal house, we could have no hope of living again.

"If Christ has not risen, they who have fallen asleep in Christ have perished"—without one ray of hope beyond the grave.—1 Cor. 15:18-23.

Baptism and its place in the Christian system is easily seen in the light of this gospel of eternal life through Christ. It is seen that Christ and His members constitute a body politic—full or complete.

"In Him dwells all the completeness of the Divine Supremacy of a body, and ye are in Him, the filled or complete thing, Who is the head of all principality and power." (How do you get in?) "In Whom ye are circumcised with the circumcision made without hands, in putting off the body of sinful flesh by the circumcision of Christ"—(which was a literal death). "Buried together with Him in baptism, and wherein ye are risen together with Him through faith in the energy of God who raised Him from the dead. And you being dead in your sins (condemned to death for sins) and the uncircumcision of your flesh, hath He made alive together with Him, having forgiven you all trespasses; having blotted out the handwriting of dogmas (dogma sin, that written on stone) which was against us, and contrary to us, and He hath removed it from the midst of us, nailing it to His cross." —Col. 2:9-14.

The law was our accuser, which Christ superseded or fulfilled in His life and death. Not one jot or tittle could pass away from the law until all was fulfilled.

"Think not that I came to destroy the law or the prophets; I came not to destroy but to fulfil," (fill full, or complete.)—Matt. 5:17.

"Christian Commission."

"As the Father hath sent Me, even so I send you. And having said this, He breathed on them, and said unto them, 'Receive ye the

Holy Spirit; whosoever sins ye remit, they are remitted unto them; and whosoever sins ye retain, they are retained.' "—John 20:22, 23.

"Then opened He their understanding, that they might understand the Scriptures; and He said unto them, "Thus it is written, that Christ should suffer, and rise from the dead the third day; and that repentance and remission of sins should be preached in His Name— (Christ's name),—among all nations, beginning from Jerusalem.' "— Luke 24:45-47.

"And He said unto them, 'Go ye into all the world and preach the gospel to the whole creation; he that believeth and is baptized shall be saved; but he that believeth not shall be condemned.' "— Mark 16:15, 16.

"And Jesus came and spake unto them saying: 'All authority is given to Me in heaven and upon earth; Go ye, therefore, and disciple all the nations, baptizing them into (eis. into) the Name (not names) of the Father, and of the Son, and of the Holy Spirit, teaching them to observe all that I have enjoined upon you.' "—Matt. 28:18-20.

Christ's commission to the apostles, as contained in the four gospels, is given in the above texts, and from these versions of the inspired writers, it is not difficult to see how the apostles were authorized to release sins—by teaching or preaching the gospel and baptizing; to represent the "form of doctrine," (Rom. 6:17) which set forth how sins were remitted by the death and reviving of Christ.

Remission of sins comes "in the Name of YAH-sous," by the believer being baptized with the proper understanding of that "Wherein the righteousness of God (or God's method of making righteous) is revealed, as proceeding from faith in order to produce faith."(Rom. 1:16, 17.) This "is the power of God unto salvation to every believer" which has been superseded by the "heaps of teachers (ordained by men) who have turned away their ears from the truth to fables." (2 Tim. 4:3, 4.) The Greek and Latin fathers inaugurated this fraud, and called it "the Church," and the whole army of ecclesiastics conspires to keep up this mercenary concern, and repudiate everything that refuses to sanction it, as "heterodox," "dangerous," "infidel," etc. They have such control of the popular ear that whatever they discountenance, the people, en masse, will run from, as "the machinations of the devil."

The form of words pronounced by the clergy over the "sacraments" was a thing unknown in apostolic times. The apostles used the NAME after this manner: "In the NAME of YAH-sous Anointed of Nazareth rise up and walk," (Acts 3:6.) Faith in that "Name" healed the "cripple." (Acts 3:16.) Again, "Repent and be baptized, every one of you into the name of YAH-sous Anointed for the remission of sins." In this Name they taught, (not in three names), "Go preach and baptize in and into the NAME," was the substance of the commission. The Samaritans were baptized, both men and women —"into the NAME of the Lord YAH-sous;" (Acts 8:12, 16) also, the Ephesians, (Acts 19:5) the company of Cornelius (Acts 10:48) and the Corinthians were, in the NAME of the One "crucified for them." (1 Cor. 1:13.) The apostles also wrought all the wonders in the same Name;—not by a strict form of the words,—instance: "YAH-sous Anointed maketh thee whole." (Acts 9:34.) Certain Jews undertook to use that Name with poor success. (Acts 19:13-17.) Here the Name was magnified, though it could not be safely used by sorcerers.

Since the days of the Apostles, there has been no new arrangement made for saving men. All the modern methods of "getting religion" are man-made, and can no more accomplish the salvation of the sinner than the Latin church process. "Repent and be baptized into the Name of Yah-sous the Anointed for the remission of sins" is no part of the improved (?) methods; yet, that was the only way the apostles did it. There are some "reformers" who talk about baptism for remission of sins. upon a bare confession that "Jesus is the Son of God." This is a modern improvement (?) entirely subversive of the primitive arrangement. It is based upon Acts 8:27, which is entirely spurious. Water, without faith, has no remitting quality. Faith took Noah into the ark, and thus, Peter says, "eight lives were carried safely through the water; of which our now being saved by baptism is the antitype; not the putting away of the filth of the flesh, but a good conscience, asking after through the resurrection of Jesus Christ." (1 Pet. 20:21.) The eight would not have gone "safely through the water" outside the ark; our faith drives us into the ark, through which we are saved from the impending destruction.

"BAPTIZED INTO."

There is an important difference between "baptizing in the Name and into the Name." The following passages will illustrate:

"Know ye not, that so many of us as were baptized into Jesus Christ, were baptized into His death."—Rom. 6:3.

"For as many of you as have been baptized into Christ, have put on Christ."—Gal. 3:27.

"For by one Spirit are we all baptized into one body."—1 Cor. 12:13.

The Greek preposition, eis, in the above, is correctly translated, and by what inadvertency the King's translator gave it "in" in the following passages. we are at a loss to say, but certainly it ought to be rendered "into."

"They were baptized in (eis) the Name of the Lord Jesus."—Acts 8:16.

"When they heard this, they were baptized in (eis) the Name of the Lord Jesus."—Acts 19:5.

"Were ye baptized in (eis) the name of Paul? I thank God that I baptized none of you but Crispus and Gaius. lest any should say that I had baptized in (eis) mine own name."—1 Cor. 1:13,14.

"IN THE NAME" implies by the authority, power, etc. 'In the name of the king, or commonwealth. Those who are "baptized into the Name of the Lord Yah-sous (intelligently), have put on Christ"—their state or condition is changed; they are induced into the life-giving Name, which makes them heirs of eternal life; and as the apostle says, "have passed from the (tou) Death into the (eis ten) Life" state. They have passed from the Adamic or condemned state, and are "free from the law of sin and death"; in other words, they have become "naturalized"—citizens of the Kingdom of our Lord. (John 5.24; Rom. 8:1, 2; Phil. 3:20; Col. 1:13: 1 John 3:14.)

CHAPTER III.

Confessions of Pious Men Concerning the Name of Our Lord.

John Bunyan says:

HRIST is the way through whom the soul hath admittance to God, and without whom it is impossible that so much as one desire should come into the ears of the Lord of Sabaoth. "If you ask anything in my name—whatsoever you ask the Father in my name, I will do it." This was Daniel's way in praying for the people of God; he did it in the name of Christ: "Now, therefore, O our God, hear the prayer of thy servant, and his supplications, and cause thy face to shine upon thy sanctuary that is desolate, for the Lord's sake." And so David, "For thy name's sake," (that is, for thy Christ's sake), "pardon mine iniquity; for it is great.' But now, it is not every one that maketh mention of Christ's name in prayer, that doth, indeed, and in truth, effectually pray to God in the name of Christ, or through Him. This coming to God through Christ is the hardest part that is found in prayer. A man may more easily be sensible of his evil works, aye, and sincerely, too, desire mercy, and yet not be able to come to God by Christ. That man that comes to God by Christ, **must first have the knowledge of Him**: for he that comes to God must believe that He is. And so he that comes to God through Christ, must be enabled **to know Christ**. "Lord," saith Moses, "show me thy way, that I may know thee."

John Wesley declared:

The inspired writers gave Him all the titles of the most high God. They **called Him** over and over by the uncommunicable name **Jehovah**, never given to any creature. They ascribed to Him all the attributes and all the works of God, so that we need not scruple to pronounce Him God of God, light of light, very God of very God: in glory equal with the Father, in majesty co-eternal."

Charles Wesley proclaimed:

Jesus, the name high over all,
In hell or earth or sky,
Angels and men before it fall,
And devils fear and fly.

Happy if with my latest breath
I may but gasp His Name;
Preach Him to all and cry in death,
"Behold, behold the Lamb!"

Spurgeon testified:

If angels were swept away, if the wing of the seraph never flapped the ether, if the voice of the Cherub never sung His flaming sonnet, if the living creatures ceased their everlasting chorus, if the measured symptoms of glory were extinct in everlasting silence, would His name then be lost? Ah, no! for as God upon the throne He sits, the everlasting One, the Father, Son and Holy Ghost;--and if the Universe were all annihilated, still would His Name be heard.

A French Ecclesiastic, Bearnard of Clairvaux, who lived from 1091 to 1151, affirmed:

No voice can sing, no heart can frame,
    Nor can the memory find,
A sweeter sound than Jesus' Name,
    The Saviour of mankind.
O, hope of every contrite heart,
    O, joy of all the meek.
To those who ask, how kind thou art!
How good to those who seek!

J. Munroe Gibson writes in his book, "Christianity According to Christ," published in London in 1888:

The name of God is that by which He has made Himself known to us, specially in the course of revelation; above all, the two great names of "Jehovah" in the Old Testament and "Jesus" in the New.

As to the name of "Jesus," while the sweetness has never been crushed out of it, as it has been out of the rich and precious Old Testament name, yet it has not been so closely identified with the Divine Being as it ought to have been. In their zeal for personal distinctions in the Holy Trinity, theologians have been too often tempted to forget such passages as these—"No man cometh unto the Father but by Me," "I and My Father are One," "I am the Truth," etc.; and so they have attempted to unfold a knowledge of God apart from His Son Christ Jesus; that is to say, a knowledge of God apart from that Name by which He has made Himself known to us."

W. W. Simpson, a missionary, states in the Latter Rain Evangel magazine of May, 1919:

The literal translation of Matt. 28:19 is, "baptizing them into the Name," etc., which means those baptized are to pass out of the dominion of self into the authority of the Father, Son and Spirit. Acts 2:38 says, "Be baptized in the Name of Jesus Christ," which means that they were to be in His authority and no longer under the dominion of self. The reason why the Father and the Spirit are mentioned in the former but not in the latter is that Jesus had not ascended, taken His seat on the Throne of God, with "all authority in heaven and earth," in His hands. "Both Lord and Christ," therefore His authority was now commensurate with the authority formerly vested in Father, Son and Spirit. There was no change in personality but a real and radical change in authority. With "all authority given into His actual possession the "Name of Jesus Christ" must include exactly as much authority as was formerly included in the "Name of the Father, and of the Son, and of the Holy Ghost."

Pierson, in The Sunday School Illustrator of Aug., 1919, remarks:

The Old Testament law was: "In all places where I record my name I will come unto thee, and I will bless thee." The New Testament law is: "Wherever believers meet in my n: me, there I will record my name. And there will I come unto them and bless them." Hence that grand companion declaration and invitation: "If two of you shall agree on earth as touching any thing that they shall ask, it shall be done for them of my Father which is in heaven. For where two or three are gathered together in my name, there am I in the midst of them."

The post-captivity Jews taught that wherever ten of them dwelt it was lawful to erect a synagogue. But our Lord says, that wherever two or three—the smallest number that can possibly assemble in His name—assemble, there is He in the midst of them.

Charles Gallaudet Trumbull, Editor of the Sunday School Times, publishes the following conviction:

The name of Jesus carries with it all the power of the triune God, for "in Him dwelleth all the fullness of the Godhead bodily" (Col. 2:9). His disciple's request that He show them the Father brought from Jesus the startlingly definite reply, "He that hath seen me hath seen the Father" (John 14:9). When John in the Revelation prophesied "They shall see His face; and His name shall be in their foreheads" (Rev. 22:4) that name and face will be Jesus', when we shall "see Him as He is."

It may well be, therefore, that the disciples in baptizing in the name of Jesus were carrying out the commission of Matt. 28:19. Certainly either form is a true baptism if the reality is back of the ceremony. In both cases there is one God and one Name. Some Christians who have felt that the spiritual reality was not in the form of baptism that they received have had the ordinance performed again and received rich blessing through it.

Testimony of a Superintendent of State Insane Asylums, with that of a missionary. (Copies from a leaflet of the Free Tract Society of Los Angeles, Cal.)

In a convention of Superintendents of State Insane Asylums, the question whether religion is a source of good or evil was discussed, and it was strongly decided in favor of religion. One of the number vehemently affirmed that if one would persistently keep the eye of faith on Jesus, insanity would be an utter impossibility; the union was a sure safe-guard; failure came when the hold was lost. At times when so pressed by opposing forces that it seemed my reason would go, the testimony of that Superintendent has been used to encourage me to continue to look to Jesus.

I had no conscious hold on Him—all was seemingly lost in the engulfing wave—but I would say, "Jesus, Jesus, Jesus." There was nothing in the words—they were empty science—but, they pointed to Him on whom I would lean; and I persisted in this, Salvation would flow in, and then nothing could move me.

If one who reads these lines is tempted, just turn wholly to the "Mighty to save" and the more abundant life is yours, for He has declared it, "Him that cometh to me I will in no wise cast out." The Magic Power of the name of Jesus is most beautifully portrayed in the following story told by a missionary who dealt with a poor unfortunate rum victim, who belonged to an aboriginal tribe. The missionary explained as best she could to the poor benighted mind, the wonderful deliverance that would come by simply trusting in Jesus. At last he seemed to grasp the thought and was able to trust Jesus fully. His joy was so great that when his wife asked him how it all occurred, all he would say was: "It all came through a name;" and upon being pressed to know what the wonderful name was, he would simply whisper." The name was Jesus." He seemed to feel that that name was too sacred to be uttered aloud.

Oh, for more of this simple, child-like faith today, **in the precious name of Jesus.**

William Lee Stroud, late Editor of Eusebia (1900) teaches concerning redemption through Christ, the following:

When "El" (God) said, "I Will Be, Who I Will Be," He proclaimed what "He Would Be" to His people, when He would be, "In the Anointed One reconciling a world unto Himself." 2 Cor. v. 13-21. In this Name, Christ's body politic are "All in Christ." "Yah-oshua" (Jesus) is the Ratifier by His blood, which is the ransom price of our lives that were forfeited by sin.

The faith of Abraham that God would certainly fulfill the promise concerning the eternal possession of the land, through the Seed, who would redeem him with all the heirs, and bring him into possession of the eternal life estate, through the redemption process, qualifies us for the burial in water into the name of YAH-oshua; when we rise out of the water, we are members of Christ, and so of the Abrahamic family. When we get into the NAME of Jesus we are in the Father's NAME; we belong to JESUS, Who is God's only begotten Son, in Whom we thus become the sons of God.

Christ is the only source of an unending life, through His redemptive work. In the untold ages of the eternal tomorrow we shall realize what we can only anticipate now, the immense results of His loving arrangement in the redemption program. Shall we make haste to join ourselves to that loving NAME of Him, in Whom God has deposited all this eternal wealth? In the faith of all this marvelous redemption work, we can pass through the waters of baptism and rise in Him who died and rose to die no more,—related to a never-ending life.

"No man cometh unto the Father but through Me." John 14:6. To understand the gospel is to understand "Who" JESUS is, and His relation to the Father and to us. A false orthodoxy confuses the whole system. The apostles did nothing in three names. Rome and her daughters do everything in three appellatives, but **no name.**

George Lansing Taylor, an American Educator, 1859, sings:

Crown Him, monarchs, seers and sages,
Crown Him, bards in deathless pages,
Crown Him King of all the Ages!
Let the Mighty anthem rise.

Hark! the crash of tuneful noises;
Hark! the children's thrilling voices;
Hark! the world in song rejoices.
Till the chorus shakes the skies.

CHAPTER IV.

The Great Christian Commission and The Name of God in Jesus Christ.

By A. D. Urshan.

OU have read the masterpiece on God's NAME in His dear Son, spoken of by these eminent Christian men who knew the original languages, Hebrew and Greek. You are undoubtedly now ready to understand better the same blessed truth which is given to us by the Holy Ghost through revelation, backed up by an abundance of Scriptures. Therefore we will come to you in the NAME which is above all names, and declare to you God's gracious dealings with us on the subject, and speak as God's witnesses from our personal experience.

Beloved, we wish thankfully to testify of the great blessing for the upbuilding of our faith in Christ with which the gracious God has favored us by flashing the glorious light of His Spirit upon the scriptures which specifically speak of what is termed "The Great Christion Commission" as recorded in Matthew 28:17-19; Mark 16:14-19, and Luke 24:45-49.

The Commission.

A commission is generally a band of specially chosen and appointed capable men, being authorized and supplied by the highest office and sent forth to perform their demanded and specified duties according to the law and requirements of their commissioners. So is the Great Christian Commission.

The Christian Commission, religiously speaking, is called "A Mission or a band of Missionaries to the home land and foreign countries," but the Bible name and language for missionaries and divinely commissioned men is "witnesses," as we read in Acts 1:8. "But ye shall receive power after that the Holy Ghost is come upon you and ye shall be witnesses unto me both in Jerusalem, and in all Judea, and in Samaria, and unto the uttermost parts of the world." Here is the Great Christian Commissioner, The Lord Jesus, sending forth His chosen and appointed commission—commanding them that they should wait until they are fully supplied and empowered from on high (Luke 24:48-49), then go forth to do only one thing, and that specific duty is applied unto His own Person; as He said "ye shall be witnesses unto me." Thus we see the definite and positive purpose and service of the Great Christian Commission, viz: "Go ye therefore and teach all nations, baptizing them IN THE NAME;" notice, please, it is not written in the names, but IN THE NAME. Just as commercial and political commissions are sent forth in the name of the highest office of the government, exactly so the divine commission from the beginning has been sent forth in the one great NAME of the Almighty God. The interesting question is then whose name is this mentioned "NAME" in Matthew 28:19, in which the great Christian commission should go forth. The following sentences answer the question. It is the one name of the T-H-R-E-E—O-N-E God (1 John 5:7), yea the NAME of the Father, of the Son and of the Holy Ghost.

The infallible record, therefore, clearly states and concludes that God, the Father, has a NAME and that this very name of the Father is the name of the Son and of the Spirit also; thus, whatsoever NAME the Son has, the Father has. Then the other important query is "What is the NAME of the Father." It is the same name that the Son has. What is the name of the Son? The answer is that it is the VERY name that the Father bears. Then the anxious heart will cry out, "Tell me, please, this one great NAME of the Father, of the Son and of the Holy Ghost, which is called 'THE NAME' in Matthew 28:19?"

Beloved Saints, when Jacob met the Lord he anxiously asked Him what was His name, (Gen. 32:29) and when Moses met God he also asked Him His name, by which he desired to go forth (Exodus 3:13). And the wisdom of God also in the Book of Proverbs (30:4) inquires the name of God and His Son. Dearly beloved, have we stopped, prayerfully and diligently searching, long enough to find out the name of our great God, like the old Saints of the Almighty, for this Gospel dispensation? If you have, please tell the world what is His NAME; by what name you and I should go forth as God's delegates and His ambassadors before all nations.

Have you found out that one hallowed NAME of God, the Father, the Son and the Holy Ghost before you baptized people into it? You may say, "I baptize them in the name of the Father, of the Son and of the Holy Ghost." Please permit us to ask you again, "What is that one NAME?" Now, let us tell you frankly and lovingly, that you have never baptized converts absolutely according to the commandments of our Lord if you have not found out first what that one NAME of God and the Lord of the Apostles is.

Many of us, through ignorance, have unconsciously misread and misinterpreted the plain commandment of our Lord, and have given a wrong impression and interpretation to the new converts for Matthew 28:19, as if it read, "Go ye therefore and teach all nations and baptize them in the name—"Father"—"Son" and "Holy Ghost." We have paid no attention to the two most important written words, "OF THE." These words "of the" should make us understand that Father is not a proper noun, but a common noun, and that the Heavenly Father has a name which makes Him properly to be known, just as your father has a name. That is why we are taught to pray "OUR FATHER who are in Heaven, Hallowed be Thy Name." We should not baptize in the name "Father," etc., but in the NAME of the Father, of the Son and of the Holy Ghost. Please let us come back to the important question again, and ask you "What is that one great, glorious and highest NAME of our T-H-R-E-E—O-N-E God for this dispensation?"

Important Question Answered.

Well, Beloved, the answer to the important query may upset the theology and the interpretation of many preachers and Christian workers, and put a ban of humility upon our boasting, for we have given the impression of having suffered for our loyal obedience to the commandment of our Lord and Savior as recorded in Matthew 28:19, and of having practiced the same faithfully; yet when we soberly study in the light and interpretation of the Holy Ghost the Christian Commission as described in Matthew 28:19, we find we have withstood, opposed and misjudged those who have actually obeyed and practiced the command of our Lord up to the last letter, just as the anointed and appointed apostles of our Lord Jesus Christ taught and practiced. Read, please, Acts 2:38; 8:12; 10:47-48 and 19:5; Gal. 3:27, etc., etc.

You may ask us to tell you the one NAME of the Father, of the Son and of the Holy Ghost. We will point you to the record of Mark and Luke, which is a part of the very same conversation of our Saviour on this great Christian Commission which Matthew wrote of. Please read now carefully Mark 16:14-19; Luke 24:45-49, with Matthew 28:19. You will clearly see, if you wish honestly to see, that Jesus Christ is that one NAME of the T-H-R-E-E—O-N-E God in which we are called and sent forth to preach repentance and remission of sins, to cast out devils and to lay hands on the sick and on the seekers to receive the healing and the baptism of the Holy Ghost. Yes, in this very NAME, the one, the single name of the Father which is also the name of the Son and the name of the Holy Ghost. If you do not accept this God-given light and testimony on this blessed commandment of our Lord in Matthew 28:19, please read the apostolic record and practice, and the Holy Ghost-given exhortation through the Great Apostle Paul for the Gentile Believers, who commands us that whatsoever we do in word and deed that we should do it all in the name of the Lord Jesus Christ, giving thanks to the Father. Amen. Col. 3:17 and etc.

The Old Dispensations And Commissions.

Beloved, God has been graciously taking us through the whole Bible and showed us His leadings and His great Commissions to His chosen people of old and that when He commissioned them or when He sent them forth He not only told them to go at His command but He gave them His great and mighty NAME to be their shield, buckler, hiding place and fortress. He taught them to lift up their banners and their swords and their voices against their enemies and that in His single and mighty NAME, by which He appeared unto them. So we read that when He commissioned our Father Abraham He appeared unto Him by His singular name "The Almighty God" and said unto Him that he should walk before Him and be perfect, and gave him also the great promise for himself and his generation. Gen. 17:1-8. So our Father Abraham went forth and conquered all his foes, prospered above all his fellowmen and became the Father of many nations and the friend of God, the Almighty.

Then we see God appearing to His servant Moses also to deliver his people from their bondage and ushering in another new dispensation and that with His new Name. So we read, "and God spake unto Moses, and said unto him, 'I am the Lord: and I appeared unto Abraham and to Isaac, and unto Jacob, by the Name of God Almighty, but by name Jehovah was I not known to them, and God said unto Moses, I am that I am: thus shalt thou say unto the children of Israel, I am hath sent me unto you." Exodus 6:1-3 and Exodus 3:13-14.

Moses did not stagger at the new name of the Almighty T-H-R-E-E—O-N-E God; he did not go around and teach the people of God that this new name Jehovah was the second name and that he and the people of God should go forth in the first and the second names of their God; as we are teaching and doing in these days;

but he simply obeyed the voice of his God and went forth in the **Name Jehovah**—Lord God—before the Pharaoh King, and before Israel. Therefore, he prospered and prevailed and conquered all his foes and finally he triumphed over death itself, and arising from his sleep he ascended into the very Heavens.

Now the vital queston is: Has the Almighty God of Abraham and of Moses ushered forth this gospel dispensation? You and all must agree with us and say Yes. Has He appeared unto us with a new name or not? You again must say yes with us. Then the important question is the same question that the wisdom of God inquired in Proverbs, 30th chapter and the 4th verse," What is His name, and what is His son's name, if thou canst tell?"

Now, dear friends, we humbly confess and testify to you and to all who may hear us that the same God of our Fathers, the Ancient of Days, hath appeared unto many saints and unworthy us also and hath told us that His proper NAME is not Father, nor Son, neither Holy Ghost, but the Lord Jesus Christ. That does not do away with the loving Fatherhood of the Almighty, nor with the gracious Sonship of the Lord, and neither does it do away with the blessed existence of the excellent Spirit of God, but it makes clear and harmonizes all the scriptures with all the fulness of this T-H-R-E-E—O-N-E Godhead summed up in this dispensation for all the human race in that sweetest of all names, JESUS, the anointed Jehovah Lord. Oh, let us use all the tongue, the voice, and the speech that we ever have by the Holy Ghost and confess and proclaim that **Jesus is the Lord**, bowing on bended knees with a humble, contrite and obedient heart and worship God, the Father, the Son, and the Holy Ghost in His new revealed NAME for this dispensation, of which the heavenly race and family is thereby named "**Christians**" or the Christ-ones. Hallelujah! God was in Christ reconciling the world unto Himself! Oh glory! He is yet with all His greatness, power and glory dwelling and manifesting Himself before the angels in that lovely Person of His Christ, the Son (see Col. 2:1-9).

The Apostolic Commission.

Beloved, this scriptural revelation makes Matthew 28:19 and Acts 2:38 equivalent, not two separate verses contradicting each other, but a blessed prophecy and command and its sure fulfillment in the power and revelation of the Holy Ghost through the teaching and practice of the chosen appointed and anointed apostles of our Lord and Saviour: thus we can with gladness read the Christian commission with one singular name of our God, viz: "Go ye therefore, and teach all nations, baptizing them **In the NAME of the Father, and of the Son and of the Holy Ghost.**" Amen!!!

This is the blessed Christian Commission of this dispensation, and here is the same great God who appeared with a single name to the patriarch Abraham, and with His new and single name to the prophet Moses; and announced through His holy prophets another new name that His people should yet know. "Therefore, behold, I will this once cause them to know mine hand and my might; and they shall know that my name is The Lord." (Jeremiah 16:21.)

"Therefore my people shall know my name; therefore they shall know in that day that I am He that doth speak: behold, it is I. How beautiful upon the mountains are the feet of Him that bringeth good tidings, that publisheth peace, that bringeth good tidings of good, that publisheth salvation, that saith unto Zion Thy God reigneth." (Isa. 52:6-7.) You notice, brethren, that future knowledge of Jehovah's name is prophesied in the sixth and seventh verses and it tells us of this very dispensation of the gospel; and the Apostle Paul repeats this very scripture in his discourse concerning the sure way of salvation by believing and confessing the name of the Lord Jesus in Romans 10:8-15. Thank God, that prophesied name of Jehovah is the name of our Saviour and Lord, Jesus, therefore the prophet Isaiah proceeds, saying, "And in that day shall ye say, Praise the Lord, call upon His name, declare His doings among the people, make mention that His name is exalted." Isaiah 12:4. (See also Ezekiel 39:7.) So to His apostles He appears not with many names or old names, but with this one new singular and sweet NAME. Brethren, you and all know that Father is not a name, nor is Son a name, nor is Holy Ghost a name; for if Father, Son and the Holy Ghost were names, then our Lord would not have said, Go and baptize the nations "in the Name," but He would have had to say, "in the names." Thank God, it is not so! It is one great powerful and glorious NAME which is above all names in Heaven or in the earth or under the earth. No wonder the apostles of our Lord preached, loved, cleaved to, suffered and died for that name, **Jesus Christ, the Lord.** See, please, Acts 11:20, 11:23, 21:13, 21:24, and 2 Cor. 4:5.

It is no wonder then that all the prophets and apostles give Jesus Christ the name and all the titles of the Almighty God of Abraham, Isaac and Jacob; no wonder our Saviour Himself could boldly say "Before Abraham was, **I AM, and, I am the First and the last, the beginning and the end, and the Almighty."** And His loving exhortation for us all, over and over is to abide in Him, which means that we should not get our heart, our mind, our spiritual vision and all we are and ever will be, out of Him, and look away from Him to see the triune God.

We gospel ministers preach and exhort the people that everything spiritual and eternal, which includes our blessed and adorable T-H-R-E-E—O-N-E God is all in the written word and that we should prayerfully and carefully study it and hide it in our hearts and bring our lives and experiences into subjection to it, for it is the only sure way of life. Then a question arises: What is all this infallible and Holy Word of God, if it is not Jesus Christ the Lord? Can a human being find a triune God out of the written word? If not, then why should we think, or try, to find God our Father apart from His Son, who is the Alpha and Omega or the whole written Word of the Almighty God!! Brethren, let us not be too proud, or imagine we can see and think beyond Jesus Christ. Let Christ, the Lord, fill our vision and be satisfied with Him.

Abraham, Isaac and Jacob, Moses and all the prophets of the Bible went forth living and proclaiming their message to the people of God, the Jews, and to the Gentiles in the NAME that was revealed unto them for their dispensation. Why should we stagger at the name of God in His Son which has been given unto us to live and to proclaim in the whole world. "GO ye therefore and teach all Nations, baptising them **in the Name,"** etc. There lies the whole secret and the power and the message of the apostles "in the **NAME."**

Confusion Over Subject Defeated.

A few days ago a lady came to our meetings, an earnest child of God. She could not grasp the spirit and the motive of the message: "the Godhead in Jesus Christ." She went home disgusted, thinking we were misleading people. But in the silence of the night the blessed Spirit spoke to her saying, "Have you a father and a son?" She said, "Yes." Then the Spirit asked her, "Is your father's name Father?" she said, "No, my father's name is Brown." "Is your son's name son?" she said, "No, it is Clarence." Then God asked her, "What is the name of your Heavenly Father?" She honestly and prayerfully thought and thought, but she could answer nothing. Then the Spirit proceeded, "What is the name of the Son of the Father?" She said, "Jesus Christ." Then the Spirit proceeded, "Has your Heavenly Father a name; if so, what is it; don't you want to know it?" And He graciously showed her that Jesus was the name of God, our Saviour, and Christ was the anointed One which stands for the Name and the fulness of the Holy Ghost in Him, and the Lord was the name of the "Father and all the Deity."

The Name of the Holy Ghost in Jesus Christ.

In the Syriac translation and also in the Greek the Holy Ghost is not called "the Comforter," as in the English version (John 14:26), but is called "the Parakleta." Jesus Christ bears this very name of the Spirit in 1 John 2:1. (See the Scofield Bible, page 1136.) The Holy Ghost is called "the quickening Spirit," so is the Lord Jesus called "the quickening Spirit." Compare John 6:63 with 1 Cor. 15:45. The Holy Ghost also is called "the Lord." Thank God, Jesus Christ is "the Lord" also. The Holy Spirit is called "the Spirit of the Lord" and "the Spirit of Christ."

Just as your spirit has not a separate name from the name you bear, but your name is the name of all that is in you, just so the Spirit of Christ bears the name of Christ, for he dwelleth in Christ (Col. 2:9) and is given to us by Christ (John 7:37), and comes forth from Christ (Acts 2:33).

The Holy Spirit is called also "the anointing," 1 John 2:27. So Jesus Christ is "the Anointed One." Hallelujah!

There have been mighty revivals and reformations by chosen men of God in the past, over some part of the truth which they declared boldly; like Luther and John Knox over their message of Justification by Faith, like Wesley and other Holiness Reformers over their teaching on holiness, like the Christian Alliance and others on divine healing in the atonement and the pre-millennial message, and like Pentecostal people over the baptism of the Holy Ghost with speaking in tongues as the Bible evidence, etc., etc., etc. Although these movements and the Reformers faced great difficulties and suffered great persecution, and many were confused and stumbled over them, nevertheless the truth that was revealed unto them prevailed and today there are thousands who have been justified, sanctified, baptized, and healed and are rejoicing in the blessed hope and the appearing of our Great God and Saviour Jesus Christ. Now this message on the name of God revealed by the power of the Holy Ghost in Jesus Christ contains more scriptures than any of the above mentioned messages. Will God let hundreds of scriptures in which His name is mentioned be obscured and not emphasized? No, he will not, and He is now putting it in our hearts with the greatest fire and zeal that we ever felt to declare, proclaim, and make mention of His name among all nations, as Moses did. Read Deut. 32:1-3. As David did. Read Psalm 22:22, 34:3, 102:21, 145:1, 148:13. As Isaiah, the prophet did. Isa. 12:4, and as the Apostles did. Read Acts 4:15-20, 5:27-32 and 42.

Loss and Suffering For His Name.

When our Lord commissioned His apostles to go forth in His name (which is the name of all Deity for this dispensation) He told

them that they would suffer greatly for His name and that they
would be hated by all men, not for their spiritual experiences, or
gift of Tongues, but for His Name. Why for His Name? Because
that was to be their message to the world, yea, the message that
stirs up not only Hell but the religious world also. Read, please,
Matthew 10:20-22, Acts 5:41, 9:14-16, John 16:20, Luke 21:17,
etc., etc. We are glad we had the privilege in Persia, before those
Mohammedans, of testifying to our Lord and God, Jesus; although
being surrounded to be butchered for His Matchless Name, yet there
was such an unspeakable glory possessing our whole being that it
made us more than glad to be tortured and die for His worthy Name.
And now it is a very small thing to us to be slandered and misunderstood and misjudged for The Name of the Father, of the Son, and
of the Holy Ghost, which is the Lord Jesus Christ.

An Evident Fact.

It is an actual fact that the revealed name of the T-H-R-E-E—
O-N-E God is not only slandered and insulted by Christian Scientists,
Unitarians and Spiritualists, Russellites and Mohammedans, but it
is a name that is not generally spoken, or taught to children, by the
so-called Orthodox Christians of our day. You go to their high
society gatherings and among Christian politicians and into the great
church pulpits, and you will hardly hear mentioned that highly
exalted name "Jesus;" but thank God the day is approaching that
every knee must bow before that name and every tongue must confess
that Jesus is Jehovah. I am glad I do not have to wait for that day
and be forced to acknowledge Him as Lord God Almighty, but voluntarily and gladly I say now, "He is my All."

If the apostles should be raised up and should come to our
churches to give their message today, they could have no entrance
into our churches and assemblies, because they, being members of
no present day denominations, small organizations or sects, could
come only in the name of their Commissioner; they would be asked
what denomination they represented and if they had the credentials
and the fellowship certificates and Pastor's references; and if they
had failed to produce these man-made papers, of course they would
have to be shut out, no matter how much and highly they could have
spoken of the Lord. That could not give them the present-day
Christian platforms. Brethren, doesn't this fact prove that our own
names and the names of our Conferences have been exalted and
trusted above the Name of our Lord and Saviour? How can we then
expect to have the power and glory of the first Apostolic Church?
Oh, let us go in His Name and for His Name alone so that it will
be said of our ministry as it is recorded in Mark 6:14, "His name was
spread abroad." The Disciples healed the sick and cast out evil
spirits, yet His Name was so spread abroad that King Herod heard
about Him.

All Power, All Things And All The Glory Of God Is Given To Jesus Of Nazareth.

Brethren, what has been already said not only proves that
Jesus Christ is all of God for us, that His name contains the name
of all the deity, and that in Him dwelleth all the fulness of the Godhead bodily and that He is visibleness of the invisible T-H-R-E-E—
O-N-E God, but the whole Bible teaches this great conclusion. Now
let us search the scriptures and see if these things are not so, for
it is not what you and I say, but what the scripture says that is
important. Here God is speaking in Isaiah 42:8, 'I am the Lord:

that is my name: and my glory will I not give to another, neither my praise to graven images." If Jesus Christ was not the very God and the only begotten Son of God and in Him all of God, He would certainly be another one, or the second Being as some think; and He would never have said what He did as recorded in Matthew 11:27-30, John 14:6, Matthew 28:18 and Rev. 1:8.

The following scriptures will prove to every honest believer of the whole Bible that the God of the Old Testament whose name was "the Almighty," "Lord God" and "Jehovah" is in Jesus Christ the Lord of the New Testament.

The Names of God In The Old Testament.

The general and the unchangeable name of the **One Supreme Being,** the great Creator, the most high and the lofty one, is **GOD** as it is written in Exodus 3:15. The next name of the Almighty God is the Lord or (Jehovah). See Exodus 15:3 and in full, God's Name is called, The Almighty God, The Most High God, The Everlasting God, The Great, the Mighty God and the Lord of Hosts. Read, please, Genesis 17:1, 14:18; Gen. 21:33; Exodus 6:3; Jeremiah 32:18.

Beloved, if you love Jesus in sincerity as the bridegroom of your eternal life and your only hope, you should rejoice greatly with us to learn that this same Holy Bible calls Jesus Christ, **"Mighty God,"** Isaiah 9:6; "The **Great God,"** Titus 2:13; "The **Everlasting God,"** Hebrew 1:8-12, Micah 5:2, Romans 9:5. "The Most High God" means the ONE far above all and over all, so Jesus Christ's present position is, as the Apostle says, that "He is exalted not only above all principalities, powers and dominions, but Far above all where the 'Most High' is," thus the apostle again could say of Jesus Christ, "who is over all, God blessed forever." Amen. Compare Romans 9:5 with Phil. 2:9, Psalm 97:9, with Eph. 4:10, 1:21. Now as to "The Lord of Hosts." Read, please, Jude 14, with Zechariah 14:5, 9, 16, 17; here you will see the Coming One is "the very Lord of Hosts," and the Apostle John also saw Him in His coming glory by his great revelation in the Holy Spirit, as Isaiah, the prophet saw Him as recorded in Isaiah, 6th chapter; see John 12:40-50 and Revelation 4:8. "And the four beasts had each of them six wings about him; and they were full of eyes within: and they rest not day or night saying Holy, Holy, Holy, Lord God Almighty, **which was, which is, and which is To Come."**

The question is, then, who is He that is coming again; Rev. 1:7-8 with 15:3-4; Rev. 16:4-7, 17:14, with 19:1-16, 11:15-7 will answer the question. As to Jesus Christ being Almighty, you have already read in Rev. 1:8.

There is another distinct name which God has and that is, Holy, "As for our Redeemer, The Lord of Hosts is His Name the Holy One of Israel." Again, For thus saith the high and the lofty one that inhabiteth eternity whose name is Holy. See Isaiah 47:4 and 57:15. Our Lord and Saviour is called over and over again by this very name "Holy," see, please, Rev. 3:7, Acts 2:27, etc., etc. As to the name Jehovah being in our Saviour Jesus, we will give you the exact words of Dr. R. A. Torrey, dean of the Bible Institute of Los Angeles, in his tract on The Deity of Jesus Christ, page 7. "In first Corinthians, 2:8, the Apostle Paul speaks of our crucified Lord Jesus as 'The Lord of Glory.' His exact words are 'Which none of the Princes of the world knew: for had they known it, they would not have crucified the Lord of Glory.' There can be no question that 'the Lord of Glory' is Jehovah God, for we read in Ps. 24:8-10, Who is this King of Glory? Jehovah strong and mighty. Jehovah mighty in battle; Lift up your heads, O ye gates; yea lift them up, ye everlasting doors, and the King of Glory shall come in. Who is the King of Glory? Jehovah of Hosts, He is the King of Glory.' And we are told in the passage already referred to that our crucified Lord Jesus was the King of Glory, therefore He must be Jehovah. In John 20:28, Thomas addressed the Lord Jesus as his Lord and his God, 'And Thomas answered and said unto Him, my Lord and my God.' Unitarians have endeavored to get around the force of this utterance of Thomas' by saying that Thomas was excited and that he was not addressing the Lord Jesus, but was saying 'My Lord and my God' as an ejaculation of astonishment, just in the way that profane people sometimes use these exclamations today; but this interpretation is impossible, and shows to what desperate straits the Unitarians are driven; for Jesus Himself commended Thomas for seeing it and saying it. Our Lord Jesus' words immediately following those of Thomas are, 'Because thou hast seen me, thou hast believed: Blessed are they that have not seen, and yet have believed' (John 20:29)."

Oh, beloved messengers of the gospel, let us rejoice over the archangel's glorious message who said, "Behold, a virgin shall be with child, and shall bring forth a Son and they shall call His name IMMANUEL, which being interpreted is GOD with us. Math. 1:23. Oh, friend, there are many false gods and false Christs which thousands of people even in this county are believing and preaching, but unto the holy prophets and apostles, there is One true God which is in His Son, Jesus Christ, in whom we have eternal life. See, please, 1st John 5:20. This message unto the ignorant and unbelievers is a great mystery of controversy, but unto us who seek to find the true God it is a great mystery of godliness without controversy. "God was manifested in the flesh, justified in the spirit, seen of angels, preached unto the Gentiles, believed on in the world, received up into glory. Hallelujah!" 1 Tim. 3:16. "He was in the world and the world was made by Him and the world knew Him not." Dear reader, do you know Him? "The people that do know their God shall be strong, and do exploits." John 1:18 and Daniel 10:32.

The Lover of the Bible.

Fellow-workers, if you love the good old Bible you will be delighted to read all the above scriptures with an honest searching, and the prayers over your study will mean a great uplift to your precious Faith and will make you a much more effectual Christian worker than you have ever been before. Therefore you should not hesitate to read the following scriptures in addition, which ascribe all the titles and offices of the God of the Old Testament, and their fulfillment, to the name and ministry of our Lord and God JESUS.

When our Lord Jesus spake of Himself to His enemies and to His own disciples, He spake Scriptures (of course, the Old Testament, for the New was not written then), so we read in Luke 24:27-45, the following: "And beginning at Moses and all the prophets, He expounded unto them in all Scriptures the things concerning Himself." "Then opened He their understanding, that they might understand the Scriptures." He also commands us to search the Scriptures concerning Him, as it is recorded in John 5:39. "Search the Scriptures, for in them ye think ye have eternal life; and they are they which testify of me." When Philip and Nathaniel found Him they said unto Peter, "We have found Him of whom Moses in the law, and the prophets, did write, Jesus of Nazareth,the son of Joseph." John 1:45.

Beloved, to know the Lord Jesus Christ in the Bible we must not only read the New

Testament, but the Old Testament also, for the New Testament is the fulfillment and explanation of the Old.

Compare with me the following Scriptures, please:

Read Law and the Prophets, and Compare with the Four Gospels and the Epistles.

"THE CREATOR"

God, the Creator—Gen. 1:1; Isa. 45:11-12; Ps. 148:5, etc., etc.

Jesus Christ, the Creator—Heb. 1:8-12; Col. 1:12-17; John 1:1-10, etc., etc.

"THE REDEEMER"

God, the Redeemer—Isa. 43:14, 41:14, 47:4; Ps. 78:35, etc., etc.

Jesus Christ, the Redeemer—Gal. 3:13; Acts 20:28; Rev. 5:9; Luke 24:21, etc., etc.

"THE SAVIOUR"

God, the Saviour—Isa. 43:3 and 11, 45:21, 49:26; Hos. 13:4, etc., etc.

Jesus Christ, the Saviour—John 4:42; I. Tim. 1:1, 2:3; II. Tim. 1:10; Titus 1:3-4, 2:10 and 13; II. Peter 2:20; I. Peter 1:11; Jude 25, etc., etc.

"THE SHEPHERD"

God, the Shepherd—Ps. 23:1; Isa. 40:10 and 11, etc., etc.

Jesus Christ, the Shepherd—John 10:11; I. Pet. 5:4, etc., etc.

"THE ROCK"

God, the Rock—II. Sam. 22:32 and 47; Ps. 62:2; Isa. 51:1; Ps. 78:35, etc., etc.

Jesus Christ, the Rock—Rom. 9:33; I. Cor. 10:4; I. Pet. 2:8, etc., etc.

"THE KING"

God, the King—Isa. 43:15, 44:6; Zech. 14:9, 16 and 17; Ps. 45; Mich. 5:2.

Jesus Christ, the King—Luke 23:3; John 19:21; I. Tim. 6:13-16; Rev. 15:1-4, etc., etc.

"THE I AM"

God, the "I Am" and Almighty—Ex. 3:14, 6:3, etc., etc.

Jesus Christ, the "I Am" and the Almighty—Rev. 1:8; John 8:58; Rev. 4:8.

"I AM HE"

God, the "I am He"—Isa. 43:10 and 25, etc., etc.

Jesus Christ, the "I am He"—John 8:24 and 28, etc., etc.

"THE FIRST AND LAST"

God, the "First and Last"—Isa. 41:4, 43:10, 48:12, etc., etc.

Jesus Christ, the "First and Last"—Rev. 1:11 and 17, 22:13, etc., etc.

"THE WORSHIPPED"

The Worshipped God—Isa. 45:23, etc., etc. Jesus Christ, the Worshipped God—Phil. 2:5-11, etc., etc.

The Lord God of the Holy Prophets and Saints—Zech. 14:5; Titus 2:13-14; John 20:28; Rev. 1:1, 22:6. Compare with Rev. 22:16 and 20.

Conclusion.

Oh, Hungry Ones, let us keep close to Christ Jesus, who is our Hope, and love Him, worship Him, Preach Him and keep His Commandments; then John 14:21 will be our experience. "He that hath my commandments, and keepeth them, he it is that loveth me and he that loveth me shall be loved of my Father, and I will love him and will manifest myself to him." "Brethren, I count not myself to have apprehended, but this one thing, I do, forgetting those things which are behind and reaching forth unto those things which are before. I press toward the mark for the prize of the high calling of God (Where is this mark of God?) In Christ Jesus. See Phil. 3:7-14. This is the great apostle's only aim and His great future ambition unto which He is running. Should we not aim at the same thing? Brethren! if you won't we will count all things but loss for the excellency of the Knowledge of Christ Jesus our Lord!!! "Give unto the Lord, O ye mighty, give unto the Lord glory and strength. Give unto the Lord the glory due unto His name; worship the Lord in the beauty of holiness." Psalm 29:1 and 2. Let us stand for Him who left all His glory and became a servant and the poorest of all, and died on the cruel cross of Calvary for our sins, and "Go ye therefore and teach all nations, baptizing them In The NAME of the Father, of the Son and of the Holy Ghost," "which is JESUS CHRIST, THE LORD."

CHAPTER V.

Some Scriptures Worthy of Special consideration concerning the Name of God.

The Secret of Great Fame.

F THERE was a famous man in the world, among the noblest of earth, it was King Solomon. His fame was so great that it not only captured the mind of the common people but of the kings and queens of the earth. As we read:

"And when the queen of Sheba heard of the fame of Solomon, she came to prove Solomon with hard questions at Jerusalem, with a very great company, and camels that bare spices, and gold in abundance, and precious stones; and when she was come to Solomon, she communed with him of all that was in her heart. . . . and there was no more spirit in her. And she said to the king, It was a true report which I heard in mine own land of thine acts, and of thy wisdom; howbeit I believed not their words until I came and mine eyes had seen it: and, behold, the one half of the greatness of thy wisdom was not told me: for thou exceedest the fame that I heard."

The question is, what made Solomon so great, and therefore famous? It was the power, excellency, and greatness applied to Solomon's life by the wisdom in the Name of God. So that the queen of Sheba heard not only about the fame of Solomon, but of this mighty Name of his God, for which the temple of Solomon was built.

"And when the queen of Sheba heard of the fame of Solomon concerning the name of the Lord, she came to prove him with hard questions." 1 Kings 10:1. Compare with 11 Chr. 9:1-6.

Every true Bible student will agree with us that Solomon's fame and reign was only a foreshadow of the great reign of our Lord Jesus Christ, the King of kings and Lord of lords, on the earth during the Millennium. If the foreshadow was so famous, what will it be when God Himself rules on the throne of David? Yea, the whole earth will be filled with the glory of the Lord, for in that day, Jehovah Himself (Jesus) will be King of the earth. Compare the above texts with Mark 6:14 and you will have prophecy and its fulfillment. When our Saviour sent His twelve disciples, two by two, he gave them power over demons, devils, sickness and death, and sent them in His Name to go and do these mighty works. Did they make a failure? No. But their prosperity was so great that King Herod heard—of them? No, of Him. Why? "For His Name was spread abroad." "And Jesus returned in the power of the Spirit into Galilee: and there went out a fame of Him through all the region round about." Luke 4:14. What a significant thought! Solomon built the temple, but the Name of the Lord was spread abroad. The disciples cast out devils and did miracles, but the Name of the Lord Jesus was spread abroad. Why is it so? Because the whole secret of great success and fame lies in the NAME OF THE LORD. Oh that we might be privileged to know and to honor the Name of the Lord in our lives as did the ancient people of God!

The Outpoured Perfume of the Alabaster Box.

When our blessed Lord was being entertained in the house of a Pharisee, there came suddenly a woman of ill reputation with something under her wide robe. As she came near to our Saviour, she took out that something, which was an alabaster box, and broke it, pouring the ointment in it upon the head of Jesus. What happened? The whole house was filled with sweet perfume. Notice, please, there was no smell of perfume before the box was broken, but as soon as it was poured forth, all enjoyed the precious savour. And some of those who were sitting with Him at once noticed the preciousness of that ointment and considered what a great price could have been obtained for that box of alabaster if it were sold. But what is that natural perfume and costly ointment, compared with the NAME of the Lord? We read in the Song of Solomon, when the Bride speaks of His excellent Name:

"Let him kiss me with the kisses of his mouth; for thy love is better than wine. Because of the savour of thy good ointments thy name is as ointment poured forth, therefore do the virgins love thee." S. S. 1:2, 3.

This savour in the Name of the Lord is the savour of Heaven; hence, the savour of eternal life of joy and divine pleasure. Also it is the savour that destroys every unclean, unhealthful odor of sin and the devil. This was the secret of the sweet grace of God in the Apostles' life and ministry, that made them to be channels of eternal life to thousands, and destruction unto the power of sin and the devil, all of which they wrought in the Name of the Lord. So we read; the great Apostle, speaking of this sweet, heavenly savour:

"Now thanks be unto God, which always causeth us to triumph in Christ and maketh manifest the savour of his knowledge by us in every place. For we are unto God a sweet savour of Christ, in them are saved, and in them that perish. To the one we are the savour of death unto death; and to the other the savour of life unto life." 11. Cor. 2:14-16. Compare with Luke 7:36-42. Oh, the sweet life of power, of glory, of excellency—the life of Almighty God, in the precious Name JESUS.

The Perfect Heavenly Blessing.

The number seven in the Bible is a divine number, which shows the completeness of the Deity, in Himself and in His Church; as, the seven spirits of God, the seven churches of God, the seven messengers of God, etc., etc. But we find another number seven in the ninety-first psalm, which is, seven heavenly blessings, or the complete blessing of the Almighty God. Where do you think this great blessing is kept in store? The psalmist says, in the knowledge of the Name of the Lord; in other words, to know the Name of the Lord and to set our affections on Him, is to have the seven blessings of God.

"Because he hath set his love upon me, because he hath known my name,

1. Therefore will I deliver him;
2. I will set him on high;
3. He shall call upon me, and I will answer him;
4. I will be with him in trouble;
5. I will . . . honor him;
6. With long life will I satisfy him;
7. And show him my salvation."

The question is, can any mortal being receive the perfect blessings of God apart from Jesus Christ? No: for the Scripture declares that "we are blessed with all spiritual blessings in the heaven—lies in Christ Jesus." And "all the promises of God in Him are yea and Amen." Hence, to know the Name of the Lord Jesus and to love it, is the condition upon which we can receive these seven great blessings. Reader, do you know His Name?

"They that know thy name will put their trust in thee: for thou, LORD, hast not forsaken them that seek thee." Ps. 9:10.

Reader, do you love that matchless Name? "They that love His Name shall dwell therein." And "The Name of the Lord is a strong tower; the righteous runneth into it and is safe." Ps. 69:36; Prov. 18:10.

We read of the fearful and gloomy day of the Lord, which shall come upon the inhabitants of the earth, which will be a day of wrath, destruction, and death, a day in which the pangs of sorrow will capture the people that are out of Christ, a day when the Almighty shall show forth his terrible wonders in Heaven above and signs in the earth beneath, blood and fire and vapor of smoke, when the sun shall be turned into darkness and the moon into blood. Reader, do you not think the inhabitants of the earth will seek a hiding place in that awful time? Oh yes, they will cry out for it. Unbelievers will cry out for the mountains to fall on them and hide them from the wrath of God. What a poor refuge! for it says that even the mountains shall be removed. But thank God! there will be a real refuge in that day. For the prophet says:

"And it shall come to pass, that whosoever shall call on the NAME of the Lord shall be saved."

Oh, reader, remember for time and eternity that there is no name under Heaven whereby we can be blessed and delivered but the Name of the Lord Jesus Christ. Compare Acts 2:17-21 with Rev. 6:12-17 and Acts. 4:12.

"In the calm of the noon-tide, in sorrow's lone hour,
In times when temptation casts o'er me its power:
In the tempests of life, on its wide, heaving sea,
Thou blest 'Rock of Ages,' I'm hiding in thee.
Hiding in thee, hiding in thee,
Thou blest 'Rock of Ages,' I'm hiding in thee."

No wonder that the prophets and apostles knew the great value of God's name and gloried not in their own names, nor in their spiritual experiences, but in the Name of the Lord. In the name of the Lord we find salvation, healing, baptism of the Holy Ghost, power over demons, and eternal life; yet people will preach and glory in all these things and forget that they all come to us for the sake of His Mighty NAME. See, please, Mal. 4:2, Mat. 18:20, Acts. 2:20, 3:16, 4:12, 10:43, 16:18, Mark 16:16, 17, John 14:26, James 5:14, 111 John 7.

A Great Religious Conference.

When a large denominational conference or a great revival meeting is held, the editors of both religious and secular papers will be there to take the record of the great gathering. That is good as far as it goes. But there is another meeting which God Almighty Himself attends, and He, being much interested in that meeting, keeps quiet and listens to the words of those who confer together. And not only does He listen, but He also takes the record of that meeting and puts it before His hallowed presence for a great memorial. What kind of session do you think this meeting is, that God is so pleased with as to become its recorder? It is the meeting of those that love and honor His Name, that come together and think how to exalt and magnify the Name of their Lord in the earth. The following Scriptures so affirm:

"Then they that feared the Lord spake often one to another: and the Lord hearkened, and heard it, and a book of remembrance was written before Him for them that feared the Lord, and that thought upon His Name." Mal. 3:16.

And what is the outcome of such a meeting

"And they shall be mine, saith the Lord of hosts, in that day when I make up my jewels; and I will spare them, as a man spareth his own son that serveth him. . . . Unto you that fear my name shall the Son of righteousness arise with healing in His wings; and ye shall go forth, and grow up as calves of the stall. And ye shall tread down the wicked; for they shall be ashes under the soles of your feet in the day that I shall do this, saith the Lord of hosts." Mal. 3:17 and 4:2, 3.

What a sweet harmony the above Scriptures have with the words of our Saviour concerning His own Name, who said:

"For where two or three are gathered together in my name, there am I in the midst of them."

What will follow such a meeting?

"Verily, I say unto you, Whatsoever ye shall bind on earth shall be bound in heaven and whatsoever ye shall loose on earth shall be loosed in heaven. Again I say unto you, that if two of you shall agree on earth as touching anything that they shall ask, it shall be done for them of my Father which is in heaven." Mat. 18:18-20.

Yet in the face of all these eternal blessings and benefits of God in His Name, which He has given to His Son Jesus Christ, for us to declare, to trust, and to glory in, some people will try to deter us from speaking so much of the name of Jesus, mockingly saying: "Don't play always on one string, and don't make the name of the Lord a hobby," etc., etc., Such remonstrances are nothing less than a dishonoring and insulting of the Name of the triune God in our only Saviour, Christ.

"No word of man can ever tell
How sweet the name I love so well;
O let its music ever swell.
O praise the name of Jesus.
'Jesus,' O how sweet the name!
'Jesus,' every day the same;
'Jesus,' let all saints proclaim
Its worthy praise forever."

The Apostolic Doctrine.

There is a great cry in the land coming up from the hearts of honest believers for the "old paths," the old-time apostolic ardor, doctrine, and teaching. Such a cry is timely, seeing that Catholicism is increasing, and Protestantism is going swiftly into Laodiceanism, Higher Criticism, and sectarianism, producing doctrines and teachings of the heathen under the name of Christ, and even the Spirit-filled people of God are drifting into formalism, legalism, worldliness, and self-sufficiency. So that, generally speaking, the whole of present-day Christendom is in a tumult of confusion. Yet there are many, yea many individuals among all classes, nations, and denominations, who are aware of this religious peril and are seeking the old-time apostolic gospel. Now the question arises, what is the gospel and the doctrine that the apostles taught? Let the holy record answer this timely question.

We read in the book of the Acts of the Apostles that "they continued steadfastly in the apostles' doctrine and fellowship." Again we read of the Pharisees, who were greatly stirred because of the doctrine and the teaching of the apostolic church, being indignant, saying complainingly, "Behold ye have filled Jerusalem with your doctrine." What was this doctrine? The leading men of Jerusalem, in their great council against the followers of Christ, decided to stop the apostles from preaching and teaching, and made a decree saying, "That it spread no further among the people, let us straitly threaten them, that they speak henceforth to no man in this Name." Did the enemies of Christ prosper? No, indeed. For we read again that the apostles "departed from the presence of the council, rejoicing that they were counted worthy to suffer shame for His name, and daily in the temple, and in every house, they ceased not to teach and preach Jesus Christ." Again we read, "They which were scattered abroad, upon the persecution that arose about Stephen, traveled as far as Phenice, and Cyprus, and Antioch, preaching the word, . . . and, when they were come to Antioch, spake, preaching the Lord Jesus." And the Apostle Paul, speaking of himself and the other apostles, says, "For we preach not ourselves, but Christ Jesus the Lord; and ourselves your servants for Jesus' sake." The solution is plain, that the apostles preached nothing else than the Lord Jesus Christ and all in His mighty Name: therefore the Name of the Lord Jesus Christ, which includes His death, resurrection, ascension, and the great glory of God, is the only gift of God to the human race, in which they should believe and thereby have eternal life. This is the apostolic doctrine and teaching. Let us, oh brethren,

Preach Jesus Christ and Him crucified;
Cleave unto Christ our Lord; Acts 9:16,
And suffer for His name. Acts 16:31.

The Divine Name of the Church.

The prophets of old, with the inspiration of the Almighty God, knew the meaning of the great Name Jehovah, and prophecied that that Holy Name of their God was to be recognized and worshipped not only by Israel but by all the nations of the earth in the future. This is confirmed by the great conference of the apostles in Jerusalem, when the question of the Gentiles had arisen in the church. We read in Acts 15:13-17:

And after they had held their peace. James answered, saying, men and brethren, hearken unto me: Simeon hath declared how

God at the first did visit the Gentiles, to take out of them a **people for His Name**. And to this agree the words of the prophets; as it is written, After this I will return, and will build again the tabernacle of David, . . . that the residue of men might seek after the Lord, and all the Gentiles, **upon whom my name is called**, saith the Lord, who doeth all these things.

Reader, note please, that the Name of Jehovah God was to be put upon believers from among all nations. The Apostle James again, after a lapse of many years, writing to the scattered people of God concerning righteous living, reminds these people of the Name of God upon them, saying, "Do they not blaspheme that worthy Name by the which ye are called?" The question is, what was that excellent Name by which the believers of that time were called? The answer is plain: that name was Christians, or the name of Christ Jesus upon the believers. Thus the Name of God Jehovah was the Name given to the Church, and that Name **was in His Son**. See, please, Acts 11:26, 26:28, 1 Pet. 4:16.

It is commonly known and affirmed that the Apostle Paul was called by God especially to be the apostle unto the Gentiles; therefore, he was the one to be used to bring out a people from among all nations for the Name of God. So the chief message of the Apostle unto the Gentiles was to be THE NAME. When Christ met him and called him to his great ministry on the journey to Damascus, we read, the Lord said to Ananias: "Go thy way (to Saul of Tarsus): for he is a chosen vessel unto me (for what purpose?) to bear my name before the Gentiles, and kings, and the children of Israel: for I will show him how great things he must suffer for my name's sake." Acts. 9:9-16. So if we should trace Paul's ministry all the way through, we should find the fulfillment of what Jesus said concerning His Name and His apostle. Paul preached nothing but the Lord Jesus Christ, and it was in that mighty Name that he did all things, and finally he suffered death for it. See Acts 19:1-17. The faithful apostle, therefore, taught the church of God (Acts 20:28) "Whatsoever ye do, in word or deed, do all in the name of the Lord Jesus, giving thanks to God and the Father by Him." O beloved, the day is coming upon us soon, when we shall be singled out and bitterly hated by all men for that worthy Name, and probably suffer the loss of everything and even death for it. Let us therefore make our decision and consecration complete, that we may be able to say boldly, like Ignatius, a martyr of the first century: "Come fire, come cross, and crowds of wild beasts; come tearing, breaking and crunching of my bones; come the mutilation of my members, and shattering of my whole body, and all the dreadful torments of the Devil, so I but attain to Jesus Christ. I would rather die for Jesus Christ than rule the world."

As we live in the fulness of the times, or the end of this dispensation, the real separation between the wheat and tares is at hand; false Christians and world politicians and commercial men are joining, making leagues, heading up to One (the Anti-Christ), who will exalt himself above all that is called God, and the people of the world will accept him as their "father" and their God and All. But think God there is another thing happening at this very time, our Almighty God, the Father of our Lord Jesus Christ, by the Power of His Spirit, is showing and revealing all His power, glory and even His Own Name, in His Son, JESUS CHRIST, the Coming KING, who shall appear in His own time, not only with His own glory, but also WITH THE GLORY OF THE FATHER; in other words the glorious God, our

Father, will shine in and through the Person of Jesus Christ, His Son, and His glorified Bride. Compare Mark 8:38 with Titus 2:13.

"And the Lord shall be KING over all the Earth: in that day shall there be One LORD and His Name ONE." Zech. 14:9.

And the Jews who have for so many centuries rejected the glorious person of their Messiah, and their God, in Him, shall see Him:

"And it shall be said (by them) in that day, Lo! this is our God; we have waited for Him, and He will save us: this is the LORD, we have waited for Him, we will be glad and rejoice in His salvation." Is. 25:9.

Beloved friends, the Holy Ghost did not come into us Christians only to make us speak in tongues and to organize religious bodies, neither came He in us to cause us to fight one another; but He came to reveal to us the excellent glory of the Father, the Son, and the Holy Ghost, in the Person of JESUS CHRIST, our LORD, and to make all our thoughts, ambitions, works of faith, spiritual dreams and revelations, and all our life, to be gathered in ONE, even CHRIST JESUS. The Apostles saw this, therefore they did not go around and preach "issues," but CHRIST AND HIM CRUCIFIED, RISEN AND GLORIFIED, and coming with all the heavenly glory; and God showed to them, that in these last days, in which we are living, there will be a special gathering of all things heading up into ONE, even CHRIST JESUS. See Ephesians 1:10.

"That in the dispensation of the fullness of times He might gather together in one, all things in Christ, both which are in heaven, and which are on the earth: EVEN IN HIM. See Heb. 12:2.

CHAPTER VI

The Great Conflict of Our Day Against God and His Word.

By Andrew D. Urshan.

E ALL should thank and praise God for privileging us to live in these last days and to behold the madness of the nations of the earth and see the great stretched forth arm of the Lord omnipotent in the kingdoms of men (Daniel 5:21-22), causing the wrath of man to praise Him, and all things to work together for the good of His people, even unto them that love Him (Rom. 8:20).

Hallelujah! God is unfolding and fulfilling the blessed promises of the Bible and He is opening the way for the soon manifestation of the Sons of God (Rom. 8:19).

While the nominal Christians with the worldly people are busy planning and striving to establish for themselves a world of peace and pleasure, we, by the revelation of the Spirit, know that the end of the times is before our Heavenly Father and that He is sitting upon His majestic throne laughing at the proud and high-minded sinners (Psalm 2:4). He is smashing the great governmental image of the Gentile's reign which the great king of Babylon, Nebuchadnezzar, saw in the vision, by His stone cut out from the mountains without hands, to establish His own eternal kingdom on the earth, as it is in heaven (Daniel, second chapter, and Rev. 1:5). Let us, therefore, continue praying, "Our Father who art in Heaven hallowed be thy NAME; thy kingdom come, thy will be done on earth as it is in Heaven."

The First Great Conflict of the Day Against God's Word.

The great war of the so-called civilized nations which took place during the last four years was a war of man against God's WORD and God's plan. This might sound like a strange utterance to some people, because they have heard so much and often that this war was a war of nations against nations; but the following facts will prove that this great conflict was to upset God's plan for the human race.

It is clearly understood now that the Central Powers were planning and preparing for this war years ago, and their sole purpose was a world-wide monarchy; therefore, they fought fiercely, aiming for a Throne upon which one would sit who would be recognized, feared and honored by all the nations of the earth as the King of Kings and Lord of Lords. Every true Bible student knows that such a human ambition is in direct opposition to the purpose, plan and WORD of God.

The Bible says there is only one King of Kings and Lord of Lords, whose name is the Word of God (Rev. 19:11-16), who is the Prince of life, Prince of glory, and Prince of the kings of the earth (Rev. 1:15). To Him belong all power, honor and dominion, not only in Heaven but upon the earth, also, because He has made all things for His own pleasure, that He may have full pre-eminence in all things. He upholds all things by the power of His WORD,—even He who died for all men, "And that He died for all, that they which live should not henceforth live unto themselves, but unto Him who died for them and arose again" (see John 1:10; Col. 1:15-20; Hebrews 1:2-11; 2 Cor. 5:15), who is the "blessed and the only potentate, the King of Kings and Lord of Lords, to whom be honor and power everlasting, Amen!" (1 Tim. 6:15-16).

The present day political enemy of God was defeated, as has been the case in all the past centuries. Hence the Allies did not conquer that great enemy by their own power and ammunition alone, but also by the Great and invisible arm of God, stretched forth among their armies. To this can testify not only those who earnestly prayed about this great war, but many soldiers and officers, as well, who actually saw the angels of God operating between the two great gigantic armies. God helped the Allies to destroy the proposed King of Kings's throne and his plan, and He also fulfilled some of His promises concerning the Holy Land.

It is very pleasing, indeed, to all Christians under the unfurled flags of the Allies to see that the Great God was pleased to use us as His chosen instruments to carry out His great purpose, in spite of our national sins and shortcomings against Him. But there is also another phase of the matter, or the other part of the truth. I am sure that with glad hearts all true Americans would say Amen concerning what we said about the Central Powers, and say that it is true. Now, if we are honest and liberal, as we claim we are, we should be willing to say Amen to the other part of the truth also, though it may hit us hard and cause us to be humiliated. Let us, therefore, speak the truth and the whole truth.

The Whole Truth.

What is the whole truth, some may ask. The truth is that some of our Allies' present plans are indirectly and unconsciously against God's plan and His WORD, also. If the League of Nations with its covenants and plans be perfected and set forth in full force, its operations will fight God and His purpose. One may ask, what is the purpose of some of the Allies through the league of nations? It is to establish a lasting peace, a law of justice, and an unbroken human brotherhood, and that through the power and influence of a society of nations.

First, all Bible students know that it is impossible to establish a lasting peace on the earth without the personal reign of the Prince of Peace—Jesus Christ, "The Lord of All" (Isa. 9:6), and that "There is no peace unto the wicked" (Isa. 48:22), and so as long as wickedness is in the hearts of men, there can be no lasting peace. Before the human family can attain an enduring peace for herself, she must have peace with God and the peace of God, and that can only come to the human race by and through Jesus Christ, the mediator between God and man. Hence to establish a lasting peace on the earth without Jesus Christ is against God's plan and His word.

Second. There cannot be an establishment of a law of justice according to the Bible without a just God. The God of Righteousness has set forth His good laws centuries ago and man has failed to walk in them; therefore, He has graciously given us "the law of liberty" which is the law of God's love unto humanity, and that through the atonement, resurrection and intercession of our Saviour Jesus Christ. Thus to establish righteousness and justice on the earth without Jesus Christ is to ignore God's voice as recorded in the Old and New Testaments, from which we will give only a few verses:

"As it is written, there is none righteous, no, not one: There is none that understandeth, there is none that seeketh after God. They are all gone out of the way, they are all together become unprofitable; there is none that doeth good, no, not one. Their throat is an open sepulchre; with their tongues they have used deceit; the poison of asps is under their lips; whose mouth is full of cursing and bitterness: Their feet are swift to shed blood: Destruction and misery are in their ways and the way of peace have they not known: there is no fear of God before their eyes."

"Now we know that what things soever the law saith, it saith to them who are under the law; that every mouth may be stopped, and all the world may become guilty before God. Therefore, by the deeds of the law there shall no flesh be justified in His sight: for by the law is the knowledge of sin. But now the righteousness of God without the law is manifested, being witnessed by the law and the prophets. Even the righteousness of God which is by Faith of Jesus Christ unto all and upon all them that believe; for there is no difference." (Rom. 3:10-18; Psa. 14.)

Here is God's own description of the characters and the nature of the whole human race from the beginning to the end. How, then, in the face of these divine facts do men dare to establish their own righteousness and justice by inventing new covenants, rules and regulations of another man-made law, except by ignoring and dishonoring God's WORD?

Third. According to God's plan set forth in the good OLD BIBLE, there can be no human brotherhood and, if there should be a seeming one, it will be temporary and that without solid foundation, and the outcome of it will be a horrible destruction. God knew from the beginning that man, because of the fall of Adam, would become selfish, jealous, proud and sinful, corrupted from head to foot; therefore, to rescue man He had to make a new covenant with new orders and promises of grace, to create a new generation. This would be through the mystery of the Incarnation, so that men and women must be born again of water and the Spirit, and that through faith in the Saviour's name (John 1:10-12), as our Master said in John 3:15, and thus become children of God or new creatures in Christ Jesus, receiving a new nature by which they alone can become true brothers and sisters. Hence, to establish a human brotherhood without the Gospel of our Lord and Saviour is to dishonor God's great and eternal plan of salvation and of true brotherhood for the human race. There can be no true love in us toward each other, except as we are first filled with the Holy Spirit and then the Holy Spirit will shed abroad in our hearts the love of God that will make us love everybody, even those that hate us. (See Romans 5:15.) The outcome of all such leagues will be a preparation for the "man of sin," who soon will appear to be head of most of the nations of the earth, whose name is Anti-Christ. He will sit in the temple of God as god, exalting himself above all that is God, to counterfeit and blaspheme our blessed Saviour, the God Man and King, JESUS; but even he, although he may prosper for a short time to head up and confirm all man-made plans and leagues against

God and His WORD, will yet suddenly fall, also, with an eternal destruction by the power and great glory of the appearance of the heavenly monarch IMMANUEL, "the Lord of Glory." (See Daniel 8:23-25; 2 Thess. 2:1-8.)

The Second Army Conflicting Against God.

Satan not only fights God as a roaring, wild, political beast, but he appears like an angel of light through the influence of his second army arrayed against God and His WORD. This second army is the false religious army or the army that contains millions of the Apostate Christians who have a form of godliness, but they deny the mystery of godliness, "God manifested in the flesh" (1 Tim. 3:16) "and deny the power of God" (2 Tim. 3:1-5). "They profess that they know God; but in works they deny Him" (Titus 1:16). "Whose God is their belly and whose glory is their shame, and who mind earthly things and turn the grace of God into lasciviousness" (Phil. 3:18-19). These "filthy dreamers," the enemies of the Cross, are using all their energy, power and talents trying to prove that not all of the Bible is inspired, tearing the Good Old Book into pieces, handling the word of God deceitfully and wresting the scriptures unto their own destruction. This army can be divided into two forces. Each force contains some of the denominational organizations of our day. One of these great forces denies in part the inspiration of the Bible, the deity of our Lord and the utter depravity of man; hence the necessity of the shed blood of Christ. This army boastingly claimed that there would be no war, such as began five years ago, but they were proved to be false prophets by the outbreak of the present war. These hypocrites and Pharisees of our day, instead of keeping quiet and repenting, are speaking more loudly than ever, that the world is growing better and that they are going to usher in the Millennial Age by the power and influence of their churches or the church corporations, so called, and other moral movements.

These Nominal Christians, the higher critics, do not preach "Christ and Him crucified, raised for our justification and coming again for our eternal salvation;" but they preach and teach that there is good (divine nature) in every man. To develop that to perfection is the salvation of man and the building up of a moral and educated society and community is the remedy by which such a salvation can be worked up. They are preaching reformation of men through the good efforts of man, instead of regeneration through the power of the Cross of Christ and the Holy Spirit. These people are denying "the Lord who bought them" (Acts 20:28) while taking His name upon them for a cover to deceive the unlearned and honest souls. From such, God says, "turn away." The picture of these ungodly men is drawn by God's Apostles 2 Timothy 3:1-10, Titus 1:10-16, 2nd Peter 2nd chap. and Jude—the whole chapter.

The second force of this same rank are those Christians who spiritualize every material thing in the Bible. They go so far as to deny the real human Person of Jesus of Nazareth and His death and His resurrection. They deny, also, the intelligent person and being of the one God. They teach that God is a higher or supreme influence or mind which is in every man and also in animals and in everything. They twist Bible Scriptures into human philosophy and science, calling themselves Christian Scientists, Spiritualists, etc.

The aim of these spirits of the Anti-Christ is to do away with the whole plan of salvation, and they are trying to make the world free from sickness, sorrow, sin and the Devil by denying the whole thing. Concerning these, the Apostle John very solemnly warns us in 1st John, 4th chapter, and the Apostle Paul in 2nd Thess., 2nd chapter, and also our Lord tells us about them in Matt. 7:15-23. It is these two forces that have helped the Jews and unbelievers of our country to vote the Bible out of our public schools; so that our precious boys and girls, instead of being taught the fear of God through the reading of the Bible and songs of the Gospel, are being taught evolution and psychology, which cause them to become twentieth century infidels.

This second subtle satanic conflict against God is the Devil's old pernicious way. When he wanted to upset God's plan at the beginning, he appeared in the garden of God not like a roaring lion, but like a refined, beautiful, wise, gentle serpent. He came to the innocent woman and asked her if God had really said unto them (Adam and Eve) that they should not eat of every tree of the garden; "and the woman said unto the serpent, "We may eat of the fruit of the trees of the garden, but of the fruit of the tree which is in the midst of the garden, God hath said, ye shall not eat of it, neither shall ye touch it, lest ye die." And the serpent said unto the woman, "Ye shall not surely die; for God doth know that in the day ye eat thereof, then your eyes shall be opened, and ye shall be as gods, knowing good and evil." (Genesis 3:2-5). Here we see plainly that Satan, in order to upset God's plan and purpose for the human race, seems to favor the man; telling him that, if he disobeys God, he will not die, but will rather be like a god, misrepresenting the word of God and misrepresenting the purpose of God. From that time on until this day Satan fights God, the WORD (John 1:1). The old enemy knows that to fight the WORD is to fight God; for the WORD is GOD and His expression, He was in the world and the world was made by Him, but the world knew Him not (John 1:10).

This so-called world-wide Church Federation, which claims to be "the church of God," taking Scriptures and putting their own interpretation upon them, is working hard, also, to propagate a world-wide gathering of tares into bundles of human unity, and will join the old religious harlot church and be headed up by a false prophet who will show forth great religious performances by the working of miracles, giving all his power and honor to the BEAST; but even he, with all his religious, organized forces shall be defeated and cast into eternal torment.

Rev. 19:19 to end: "And I saw the beast, and the kings of the earth, and their armies, gathered together to make war against Him that sat on the horse, and against His army.

"And the beast was taken, and with him the false prophet that wrought miracles before him, with which he deceived them that had received the mark of the beast, and them that worshipped his image. These both were cast alive into a lake of fire burning with brimstone.

"And the remnant were slain with the sword of Him that sat upon the horse, which sword proceeded out of His mouth: and all the fowls were filled with their flesh."

Note.—The following startling and pointed remarks on this truth are taken from a booklet entitled "A Message to Christians and to the World," by T. P. Douglas, forwarded by Philip Mauro of London, England:

THE EFFECTS OF MODERN EDUCATION AND EXPLANATION OF THE UNIVERSE, AND MODERN HUMAN LAWMAKING NULLIFYING THE WORD OF GOD.

"But few, if any, writers or speakers sufficiently recognize the fact that our modern system of 'scientific' education is also undermining the former religious beliefs of our own people; that it is destroying that respect of children for their parents, of servants for masters, and of the people for their rulers, which Scripture enjoins; and that it chiefly underlies the seething unrest in our own nation. These results must needs follow in the train of modern education, for anything that overthrows the **authority of God and His Word,** necessarily tends to destroy ALL AUTHORITY. It has been truly said that a striking characteristic of our times is the 'decay of authority.'

"Science gives no confession whatever of the truth that **the Creator of all things has appeared as a Man upon this earth;** and that non-confession of science clearly betrays its real character and purpose, which have long been carefully concealed from men (1 John 4:3). Its real character as revealed in that non-confession is seen to be a complete manifestation of the Anti-Christ; and its real purpose is. on the one hand to disown and dishonor Jesus Christ, and on the other hand to deceive and destroy men. It robs Jesus Christ completely of the honor that is due to Him **as the Creator and Upholder of all things;** and in robbing Him of that honor it robs Him of all that qualified Him to become the Redeemer of mankind. As the welfare of all men is bound up in what Jesus Christ is, and in what He has done for men; so the blinding of the minds of men to His supreme excellency of character and of purpose is the surest way by which to accomplish their ruin.

"**The apostles saw Jesus as God manifest in the flesh, as the One by Whom and for Whom all things were created, and as the new Sinless Head of the whole human race; and THEY SAW ARIGHT.** But in these 'last days' learned men have almost 'hunted God from His own Universe,' and have well-nigh banished His Name from the speech of men. Man, the creature, has disowned his own Creator, and for the second time he has cast out the Heir and has seized His inheritance.

'God has never given authority to His people to make compulsory laws, and Christians can neither make, nor assist in making a national law that does not add to, or take from, or nullify some one or more of the commandments of the Lord Jesus or of His apostles. Christians are, or should be, under 'the law of Christ.' But the so-called 'Christian nations' have no regard for the law of Christ. Hence they are, one and all, occupied in turning out an endless succession of laws, all alike futile, to suppress or control the rising tides of evil and lawlessness. Long ago the Jewish leaders had made the Word of God of no effect.' through commandments of their own devising, and man's law-making is always in opposition to the teaching of Jesus Christ. For many centuries the legislation of Christendom was dominated chiefly by the Church, and all legislation so dominated was anti-christian. Now the legislation of the whole civilized world is dominated chiefly by science, and all of it is anti-christian.

"Today, in this country (England) and other countries, believers and unbelievers, Jews and Agnostics, Protestants and Roman Catholics, in an unholy alliance, **are almost incessantly making new laws,** all of which are anti-christian; and the truth of that terrible charge is easily established. The light cannot be shut out of a room without the darkness being shut in; neither can Jesus Christ, Who is the Light of the world, be shut out from any, or from every department of knowledge (and He is shut out in compulsory education, and in all other matters on which legislators exercise their functions) without the Prince of darkness being shut in. If He 'Who is the Truth' is shut out, then the Liar must be shut in.

"Lawmaking is one of our many modern ways of saying 'We will not have this man to reign over us.' The second Psalm is as true of world-rulers now as of those who crucified the Lord of Glory long ago; and the Devil is the prince, or god, of this world now as then. But today many preachers of the Gospel (so-called) and their hearers appear to be almost as blind as the world itself is to these awful truths, and to the deadly antagonism that exists between the world and Jesus Christ. **Hence, preaching is powerless,** and a condition of dead indifference to eternal things is almost universal.

"In the present awful apostasy the time seems to be ripe for a world-wide and a final answer to a **challenge** like that given by Elijah to the people of Israel on Mount Carmel long ago. That challenge now takes this form: IF THE LORD JESUS CHRIST BE GOD, FOLLOW HIM; but if Nature, or Gravitation, or Evolution, or a Democratic State, then follow that; and the God that answereth by the Fire of Truth, let Him be God. And in response to that challenge. Scripture. and reason, and common-sense, and all past history, and the present universal unrest, and the abounding destitutions and distresses of this time, and all true voices in heaven and earth, with one accord exclaim:—**'Let God be true and every man a liar.'**

"In view of what is here written the urgent and universal call to Christians is to **'save yourselves from this untoward generation,' and be**

ready for the coming of the Lord. And the urgent and universal call to the world is to repent, and **believe on the Lord Jesus Christ,** for the Kingdom of God is nigh at hand, even at the doors."

Another Army Arrayed Against God's Word.

The third army is Laodecean, that is conflicting with God. There is still another body of Christians arrayed against God and His WORD —yea, against Him who loved them and gave His life for them— Jesus Christ, the AMEN and the faithful WITNESS. This army formerly was the people of God; but they gave place to the spirit of the world, love of riches and human honor—so much so that they grieved Christ away from their midst, and they gradually became so blinded spiritually that they think they are rich and increased in goods, in spite of the fact that they are wretched, naked, miserable and blinded, and also without Christ; for we see our Lord outside of the door of that church. He is not only thrown outside of it, but the door is locked behind Him and He cannot enter in to sup with them and bless them. He is standing outside, knocking and pleading for entrance. (Read, please, Col. 1:1 and 4:12-16; Rev. 1:11. Compare with Rev. 3:14-20.)

This army of the "lukewarm" Christians contains two forces, also, namely: post-millennialists and the "foolish virgins." Many of the post-millennialists work hand in hand with the higher critics on the theory of the development of the world by the power of the present-day civilization and Christianity—and that **without the second personal coming of our Lord;** so they are busy with their human plans, programs, wealth and achievements, trying to patch "the Old Man" and make him appear good, and bring peace on the earth. These backslidden Christians, although they believe in many Bible fundamentals, yet they do away with hundreds of scriptures which specifically and clearly speak of the thousand years' reign of Jesus Christ with His church **on this very earth,** the restoration of Jews to their God and **Messiah,** and their reign on the earth through the power and appearance of Jesus Christ, their King, with the Queen, His Redeemed Bride. These people tear the Bible into small pieces while the higher critics tear it into big pieces. The higher critics say, "We believe this book of the Bible is inspired and the other book is not inspired." So they put away or ignore a number of books of the Bible and make the people believe that part of the books of Genesis and Exodus, the book of Job, of Daniel, of Jonah and Revelation, and many others, are simply symbolical and dead men's stories. But the post-millennialists, while they say all the Bible is inspired, yet say, "We do not believe in the divine healing, in the atonement and in the holy and overcoming life in this world and we do not believe in the second personal advent of the Lord, and we do not believe in the baptism of the Holy Ghost, speaking in other tongues, or of restoration of the apostolic gifts and miracles; because (they say) the days of miracles are past." So they misinterpret and misrepresent at least two thousand scriptures in the Bible on the above subjects: fighting God and His WORD while boasting in their knowledge of God and their Christian profession, which is half dead.

The Army of The Foolish Virgins.
(See Matt. 25:1-13.)

The "foolish virgins" (Christians), although they believe in Christian chastity through the atonement, and although they cling to their Bibles (their lamps, Psa. 119:105), and believe also in the second coming of the Lord, and seemingly look for His appearance; yet they have fought, and are even now fighting, the Apostolic baptism of the **Holy Ghost.** They have their lamps (the Bibles), but no oil (Holy Ghost) in their vessels (body—2 Cor. 4:6-7; 1 Cor. 6:19, 29).

Some fourteen years ago, when the drought was prevailing in the Protestant church everywhere, God graciously answered the prayers of His faithful people (the individuals) and caused the showers of the Spirit to fall in Wales; and the Welsh revival took place. Of course, that created a great hunger and thirst in many hearts everywhere; so the people began to seek God for an outpouring of the Holy Ghost in this country. I well remember at that time, when I was in Chicago, that there were held special prayer-meetings in many different Protestant churches. They were preaching and seeking one thing, and that was the **Holy Ghost outpouring.** I actually saw some of the ministers, with tears in their eyes, on their bended knees praying to God: "Oh Lord, repeat the Pentecost! Pour out Thy Holy Spirit once more, as Thou didst in the beginning!" and many similar utterances. God graciously heard those prayers, and in just a few months He began to pour out His blessed **"Latter Rain."** But it came **in His own way** and not in the way of the fixed theology of those preachers on the baptism of the Holy Ghost. What happened? These very people began wildly fighting the very answer to their prayers! Yea, fighting the triune God in that out-pouring of the Spirit! They mockingly and vehemently denounced this blessed Scriptural latter rain (see, please, Ezek. 10:1; Joel 2:23; Hosea 6:3; Psa. 68:9; Acts 14:17; James 5:7), calling it "the latter day delusion, hypnotism, mesmerism, spiritualism, the tongues movement," etc., etc. They warned and scared away many honest and hungry souls from God, the Spirit. Now some of those preachers, who were once God's pioneers in His church, have grown dry, cold or lukewarm, thinking they are wise; but they are proved to be the foolish virgins. For these people, we (spirit-filled people) dearly love and earnestly pray. They preach a great deal on the spirit-filled life and the baptism of the Holy Ghost, and anointings; but they do not have these things. Why? Because they have not the essence of their message.

Beloved friends, Jesus said, The wise man is he who not only preaches or hears the Word, but **"doeth it,"** or he that gets the life and the spirit of the word, and, therefore, is able to perform it. **He is the** one that builds the house of his faith upon the Rock and it is durable. (See Matt. 7:24-29.)

The above dear people, made it very hard for thousands of their best church members, because we received this baptism of the Holy Ghost with the sign of tongues, and we had to come out of their churches and become a people by ourselves, and are known now all over the world as Pentecostal people, etc., etc. These foolish virgins prophesied that those who spoke in tongues in the beginning (twelve years ago) were spiritually insane and would all soon be put in asylums, so that the thing would die in a few months; but their prophecies have not been fulfilled, because nearly half a million people, among whom are thousands of ministers and missionaries, have received this blessed Holy Ghost outpouring among all nations all over the earth. Although this great Pentecostal family has had its failures, as we will show later, like the Apostolic church of Corinth, yet the testimony of Jesus Christ and the gifts and operations of the Holy Spirit have been in action and have been confirmed by God Himself more than any other advanced Christian movement and revival of the past since the days of the Apostles of our Lord Jesus Christ.

These anti-Holy-Ghost-Tongues people are misrepresenting and misinterpreting many Scriptures which plainly prove that the baptism of the Holy Ghost must be accompanied by the speaking in tongues as the Spirit gives utterance (see, please, Mark 16:17-18; 1 Cor. 14:22; Isa. 28:11-12; Acts 2:4, 10:45-46, 19:6, etc.) and shaking of the body, and prostration under the power of the Spirit. (See, please, Psa. 119:120; Jere. 23:9; Habak. 3:16-17; Job 4:13-15; Dan. 10:7-15; Acts 4:24-31, 9:5-6, 10:10; Rev. 1:17, etc.) These people are unconsciously calling the author of the movement (Jesus Christ) "the Hypnotizer" or "Mesmerizer." The Scripture says, Jesus Christ is alone the Baptizer with the Holy Ghost and fire (see Matt. 3:11-12). Since Jesus Christ baptizes with the Holy Ghost and with fire, He thus becomes an object of reproach to these people. Yea, these very people are fighting the Lord Jesus Christ in this present day Pentecostal body. In behalf of these people we must earnestly pray that thousands of them will become wise and receive the true and scriptural Holy Ghost baptism, and be ready for the soon coming of our God, the Saviour (Jude 25:1; Timothy 2:3; Titus 2:13).

It should be remembered, friends, that not only these visible great human armies are fighting God and His WORD, but there are many invisible armies in the high places, also, influencing these earthly armies against God, our Creator and Saviour. Therefore, it is most important for us all who know these startling facts, to keep under the precious blood of the Lamb, giving ourselves to prayer and walking humbly and softly before God, lest we be found fighting God and His WORD; for it is evident that already many of us Pentecostal people have been influenced in a great measure by the same invisible demoniac forces that have captured the present-day politics, false religions and lukewarm Christians, and have raised them up against Jesus Christ, and these very evil spirits are causing us, also, to fight one another, and God's advanced dealings with some individuals among us.

The fate of the ungodly armies arrayed against God, we showed, in a measure, in the above Scriptures; but the fate of the lukewarm Christians and the foolish virgins, although it will not be as hard as that of the higher critics, yet it will be sad enough when they miss the rapture of the saints and the marriage supper of the Lamb, and the great rewards of the eternal King who shall decorate His heroes, even those who fought not against Him and His WORD, but who fought a good fight of faith and kept His WORD and denied not His Holy and Sacred NAME. These foolish virgins, at the coming of the Bridegroom, will see the doors of the skies closed unto them if they remain foolish. They will miss that power of the Holy Ghost in their bodies which otherwise would have translated them "in the twinkling of an eye," taking them up into the highest, to meet and see the great King, and they will find out, amid sighing and sadness, that the faithful ones have left the earth and gone; they shall find themselves in the midst of the great tribulation, surrounded not only by the wild, mad human forces combined against their Redeemer, but also by Satan himself, thrown down from the air unto the earth with all his demoniac hosts. Oh! what a day of gloom, of disappointment, despair and sorrow! Yea, the day of death; for many of these dear people will suffer torture and martyrdom in those days because they rebelled against God and His WORD.

Suffering Awaiting the True and Loyal People of God Just Before the Rapture.

There are various opinions about the saints' passing or not passing through the great tribulation; but one thing I know, and that is, all we who claim to be the true people of God of these days shall and must pass through persecutions severe enough to make us yearn for those among us who are baptized into the same body by one Spirit. We need a real persecution, too to separate us and purify us from every bit of the love of the world, money, property, reputation and easy living. Sometimes God causes all these things to be taken away from us, and even allows us to be driven away from the very community where we live, and into a real wilderness, as have been the Armenians and my people in Persia, who have been during the last four years made destitute and robbed of everything of this world's goods—even of their lives and loved ones. Then God will come and show us His real and abundant glory in His presence, and through that He will allure us unto Himself (Hos. 2:14). This was the very reason why He took His ancient people out of Egypt and led them into a forty-year wilderness experience. Those of them who were proved to be worthy to inherit His great future promises and the blessed promised land were made ready for their God-given inheritance and became, through a personal acquaintance with their God and their Redeemer, able to minister unto Him acceptably before all the other nations in the promised land. So we must be trained more fully and become more closely acquainted with our God in His Son, Jesus Christ, and His ways and leadings before we can be rulers and the leaders in the new Earth which God has promised to make for the new creatures in Christ Jesus (Rev. 21:1-5).

We need special persecution, also in order to bring upon us such an awful dissatisfaction with this world and the life of the flesh, and make us so terribly lonesome for the Bridegroom of our souls that we will day and night, like the Elect of God, cry out that He may come soon and avenge us by His glorious appearance. (Read, please, Luke 18:1-9.)

Our wise God dealt with His dear Apostles and the first-century Christians in this hard and awful disciplinary manner. The world was looking upon them with pity, thinking they were too loyal to a God that did not protect them from the terrible martyrdom they suffered at the cruel hands of the old Romans; but God was working in this way for their own eternal glory and reward, although it was hard for them to bear in the flesh. If God did not spare His ancient people and the faithful Apostolic Christians from the terrific persecutions of those days sent to make them ready to serve Him in the ages to come, I do not think He will spare us—rather, He will allow us to go through it in some way, if not to the same extent; we shall suffer a martyrdom (being killed to everything), similar to it, so that we may in eternity come to appreciate His loving prunings and purifings and His great rewards for us that endure to the end.

We claim that we are waiting for His blessed appearance; but we are living far below the deep spirit and devotional life of such an expectation. God had to take the beloved Apostle John and put him in the midst of the great waters, on the island of Patmos, probably in the midst of wild beasts, and there He showed him his glory to come, and made the old Apostle so lonesome for Himself that he had to cry out: "Even so come, Lord Jesus." Exactly so it shall be done with us before the Rapture.

The Essence of Our Faith.

But the question is, on what point of our faith shall we be persecuted or for what part of our profession? This question is clearly answered in the book of Acts, the Epistles and early Church history. We read that the Christians of old were hated, threatened, persecuted and martyred, not for speaking in tongues or for their good experiences, or for their good lives, but for their message, which was the preaching of peace, pardon, deliverance, salvation and protection for all the human race that depended solely upon the faith in the NAME of the LORD JESUS CHRIST. Of course, such a message meant that the great Roman Empire and the imperial worship of the innumerable gods of Caesar were available for nothing, and that they were only human laws, rules and regulations which were causing men to go astray from the knowledge of the true God. The proud Romans could not stand such a message through such a small and despised band as that called "Christians," and, seeing their people being converted, they thought that to kill them and burn their houses and capture their substance was a loyal service for the benefit of the country and community.

The Apostolic message in the name of the Lord indirectly opposed the proud religious Jews, also; so the leading men of Jerusalem had to come together to hold a council as to what to do with these people called by the name of Christ Jesus, who claimed to be Lord and King of the Jews before His crucifixion and whom they hatefully rejected before Pontius Pilate. So they said to each other, 'That it spread no further among the people, let us straitly threaten them that they speak henceforth to no man IN THIS NAME. And they called them (the Apostles) and commanded them not to speak at all, nor teach in the name of Jesus." (Acts 4:17, 18; see also Acts 5:28.) It was that great political and religious pressure against God's people in their day that made them unitedly with one heart and voice to cry to God saying, "Lord, Thou art God, which hast made heaven, and earth, and the sea, and all that is in them: Who by the mouth of Thy servant David hast said, 'Why did the heathen rage, and the people imagine vain things?' The kings of the earth stood up and the rulers were gathered together against the Lord and against His Christ. For of a truth against Thy holy child Jesus, whom Thou hast anointed, both Herod, and Pontius Pilate, with the Gentiles and the people of Israel, were gathered together for to do whatsoever Thy counsel determined to be done. And now, Lord, behold their threatenings; and grant unto Thy servants that with all boldness they may speak Thy WORD" (Acts 4:25-29).

The Apostolic Church suffered for the Name of the Lord ("Yahsous") Jesus and the Gospel preached in His Name—that was the delicate point of the hatred of them by all men (politicians and religious people), and our Lord prophesied about these very days in which we are living and said that He will have witnesses, yea, "a people for His NAME," that must suffer greatly in the hands of the politicians and religious armies of our day, and that for His NAME. The question is now, who will voluntarily dare to enter this great battle against all human and hellish forces "and fight the good fight of the faith," deny not the name of the Lord Jesus Christ, and speak the truth and the whole truth in His mighty NAME!

The truth which is contained in this letter to you, dearly beloved people of God, is just a little hint of what you and I must preach more fully if we would remain loyal to the Holy Ghost teachings and lead-

ings; and, believe me, we shall not have an easy time with the people
of our day when we proclaim that Jesus Christ is all and everything
to all the human family, in time and eternity, and that apart from Him
there is no true God, true religion, true civilization, true brotherhood,
and that His NAME must be exalted above the names of all leagues,
denominations, federations, presidents, kings and nobles of earth
and heaven: "That at the name of Jesus every knee should bow, of
things in heaven, and things in the earth, and things under the earth;
and that every tongue should confess that Jesus Christ is the Lord
(Jehovah) to the glory of God the Father (Phil. 2:10-11).

The Last Days' Faithful Remnant.

God has never left Himself without witnesses; but He has in
all ages preserved a remnant for Himself, a people out of His own
people, faithful to witness for Him.   Bible history proves this fact.
Take your concordance and look up the word "Remnant" and you will
see God's special chosen people all through the Bible.   Isaiah, the
prophet, shows the value of such a people, not only for the glory of
God, but for the benefit of the backslidden people of God, when he
says: "Except the Lord of Hosts had left unto us a very small
remnant, we should have been as Sodom, and we should have been as
Gomorrah" (Isa. 1:9).   Herein he shows that the deliverance of
Israel lies in the remnant, though it be very small.

When Elijah, the prophet, saw the terribly backslidden condition
of God's people with their queens, kings and prophets serving Baal and
killing the true prophets of God, he thought he was left alone and he
wanted to be taken away, also; but God showed him his true people,
the remnant of seven thousand who had not bowed to any other
gods, but the true God.   When Jesus Christ came in the flesh, the
power of paganism was ruling the world and man-made tradition was
leading the people of God.   Everything was dark and gloomy spiritually speaking.   It was then and there that the star of Bethlehem
shone.   He was born of the Virgin Mary, who belonged to a poor crowd,
but who were alas! the true people of God.   When the Jews had be-
trayed and killed the Lord Jesus they thought they were rid of Him
and His followers, because He was dead and buried and His disciples
scattered; but forty-nine days after His resurrection the entire city of
Jerusalem was stirred by the power of God and brought to hear the
testimony of the Apostles.   So God had even then His remnant from
among His backslidden people.   It was then Peter said, 'Who in times
past suffered all nations to walk in their own ways, nevertheless
He left not Himself without witness, in that He did good, and gave
us rain from Heaven and fruitful seasons, filling our hearts with food
and gladness" (Acts 14:16-17).   So in these last days of the Gospel
dispensation in the face of all these human armies, and the darkness
prevailing in the hearts of the people,—even His own church of
Laodicea has gone back on Him;—yet we see He has His remnant
and He is now revealing Himself to that remnant and speaking words
of comfort to their hearts.   One may ask, "Who is that remnant of
God in these last days?   It is the Church which is called the Church
of Philadelphia.   It is worth while, therefore, to take a little time to
see the character of this last faithful Remnant of God and the promises
of God for them.

The Philadelphia Church.

"And to the Angel of the church in Philadelphia write: these
things saith He that is holy. He that is true, He that hath the key

of David, He that openeth and no man shutteth; and shutteth, and no man openeth. I know thy works: behold I have set before thee an open door and no man can shut it; for thou hast a little strength, and hast kept my word, and hast not denied my name. Behold I will make them of the synagogue of Satan, which say they are Jews, and are not, but do lie; behold, I will make them to come and worship before thy feet, and to know that I have loved thee. Because thou has kept the word of my patience, I also will keep thee from the hour of temptation, which shall come upon all the world to try them that dwell upon the earth. Behold, I come quickly: hold that fast which thou hast, that no man take thy crown." (Rev. 3:7-11).

One of the first precious things we find in this message to this Church is the opening of a door for it. "Behold, I have set before thee an open door which no man can shut." Why did Christ say this to that church? Our present experience, with the experiences of many who have stood loyal to their Saviour and His NAME, shows the need of this promise of favor to His loyal Remnant. Let every honest minister or saint be true to the words of Jesus through His Apostles, proclaim His matchless NAME alone and renounce every man-made theory and theology on the God-head, and He will soon see that the doors of all assemblies or churches organized and controlled by rules, regulations and creeds invented and confirmed by the vote of their conferences will soon be shut to him, just as the church of Laodicea was to Christ. When they chose popularity, wealth and the approval of men of the world, they had to throw Christ outside of the church and shut and lock the door in His face; but, thank God! the blessed Lord has the royal keys (keys of David) and He can and He will set an open door that no man can shut. Hallelujah!

Permit us, please, to be a little personal. We wish we did not have to be, but the occasion compels us to do so. Since we have come forth publicly speaking that which God wants us, and mean to be loyal to the words of our Lord through His prophets and apostles (as recorded in the Book of Acts) and have taken a stand for the name of the Lord Jesus Christ, the General Council, which is a Pentecostal people's organization, are trying to close the doors of their assemblies and to prejudice the hearts of all the people of God against this glorious message of the Church of Philadelphia (which is the message of God entrusted to his faithful remnant in these last days) by accusing us through their magazines of wrong doing, seeking to stain our God-given character. Thank God, judgment has already begun at the house of God; although man tries to shut the doors to the Philadelphia Church, the Lord is opening His own door, which no man can shut.

The second thing to be noticed in the message of the Lord to that church is its little strength. It has not a great human "pull", but that which it has is strong enough to make it loyal to its message. What is the message of this church? The Lord Himself answers this question: **Thou . . . hast kept my word and hast not denied my name."** Did this church read the four Gospels which some people think are the only words of Jesus, affirming that the teaching in the book of Acts is not the word of Jesus, but of the Apostles? No. The Gospels were not written at this time. Evidently, just as the other churches in Asia were builded up by the Lord through His apostles, so this church also must have been one of the Assemblies that God caused the Apostles to build. Therefore, "You have kept my word" refers to the word and teaching of Christ through His Apostles. These faithful people kept to the message of the Apostles, which was preaching Jesus Christ, the Lord. (Please see 2 Cor. 4:5.)

"Thou hast not denied my name." Why the Lord did so specifically mention here His own NAME and the loyalty of this church toward it is a question for deep consideration. It is because, as we showed before, the battle is against the person, the deity, the atonement and the NAME of the Lord and Saviour, the soon-coming "King of Glory." This church evidently was tried, tempted and persecuted for those two things, namely, the WORD of God and the NAME of Jesus Christ. Although everything was dark and gloomy around that early church of God, which was one of the last existing in faithfulness —the church of the Apostles—yet the Lord of the church appears with a glorious promise to His faithful remnant and says, "Behold, I will make them (false professors) to come and worship (Jesus Christ) before thy feet, and to know that I have loved thee,"

The Philadelphia church was also a forshadow of the last remnant, the faithful and true people of God. The following scripture proves this: "Because thou hast kept the word of my patience, I also will keep thee from the hour of temptation which shall come upon all the world to try them that dwell upon the earth. Behold I come quickly: hold that fast which thou hast that no man take thy crown." This proves that there must be another band of the people of God who will bear the same testimony that the Church of Philadelphia had, and that they will also suffer for that message just before the hour of great Tribulation and the coming of the Lord from heaven. I am happy in these last days to be worthy of being one of those who are despised, not for our own names and our own words, but for the WORD of God and the NAME of Jesus Christ, the Lord. Our Lord says to us, "Hold fast that which thou hast." Let us answer Him, saying, "Lord, I will. Help me for thy name's sake."

The Invisible Forces or The Demoniac Anti-Christ Armies Affecting The Pentecostal Movement.

We Pentecostal people have showed forth the failure of the church people during the last twelve years almost enough, and now it is about time for us to judge ourselves. "For, if we would judge ourselves, we should not be judged" (1 Cor. 11:31). We have spoken about the denominations from which we came out, or rather, were thrown out; how they misrepresented and mistreated us, because of our advance in spiritual experiences, namely, believing in the Holy Ghost baptism with speaking in tongues. We have declared their formality and backslidden state; we have noted their worldliness, their organizations and man-made fundamentals (creeds). We have been grieved over their limiting of God by the rules and regulations they have made that hinder the people of God from going into deeper truths. But are we not guilty of the same things now? God knows we are, and we know it, too. Now let us honestly confess our shortcomings, and speak the truth about ourselves.

1st. **Russellism amongst the Pentecostal People.** There are many among us who have gone into what is called "Russellism," who do not believe that Jesus Christ was the very God before He came in the flesh, neither do they believe in eternal punishment. Why did this come among us and why does it prevail in great measure? Because we did not preach the deity of our Lord and Saviour, and if we do not watch and pray and preach that Jesus Christ has come in the flesh (1 John 4:1-4) and that Jesus Christ is the very God who came in the flesh (1 Tim. 3:16 and John 1:1-14), as well as Son of God and the Son of Man, many others will go into these errors and join the other armies who are conflicting against God and his WORD.   The spirit of Russellism and Unitarianism among us is being uncovered since this message of the Philadelphia church has been going forth. May God help us to wake up!

2nd.   **Legalism controlling many of the Pentecostal people.**

The organization of the General Council has rules, regulations and a creed (fundamentals) which have been formulated and confirmed by a vote set forth in print, just like all other denominations. and no one can join that organization now if he does not keep within the borders of their set doctrines.   If one should go ahead of their creed, as he is led by the Holy Spirit he is cast out and pronounced dangerous.

3rd.   **Worldliness among the Pentecostal people.**

Let a man of God go and visit the Assemblies of God, so-called, and he will see not only a great deal of fanaticism on one side and formality and dryness on the other, but the worldly dressing, worldly conversation and worldly pride, in some cases exceeding the other religious movements.   We need not speak about luke-warmness and the backsliders among us, which are in abundance.   May the gracious God save us all from the ambition, and formality now prevailing in the world which is working among us, thus causing us to fight one another!

The Spirit of the Higher Critics Among Us.

We personally have been shocked in Los Angeles alone to see the terrible working of the spirit of the higher critics among us Pentecostal people, some boldly from the platform having warned the people not to take as seriously the words of the Apostles in the Book of Acts, and in the Epistles, as the four Gospels, for the four Gospels, they say, contain the voice of God from heaven, who said Jesus was His Son, and Matthew 28:19 is a commandment of our Lord.   Some of these men, who are considered to be good, have said, "I prefer the words of Jesus Himself, rather than what is written in the Book of Acts and the Epistles."   If this is not what the higher critics say we ask, what is it? May God help us to remember that the greatest proofs and confirmation of our baptism in the Holy Ghost are in the Book of Acts, that the Book of Acts is the pattern of the true Church of God, and that the Apostles spoke as they were moved by the same Spirit of God that moved Jesus to speak.

Let us begin as the true Church, in the upper room, and follow the Apostles of God, as they followed Jesus Christ, our Lord, in the power of the Holy Spirit.

God's Plan Set Forth in Scriptures.

Christ gave Himself for His church "that He might sanctify and cleanse it with the washing of water by the WORD; that He might present it to Himself a glorious church, not having spot or wrinkle or any such thing, but that it should be holy and without blemish" (Eph. 5:25-26).

God will not let us stay in our present miserable state.   He will have us purified and made straight under heavy, hot irons of persecution.   Every bit of worldly spirit and all the higher or lower criticism of His Holy Word must be taken out of us.   He will have a people that will hear and do every command up to the last letter.   He is going to make us practice the Bible principles and the doctrine of Christ up to the last jot and tittle before He can lead us into perfection. Christ never commanded His apostles to baptize those that believe in His name into the Father, the Son and Holy Ghost, but into "The NAME" of the T-H-R-E-E—O-N-E GOD. He is going to make us quit thinking that the Apostles baptized as the modern Theologians do. But He will humiliate us, so much that we will be glad to do exactly like His chosen and commissioned Apostles, exactly as it is written in the book of Acts, the pattern of God's church. It is the spirit of obedience God has put in our souls that caused us to go into the water in nothing less than the NAME Lord Jesus Christ. We knew well that it would cost us something, and we are now being judged and misrepresented for following God's word in full, but we are glad and full of praise to Him for counting us worthy to suffer shame for His NAME. And the end is not yet, for persecution is still coming and it is going to increase in hatefulness if we cleave to the precious NAME. They that wish to build homes, reputation and temples, cannot stand the pressure for His Name's sake; but I for one have decided for time and eternity that I will go through with Him, if need be I should do secular work for a living; for I love to keep busy and make an honest living and glorify Jesus, "the Lord of Glory."

Finally, Brethren: There is enough sweetness and grace and love in the matchless name J-E-S-U-S. If any of us lack the divine virtues, we can obtain grace and mercy from God that will make us more than conquerors and to be faithful to the end to God and His message in and through His Son, JESUS, the NAME that shall endure forever and forever. Amen.

CHAPTER VII

The complete fulness of the Deity in Jesus Christ.

By A. D. Urshan.

OU have read and probably have already seen the significance of God's purpose in revealing His mighty NAME to His ancient people as "EL SHADDI" and "YAH-WEH," and to the whole world as the "LORD JESUS CHRIST," as you have seen in our five previous letters.

But there is another crowning truth which we all ought to know and proclaim, and that is, Jesus Christ not only has the Name of the Deity in Him, but also the **fulness of the Deity** dwelleth in Him, and that He is the **embodiment and visibleness of the invisible God** Therefore we read in Hebrews, first chapter:

"God, who at sundry times and in divers manners spake in time past unto the fathers by the prophets,

Hath in these last days spoken unto us by His Son, whom He hath appointed heir of all things, by whom also He made the worlds;

Who, being the brightness of His glory, and the EXPRESS IMAGE of His person, etc."

Again: "Who (Christ) is the image of the invisible God; the firstborn of every creature." Col. 1:15.

Over and over, repeatedly, the Three-One God, or the Deity, is spoken of as an invisible Being, a God that can never be seen as He is; that is, in His full, great and infinite majesty; for God is a Spirit, according to the words of our Lord in John 4:24. The following Scriptures prove this,—Ex. 33:20-23; Jno. 1:18; I Jno. 4:12; Heb. 1:3; Col. 4:4; Heb. 11:27. And in I Tim. 6:16 we read that the Deity is a LIGHT, "the light which no man can approach unto, whom no man has seen nor can see; to whom be honor and power everlasting. Amen." Here the Apostle plainly says that God was not only invisible in past ages and no man could see Him then, but that He is a God that never can be seen. So in this Scripture we have a God invisible in the past, invisible in the present and invisible in the future, an unapproachable, mysterious, incomprehensible hidden, **spiritual BEING.**

But some may say that the Scriptures declare that Adam and Eve saw God (Gen. 3:8). Abraham saw God when He appeared with His two angels in the plains of Mamre (Gen. 18:22). Jacob saw God and wrestled with Him and said, "I have seen God face to face and my life is preserved." (Gen. 32:30). The nobles of Israel saw God and did eat and drink. (Ex. 24:9-11). And we read that Moses spake with God face to face, as a man speaks unto his friend (Ex.

33:11), etc., etc. Yes, the Scriptures speak thus, but if you read the context carefully, you will see that these ancient people saw the Lord, not in the fulness of His glorious Deity, but in His own different revelations and manifestations, such as in the form of an angel, in clouds, in fire, whirlwind, etc. For we read God's own declaration unto His servant Moses, who anxiously desired to see the real face of God, but unto whom the Lord said: "Thou canst not see my face; for there shall no man see me, and live." (Ex. 33:20). However, the Lord showed Moses the type, or the fore-shadow of His future full manifestation: He asked him to go into a cleft of a rock, and He shewed Moses His "back parts." In this typical revelation of God unto Moses, we see the twofold prophetic type, or shadow, of "God manifest in the flesh" (I Tim. 3:16)— the broken rock represents the crucified Jesus Christ; "back parts" represent the male, or God becoming a man, to save man. Moses could see only the back of the Lord, because he was in the old covenant; but the new covenant is a better covenant, much more glorious. Therefore, as the Apostle says, we can see the Lord, not His back parts, but "with an open face, beholding as in a glass the glory of the Lord, (we) are changed into the same image, from glory to glory, even as by the Spirit of the Lord." II Cor. 3:18. No, dear reader, the old-time people of God did not see God, although they longed to see Him. If they had actually seen Him, John the Baptist would not have said, "For the law was given by Moses, but grace and truth came by Jesus Christ; (and) no man has seen God at any time; the only begotten Son, which is in the bosom of the Father, He hath declared Him. And this is the record of John, when the Jews sent priests and Levites from Jerusalem to ask him, Who art thou?" (Jno. 1:17-20). And as we read before, the Apostle Paul also said that God, whose being is a marvelous and glorious LIGHT, has not been and cannot be seen by any man. In the mouth of these two witnesses of God the truth is confirmed.

The Gracious Manifestations of God.

This lofty and glorious Being of beings, the infinite ONE, is so gracious and so loving that He could not hide Himself from His creatures eternally. And so He created the first man (Adam) in His own image, and after His own likeness. It is very significant that we never find in the Bible that angels were created in the image of God; although they have intelligence and free will as we have; but we do find concerning man that "in the image of God created He him; male and female created He them. And God blessed them, and God said unto them, Be fruitful and multiply, and replenish the earth, and subdue it" etc. (Gen. 1:26-28). Many Christians think that the first promise of the gospel was given when God said con-cerning Eve, that her seed should bruise the head of the serpent. But they forget that the very creation of man and woman, and the seed in them, was in itself a promise of the gospel of grace typically, because God was to come forth in flesh and blood, in the likeness of man to redeem him, and be called the second Adam, "the Lord from heaven" (I Cor. 15:47), who was to die on the cross, and from whose riven side should be formed a Bride, and that these two, Christ and His Bride, should multiply and replenish and subdue the earth unto God. So Adam and Eve were created in the image of the God-man, with His church, and His seed in Him, even Jesus Christ, "God manifest in the flesh," and their creation was the first prophecy and type of the God of grace who was coming to save the fallen race.

The following is quoted from "Lectures on Messianic Prophecy," by Mark Lev, a Hebrew Christian, late Editor of "Immanuel's Witness:"

"It is commonly taught, that the first Messianic prophecy is contained in the promise of the seed of the woman in Gen. 3:15. But Gen. 3:15 is the Betha, not the Alpha of Messianic Prophecy. A prayerful and scrupulous searching of the Scriptures will reveal to us the foundation of God's plan for the redemption of our fallen race prior to the fall of Adam, long before he was created." (This is the first promise of redemption through prophetic type.) "The Alpha of Messianic Prophecy, the so-called protevangelium is found not in Gen. 3:15, but in Gen. 1:26, 27. This may seem a strange assertion; but let the Bible student dig patiently and prayerfully into the depth of Messianic Prophecy, and the Holy Spirit will make this great fundamental truth plain to him."

Beloved friends, I personally cannot refrain from believing that there is a plurality in God's mysterious Being, and that this plurality is shown as a three-ness, not three separate, distinct Beings or Persons of God, but a mysterious, inexplicable, incomprehensible three-ness, as it is expressed by the Apostle in I Jno. 5:7 and Mat. 28:19, and that the triune office of this one God is shown in I Cor. 12,—not three offices of three Gods but one office of one God with three branches (I Cor. 12:4-6). Again, in Eph. 4:4-6, we find this three-one God, who is called "One Spirit," "One Lord," "One God (the Deity) and Father of all, who is above all, and through all, and in you all." And the first expression or image of this Three-One God was Adam and Eve and that which was in them, a foreshadow of the coming One. We find this Three-in-One all through the Old Testament Scriptures, expressed by types and shadows pointing to God in Christ; for instance, observe Noah's ark; there was one ark, with three compartments; but the middle compartment, or central room, had the only entrance, through which alone Noah could enter the whole ark. What a beautiful type of the triune God, Christ being the central compartment, with whom the first and last compartments are connected, through whom alone we can enter into the Holy Spirit and the Father, and through whom alone, the center of this marvelous God of gods, the Father and the Spirit can benefit us. That is why, when the Lord told the disciples that He was going to His father, and Thomas said unto Him, "We know not whither thou goest, and how can we know the way?" Jesus answered, "I am the way, the truth, and the life. No man cometh unto the Father but by me." (Jno. 14:1-6). Again, the Bible student will note that the tabernacle, made by Moses, and the Temple, built by Solomon, each had three compartments, with all the appurtenances thereto, such as the High Priest, the sacrifice, the altar, the shewbread, and everything within,—all these being in types and shadows manifestations of the invisible, triune God, pointing to the future full manifestation of the God of Israel. In the same way, all their religious activities were ordained by God for His people in order to teach, lead, and prepare them for the coming One, whose highly exalted Name was to be "YAH-OSHUA" (Jesus), the Jehovah-Saviour or Immanuel. Hallelujah!

The blessed God revealed Himself not only to His chosen people through these divine types and shadows which He delivered unto them, but He revealed Himself also unto the Gentiles, as we read in Rom. 1:19, 20. "Because that which may be known of God is manifest in them; for God hath shewed it unto them. For the invisible things of Him from the creation of the world are clearly seen, being understood by the things that are made, even His eternal power and Godhead (Deity) so that they are without excuse."

Reader, you will remember that the Apostle Paul said that God is a light that cannot be seen, neither can it be approached unto; and the Apostle John says the same thing, that "God is light, and in Him is no darkness at all." God had a double purpose in creating the natural light and the sun: they were not only to give light and life to man and the animal, vegetable and mineral world; but they were also to present a type and forecast of Him who Himself said, when He appeared, "I am the LIGHT OF THE WORLD; he that followeth me shall not walk in darkness, but shall have the light of life." (Jno. 8:12) The prophet Malachi calls the Lord God "the Sun of Righteousness." "But unto you that fear my NAME shall the Sun of Righteousness arise with healing in his wings" (Mal. 4:2). So the heathen could lift up their heads and look upon the heavens, and discover in the sun, moon, and stars foregleams of the Deity, or "the Godhead," as the English translators have put it, and worship the Invisible One and seek His full revelation and glorious face by faith. So they are without excuse, for they could know Him and see Him clearly, "He being understood by the things that are made, even His eternal power and Godhead."

Inexcusable Ignorance.

Dear reader, if God will not excuse the heathen for failure to understand the revelation and knowledge of Him through the things He has created, and to pay Him due worship, how much more inexcusable shall we be for our ignorance of God's Being and His gracious manifestation! For it is evident that millions of Christians and Jews, who have been crowned with many gracious manifestations of God through the types and shadows in the Old Testament and at last in His Son Jesus Christ, are yet ignorant and confused concerning the Three-One God, our Father, our Creator, our Saviour, and our All. Let this be known unto you, reader. God the Father is light; the Son is light; the Holy Spirit is light,—not three lights, but one self-same Light with three rays (manifestations or revelations); and this great Triune Being of the excellent light of eternal life can be seen, and His blessings, gifts, and promises received, only in and through Jesus Christ, "the Son of the Father." And our purpose and prayer in writing the messages in this last letter, is that you may take your eyes away from men's traditions concerning the Godhead (Deity), and put them upon Jesus Christ, who is "the express image and shining-forth glory" and visible embodiment of the invisible three-one God.

The pastor of the First Baptist Church of New York, I. M. Haldeman, gives a beautiful explanation of God, who dwelleth—revealeth Himself—in the Person of His Son. He deals with this important subject from the standpoint we have seen in the Scriptures, namely, the invisible Being of God as expressed by the light and the sun. So he proceeds on the subject in his tract on "God's only Begotten Son," as follows:

"Wonder of the Three Light-Rays.

"The first Ray is neither seen nor felt; the third Ray is not seen but is felt; the second Ray is both seen and felt.

"Likewise the Father can neither be seen nor felt: (See Col. 1:15 and Heb. 1:3; also I Tim 6:16). The Spirit can never be seen, but is felt; while the Son can both be seen and felt.

"The second Ray is the revelation and manifestation of the first and third Rays, therefore the embodiment and fulness of the Light. "The Son of God is the revelation of both the Father and the Spirit, therefore the embodiment and the fulness of God; as it is written, "In Him dwelleth all the fulness (Deity) of the Godhead bodily." Col. 2:9.

William Bridge, an English divine (1600-1670) also explains this wonderful Bible theme of the Deity revealed in the Son, in these beautiful words:

"All the sweets that are in the flowers of the field and in the garden are brought in by the bees, and are there embodied in one hive; so all the attributes of God and the sweetness of them all are hived in Christ, in whom all the fulness of the Godhead dwells bodily."

Baruch Spinoza, a Dutch philosopher (1632-1677), speaking on the same subject says:

"This is the highest thing which Christ said of Himself, namely that He is the temple of God, since God chiefly ministered Himself in Christ; as St. John said, that He might express it more efficaciously, clothed in the expression that 'The Word was made flesh.' "

The Editor of the Christian Evangel (a Pentecostal paper) also gives a proper answer to puzzled minds on this subject, in his column devoted to "Questions and Answers":

The questioner here asks: "Please explain I Jno. 2:23: 'Whosoever denieth the Son, the same hath not the Father: (but) he that acknowledgeth the Son hath the Father also.' " Ans. Worrell renders this verse as follows: "Every one who denies the Son has not the Father either; he who confesses the Son has the Father also." This means that men can now know and have the Father only through Jesus Christ, and the Father is in Christ and gives Himself with the Son to all who accept Jesus. Jesus said the same in saying, "No man can come unto the Father, except by Me." This is still the only way to the Father today.

The second question asked for an explanation of John 14:9. which reads, "Jesus saith unto him, Have I been so long time with you, and yet hast thou not known Me, Philip? He that hath seen Me hath seen the Father; and how sayest thou, then, Shew us the Father?" Ans. This means that the Father is to be seen only in Jesus, that He reveals Himself to men only in and through the Son, as I have explained in the above answer. Jesus explained it Himself in the next verse, saying, "I am in the Father, and the Father in Me." He did not say, "I am the Father." There is a world of difference between saying He was in the Father and the claim that He is the Father. Until people learn the difference between Is and In, there is no hope of their understanding this deep matter. No man knoweth the Father save the Son and He to who Son reveals Him. Hallelujah! We are glad of it, for we do not want to dodge Jesus and climb up some other way. He is not only the way, but He is the only way.

J. Monroe Gibson, M. A., D. D., still more clearly and in detail explains the Godhead in Jesus Christ. The following is copied from his book, "Christianity According to Christ," published in London, England, in 1888:

The Godhead.

The Father, Son and Holy Ghost are all in Jesus Christ. "I am the Way, the Truth and the Life." Father, Son and Holy Ghost are all here, each found in Him, so that our thoughts are not to leave

Christ when they pass to the Father or to the Holy Spirit. **Christ is all—in Him dwelleth all the fulness of the Godhead bodily.**

Now this is manifestly the way in which we are intended to realize to ourselves the truth about God as Father, **as Son, as Holy Spirit—not by wandering away into the infinite, but sitting at the feet of Jesus and looking up into His face.**

The reason why some get into difficulty and perplexity is their perverse determination— notwithstanding all the directions and cautions the Master has given—to seek a separate knowledge of the Father, Son and Holy Spirit. They wish to know God the Father, and in order to find Him, they look away from Christ, instead of at Him. **They gaze into the infinite unknown instead of looking at the face of Jesus.** And when they think of the Spirit, **again they must** have this as a separate region of theological lore.

So again they look away from the face of Jesus to find somewhere else God the Holy Spirit. If they would have what they are vainly seeking, they would have three Gods instead of one, **as practically many Christians have, for they actually have great difficulty sometimes as to which of the three to go to.**

It is very easy to show how utterly needless all this perplexity is, and how thoroughly unscriptural are all these notions out of which it grows. There is only one Person to whom any one can go, and that Person is Christ. **We should go to Him always, under all circumstances, with our prayers, with our tears with our longings, with our doubts, with our difficulties, with our troubles, with our innumerable wants.**

When we say "Our Father" **we must look to Christ,** for He plainly tells us that we cannot reach the Father but by Him. Christ Himself says, as plainly **as tongue can express it,** that it is impossible to know the Father apart from Him. "No man cometh unto the Father but by Me." And when even after that plain statement the still puzzled disciple says, "Lord, shew us the Father, and it sufficeth us," what can the Master do but repeat the same truth in still more emphatic terms, **"He that hath seen Me hath seen the Father." "Do you not know Me yet?" Who can suppose that Philip retained his perplexity after so clear an answer? Why should any one be perplexed now?**

Christ is the only way, and those who turn away from Him set their faces to the outer darkness. The same considerations **apply to** those who perplex and confuse themselves by trying to have a knowledge of the Spirit apart from their knowledge of Christ. Our Savior claims Himself to be the Life, as well as the Truth.

He speaks of the giving of "another Comforter," **but when He comes, He will not speak of Himself, but "He shall take of the things of Mine and show it unto you."** So complete is their identification that the Lord speaks of His coming as His own coming: "I will not leave you comfortless; I will **come to you.** "At that **day ye shall know that I am in the Father, and ye in Me, and and I in you."**

"I am in the Father"—there is the doctrine of the Father. "Ye in Me"—there is the doctrine of the Son. "I in you"—**there is** the doctrine of the Spirit. If we think of the Father, there is Christ—"I am in the Father, and the Father in Me." **If we think of the Son, union to Christ is the practical thought—"ye in Me." If we think of the Holy Spirit, the practical thought is Christ in us—** "I in you."

It comes to this, that practically Christ is **all in all.** ' am the

Way, the Truth and the Life." It is "I am" all the way through. The divine NAME is all in Christ. "Hear, O Israel! The Lord our God is one Lord." The unsearchable God has made Himself known to us as Father, Son and Holy Spirit. But all that there is for us in Father—all that there is for us in the Son—all that there is for us in the Holy Spirit—is manifest in Christ.

He is all and in all. All praise and glory to Christ the Son—the only Revealer of the Father—the only Fountain of the Spirit. Let our prayers always be to Him, whether we are looking at the Father as revealed in Him, or whether we are looking to Him, as the source whence flow the streams of the Spirit's life.

Whether we are thinking of the invisible God quite out of our reach, or the invisible Spirit proceeding from Him and entering into us, the eye of our faith is ever directed to Him who is for us the face of God. "God, who commanded the light to shine out of darkness, hath shined in our hearts, to give the light of the knowledge of the glory of God in the face of Jesus Christ."

Light shining out of darkness suggests the Father; shining in our hearts suggests the Spirit; shining reflected from the fact of Jesus Christ—there is the Son. There is only one face to look at—only one direction for the eye to take. "Looking unto Jesus Christ, the author and finisher of our faith." Heb. 12.

The Face of God.

We have carefully and prayerfully looked into the passages in the Bible on "the face of God." We find God Himself, with His prophets and apostles, speaking of His face always in the singular number, or as having one form (Ph. 2:6), one Being (Heb. 1:3). The ancient people of God all believed in one God having one personality (Job 13:7, 8), and one glorious face. They did not believe like the apostate Roman church and presentday theologians, in a God with three forms and faces, or a God of three distinct and separate persons, putting the great and mysterious God into their arithmetical terms, 1st Person, 2nd Person, and 3rd Person, which is absolutely unscriptural, being man's feeble, confusing conclusion on the Deity (Godhead), causing believers to think that Christ is inferior to God and giving Him a second place in their minds, in the face of the truth which our Lord proclaims: "I am the first and the last." If God is three separate and distinct persons, then He must have three distinct, separate faces. But the Scriptures are contrary to such misleading teaching.

When Cain, the son of Adam, was punished by God for the murder of his brother, he said to God: "Thou hast driven me out this day from the face of the earth; and from thy face (not thy faces) shall I be hid." (Gen. 4:14). When Jacob speaks about the face of God, talking to his brother Esau, he says: "Therefore I have seen thy face as though I had seen the face (not faces) of God." (Gen. 33: 10.) Moses also believed like these men in one Being, Person and face of God, as we read in Ex. 33. He anxiously desired to see the face of God (not faces). What did the Lord say unto him? Did He ask him, Which one of my faces do you want to see? No, indeed; but He said, "Thou can'st not see my face (not faces), for there shall no man see me (or my face) and live." Here God plainly says to His servant that He has but one face. In Numbers 6:25, when the messenger of God gives blessing to His people, he says, "The Lord make His face (not faces) to shine upon thee, and be gracious unto thee." The Psalmist, cries vehemently, "How long wilt thou hide thy face (not thy faces) from me?" Again, God Himself says, concerning His backslidden people," "I will set my face against you for evil." So all the way through the Old Testament, His people seemed to have a clear understanding that their God was one Lord and His FACE one. For the Lord appeared unto them as such, and taught them this truth through His messengers and prophets.

Christ The Face of God.

When Moses came down from his forty days' communion with God, he had to put a veil over His face, because the Israelites could not endure its shining brightness. Yet this was only a reflected glory of God, even as the moon reflects the glory of the sun. How much more need was there, think you, that when the Sun of Righteousness, the Lord of Glory, came down to His people, He should put a veil over His face! And that veil was the humanity of Jesus, as the Apostle plainly tells us in Heb. 10:20, where he calls the flesh of the Lord a veil. And as Moses went veiled among his people that he might reveal to them God's law, so the man Christ Jesus veiled the glory of God in Him, that He might reveal to His people God's grace and love and all the divine attributes in His own Person and His mighty works (John 14:10). The Scriptures clearly teach that the Lord Jesus Christ is not only the Son of God, but the visible embodiment, and the **very face of God.** He is therefore the only true and full revelation of the invisible ONE.

Concerning John the Baptist, the messenger of Christ, it was prophesied that he should be the messenger of Jehovah God, as we read in Matt. 11:10: "For this is he, of whom it is written, Behold, I send my messenger before thy face (not thy faces), which shall prepare thy way before thee." If John the Baptist was the messenger of God, and if he was sent before the face of God (Isa. 40:3) and since he was, according to the New Testament, the messenger of Christ, going before the face of Christ then the **face of God must be Jesus Christ.** This wonderful truth is proclaimed clearly and definitely by the Apostle Paul, when in II Cor. 4:6 he speaks of God revealing Himself in us: He says: "For God, who commanded the light to shine out of darkness (the Creator), hath shined in our hearts" (why? The answer is) "to give the light of the knowledge of the glory of God" (where?) **"in the face of Jesus Christ."** Here it is again, God in Christ, and Christ in us. Hallelujah! Christians say they are temples of God. But do we ever stop and think how we are temples of God? It is only because Christ dwelleth in us and God is in Christ; otherwise God could never dwell in us, because without Christ in us, we are unregenerated and unclean. So before God the Father can come to dwell in us, He puts the divine germ or life of His Son (the good seed) in us; then He comes, by His Holy Spirit, into His Son in us. Then, and not until then, we become the temples of the living, three-one God in the Person of Jesus Christ.

The Face of Deity Shining Forth in the Person of the Son of Man.

The wonderful description the Bible gives us of the face of the Son of Man and Son of God ought to convince us that it would be nothing less than the face of God. Such excellent brightness, glory, power and majesty as are pictured in that face must be the shining forth of One who is Almighty and Infinite. For instance, the Apostle Paul, speaking of a mystery, says that "in a moment, in the twinkling of an eye, at the last trump, ... we shall be changed." Now, the question is, what will cause us to be changed from corruption into immortality—spirit, soul and body—and become like the glorified Christ forever? The Apostle John explains the secret of this mysterious change in these words: "When He shall appear, we shall be like Him, for we shall see Him as He is." Compare I Cor. 15:51-53 with I Jno. 3:2. Think, friends, what a powerful glory there must be in the face of Jesus Christ, to change us in the twinkling of an eye and make us like Him! It was this invisible glory of the Deity which Moses beheld through darkness, on the mountain of Sinai, which caused his face to shine with such a brilliance that he must needs veil it before the people. It had happened to Moses according to the words of the psalmist, "they looked unto Him and were radiant." (Psa. 34:5, R. V.)

Speaking of the manifestation of the son of perdition with his power to deceive, in his reign over the whole earth as Anti-Christ, the Apostle tells us of the end of this great monster, his instantaneous destruction. What do you think will destroy that great false god with his tremendous influence and power The Apostle says it will be "the brightness of His coming." Some people think that Jesus Christ will come leading a great army, with swords and spears, to fight against Anti-Christ and his multitudes. Oh, no! when the nations gather around Jerusalem to destroy the people of God, suddenly the heavens will burst asunder and there will appear the Great King with such heavenly brightness that it will smite the Anti-Christ and his army with blindness in a moment of time and the only weapon Christ will need to use will be the sword of the Spirit, which is the word of God. Just a few words from Him will be so powerful as to pierce millions of God's enemies, consume all their strength and make them like corpses. "And then shall that Wicked be revealed, whom the Lord shall consume with the spirit of His mouth, and shall destroy with the brightness of His coming" (2 Thes. 2:8). Saul of Tarsus, when he thought to put an end to the followers of Jesus of Nazareth, was privileged to get a glimpse of this glorious face of God in Christ, when "suddenly there shined around about him a light from heaven, and he fell to the earth (blinded), and he heard a voice saying unto him, Saul, why persecutest thou Me? And he said, Who art thou, Lord? And the Lord said, I am JESUS whom thou persecutest. . . . And he trembling and astonished, said, Lord, what wilt thou have me to do?" This Apostle had tasted a little "of the power of the world to come," of the light of that glorious and marvelous FACE, so that he could experimentally speak of the glory of God in Christ which is to destroy sin and the devil and fill the earth with light. Compare II Thess. 2:7, 8 with Isa. 11:9, and Isa. 6:3 with Jno. 12:40.

When the glorified God-man sits upon His throne as Judge of quick and dead, there will be such majestic glory in His face as to cause the heavens and the earth to flee away in a moment of time. Such will be the power of divine justice and indignation against everything and every creature soiled by sin, the sin of rejecting Him and persecuting and killing His followers. Rev. 20:11 reads as follows: "And I saw a great white throne, and Him that sat on it, from whose face the earth and the heaven fled away; and there was found no place for them." Oh, what glory and majesty! What power in the Face of our great LORD, in which all Deity shineth forth!

The Unchangeable Revelator.

The Lord Jesus Christ has been and will be forever the manifestation and revelation,— the face of God. Before the Word was incarnate. God created all things and manifested Himself to all His creatures by the prophetic WORD, now called the written word, and Christ takes all that Word to Himself when He says, "I am Alpha and Omega," which means all the written word from A to Z. Glory! When, in the fulness of time, God again manifested Himself, and that in and through the Incarnate WORD, we read, "In the beginning was the WORD, and the WORD was with God, and the WORD was God. . . . The WORD was made flesh and dwelt among us, and we beheld His glory, the glory as of the only-begotten of the Father, full of grace and truth." Is it a wonder, then that Christ so plainly and emphatically explains to His anxious disciples the visibleness and manifestation of the Father, when He said to them: "He that hath seen me hath seen the Father. I am in the Father and the Father in Me, and from henceforth ye know Him (the Father) and have seen Him (the Father)?" (Jno. 14:5-11.) In other words, Jesus says, "I am the Son, the image, and the face of the Father. So don't look away from Me to find the Father; for I am the way to the Father, and the Father c n only reveal Himself to you, His children. in Me and through Me." For "no man knoweth the Father save the Son, and he to whomsoever the Son will reveal Him." Matt. 11:27. We already have read in II Cor. 4:6 that in this dispensation of the Holy Spirit, the triune God dwelleth and manifesteth Himself through His people, and that in the FACE of Jesus Christ in us. But some may say, as many unlearned do say, that when we get to Heaven, we shall see the face of the Father, the first Person, the face of the Son, the second Person, and the face of the Holy Ghost, the third Person, each one separ tely. In other words, when Christ comes to take us away, He will come alone and take us up and present us before another Being, God the Father, distinct from Himself. Oh, no! The Scripture does not teach this at all, but it says that when we get to Heaven, "we shall see His FACE" (not their faces),—it uses the singular number,—and His NAME shall be in our foreheads. "And there shall be no night there; and they need no candle, neither the light of the sun; for the Lord God giveth them light; for the glory of God will lighten it." How will the glory of God lighten our eternal Habitation? The Scripture says: "And the Lamb is the light thereof." So we see that the light of Heaven is the Lord God shining through the Person of His Son. Compare Rev. 21: 22-27 with Rev. 22:4, 5.

In the book of Revelation, which is "the revelation of Jesus Christ," the Lamb always represents the sacrificial body of the WORD, or that human form which God created for Himself, His WORD, and His Spirit to dwell in, not only to work His great redemption for the human race, but through that very body. "the Lamb," to manifest His eternal grace and excellent glory before all His angelic and human creatures. And so JESUS CHRIST is the only express image of the invisible God for time and for eternity, in both earth and Heaven. Thus, beloved friends, when we get up yonder, we shall see the Father and the Spirit shining forth with such glory in the face of the Son of Man and Son of God as not only to change us in the twinkling of an eye and make us perfect beings, to rule and reign with Him through the ages to come, but also to cause us to be swallowed up in it, as in a great ocean,—that glory of the triune God, proceeding like many mighty streams through those eyes that John saw like two pillars of fire, and through that glorious face, shining like the sun in its glory, and through that beautiful hair, white like pure wool,— yes, through that glorified Man of Calvary in whom dwelleth all the fulness of the Godhead bodily (Deity). Glory and honor be to His Name forever and ever.

> "Holy, holy, holy, Lord God Almighty,
> Early in the morning our song shall rise to Thee.
> Holy, holy, holy, merciful and mighty,
> God in Christ Jesus, blessed Deity!"

Jesus Christ the Image and The Temple of God and the Object of Our Worship.

"But if our gospel be hid, it is hid to them that are lost: In whom the god of this world hath blinded the minds of them which believe not, lest the light of the glorious gospel of **Christ, who is the image of God,** should shine unto them."

The above Scripture, and many other Bible passages, clearly teach not only that God Himself is invisible, but that His visibleness is made possible only in and through His own glorious Habitation, which is the body and Person of Jesus Christ. Therefore, the Son of God is both the express image of His Father, and the living temple of the entire Holy Deity. It is very important that we should worship God aright, as well as seek Him diligently,—that having learned where to find our God dwelling, we should enter into His house like the psalmist of old, "to behold the beauty of the Lord and inquire in His temple." (Psa. 27:4). It is blessedly true that God is seeking true worshippers, but it is no less true that He commands His people to worship Him in the places of His appointment, the places where He puts His NAME and shows His shekinah glory. He wants His people to enter those places and there to worship Him in the beauty of holiness. It was for this reason He brought His people out of Egypt: He did not want them to worship Him there, but to come out of Egypt and be free with Him alone in the wilderness. And in that wilderness He caused to be built a tabernacle which He called His house. Into this He commanded His people to enter to worship Him and be blessed by Him. This tabernacle led the people of God to a still more lofty place of worship, which was the temple that Solomon built for God's Name in the Holy Land. God wanted His people, in order to worship Him acceptably, to build Him that holy temple; He called it His house, and He desired that they should come from all over the earth once a year, not only to meet each other, but also to meet their God and receive the blessing that comes through worshipping Him in His own appointed place, where His glory dwelt. That place of worship, wherever it might be, was so significant and important to the Lord's people of old that it made them, when they were far away in heathen countries, to turn toward the Holy City and the Holy Temple at the time of worship, in order to be accepted of God and to get answers to their prayers.

What were all these ancient religious observances, if not schoolmasters to teach the people of God the perfect worship and lead them into the perfect temple, even His Son? That is why Jesus stood by the temple and said, pointing to His own body, "Destroy this temple (of God) and I will build it up in three days." There was the great fulfillment of God's eternal plan through which He would bless His beloved people, a temple that should stand as long as eternity, a temple that should be raised up after its destruction (the crucifixion), a temple in which the true and living God should dwell. No more should it be necessary that the worship of God should be confined to Jerusalem and the mount of Samaria, but all men everywhere might come into the true temple, Christ Jesus, and worship God in Spirit and in truth. For such worshippers Christ said, "my Father seeketh." But the poor,, deceived Jews did not recognize this wonderful truth. They still clung to the types and shadows, and rejected their Messiah, thus rejecting the Father in the Son, and grieving the Holy Spirit. But alas! we need not go back to those days to see the blindness of the people of God to this truth. The same devil is blinding God's people in these very days and causing them to follow the traditions of men on the Godhead, and to seek and worship God the Father apart from His Son, despite the fact that His Word says that in Him (Jesus Christ) dwelleth all the fulness of the Godhead bodily, and that the Father is pleased that this fulness should so dwell in Him, and is seeking worshippers that will come into Jesus Christ, to worship God in Him. Now, the sole purpose of God's gracious dealings with the human race, the purpose for which redemption was provided, was to bring fallen man to meet God, to fellowship God, and this was to be in the place where God desires and delights to dwell, and to bless all who come to worship Him in spirit and in truth. But our Lord solemnly warns us that there is such a thing as vain worship, a worship which God will not accept and from which He will turn His face away, a worship that will bring a curse instead of a blessing, no matter how much earnestness and sacrifice may be attached to it, and He tells us that the end of those who render such worship will be destruction forever and ever. The reader may ask, what is that worship? We will let the Lord Jesus answer, in Mark seventh chapter and seventh verse: "Howbeit, in vain do they worship me, (why in vain?) teaching for doctrines the commandments of men." Oh, may God help us to be saved from vain worship, thinking we are following God and pleasing Him, and yet being found, after all, to have been following men's traditions instead of seeking God in His beloved Son, Jesus Christ.

Jesus Christ The Only Object Of The True Worship.

It is noteworthy how boldly the Apostle says that all homage, or worship, should be given to God before the presence and in the Name of the Lord Jesus Christ. Hear His words: "Wherefore God also hath highly exalted Him, and given Him a NAME which is above every name; that at the Name of JESUS every knee should bow, of things in heaven, and things in earth, and things under the earth; and that every tongue should confess that Jesus Christ is LORD, to the glory of God the Father" (Ph. 2:9-11). Reader does not this Scripture demand all the worship that can be offered to God, to be offered to the Person of Jesus Christ? If "every knee should bow"—are there any knees left to bow to any other God apart from Jesus Christ? If "every tongue should confess," is there any tongue left to confess any other than the One that dwelleth in Jesus Christ? No! I have one tongue and two knees which God gave me to use in worship and for His Glory. The Scripture commands me to bow, not one knee, but both (every knee) before the presence of Christ, and acclaim, like Thomas of Old, "My Lord and my God!" Is God the Father robbed of His due worship when we bow before Christ and confess Him as the only Lord? No. We worship God the Father when we worship His Son Jesus Christ, for the Father dwells in His dear Son and His Son is His living and Holy Temple; and it is written: "Whosoever denieth the Son, the same hath not the Father: but he that acknowledgeth the Son hath the Father also" (1 John 2:23). It is no wonder, then, that Jesus said, that "all men should honour the Son, even as they honour the Father. He that honoureth not the Son honoureth not the Father which hath sent Him" (John 5:23). No wonder that, "when He brings the first born into the world, He says: 'And let all the Angels of God worship Him (Christ)'" (Heb. 1:6). No wonder the wise men from the East and the shepherds from the field came and bowed and worshipped, not only with all their hearts and minds, but with their best gifts, although the great Saviour was yet a babe. And we read over and over that our Lord, when during His earthly ministry He was worshipped by those who came to Him for help, accepted their worship. We never read that He stopped them, saying, "Do not worship me, worship God alone." And when the devil was tempting Him in the wilderness, Jesus said unto him: "Thou shalt not tempt the Lord, thy God." The devil was not tempting God in Heaven, but he was tempting Jesus Christ. And Jesus Christ said to the devil that He is his Lord and his God, (God-man in the flesh) and in the next breath He says, "Thou shalt worship the Lord thy God, and Him only shalt thou serve." (Matt. 4:7-9). Then the question is, have we two or three separate Gods to worship? No; but three in one, the God of the Bible, who is the Father, the Son, and the Holy Ghost, who indwelleth, manifesteth Himself unto, and blesseth all His creatures in and through Jesus Christ.

In a note in The Sunday School Lesson Illustrator of August, 1919, this worship of God in the Person and the Name of the Lord Jesus Christ is well described and explained by Pierson:

"The O. T. law was, 'In all places where I record my NAME, I will come unto thee, and I will bless thee.' The N. T. law is, 'If two of you shall agree on earth as touching anything that they shall ask, it shall be done for them of my Father which is in Heaven.' Why? 'For where two or three are gathered together in my NAME, there am I in the midst of them.' In other words, wherever believers meet in my NAME, there I will record my NAME (Jesus Christ) and there will I come unto them and bless them. If we put the two laws side by side, the contrast will be the more apparent."

Just as the Old Testament Jehovah God of Israel concentrates all the worship of His people upon His name and in the place where He had put His name, so Christ Jesus, His Son, comes from Heaven and gives the full light and life to true worship, of which the prophets prophesied: Thus the Name of Christ and the life of Christ are the place and object of all true worship of the God of the Old and new Testaments.

On the Mount of Transfiguration, when Jesus gave a foregleam of the glory of His future Deity to His three disciples, Peter, seeing that earnest of the glory of the Lord, felt the power of the law (Moses) and of the Prophets (Elijah), and of Grace (Incarnate Word); he felt urged by his human emotions to make three tabernacles, wherein Law (Moses), Prophecy (Elijah), and Grace (Jesus) might dwell; just like many believers in three days, who are not satisfied with one tabernacle and one temple of God, wherein dwelleth the righteousness of the Law, the fulfillment of Prophecy, and the fulness of Grace and Truth. They are moved by their human emotions to build up by their doctrines and traditions three separate, distinct, divine temples of One God. They say, "God is One in Three," in spite of the truth that "In Him (Jesus Christ) dwelleth all the fulness of the Deity bodily." Beloved, let us quit making three tabernacles for one God, and be satisfied with His own pleasure, as it is written, "It pleased the Father that in Him (Christ) should all fulness dwell," and obey His voice from Heaven, which said, "This is my beloved Son. Hear Him." And let us go to His Son and hear Him saying: "He that seeth me seeth the Father: for I am in the Father and the Father is in Me," and be satisfied, bowing at the feet of Jesus. Let us worship God the Father, the Son, and the Spirit in our glorious Lord.

God, in His foreknowledge, knew of the day of perfect worship, hence the perfect blessing that was coming to His people, and that through His incarnate WORD. Therefore, with great solemnity, He commanded His people of old not to make any statue or image of Him, as we read: "Thou shalt not make unto thee any graven image, or any likeness of anything that is in Heaven above, or that is in the earth beneath, or that is in the water under the earth." Why did God warn His people not to make an image of His invisible Being and worship Him in that way? Because He had in His mind, away back in eternity, that He was to be manifested in the flesh, or that His eternal WORD was to come in the form of a unique and perfect man, and that the Father would dwell and show forth His great glory in and through that God-man, and thus would become to Himself His own image, in His own substance, His Son, a living image and a true expression of His omnipotence, omniscience, and omnipresence and all His glorious divine attributes. Christ Jesus is therefore that image of the living Three-One God, which I, for one, am glad to worship day and night, and to praise all the days of my life, and to see in the glory to come, my Heavenly Father shining forth with His eternal, divine life and blessings in and through the glorified presence of His Son, who is my All.

> "O come let us adore Him,
> O come let us adore Him,
> O come let us adore Him,
>   Christ, our LORD.

> "For He alone is worthy,
> For He alone is worthy,
> For He alone is worthy,
>   Christ, our GOD."

In The Lord Jesus Is Our All.

Dear friend, you must, with me, remember always that at our very best we are but creatures, and a creature means a needy being. There is only One that needs nothing, and that is God, who is all-sufficient both for Himself and for all His needy creatures. This gracious God and Father knew of our great temporal and spiritual needs and He hastened lovingly to supply them, and that in and through Jesus Christ, His only Son. The question is, then, what is the chief need of a human being? All enlightened Christians will agree with me, that it is God Himself. Many of us know that, even though we have had miraculous supernatural experiences and gifts, there is still a longing, a hunger in our souls that is greater than ever before. A longing for what? The true Christian knows that it is for the GIVER. This is the longing not alone of Christians, but of heathen, too; this is indeed, the cause of their innumerable gods. The next question is, did God, who loved the world and gave His Son for it, provide for His creatures the supply of this great need of their hearts,—the need of Himself? He certainly did. That is why the Apostle could say to Christians: "My God shall supply all your need, according to His riches in glory (how?) by Christ Jesus," and "blessed be the God and Father of our Lord Jesus Christ, who has blessed us with all spiritual blessings in heavenly places (where?) in Christ Jesus." Reader, is it not one of your chief needs and longings, to know and to see God, the Father? I have no doubt it is, if you are a seeker after God, and I doubt not that, like Philip of old, you often say, "Show us the Father and it sufficeth us" (Jno. 14:8). According to the Scriptures, Christ supplies that noble desire in His own Person and presence. Hallelujah!

The Scriptures declare that all things—and this includes us— were made by Christ and for Christ; therefore they are delivered to Christ. (Jno. 1:1-3; Col. 1:14-18; Matt. 11:27.) All power in Heaven and earth, over principalities, dominions, and all flesh, belongs to Jesus Christ (Matt. 28:18; Jno. 17:1-3). All the promises of God mentioned in the whole Bible are to be fulfilled for you and me in Jesus Christ. (II Co. 1:20.) All the revelations of the invisible God and the treasures of knowledge and wisdom and understanding are hid in Jesus Christ (Col. 2:3). All the spiritual body or temple of God is to be fitted together and grow into perfection in Christ the Lord. (Eph. 2:19-22.) I suppose, reader, you want also "the Lord over all." He is that also for you. (Rom. 10:12, 13.) He is not only Lord over all for you, but "God over all" for you also. For in Him dwelleth all the Deity. (Rom. 9:5; Col. 12:19.) Therefore, we are all to live, to die, and to be raised again to live, for time and eternity, for Christ. (II Cor. 5:14, 15.) Hence it makes Christ our ALL AND IN ALL. Therefore we should do all things in the NAME of Jesus Christ, giving thanks to the Father. Hallelujah for Christ Jesus, who is made of God unto us righteousness, sanctification, wisdom, redemption, the power of God, the hope, the peace, the eternal life, the Alpha and Omega, the first and the last, the beginning and the end, the author and the finisher of our salvation. Can you, dear reader, look beyond such a great Saviour, or imagine beyond His Diety and divine fulness Will you dare to put Him to one side, taking the eyes of your faith away from Him, and look in some other direction to find God for yourself? No, do not do this, please, but obey the gracious exhortation of the Holy Spirit, while running your race in this life, putting off sin with its ways, LOOK UNTO JESUS CHRIST.

Looking and Hoping.

Hope is expectation for the future. Our Christian hope is, the life beyond, the divine things which we shall see, meet, receive and enjoy when we go into Heaven. We have already learned from Scripture that the Name of God and the salvation of God and the fulness of God, in fact, all of God for us in this life, is in Jesus Christ; but we wish you, dear reader, to see in the coming world also, and that there we shall find and see all of God in Him and through Him for us. Therefore, Christ becomes our only Hope. The Old Testament saints, who had the light of God; who were spiritually advanced greatly beyond the common people of God of their time, declared over and over that Jehovah was their salvation and hope. So they cried out: "Be not a terror unto me; thou art my hope in the day of evil." (Jer. 17:17). "But Jehovah will be the hope of His people, and the strength of the children of Israel." (Joel 3:16.) "For thou art my hope, O Jehovah, God: thou art my trust from my youth" (Psa. 71:5), etc. The saints of God in the New Testament speak of Christ as being the LORD of their hope. The Apostle Paul says, "To whom God would make known what is the riches of the glory of this mystery among the Gentiles: which is Christ in you, the hope of glory." (Col 1:27.) Again, "Paul, an apostle of Jesus Christ by the commandment of God our Saviour,

and Lord Jesus Christ, which is our hope." (1 Tim. 1:1.)   And again,
"That by two immutable things, in which it was impossible for God
to lie, we might have a strong consolation, who have fled for refuge to
lay hold upon the hope set before us." (Heb. 6:18.)   Since Christ
is our hope, or our future expectation of divine glory, it behooves us not
only to put off all sin, denying ungodliness and worldly lusts, that we
should live soberly, righteously and godly in this present world, but
also to keep "looking for that blessed HOPE and the glorious appearing of the great God and our Saviour Jesus Christ." (Tit. 2:13.)
And again, "So Christ was once offered to bear the sins of many; and
unto them that look for Him shall He appear the second time without
sin unto salvation." (Heb. 9:28.)   Again, "Looking for and hasting
unto the coming of the day of God, wherein the Heavens being on
fire shall be dissolved." etc.   (II Pet. 3:12.)

In the Old Testament we read that God is calling upon His faithful,
people to turn their whole attention and gaze unto Him: "Hearken
to me, ye that follow after righteousness, ye that seek the Lord: look
unto the rock whence ye are hewn, and to the hole of the pit whence
ye are digged." (Isa. 51:1.)   Again, "Tell ye, and bring them near;
yea, let them take counsel together; who hath declared this from
ancient time?   Who hath told it from that time?   Have not I the Lord?
and there is no God else beside me; a just God and a Saviour; there is
none beside me.   Look unto me and be ye saved, all the ends of the
earth: for I am God, and there is none else." (Isa. 45:-21, 22.)
The same Lord God of the Old Testament saints, by the same Holy
Spirit, tells us through His Apostle, that although we are compassed
about with so great a cloud of witnesses, who did those wonderful
things as described in the eleventh of Hebrews, yet we should not look
upon these people, but, taking our eyes away from everything, should
put them on the Lord Jesus.   For He says: "Let us run with patience
the race that is set before us, looking unto Jesus, the author and
finisher of our faith." (Heb.. 12:1, 2.)   Peter, when walking miraculously on the water, took his eyes away from Jesus and began to sink.
There are thousands upon thousands of Christians who, having attempted to fix their eyes on three separate, distinct Persons, according
to the theology taught them, and becoming greatly puzzled and confused thereby, Christ and His divine fulness being obscured from their
sight, have forsaken that teaching and gone into Unitarianism, or the
teaching of what is called One God, the Father; and little by little,
these people, who never had clear sight of the Lord and God in His
Son, have lost even that poor theological sight of Jesus that they had,
and the outcome of it all is, they are deceived and out of THE WAY.
They think they have God the Father apart from His Son Jesus Christ,
and thus they are sinking into error and eternal perdition.   Some day
they will wail and mourn that they did not see Him in the Holy Ghost,
according to Holy Writ, and missed eternal glory.   May God help
us who are clinging to the traditions of men, to get loose from them
all, and hold onto the Head, in whom dwelleth all the fulness of
the Godhead bodily!

Reader—
"I want to see Jesus, don't you?
My Saviour so faithful and true;
When I reach the strand of that love bright land,
I want to see Jesus, don't you?
He is fairer than lily or rose to me,

And His blessings fall soft as the dew;
O my heart, how it longs His dear face to see;
I want to see Jesus, don't you?

"When I tread the crystal pavement of the New Jerusalem,
Where my Saviour has prepared for me a place;
Where the angel choirs are singing praise and glory to the Lamb,
O then I'll see My Saviour face to face.
O I want to see my Saviour face to face,
Who hath loved me and redeemed my by His grace;
In His kingdom, crowned with glory, on His everlasting throne,
I want to see my Saviour face to face."

Christ Our End.

Jesus Christ is not only our all and our hope, but He is also our end. He is not only the end of all law unto us, and the end of all righteousness, but He is in Himself the one to confirm us unto the end. (Rom. 10:4; 1 Cor. 1:8.) St. Paul's hope and the end of all his future expectation of glory and joy was to be with Christ after his departure from this life. (Not with three separate Gods.) And so he says: 'For me to live is Christ, and to die is gain. . . . For I am in a strait betwixt two, having a desire to depart, and to be with Christ; which is far better." (Ps. 1:21. 23.) The Lord Jesus was the apostle's aim, his highest ambition, his eternal goal, for he says: "I press toward the mark for the prize of the high calling of God (where?) in Christ Jesus." (Ph. 3:14.) The Apostle Paul never taught the Christians of old, like some of the apostate Catholic and Protestant leaders, that when we get to Heaven, we shall see three separate and distinct Persons, and that Jesus Christ is one of those three Persons, sitting side by side with the Father (the First Person). No, this is human philosophy concerning Christ and the mystery of God. But the Apostle rather warned them against such teaching, and said, "Beware lest any man spoil you through philosophy and vain deceit, after the tradition of men, after the rudiments of the world, and not after Christ. For in Him dwelleth all the fulness of the Godhead bodily." The Apostle Peter says: "Whom, having not seen, ye love; in whom, though now ye see Him not, yet believing, ye rejoice with joy unspeakable and full of glory: receiving the end of your faith, even the salvation of your souls." (I Pet. 1:8, 9.)

O, beloved fellow-Christians, remember, for time and eternity, that Jesus Christ is not only the DOOR through which alone we can enter into the eternal mysteries of the Deity, but He is also the WAY in which we shall walk in the ages to come, and as we walk in the light and glory of Him over there, we shall find Him also to be THE END. Therefore, we beseech you, take your eyes away from the best men that ever lived on the earth, and ask God to cleanse your mind from all the traditions of the so-called Church Fathers, and let the Holy Spirit, who has come into you, teach you all the truth (Christ) as it is in the Scriptures; let Him take from Christ and show unto you the things that "eye hath not seen, nor ear heard neither hath entered into the heart of man, the things which God has prepared for them that love Him," and hear the Spirit saying unto you, or Christ in the Holy Spirit:

"And He that sat upon the throne said, Behold, I make all things new. And He said unto me, Write: for these words are true and faithful."

Of Jesus' love I'm singing,
I praise Him every day;
He is my all in all, all in all;
He frees my soul from bondage,
He takes my guilt away,
Jesus is my all in all.
A strength in time of weariness,
A light where shadows fall;
All is all, all in all,
Jesus is my all in all.

Your unworthy brother, in Him who is my LORD, my God, my hope, and my All, a child of the Father who dwelleth and manifesteth Himself in the Son, a servant of Christ, and one who needs your earnest prayers, that I may be filled with all the fulness of God, according to Ephesians third chapter and nineteenth verse,

ANDREW D. URSHAN.

CHAPTER VIII.

The Fatherhood of God.

By A. D. Urshan.

THERE is some confusion among the people of God concerning the fatherhood of God, and the cause of such confusion is the conclusion of men on the mystery of godliness, who try by their limited thinking to explain the Deity (Godhead). If we had not such man-made creeds on the Godhead, the subject could be far better understood by the honest seekers after God, from the Bible itself. It must be remembered that the Bible clearly teaches that there is only one God, and that God is the Father. So we have one Father, God, whose lofty habitation is high Heaven. As our Lord instructed His disciples: "Call no man your father upon the earth; for one is your Father, which is in heaven." And the apostle also tells us: "But to us there is but one God; the Father, of whom are all things, and we in Him," etc. And in Ephesians fourth chapter the Apostle tells us who this Father is. He speaks of the Deity as "one Spirit"; "one Lord," "one God." Now the question arises, is the Holy Spirit God, and is the Lord, God? Yes, indeed. For God is the Father, the Lord Jesus (the Son), and the Spirit. All this three-one God is called "the Father of all, who is above all, and through all, and in you all." (Verses four to six.) The Scriptures teach that the whole Deity is the Father; that is, not only is the Father of our Lord Jesus Christ our Father, but the Holy Spirit is our Father also; and our Saviour taught us so, when He said: "Except ye be born of the Spirit" (John 3:5, 8). The WORD is our Father also, because we read that we are "being born again, not of corruptible seed, but of incorruptible, by the Word of God, which liveth and abideth forever." Again, "Begotten through the Word" and "Born of the Word" etc. I Pet. 1:23.

So when we are born of God, we are born by the Spirit, through the Word, the Spirit and the Word of the Father of our Lord Jesus Christ, hence, born of the three-one God. But the most important question concerning this heavenly relationship is, how and when are we born of God, and how and when does God become our Heavenly Father? We are not born of God until we accept the Son of God as our Saviour, Lord, and all. When we rightly do the accepting, God does regenerate us. Hence, we are born "not of blood, nor of the will of the flesh, nor of the will of man, but of God." And all this is done by his Holy Spirit, and that through faith in the Name of our Lord and Saviour. Thus we can be the children of God only "by faith in Christ Jesus;" for as many of us as have been baptized into Christ have put on Christ. There is neither Jew nor Greek, there is neither bond nor free, there is neither male nor female, for we are all "one in Christ Jesus." See Gal. 3:26-28. The modern teachings which affirm that all the human race are the children of God, and that God is the Father of all, regenerated and unregenerated, men and women, is absolutely contrary to Holy Writ; for there is only one family of God, and that family is being born again only in and through Jesus Christ.   Just as it is impossible for us to become the children of God apart from Jesus Christ, so it is impossible for God to become our Father apart from His Son Jesus Christ.   Hence we have a Father-God, and He is found in His Son, Jesus Christ our Lord.

This glorious, divine relationship gives the Deity's most blessed and gracious title, FATHER, to Jesus Christ; thus Jesus Christ "shall be called the Everlasting Father," as the prophet Isaiah said (Isa. 9:6).   Some people shrink from confessing Jesus Christ as their Father.   This shrinking is caused by the fear of men, who have concluded that Jesus Christ is the Son of God, therefore He cannot be called our Father-God.   But if one is willing to suffer the contradiction of all, and go to the Bible, he will easily see that Jesus Christ is our Father, because we are not only born of Him (the Word), but because His Father begets us in and through Him, and therefore becomes our Father only in His Son.   For we see in Isaiah fifty-third that the prophet speaks of our Saviour as of one who has a generation, saying: "He was taken from prison and from judgment, and who shall declare His generation?"   Again: "When thou shalt make his soul an offering for sin, He shall see his seed."   Who can have the seed and generate but one who is a father?   These two Scriptures make our Lord a father.   Is. 53:8, 10.

Again, the Apostle calls our Saviour "the second Adam, the Lord from Heaven."   If we all are the offspring of the first man Adam concerning the flesh, could we be concerning the Spirit, the children of any other one but the Lord Jesus, who is the second Adam, or the Father of the new race?   No, indeed.   As the old Adam is the father of the human race, so Jesus Christ is the father of the Heavenly race. I Cor. 15:45-48.

Again, the same Apostle, speaking of the Jerusalem which is above and is free, says, she is "the mother of us all."   See Gal. 4:26.   And if you trace that name Jerusalem all through the Scriptures, you will see it represents the Spirit in Zion, which travaileth and bringeth forth, and it also represents a heavenly mystery, the New Jerusalem being the wife of the Lamb.   Now, if JERUSALEM is our mother, and she is the wife of the Lamb, then we must be the children of her husband, who is Jesus Christ, the Lamb.   See Rev. 21.   Again, Our Saviour plainly announces Himself as being the Father of the overcomers; in the same chapter.   He says: "It is done.   I am Alpha and Omega, the beginning and the end.   I will give unto him that is athirst of the fountain of the water of life freely.   He that overcometh shall' inherit all things; and I will be his God, and he shall be my son."

Well, the backslidden Christians, who naturally entertain themselves with men's ideas and theology, are sometimes too shallow to understand the hidden mysteries in Christ Jesus, who is our All.   But the day is coming soon when the Son of Man comes with the great glory of the Father; then He shall be called by the overcoming Christians their Father-God, and He shall say unto them: "I am your God and you are my children."   Hallelujah!   This is not doing away with the identity of the Father of the Son, nor does it make Jesus Christ His own Father; but it confirms His own saying, that "the Father dwelleth in me," and "He that seeth me seeth the Father," and the teaching of the apostles, who pronounced Christ to be the image and revelator, hence the temple of God, in whom the Father of Lights dwelleth and manifesteth His full grace and glory. To Him be honor everlasting. Amen.

Again, when the Apostle, in the first chapter of Hebrews, in his great discourse concerning the Deity of our Lord, says: "But unto the Son he says, Thy throne, O God, is forever and ever" etc., he goes on to prove the greatness and high position and personality of the Son of God, by quoting a part of the forty-fifth psalm. The one who reads that psalm can see clearly that it is a prophecy of the King, Jesus, and His glorious Bride, and points to a great day when that King shall reign with His Bride, and then shall he be recognized by all the patriarchs, such as Abraham, Isaac, Jacob etc., as their divine Father. This might sound strange to us, knowing that Christ after the flesh is the Son of Abraham and the Son of David; nevertheless, the Scriptures, that cannot be broken, declare concerning Him:

"Instead of thy fathers shall be thy children, whom thou mayest make princes in all the earth. I will make thy name to be remembered in all generations: therefore shall the people praise thee forever and ever."

Here we see plainly that the fathers of our Saviour are become His children. How is that? We do not know. It is indeed a mystery beyond us, but we do know that the Scripture says so, and it is for us to believe it, putting away our own notions of theology, accepting and recognizing Jesus Christ as our all, to the glory of His Father which dwelleth in Him. Again, some may question that Jesus Christ is declared by the Scriptures to be "the Son and offspring of David." Yes, to this all the prophets and apostles agree, that He is the Son of David after the flesh. But it must not be forgotten that the Scriptures also declare Him to be "the root of David." (See Rev. 5:5 and 22:16.) Every gardener knows that the fruit of a tree is the offspring of the root: hence, the root is the father of the tree. So Jesus Christ, being the root of David, must be the father of David, and the Lord of David. Hallelujah! All these things show that we have a great and mysterious and eternal SAVIOUR, in whom we are complete, and He in us is the hope of glory. But one may ask, why do the Apostles never call Him the Father in all their epistles? It is because the message of the Gospel is to believe on the Son of God; for the Son of God came in the flesh, to save us and reconcile us and to bring us to a place where we shall be able, sometime in the coming age, to see this deep truth. Therefore Isaiah 9:6, and our Saviour's own declaration in Revelation 21:2, with Psalm 45:16 are prophecies yet to be fulfilled. And the fulfillment of the same will be at the second coming of Him "which is, which was, and which is to come." I, for one, am not led to preach Jesus Christ my Heavenly Father now; although I love to quote the above Scriptures and believe them with my whole heart; but I truly believe that, when we shall see our Saviour face to face and see the fulness of the Deity in Him and through Him shining forth with eternal glory. we shall not shrink then from calling Him "our Father" as well as "Lord God Almighty" in the ages to come. In the meantime, brethren, let us preach the Gospel that the Apostles preached, and also believe all such Scriptures making Jesus Christ even our divine Father, and worship His Father and our Heavenly Father in Him, putting away theological controversy on the Godhead, using only the terms that the Apostles used concerning the Deity. I have no doubt that, in doing so, we shall please God, the Father, the Son, and the Holy Ghost, and that He will bless us all in and through Jesus Christ, our All. Amen.

THE REVELATION
OF
JESUS CHRIST

BY

FRANK J. EWART

SYNOPSIS OF CONTENTS

Published by

PENTECOSTAL PUBLISHING HOUSE
3449 S. Grand Blvd.
St. Louis 18, Mo.

FOREWORD

The material in these pages first appeared in the Pentecostal Defender. Their re-appearance here, is not only because of the numerous urgent requests that they be published in book form, but, rather because of a profound conviction by the author that in this form they could have a real ministry in the Word.

The revelation of Jesus Christ that the Apostle Paul received to deliver to the church, was that Christ was the "mystery of God" (Col. 2:2, R.V.). In other words, according to Paul, Jesus Christ was the one, true God, veiled in flesh. I Tim. 3:16, "And without controversy, great is the mystery of godliness: God was manifest in the flesh." Paul earnestly warns the church, "Beware lest any man spoil you through philosophy and vain deceit, after the tradition of men, after the rudiments of the world, and not after Christ. For in him dwelleth all the fulness of the Godhead bodily" (Col. 2:8-9).

Now, this is the mystery that we are commanded to fellowship. It is the only possible way to sustain the absolute oneness of God. This revelation enables us to fellowship to the mystery of Jesus Christ's teachings: He disclaims any of the glory belonging to God, the Eternal Spirit, within Him. Jesus Christ was the last theophany: "God, who at sundry times and in divers manners spake unto the fathers by the prophets, hath in these last days spoken unto us in a son" (Heb. 1:1-2).

The seeming "separate identity" of Father and Son, is owing to the fact that Jesus invariably spoke from two distinct standpoints: That of the Son of God, our example in the flesh. As such, He was the "Sign Son." Then He spoke from the standpoint of the deity. Jesus tried to forestall this confusion in the minds of men, by the emphatic statements, "I and My Father are one," and, "I am in the Father and the Father is in me."

To the earnest request of Philip, "Lord, show us the Father and it sufficeth us," Jesus answered, "have I been so long time with you and dost thou not know me, Philip?" (John 14:9, R.V.). Philip's request was based on the statement of Jesus in the seventh verse; "If ye had known Me, ye would have known My Father also, and from henceforth ye know Him and have seen Him." Jesus Christ, here gave the most revolutionary "NO" in human thought, to the universal tendency of all Christendom, to separate the Father from the Son. "No man knoweth who the Son is but the Father; neither knoweth any man who the Father is but the Son, and he, to whomsoever the

Son will reveal Him." The marginal reading of the best Bibles, sustained by the Greek, puts "It" in place of "HIM" in this text. The word, "IT" relates to the Mystery of the Father in the Son. Jesus' own explanation is: "I am in the Father and the Father is in Me." So, William Phillips Hall, states, that the revelation of the Fatherhood of God is exclusively confined to the SON. If there was a separate identity of Father and Son as to individuality, Jesus would have answered His disciple Philip's query altogether different. His answer absolutely prohibits any separate identity. He was not here to hide the Father, or enshroud Him with mystery, impenetrable: He was here to reveal Him. The other disciples all shared in Philip's dilemma; but, after Pentecost this mystery of mysteries was perfectly clear. This was the fulfilment of His promise: "These things have I spoken unto you in proverbs: but the time cometh when I shall no more speak unto you in proverbs, but I shall show you plainly of the FATHER" (John 16:25).

To this pertinent question, on human lips ever since Jesus left the earth, "Who was Jesus Christ?" only one answer is scriptural: That is, He was God manifested in flesh. Theologians call this union, the "God-Man." But, the sad part of their vain theory about the Deity is, that they make Jesus a separate individual in Spirit Form from the Father—the SECOND Person—if you please. Bless His Name, He is not the second. He is the FIRST and the LAST—"God Over All, blessed, forever, Amen."

Every man in pulpit or pew, in priestly or preacher's garb, or otherwise arrayed, the voice of a creed or a free-lance, who teaches that Jesus Christ was not the Eternal Spirit—the Creator, manifested in flesh, labors under the same misapprehension of Him, as Philip and the other disciples, before the Spirit's revelation on and after the Day of Pentecost. The pathetic complaint of the Master, "Have I been so long time with thee, and yet hast thou not known Me," is directly applicable to them. To all who say that Jesus Christ is a second Person, making Him a secondary consideration in any sense whatsoever, Jesus is the "unknown God." Whom, therefore, they ignorantly worship. The pathetic and tragic statements made by the leaders in trinitarian circles, that they worship each one of the three persons or Gods separately, and that they know when they quit talking to one and commence talking to the other, shows what abysmal ignorance characterizes their doctrine of true worship. It is written, "Thou shalt worship the Lord, thy God, and HIM ONLY, shalt thou serve."

Paul preached God to these Athenian philosophers—"God that

made the world and all things therein." If that God was not Jesus Christ—the Logos, then John labored under an illusion; for he states: "He (Jesus) was in the world and the world was made by Him, and the world knew Him not," and lest anyone should be mislead about who created all things, he says, "All things were made by Him, and without Him was not anything made that was made."

With this blinding flash the cross of Calvary becomes too big for human apprehension—words fail to express the love and grace manifested there. God the eternal Father, did not send another, apart from Himself; it was He, Himself, that sacrificed His body! I John 3:16 declares that "God gave Himself for us." Calvary unlocked the flow of God's love, which is God's very nature, into the hearts of His creatures, making the "New Birth" possible. It is to the fuller unfolding of this "Mystery of Mysteries," the following pages are dedicated.

THE SOLITARY ONE

God is the final, certain, solitary ONE! A champion of the "Three-person God" recently made the statement: "The oneness of God is not and never was numerical." He triumphantly asserts that this is an end to all controversy on the Godhead question—a consummation devoutly to be desired; for, "**without controversy** great is the mystery of Godliness" (1 Tim. 3:16). So we can wipe our perspiring foreheads and say with the bewildered Isaac, "How hast thou found it so quickly my son?" (Gen. 27:20). This dear brother says, "these new-issueites are making a distinction without a difference." No, brother, we are simply insisting that there is a difference between venison and goat meat. The deceiver, Jacob, answered his blind old father, "Because the Lord thy God brought it to me." This assertion is made regarding the origin of the trinitarian doctrine, but unlike blind old Isaac, we turn away from it. We have meat to eat that they know not of. And since we have tasted of this meat, Rebekah (the backslidden church) cannot deceive us with her savory counterfeit dish.

The whole economy of divine government gathers round Deuteronomy 6:4, "Hear O Israel: the Lord, our God is one Lord!" This was the special truth that was committed to Israel to preserve among the nations of the earth. "GOD IS ONE!"

The sacred stewardship of this mystery must have been deeply impressed on the heart and mind of every devout Israelite; for we find James, Bishop of the first Christian Church, said, "You believe that God is one, and you are right: evil spirits also believe this and shudder." (Weymouth.)

If God is not a numerical one, why does He declare in Isaiah, "Thus saith the Lord, the HOLY ONE of Israel"? Why does He declare, "I am God and there is no God beside me"? Why does He claim to have performed the work of creation alone? When John 1:3 says, "All things were made by Jesus, the Logos, and without him was not anything made that was made"? If God is not a numerical one then why is it written, "Thou shalt worship the Lord thy God and Him only shalt thou serve," when Jesus received worship and commended Thomas for doing it? If God is not a numerical one, why did Jesus, who is supposed to be the SECOND PERSON in this trinity of Gods, claim to have power to forgive sins—the absolute prerogative of God?

The scriptural triunity of God is THREE IN ONE; not one di-

6

vided into THREE PERSONS — equal in essence, dignity and eternality. The writer was visiting a Trinitarian church recently and he noted a statement of their faith above the platform: "We believe in the Holy Trinity—Father, Son, and Holy Ghost." He began to muse and the fire of revelation burned: The Father is the first Person; the Son is the second Person, and the Holy Spirit is the third Person. Then the Father is the First and the Holy Spirit is the LAST, according to the carnal mind; but Jesus—the wisdom of God, said, "I am the FIRST and I am the LAST!" Everybody credits Him with being the SECOND, so we conclude He must be the whole THREE-IN-ONE.

If God is the HOLY THREE, then the Scripture, to be consistent, would have to speak of **THEIR FACES** instead of **HIS FACE. Their Names** instead of **HIS NAME** or **MY NAME,** as Jesus did. The Apostle Peter said, "Neither is there salvation in any other; for there is none other name under heaven whereby we must be saved. Weymouth translates "No SECOND Name." Matthew 28:19 cannot teach three names into which repentant sinners should be baptized or the entire Apostle band would never have baptized by immersion into the Name of Jesus Christ. One exponent of the Trinity theory declares that Acts 2:38 simply means that they were baptized into the Name of the Father and of the Son and of the Holy Spirit, in the Name or authority of Jesus; but Acts 19:5 reads, as every Greek scholar knows, "On hearing this they were baptized into the Name of the Lord Jesus." (See Weymouth.) Every student of Trinitarianism knows that they base their entire reasoning on Matt. 28:19, and yet that Scripture was never repeated—but always expounded—in every isolated example of Christian baptism in the Book of Acts. Why not be honest? Why try to evade a palpable conclusion that bats you in the eye as soon as you open the New Testament? Why turn the most sacred and complete picture of the cross work of Jesus—Christian Baptism—into something that divides the Deity and perpetuates a Roman Catholic dogma?

Jesus stated that He had declared the Name of the Father to the world. He calls this name, MY NAME, and says that repentance and remission of sins should be preached in MY NAME beginning at Jerusalem. This was precisely what took place at Pentecost. William Phillips Hall in his book, "A Wonderful Discovery," says, "Matthew 28:19 was never used as a baptismal formula by the Apostles." The nominal Christian church has confirmed his findings, and yet they continue doing a thing which they confess the Apostles never did.

Paul says, that even the heathen are without excuse for not believing in the ONE GOD Deity. He says the invisible things—even His eternal power and Godhead—can be understood by the things which are made. Look at the physical universe: It is crammed full of proofs of the Oneness of God. Take a tree: there's the sap, the wood and the bark—but brother, there is but ONE TREE. Take a light: It has three distinct properties, the antenic, calorific and luminiforous— but, brother, these three properties are one and indivisible. Remove one of them and you have no light.

All mathematical science may be reduced to a common factor— ONE! When you have said that you have said two. When you have said a million you have said one. You cannot dispense with or get beyond one. One is essential, two is accidental. God is behind everything, the final certain ONE. You cannot analyze or divide or explain HIM, yet He is ONE, all comprehending and invisible. When you have said that you have said all, when you have omitted that you have left everything out, and you simply babble only in chaotic confusion. Every intelligent Christian should exult in this one essential, impregnable, eternal truth. "I am the Lord, I change not, therefore ye sons of Jacob are not consumed." Israel was commissioned to give this greatest of all truths to the world as a nation, to produce the Christ in the flesh to manifest it; to write and preserve the Scriptures to prove it, and to manifest to the world the benefits of believing in the ONENESS of God instead of having Gods many and Lords many.

JESUS IS THE TRUE GOD

The Maker of the universe,
As man for man was made a curse.
The claims of law which He had made,
Unto the uttermost He paid.

His holy fingers made the bough
Which grew the thorns that crowned His brow.
The nails which pierced His hands were mined,
In secret places He designed.

He made the forest whence there sprung
The tree on which His body hung.
He died upon a cross of wood,
Yet made the hill on which it stood.

The sky that darkened o'er His head,
By Him above the earth was spread.
The sun that hid from Him its face,
By His decree was poised in space.

The spear which spilled His precious blood,
Was tempered in the fires of God.
The grave in which His form was laid,
Was hewn in rocks His hands had made.

The throne on which He now appears
Was His from everlasting years.
But a new glory crowns His brow,
And every knee to Him shall bow.

—Author unknown.)

GOD'S HIDDEN THINGS

"It is the glory of God to conceal a thing: but the honor of kings to search out a matter" (Prov. 25:2). When the blinding light flashed on Simon Peter, that Jesus was the Christ of God, Jesus said, "Blessed art thou, Simon Bar-Jona, for flesh and blood hath not revealed it unto thee but my Father which is in heaven." A marvellous commentary on this event is to be found in Luke 10:21, "In that hour Jesus rejoiced in spirit and said, I thank thee, O Father, Lord of heaven and earth, that thou hast hid these things from the wise and prudent and hast revealed them unto babes: even so, Father, for so it seemed good in Thy sight."

Jesus knew the limits of flesh and blood (the carnal mind). He knew that this transcendent truth was beyond the grasp of flesh and blood. The carnal mind cannot rise above the level of comparative knowledge: "Some say, thou art John the Baptist, some say Elijah, some say Jeremiah, or one of the prophets." This is **speculation** versus **revelation.** This is truth that is ever and must be revealed. Every solitary soul that knew it in the days of Jesus, received it by revelation from the Father. It was revealed to Simeon that he should not die until he had seen the Lord's Christ. Anna, the prophetess, got it by revelation. John the Baptist, the Apostle Peter, and Mary of Bethany all received the revelation. To all others Jesus was an inexplicable mystery.

Indeed, it is exactly the same today: Take such books as "The Man Nobody Knows," by Bruce Barton. He makes all kinds of human comparisons of Jesus. Eulogizes Him as the wisest and best of men, but only a man. He makes the emphatic declaration that Jesus was the son of Joseph and Mary, and triumphantly asserts that the Bible teaches this. He quotes Philip, a man with no revelation of who Jesus was, at that time (see John 1:45). The book leaves Jesus dead on the cross—there is no resurrection—so the greatest thing, and the very thing that proved Jesus to be the Son of God, is left out. Never was the carnal mind of man placed at such a disadvantage as when it approaches this question: "Whom do men say that I, the Son of Man, am?" The answer to that question is one of the things which it is the glory of God to hide.

The things that Jesus referred to when He said, "I thank thee, O Father, Lord of heaven and earth, that thou hast hid these things from the wise and prudent and hast revealed them unto babes," involves this very thing we are discussing: "No man knoweth who the Son is but the Father; and who the Father is but the Son, and he, to whomsoever the Son will reveal Him." Now, in Weymouth's translation, the word "Him" is "it." That means the mystery that Paul called "Confessedly great" and said, "God was manifest in the flesh" (see 1 Tim. 3:16). It is the mystery described by John, when he said, "And the logos (God) came in the flesh. The mystery of God even Christ" (R.V.). It is the most sacredly guarded secret. The only being in the universe who knew the Son was God, Himself: "No man knoweth who the Son is but the Father." So when Peter got the tremendous truth in one blinding flash, Jesus said, "Peter, you got that not from flesh and blood, but from my Father." Because, no man knows the secret but Him.

Now let us take a deeper step into this revealed mystery: "Neither knoweth any man who the **Father** is but the **Son.**" A double revelation. The two go together, because these two are ONE. You cannot get a revelation of the Son without a revelation of the Father, the Father reveals the Son. Philip went to the Son for a revelation of the Father and got it. Peter went to the Father for a revelation of the Son and he got it—Yes, got it so perfectly clear that Jesus confirmed it, and revealed its source. "Whosoever denieth the Son, the same hath not the Father: he that acknowledgeth the Son hath the Father also" (I John 2:23). If it had been possible to know the Son apart from the Father, when Philip asked Jesus, "Lord, show us the Father and it sufficeth us," Jesus would have done so. On the contrary, He startled Philip and the other disciples by asking, in tones of reproof, "Have I been so long time with you, and yet hast thou not known me, Philip?" If Jesus wasn't reproving the disciples for seeking a knowledge of the Father apart from Himself, then these words are utterly inexplicable. They certainly give a head-on collision to the doctrine of **two separate identities.** To accommodate that untenable theory, Jesus would have said: Philip, I and the Father are TWO. I am not the Father clothed in flesh, but the second person of the trinity veiled in flesh. Instead, we have words which make the most absolute "NO" to all this: "He that hath seen ME hath seen the Father, I am in the Father and the Father is in me. The words that I speak unto thee I speak not of myself, but the Father which dwelleth in me, he doeth the works." No separate identity there!

Thank God for the supplement to that startling, breath-taking statement of Jesus: "And he to whomsoever the Son will reveal it." Reveal what? The mystery "That God was in Christ reconciling the world unto Himself." "That I am in the Father and the Father is in me." That is the way Jesus explained the mystery. If people would receive that explanation just as it stands, and **fellowship the mystery,** there would be no painful division over the Godhead question. Then, everybody would know the Son, according to Jesus' revelation of Himself. "If ye had known me ye should have known my Father also: and from henceforth ye know **Him** and have seen **Him!** To accommodate the Trinitarian theory Jesus should have said, "And from henceforth ye know US and have seen US." This may seem irreverent. It is not so intended. It is stated thus to show that logically, if the separate identity theory is true, that is exactly what Jesus must have said in order to tell the exact truth.

Now, to apprehend what the disciples understood by Jesus' words, we set down a statement from the pen of one who was present and recorded what he said: "And we know that the Son of God is come and has given us an understanding, that we might know Him that is true, and we are in Him that is true, even in His Son, Jesus Christ. He is **the True God,** and eternal life" (1 John 5:20).

Another of the hidden things of God is the hidden wisdom. No man that lives or ever did live can solve "The mystery of God—even Christ," without this hidden wisdom. "But we speak the wisdom of God in a mystery, even the **Hidden Wisdom,** which God ordained before the world unto our glory, which none of the princes of this world knew: for had they known it, they never would have crucified the Lord of Glory" (1 Cor. 2:7-8). Jesus, on the cross prayed, "Father, forgive them; for they know not what they do." Jesus understood! He knew that if the secret of His identity had been disclosed to these religious leaders they never would have crucified Him, and the Scriptures would remain unfulfilled to this day. That is the reason why Jesus invariably warned His disciples to tell no man that He was the Christ.

"Now, this wisdom that cometh from above is pure, peaceable, gentle, and easy to be intreated, full of mercy and good works, without partiality and without hypocrisy" (Jas. 3:17). It is the gift of God. And it is given unto us that we might understand the hidden things of God. "For the Spirit searcheth all things, yea, the deep things of God."

This great truth is exemplified in the words of Agur, the son of Jakeh. He was evidently exercised about the hidden things that puzzle the carnal minded of today. He knew his utter inability to read aright this most inscrutable of all mysteries. So he breaks forth: "Surely, I am more brutish than any man and have not the understanding of a man. I neither learned wisdom nor have the knowledge of the Holy." Then he discloses his problem: "Who hath ascended up into heaven or descended? Who hath gathered the winds in his fists, and who hath bound the waters in a garment? Who hath established all the ends of the earth? **What is his Name and what is His Son's Name, if thou cans't tell?**" (Prov. 30:1-4). Paul said, "Now he that ascended is the same that descended, first into the lower parts of the earth." He also tells us that this same one ascended far above all heavens, that He might fill all things with Himself. Everybody acknowledges that Agur and Paul are speaking of the same Eternal ONE, and Paul tells us that this ONE is Jesus.

The ONE NAME of the Deity—Father, Son and Holy Spirit— forever settles the Oneness of God. Every well instructed Trinitarian will tell you that the theory stands or falls with Matthew 28:19. However, this Scripture cannot be understood in the light of Apostolic precept and example if the NAME mentioned there is to be understood as Three Names—"Father, Son, and Holy Spirit." Jesus said that He had God's Name and had revealed it to His disciples. Peter said, "There is no other name given among men." God said in Isaiah, "I am Jehovah (or Yahweh), that is My Name." Jesus in the Greek is Yahweh in the Hebrew. It means, The Lord Who Saves. And so it is written in Matthew about the Babe of Bethlehem, "His name shall be called Jesus, because He shall save His people from their sins." So the Hidden Wisdom in a mystery reveals Christ as the mystery of God. **"The mystery of God, even Christ"** (Col. 2, R.V.).

THESE THREE ARE ONE

We have been accused of ignoring the threeness of the Deity which is emphasized everywhere in the Scriptures. This charge is based on the useless contention over what the Threeness, or Trinity of the Deity means. The word "TRINITY," as explained in Webster's Dictionary, is based on its usage in Catholic and Protestant Churchianity: "Three persons in individuality; One in essence." If Webster had explained the word, according to the Bible manifestation of what such a word means, his explanation would have rocked all Christendom, and probably made his dictionary exceedingly unpopular. Tacitly, it would have appeared thus: "ONE, in essence, with a three-fold manifestation."

It is the interpretation of the manifestations of the ONE ETERNAL SPIRIT, that has violated and disrupted the unity of the Godhead. This palpable threeness, in the manifestations does not prove the Deity is composed of three separate individuals. This is unthinkable; for it would contradict Jehovah's statement of Himself: "Hear, O Israel, Jehovah, our Elohim, is ONE Elohim." We are blandly told regarding this conclusive statement that God does not mean to say that He is only ONE, because He is really THREE, He is only ONE in essence—ONE WITH THE OTHER THREE. But God declares again: "I am the Lord, and there is none else, there is no God beside me" (Isa. 45:5). And again, Jehovah declares, "I am God, and there is none like me" (Isa. 46:8). Tradition says there are two others exactly like Him. Exactly alike in dignity, essence and eternality! If God is not the isolated, solitary ONE, then Scriptural language is inexplicable.

As to the threeness, about which traditional teachers have said so much, such as, "Sun, moon and stars, the three-decked Ark, the three Angels that appeared to Abraham, and to the Father, Son and Holy Spirit, of the Apostolic benediction." Every intelligent student revolts from any inference that these expressions involve a multiplicity of Persons in the Deity. The three decks in the Ark make but ONE Ark. Sap, bark and wood make but ONE tree. Body, soul and spirit, make ONE man. Father, Son and Holy Spirit make ONE God. When God said, "Let US make man in our own image," He used the word US like an editor uses the word WE. The US in the first case signifies Father, Logos and Spirit; the WE in the second signifies the body, soul and spirit, of every real man. If you interpret the words "US" and "OUR" of the 26th verse of Genesis 1 to

14

mean more than one individual, then the 27th verse contradicts your interpretation: "So God created man in HIS OWN IMAGE." We readily admit that there is a great mystery involved in these statements of Scripture regarding God. Which horn of the dilemma will you take? Paul declares, "Great is the mystery of Godliness," and he exhorts us to "fellowship the mystery."

The normal mind of man revolts from the thought of there existing from eternity more than ONE Creator, First-Cause, Redeemer, or Saviour. The absolute ONENESS of God finds its complete exemplication in Jesus Christ, who insisted and reiterated the great truth, "I and my Father are ONE." James indorsing the faith of the first disciples, says, "You believe that God is ONE, and you are right; demons also believe it and shudder" (see Weymouth). Paul calls Jesus "The ONLY WISE GOD," and John declares, "He is the TRUE GOD and eternal life." We have not presented all our evidence on this vital controversy, but enough to rest our case for the impartial consideration of any spiritually minded jurists.

The name and nature of God are synonymous, and there is a significant harmony in the Scriptural language used about God and His Name. It is pertinently significant that the ablest defenders of the Trinitarian position will admit that Matthew 28:19 is their strongest Scriptural proof of the "Three Person Trinity Godhead." They have to simply ignore the facts that in the Greek the word "NAME" is singular, which is in keeping with its use throughout the New Testament Scriptures. God's name is never plural. The contention that Elohim should be translated "The adorable ones," is utterly absurd, either from a Scriptural or scholarly viewpoint. Elohim kept very bad company back in the Old Testament. It was used to designate heathen gods, and in some cases demons were called Elohim. The word was simply used as the Hebrew for God or Deity.

As every honest student must admit, the great commission as recorded in Matthew 28:19, should read, **"Baptizing them into the NAMES,"** in order to accommodate the Trinitarian theory of the Deity. Even if this changing of the singular to the plural illusion is winked at, still they are faced with the inexplicable dilemma of three names to accommodate their three individualities, when God's Word declares that there is only one name. Yahosua, or Yaweh, means Saviour in the Hebrew; Jesus means Saviour in the Greek. God said to Moses, "This is my name and this is my memorial to all generations" (Ex. 3:15). Peter said that Jesus Christ was the only name given under heaven among men, whereby we must be saved. Paul said, "God highly exalted Jesus, and gave him THE NAME which is above every name, and, in that Name every knee should bow and every tongue confess that Jesus Christ is Lord of all, to the glory of God the Father." He wrote to the Colossians, "And whatsoever ye do in word or deed, do all in the name of the Lord Jesus, giving thanks to God and the Father by Him."

It is a little short of impiety to maintain that there are three distinct names (no matter what theory you wish to propagate) when God's Word so explicity and emphatically declares that there is only ONE NAME. Again, such an interpretation of the great commission logically involves its proponents in the untenable theory that Father, Son and Holy Spirit are three names of the Deity. It will pay us to be honest with our enlightened consciences: God's law demanded three witnesses to any truth. Nowhere in the Bible are these three words called names, nor is there a hint at baptism being performed in the formula of "Father, Son and Holy Spirit," throughout the Acts of the Apostles. If one single, isolated example of Christian baptism could be found in the Bible to fit the trinitarian interpretation of the Great Commission there would be some excuse for intelligent people adopting it; however, just as Brother E. N. Bell, in defense of baptizing in Jesus' Name, said, "I believe that the Apostles knew how to interpret Matthew 28:19," we also believe and therefore have we spoken.

If, as the ablest of exponents of the three-name-baptismal-formula assert, that this mode of baptism is the greatest proof of the three person Godhead, then that theory is refuted by the Apostles every time they baptize repentant sinners into the name of Jesus Christ.

Would it be an impertinent deduction from Apostolic example to say that every time a candidate for baptism is baptized into the name of Jesus Christ by God's ministers today, it is a continued refutation of the theory that God subsists in a three-fold-personality, which demands three individual names? Let every honest Christian think of that! The writer has baptized literally thousands into the name of Jesus Christ and continues this practice today. And everyone he so baptizes, in his judgment, is God's repudiation of any theory that divides Him into three individuals, which are known by three separate names, which must be used in Christian baptism.

The writer was talking to a minister of the Brethren of Christ Church recently and enquired humbly, and for his own information, why their theology led them to baptize believers three times, face downwards. The brother, a very humble and very earnest man of God, replied that it was considered the only form of baptism that would fit their belief in the three-person-Godhead. He went on to explain that these three persons, if they existed, must be equal in essence and majesty, therefore they should bury or baptize the believer in each of the three separate names. I enquired further about the custom of baptizing them face down, and was informed that as baptism was stated to be in likeness of Christ's death and He died with His face down, they believed that this form was the only way to carry out the exact likeness of His death in baptism. This mode of baptizing is called "Trine-Immersion" and is ridiculed by the great majority of Trinitarian ministers; but let them look to their laurels as true exponents of the mind of God, for if the three persons are distinct as to individuality, and yet equal in dignity, majesty and honor, the practice of the Brethren Church is more correct than is their own. A more absolute refutation of the three person or three name baptism, could hardly be imagined than Paul's question to the Corinthians: "Was Paul crucified for you, or were you baptized in the name of PAUL?"

GOD ONE IN NAME AND NATURE

The English word "God" is the equivalent of the Hebrew "Elohim." Elohim simply means a god, or deity. It is applied to the heathen gods as well as to our Elohim (God). If the Apostle Paul had been writing his first letter to the Corinthians in the Hebrew language, he would have written down the famous announcement of chapter 8, verse 4, "And there is none other Elohims, but one." Again in the 5th verse, "For though there be that are called Elohims, whether in heaven or in earth . . . but to us there is one Elohim." In Galatians 3:20, "But Elohim is one," In James 2:19, "Thou believest that Elohim is one, thou doest well, the devils believe also and tremble." There are many more Scriptures, but the law of God only demands three witnesses in order to establish a truth; so here are the witnesses to establish the important truth that GOD IS ONE. That is intrinsically ONE. He cannot be a multiplicity of Deities and sustain the inerrancy of His own declarations about Himself. "Hear, O Israel, Jehovah, our Elohim, is ONE ELOHIM."

A dear brother made the statement that God is essentially One in essence but three in manifestation. This is substantially correct; but these three are the ONE ELOHIM in dispensational manifestations. The Holy Spirit is the one eternal Spirit that brooded over the face of the deep in creation. There is none other. Jesus said, "God is a Spirit" (John 4:24). Paul said, "Now the Lord is that Spirit" (2 Cor. 3:17). So we would identify the one Elohim as the Holy Spirit who came on the Day of Pentecost according to the promise of the Father, and inaugurated a new dispensation, called the dispensation of the Holy Spirit. When Jesus said, "He that seeth me seeth the Father." And again, "I will not leave you without a COMFORTER, I will come to you" (John 14:9, 18). In other words, the secret is revealed: God, who appeared as the Son, and later as the Holy Spirit, was and is the one eternal Elohim. The Theophanies did not multiply HIM. Neither did His dispensational manifestations of Himself. The literal of Hebrews 1:1-2 reads, "God hath in these last days spoken out of a Son."

Elohim, the ONE, is exceedingly jealous lest His people should be foolish enough to try and make Him three. Therefore, He has caused it to be written, "It is the glory of God (Elohim) to conceal a thing: but the honor of kings to search out a matter" (Prov. 25:2).

"No man can say that Jesus Christ is Lord (Jehovah) but by the Holy Spirit" (1 Cor. 12:3). This involves the antithesis that no man can say that Jesus is not Jehovah (God) and speak with the inspiration of the Holy Spirit. So, if God (Elohim) is essentially one in essence He cannot possibly be regarded as three in manifestation. The doctrine of the Trinity insists that there were three in heaven from eternity; not three persons as to corporeity—to be sure—but three Spirit Beings as to individuality. That there were three from eternity, and the middle one, or the second person, left the other two and came down and was incarnated through the Virgin birth, and died on the cross, not as God, but as the second person of the eternal Trinity. If the victim of Calvary really existed from eternity, and was equal with God in dignity and essence, yet He was separate from the Father as to individuality, this is a flagrant violation of the unity of the Godhead.

When we consider the ONENESS of God from the standpoint of His Name, we have the same irrefutable confirmation as we have in the consideration of His Oneness from the standpoint of His nature. Indeed, the confirmation is so overwhelming that we are amazed how any intelligent and spiritual person, who can weigh the value of Scriptural evidences, can possibly fail to see the truth.

No man could possibly have put the interpretation on Matthew 28:19 that Peter put on it, confirmed by the Eleven who stood up with him, if he had spoken from the human standpoint. If he had not tarried until, but went forth before he was endued with the Spirit of truth, sent to lead us into all the truth, especially concerning Jesus, then he would most assuredly have done what people are doing today who have not waited on God in the spirit for the revelation of the truth. People realize this palpable conclusion, and try to evade it by saying that the formula used invariably in the Acts of the Apostles, is not the same; it is sometimes Lord Jesus, as in Acts 19:5, and sometimes Jesus Christ, as in Acts 2:38. Once "In the Name of the Lord," as in Acts 10:48.

Now what are these people trying to prove by this assertion? Simply that the repentant believer was not baptized into the Name of the Lord Jesus Christ, but by the authority of Jesus Christ, into the Name of the Father and of the Son and of the Holy Ghost. There can be no other motive in using the argument. However, the fact which is confirmed by the scholarship of Christendom, mentioned by William Phillips Hall, in his book, "A Remarkable Biblical Discovery—The Name of God," namely, is that the further you go back in manuscript research, you will find that the full name, the Lord Jesus Christ, is used in connection with Christian baptism.

Look at the other horn of the dilemma: That the formula, "Into or in the Name of the Lord Jesus Christ," means not a formula for baptism, but the authority in which they were baptized, into the Name (singular) of the Father, Son and Holy Ghost! Such a presumption is absolutely foreign to the Apostolic precept and practice. It is an ingenious invention to offset the Apostolic practice of baptizing believers into the Name of the Lord Jesus Christ. However, like all other inventions of the mind of man, it dwindles in the light of Scripture.

Take the Ephesians for an example. "Into what were you baptized?" Paul asked. "Into John's baptism," they replied. "John," he said, "administered a baptism of repentance, bidding the people believe on one who was to come after him; namely, on Jesus." On hearing this they were baptized into the Name of the Lord Jesus. (Weymouth's Translation.) There is not an accredited translation of the Scriptures, which exchanges the word "NAME" for the word "AUTHORITY." Yet we are blandly told that the word Name means authority. According to this reasoning, the Lord's Prayer should read, "Our Father which art in heaven: Hallowed be thy authority." How silly! The argument only needs to be mentioned in order to be rejected by every honest exponent of the Word of God. Yet, when the writer first commenced to preach baptism into the Name of Jesus, over 27 years ago, he was met with this absurd argument.

Again, if you interpret the phrase, "Father, Son and Holy Ghost," to be names, then you are giving God three names, when the Scripture emphatically declares that He has but one name. The name that God gave Moses out of the burning bush, translated, "I AM," is declared to be His name and His memorial unto all generations. That name is carried on in the Hebrew name, "Yahoshua," and "Jesus" is the equivalent in the Greek. Jesus Himself claimed that God gave Him His Name. That He had declared it to His disciples, to be declared by them to the world. No wonder we find such an emphasis on the name of Jesus in the early chapters of the Book of Acts.

The Scofield Bible has a heading above Acts 4:17 called: "Teaching in the Name of Jesus Forbidden." How significant! If, as we have been advised, the words Father, Son, and Holy Ghost, are the names of the Trinity of persons in the Deity, why is there an unbroken silence maintained about baptisms in these names in the entire Book of Acts? Why is there no mention made of Father, Son and Holy Ghost, in any formula of baptism known and used by the Apostles? If, as Dr. Scofield says, "Father, Son, and Holy Ghost, is the final name of the one true God," Why do we never find it mentioned in connection with the work of the ministry? If Dr. Scofield's statement is correct, then we would find the Apostles praying for sick people in this threefold name, baptizing into it; for that is exactly what Jesus commanded them to do—if His words can be interpreted in the literal. We find no hint at such a procedure; on the contrary, we find Paul commanding, "And whatsoever ye do in word or deed, do all in the name of the Lord Jesus, giving thanks to God and the Father by Him" (Col. 3:17). So we see that the unity of God is sustained by the absolute unity or oneness of His name as taught and practiced by Jesus and the Apostles. So palpable is this truth to honest Bible students that even ardent Trinitarians are teaching baptism into the Name of the Lord Jesus Christ. One of them writes, "If this revelation be not true, then the first outpouring of the Holy Ghost resulted in the most colossal contradiction of all time."

PREROGATIVES OF THE DEITY

The One True God has declared, "I am Jehovah, that is my name: and my glory will I not give to another" (Isaiah 42:8). This Scripture reveals God's burning jealousy in regard to His exclusive, solitary, unshared glory. Since His glory means His honor, veracity, purity, wisdom, and omnipotence, and He could not claim to be absolute Deity without these peerless attributes, we can see at a glance the reason He jealously claims glory that belongs to the solitary, superlative ONE TRUE GOD.

So God is revealed as the guardian of three prerogatives of Deity: Creator-ship, forgiveness of Sin, and Worship. The glory of God consists of these and other exclusive rights. Let us examine them!

Little need be said regarding the first of these three. The Bible opens with one telic statement that involves two astounding facts, namely, God's being and His creatorship: "In the beginning God created the heaven and the earth." So Moses wrote, "In the beginning God." John wrote, "In the beginning was the Word (Logos)." Which is right? John settled the matter, in his next statement: "And the Logos was God." Then John declares that the Logos was the Creator: "All things were made by him and without him was not anything made that was made."

The Trinitarian theory absolutely violates the unity of the Godhead in creation. If there are three separate Persons in the Deity, then, when John declares, "and the Logos was God," we naturally interrogate, "Which Person or God?" This interrogation would be perfectly valid and reasonable in the light of Orthodox Theology; but in the light of revelation it is arrant blasphemy. John says, "The Word (Logos) came in the flesh." And it is written in 1 Tim. 3:16, "God was manifest in the flesh." The inescapable conclusion is that God, the eternal Spirit, was incarnated in the person of His Son. Instead of the second person of the Deity being incarnated it was God, Himself, the whole Deity. Paul declares, "For in him all the fulness of the Godhead was pleased to dwell" (Marginal reading) (Col. 1:19). This explains why Jesus persistently declared, "I and my Father are one," and again, "He that seeth me sees the Father." It is the explanation of the first and great commandment "Hear, O Israel, the Lord our God is ONE Lord." The correct translation of James 2:19 reads, "You believe that God is ONE, and you are right." Not as in the Authorized Version, "You believe that there is one God." Every Trinitarian professes to believe that, but, alas, how

22

many hold to the old time-worn traditional dogma that denies that GOD is ONE! The preponderating evidence of Scripture denies that there were three separate persons operating in the work of creation; for every statement of the Bible confirms Genesis 1:1: "In the beginning God created the heaven and earth."

The next in order is God's exclusive prerogative of absolving sin. The Old and New Testaments unite in the declaration that God alone can forgive sins. Sin is essentially foreign to the nature of God. It is mutiny in the family of God, the Father. However, God never absolves in apart from the sacrifice of Calvary. God declares that He is Israel's Redeemer, but He redeemed the world by the blood of Jesus on the cross. Paul calls this blood the blood of God. "Feed the church of God which He hath purchased with His own blood" (Acts 20:28). It is significant that this passage is the same in the Revised Version. The cross of Calvary was no after-thought with God. Christ was the Lamb slain from the foundation of the world. He shed His own blood not for our sins only but for the sins of the whole world. On the cross Jesus filled two roles: He was the High Priest after the order of Melchisedec, and He was the Lamb of God that the High priest offered in sacrifice. Even on the cross Jesus assumed the prerogatives of the Deity. He forgave the sins of the dying felon at His side: "Verily I say unto thee, today shalt thou be with me in paradise."

When the man with the palsy was let down through the roof before Jesus, He, knowing the reasoning of the Pharisees, said, "Son, thy sins be forgiven thee." Then the Pharisees cried out, "This man speaketh blasphemies. Who can forgive sins but God only?" Then Jesus asked them, which was easier, to heal his sins or his deadly malady. This is followed by the stunning statement: "But that ye may know that the Son of Man hath power on earth to forgive sins (He saith to the sick of the palsy) 'I say unto thee, arise, take up thy bed and go forth into thine house'." This man came to the Lord with his back on the bed, but went home with the bed on his back, and the people said, "We never saw it on this fashion before." Jesus was the Lamb of God that taketh away the sins of the world. It was impossible for the blood of bulls and goats to take away sin. Jesus on Calvary was the finale of the sacrificial system. "He put away sin by the sacrifice of Himself." John the Baptist said of Him, "Behold the Lamb of God that taketh away the sin of the world."

The third sacred prerogative of Deity is the honor to receive worship. It would seem self-evident that God is the only isolated being in the universe to be worshipped, and yet idolatry was one of the most common sins of Israel. To worship an idol god is no worse in God's sight than to worship a mere man like Father Divine. We have several instances in the New Testament where worship was offered the Apostles and they disowned, disclaimed and repudiated such honor. God's anger was kindled against His people when they bowed down to gods of the heathen and worshipped in the high places.

Israel's great temptation to idolatry came through their desire to worship a god that they could see. When they thought Moses had left them, they made a golden calf and worshipped that. So God came down to earth in the form of a man. God's appearance in the form of angels and men were typical of the final theophany. He laid aside His unapproachable glory, and robed Himself in Adam's clay. He fulfilled His own law, paid the penalty it demanded, took the body that was prepared for Him to Calvary and sacrificed it, then after three days and nights, raised it up again, took it into heaven, and Paul says, "In Him dwelleth all the fulness of the Deity bodily."

Jesus said to Satan, "Get thee hence, Satan, for it is written, thou shalt worship the Lord, thy God, and Him only shalt thou serve."

Jesus is called "The only wise God" and "The True God" (Jude 25, 1 John 5:20).

Jesus received worship on earth. He said, "That all men should honor the Son even as they honor the Father." When Thomas fell at His sacred feet and cried, "My Lord and my God," Jesus did not rebuke him. He said, "Thomas thou hast believed because thou hast seen; blessed are they that have not seen, yet have believed." We ask, what was He talking about? Believed what? There can be but one answer: Believed that He was the one true God that alone could be worshipped. The syrophenician woman worshipped Jesus, and the blind man whom He healed worshipped Him. Paul tells us that in the great finale every knee shall bow in worship and every tongue will confess what we are trying to prove here: "That Jesus Christ is Lord of All, to the glory of God the Father." We close this brief article with the last words of the last Apostle: "And we know that the Son of God is come and has given us an understanding (not a misunderstanding) that we might know Him that is true, and we are in Him that is true, even in His Son Jesus Christ. He is the true God and eternal life. Little children, guard yourselves from idolatry. **Amen."**

THE TRINITY EXAMINED

The orthodox explanation of the doctrine called the Trinity has never varied since its introduction by the Roman Catholic synod back at the beginning of the third century: "One God in substance, dignity and eternality, three Persons as to individuality." To illucidate this explanation it is officially stated that God the Father, is the first person; Jesus, the Son, is the second Person; and the Holy Spirit is the third Person. Jesus Christ gave the most revolutionary "NO" in the history of thought to this flagrant disruption of God's Oneness. He, in His final message to the church, said, "I am the first and the last" (Rev. 1:11). We paraphrase thus: Orthodoxy say the Father is the first, the Son the second, and the Holy Spirit the third; but Jesus declared that He was the First and the Last and He is universally acknowledged to be "THE SECOND," therefore He must be the "THREE IN ONE." Paul's explanation of the Deity is: "For in Him dwelleth all the fulness of the Godhead bodily" (Col. 2:9).

The word "TRINITY" is not a Bible word. That wouldn't matter if the meaning given to the word scripturally defines the DEITY. It is admitted by all Christendom that the Deity is "THREE IN ONE," but the great difference is regarding the identity of that ONE. Jesus declared that the Father was dwelling in HIM. He likewise claimed that the Holy Ghost was dwelling in Him, but not apart nor separate from God, the Father; for the Holy Ghost is God.

It is admitted that the word "Person," or indeed "Persons," cannot be found in the Bible for defining either God or what people call the Godhead or Deity. Every Greek scholar admits that Hebrews 1:3 should be, "the expression of his substance." As for the plural word, "Persons," the only place I can find it with any relevancy to the Deity is, "He will surely reprove you, if ye do secretly accept persons" (Job 13:10). I therefore suggest a platform for all Christendom, especially that small part of it called Pentecostal, to unite on: Dismiss unscriptural words. Use "TRIUNITY" instead of "TRINITY"; "Substance" instead of "PERSON," and "Entities" instead of "Persons." Accept the Bible definition of God at face value: "For it is in Christ that the fulness of God's nature (or substance) dwells embodied" (Col. 2:9; Wey.). If we must use the word "TRINITY," give it a scriptural meaning. Make God the "THREE IN ONE"; not the "ONE IN THREE." Conform to Jesus' teachings that HE is the ONE. Trinity means "Three in One"; not One in Three, as the Roman

Catholics decided, and the Protestants blindly followed them in their official definition.

What makes this doctrine so subversive to the teaching of the Apostles and Jesus, is not only owing to the fact that it divides God, the Creator, up into Three equal Persons, but maintains that there was always three in heaven and that the middle one (the eternal Son) left the other two and came down to be incarnated in the Son of Mary, who was born in Bethlehem's manger. This is confusion worse confounded; for if Jesus of Nazareth was the second Person of the Trinity, incarnated, then the "Eternal Sonship Theory" is true, and since the Scripture of truth declares that the Child born to Mary was to be called the **"Mighty God and the Everlasting Father;"** now who was Jesus Christ—the Eternal Son or the Everlasting Father? John 3:16 declares that God gave His Only Begotten Son. Jesus was begotten in the womb of the Virgin Mary by God, the Holy Spirit, and named before He was born. We ask the adherents of this theory, when was this ETERNAL SON begotten? They answer, away back in the beginning." Impossible! The Son of Mary was **God's only begotten Son.** It is true that a small minority of those who believe in the Trinity as popularly held and taught, do not agree that Jesus Christ was merely the second Person of the Godhead or the Eternal Son, but the theory as received from the Roman Catholic Church and taught by the vast majority of Protestant churches, is substantially that there were always three Persons in heaven and One submitted to incarnation by the Virgin Birth and died on Calvary.

The doctrine of the Trinity in its introduction as a fundamental tenet of the faith, in the third century, kept very bad company. Transubstantiation, indulgences, Mariolatry, Infallibility of the Pope, Purgatory, and many others companied with the Trinity. These tenets of the Roman Catholic creed held the field from Constantine to Luther. After the reformation their imposition was resisted at the cost of martyrdom.

Subsequent to Luther, Protestants have repudiated all the above fundamentals of the Catholic Church, with the noted exception of the doctrine called The Holy Trinity. The Athanasian Creed, adopted at the Nicean Council in 325 A.D., made the Trinity a fundamental tenet.

Now Jesus, the Head of the church could not be obvious to the most tragic crisis in the future history of the One Body or Church He died and rose again in order to build. He therefore warned us of it in the parable of the woman (Roman Catholic Church) who took leaven (corrupt doctrine) and hid it in **THREE** measures of meal, till the whole was leavened. (Matt. 13:33.) She made a perfect job of it—never stopped till the whole was leavened. There is not a creed among the many in Christendom today, of recognition among the great imposing religious organizations from the Roman Catholic down to the Pentecostal movement, that has not been affected by the leaven. In 1914 God made His final move to raise up a people to restore the One Body or Church of the Apostolic Age. The revelation on which the New Issue (so-called) was formed, struck right at the very heart of what the WOMAN in the parable (The Nicean Council) did. Then God raised up His witnesses, "That I am GOD and there is none other." This was their battle cry. Luther's battle cry was, "Back from the **Pope** to the **Bible.**" Ours is "Back from **Pope to Christ.**" These stalwart witnesses have received a new vision, and their protest against the Woman hiding the deadly leaven in THREE measures of meal has been heard all throughout Christendom. They will never hold their peace until the last vestige of this leaven is purged from the Gospel message and we have the pure, unadultered, unleavened faith that was **once** for all delivered to the saints.

We have already gained the first-line-trenches. The startling book, "A Remarkable Biblical Discovery—The Name of God," by William Phillips Hall, was written in response to the cry of Protestant Orthodoxy, headed by Doctor Gaebelien, as the preface asserts, for more light or revelation on the Name of God. This discovery that startled Christendom is "That the Name of the Father, Son, and Holy Ghost is Lord Jesus Christ." This book has had a ready and remarkable sale. In it the author declares "That if the Great Commission in Matthew 28:19 had been universally interpreted in harmony with Apostolic precept and practice, and believers baptized into the Name of Jesus, the absolute Deity of Jesus Christ would never have been questioned." The greatest leaders in Protestant Christendom have praised the findings of the author of the above book, and acknowledged their validity in the light of the Scriptures. Many of these Great Men have been honest enough to confess their belief that the word "PERSONS" when used regarding the Godhead, does violence to the absolute ONENESS OF GOD. Truth marches on! Let us thank God and take courage.

We now present the scriptural definition of the Deity and show how impossible it is to fit the picture of the Trinity of Persons into the Bible frame. The Scriptures in accommodating the concept of God to human idioms, never speak about THEIR hands, feet, eyes, or

faces. It is invariably, "His hands, His feet, His eyes, His face."
Abundance of Scripture is available to confirm this, and it is a very
pertinent suggestion for Trinitarians to consider. If the serious and
approachable adherent to the Trinitarian doctrine is asked in what
sense are we to take the multiplied declarations of God that HE IS
ONE? He will reply, The three persons are one in Holiness, love,
glory, eternality, wisdom and power. But we never read in the Scriptures regarding the Deity, of THEIR Holiness. We read there about
the HOLY ONE, nowhere do we find the Holy Three. His love, not
THEIR love. His glory, not THEIR glory. God declares that His glory
He will not share with another. (Isa. 42:8.) The everlasting ONE, not
the everlasting THREE. Indeed the Word declares, "Thou alone, Oh
God, art eternal." Neither do we read anything about the only wise
THREE, but "the only wise God." As for power, the language of
Scripture is, "Thy power," not "Their power." David said, "Once have
I heard this, that power belongeth unto God."

The great commandment to Israel was, "Hear, O Israel! the Lord
our God is ONE Lord." To prove how the Apostles understood this,
we have only to turn to James 2:19: "You believe that God is one.
and you are quite right: evil spirits also believe this and shudder."
(See Weymouth.)

God is revealed in the Scripture as jealously regarding His prerogatives: These are: Forgiveness of sins, Creatorship, and Worship.
This was the belief of the people of God. "Who can forgive sins but
God only?" The first verse of Genesis reads, "In the beginning God
created the heavens and the earth." Again it is written, "Thou shalt
worship the Lord thy God and him only shalt thou serve." We recently heard a preacher whose name in America is a household
word, say, "that he worshipped the Three Persons of the Trinity
separately, and he knew when he quit talking to one and commenced talking to another."

After the meeting this preacher was interrogated about this
statement, and he dogmatically stuck to it, and declared that the
worshipper has not advanced very far in the knowledge of God if
he didn't know which of the Divine Three he was worshipping. Thank
God, we have not so learned Christ! The last verse in John's general
letter, says, Jesus Christ is the true God and eternal life. Little children, keep yourselves from idolatry. Since idolatry is worshipping
another than the "True God," and Jesus Christ is declared to be, "The
True God," the scriptural conclusion is unescapable, namely, that
they who worship God apart from Jesus Christ are in idolatry.

MY PRAYER

God give my eyes the inner sight
To see the world and men aright,
To find the good, the true, the fair
In everybody everywhere.

God give my ears the power to hear
The still small voice so strong and clear,
That speaks of truth and tells my soul
To gain the Spirit's shining goal.

God give my heart, that inner place,
The strength, the purity, the grace
So in each path where duty leads
I'll follow God outside the creeds.

—F.J.E.)

THE ONE NAME OF THE ONE GOD

The ONE TRUE GOD has one Name. He cannot and will not divide it with another or others, any more than He will share His glory. His glory and His Name are inseparable. Elohim distinguished the one name given to Moses out of the Burning Bush which is translated "I AM," and said, "This is My Name and this is My memorial unto all generations." The same Elohim declared through Isaiah 48:11: "For how should My Name be polluted?" and "I will not give My glory unto another."

The one name of Elohim in the Hebrew is Yahoshua. It means Saviour or Salvation, and Jesus is the Greek form of the same word. In his effort to buttress his own idea that Jesus and the Apostles substituted the word "LORD" for the one name that God gave Moses, Mr. Hall has triumphantly quoted, "I am the LORD, that is My Name." If this text read that way in the Hebrew it would mean an end of all controversy on the point, but unfortunately it reads: "I am Yahoshua, that is My Name." As every Hebrew scholar will confirm, Jehovah is a corruption of Yahoshua.

This one "ineffable or terrible name" of which Yahwe in the Hebrew language and Jesus in the Greek are the most perfect synonyms, is capable of seven compound applications, such as Jehovah-Jireh, "The Lord will provide," (Gen. 22:13-14); Jehovah-Rapha, "The Lord that healeth," (Ex. 15:26); Jehovah-Nissi, "The Lord our banner," (Ex. 17:8-15); Jehovah-Shalom, "The Lord our peace," (Jud. 6:24); Jehovah-Ra-Ah, "The Lord my Shepherd," (Psa. 23); Jehovah-Tsid-Kenu, "The Lord our righteousness," (Jer. 23:6); Jehovah-Shammah, "The Lord is present," (Ezek. 48:35). It is very significant that these seven compounds of Jehovah or Yahwe, start in with "The Lord will provide," and end with "The Lord is present." Signifying God's abiding presence with His people: "The Lord will tabernacle with them and be their God" (Rev. 21:3). It is also amazingly significant that the English name "I AM" translated from that ineffable name, is capable of being constructed into a complete supply of all the Lord's people's needs: You fill in your needs, Jehovah has promised to supply them. He knows what we need. He is the great "I AM" . . . Put the significant Name in front of your need today and draw from Him. I AM your joy, peace, strength, righteousness, wisdom, power, and holiness and glory. In other words, God's Name is the storehouse from which His people may draw the supply of all their real needs. His Name is His glory, and through

His Name He commits Himself unto us and it is His desire that no one lack, but that we might be filled with all the fulness of God. We get nothing from God apart from His Name.

The Acts of the Apostles is nothing but a record of this greatest of all facts being fully demonstrated. Before Jesus left them He instructed them that it was through His Name which was and is the Father's Name that they were to have all their equipment for service and all their spiritual and temporal and physical needs supplied. He gave them the power of attorney to use that Name. How thoroughly they apprehended His meaning! What a great play the Scriptures make on that same NAME after the day of Pentecost, right on till the end of the Sacred Record! The Acts of the Apostles is nothing but a fulfillment of His great promises: "Hitherto ye have asked nothing in My Name, ask and receive that your joy may be full," and "These signs shall follow them that believe in MY NAME: they shall cast out devils, they shall speak with new tongues; they shall take up serpents; and if they drink any deadly thing it shall not hurt them; they shall lay hands on the sick and they shall recover."

One precious but deluded brother in the early days of the preaching of this transcendent truth, said to the writer: "Brother Ewart, I am carrying out literally what Jesus commanded: He told me to anoint and pray for the sick in His Name, and I do that; but He also told me to baptize repentant people into the Name of the Father, and of the Son, and of the Holy Ghost, and I do that." I was compelled to tell him that by such a course he was doing violence to the Apostolic ministry, as everyone of them performed all the acts of the Christian ministry in the Name of the Lord, which is Jesus. How sad it is that people will unwittingly perpetuate a man-made administration that does violence to the unity of the Deity and the Apostolic precept and example! Paul said, "If any man think himself to be a prophet, or spiritual, let him acknowledge that the things that I write unto you are the commandments of the Lord," and he wrote or commanded, among many other plain precepts regarding the Name of Jesus, "And whatsoever ye do in word or deed, do all in the Name of the Lord Jesus, giving thanks to God and the Father by Him" (Col. 3:17).

In the colleges we learned that the great proof text of the tri-personality Godhead or Deity was Matthew 28:19. This statement shows how exceedingly hard pressed the proponents of this theory are to produce scriptural support for it. The Law of God demands three witnesses, and every honest man must confess that Acts 2:38 has many witnesses; but Matthew 28:19 as a formula for baptism, hasn't one single solitary witness throughout the New Testament. To say that Acts 2:38 is not the complete fulfillment of Matthew 28:19 is to assert that the Church of Jesus Christ was built on the most colossal contradiction of history.

Many, trying to evade this palpable conclusion of every honest soul, will say that "In the Name of the Lord Jesus Christ" simply meant that by the **Authority** of Jesus they baptized into the Name of the Father, Son, and Holy Ghost. That doesn't even make sense. It is a point-blank contradiction of the Great Commission from the lips of Jesus as recorded by Luke, "That repentance and remission of sins should be preached in His Name among all nations, beginning at Jerusalem." Mark records, "He that believeth and is baptized shall be saved, and he that believeth not shall be damned (condemned)." Then he deliberately promised that five signs shall follow the use of the Name Jesus, into which they had been baptized. All these signs, without exception, were demonstrated in the early Apostolic ministry. If this argument is a scriptural fact, then the Apostles baptized their converts into three names, denoting three separate persons in the Godhead, and prayed for the sick and cast out devils, raised the dead, and in fact did everything else in the Name of Jesus but the one pivotal cardinal act of Christian baptism, by which they "PUT ON CHRIST" (Gal. 3:27). "Baptized into His death" (Rom. 6:3). According to this untenable theory this "ACT" or "DEED" had to be done using the formula, "Into the Name of the Father and of the Son and of the Holy Ghost," to make it scripturally valid.

Paul declared that Jesus received the Father's Name (Heb. 1:4). Jesus declared, "I am come in my Father's Name" (John 5:43). Jesus also stated He had declared that Name to His disciples. He commanded them to pray in that Name, cast out devils and heal the sick in His Name. It is absolutely unthinkable then, to assert that Jesus would contradict Himself and command them to baptize their converts into three names.

Jesus is the only name given under heaven among men whereby we must be saved. It is the name we are commanded to use in both word and deed; it is the name to which every knee will bow and in which every tongue shall confess that Jesus is Lord of all; it is the name in which the whole family in heaven and earth is named. It is the name above every other name.

The Scriptures reveal that God always works in cycles. He ends up where He starts in. As it was in the beginning, so shall it be in the end. In the beginning God; in the end God. All in all. "As it was in the days of Noah, so shall it be in the day when the Son of man is revealed." As it was in the beginning of the church, when the Name of Jesus was so emphasized in the Apostles' preaching, and glorified in working miracles by them, so that its very use was prohibited on the threat of death; even so it will be in the end.

After all other subordinate arguments have been used to substantiate this transcendent truth from the Scriptures . . . that Jesus the Son of God, was also God, the Eternal Spirit, manifested in flesh, we must come back to the ONE NAME as the absolute proof of it.

God declares in regard to differences of doctrinal belief, that when He brings again Zion we shall all see eye to eye. That He will eliminate every discrepancy and seeming difference in the great and grand finale, it is absolutely certain. If the Scriptures of truth will not absolutely prove that there is only ONE NAME, neither will they prove absolutely that there is only ONE GOD. It should be emphasized, however, that our contention is not specifically that there is ONE GOD. The most ardent Trinitarian, with amazing inconsistency, emphatically declares his belief in ONE GOD. But our contention indicates a significant distinction: James declared, "You believe that God is one." This is the correct translation of that much used text. He is referring back to the great commandment to Israel, "Hear, O Israel, the Lord our God is One God." That is, GOD is ONE, not THREE. That should settle the controversy—a consumation devoutedly to be desired; for then we could as Pentecostal people present an unbroken and undivided front to the enemy. Then we could quit wrangling and arguing and go fishing for the souls of men. Surely, this would be a more lucrative and delightful occupation.

God is the great FIRST CAUSE, and HE takes on Himself the full responsibility for the final ultimatum. He is heading towards a premeditated, and predetermined objective. It is stated clearly in the Scriptures, and is to be found in Zechariah 14:9, "In that day there shall be ONE LORD and His NAME ONE." Nothing could be more significant than to find that statement here and it should make an end of all controversy to every humble and earnest child of God.

We here freely quote Col. 1:15-19.

"He is the exact impress of God's substance. First of all spiritual beings, Creator of the invisible things in heaven, and visible things on earth, of all principalities and authorities. He is the Origin and Original, the Ideal and the Goal; for all was created, exists by, through and for Him. HE IS before all things, and in and through Him the universe is one harmonious whole, or, holds together. HE

IS the Head of the New Creation, the Church, HE IS the Beginning, Firstborn from among the dead in order that He might become in all things Himself pre-eminent, or hold first place, because in Him was **all** the Fullness (Gr. pleroma) pleased to dwell, **through Him** to fully reconcile all things **unto Himself,** (by) having made peace through the blood of His cross."

These utterances are stupendous, but Paul follows them with another just as great: and adds a warning besides:

"Take heed lest there shall be anyone that maketh spoil of **you** through his philosophy and vain deceit, after **the tradition of men,** after the rudiments **(notions)** of the world, and not after Christ: for in Him dwelleth **all** the fulness (pleroma) of the Godhead **(Deity)** bodily" **(Col. 2:8-9).**

WHAT JESUS SAID ABOUT HIMSELF

However men may try to explain the fact that Jesus' theme was invariably HIMSELF, there it stands, facing the Bible student as soon as he opens the New Testament.

"And whither I go ye know, and the way ye know. Thomas saith unto him, Lord, we know not whither thou goest and how can we know the way? Jesus saith unto him, I am the way, the truth and the life. No man cometh unto the Father but by me."

This statement amazed the disciples, but the very next one Jesus made intensified their utter bewilderment: "If ye had known me ye would have known my Father, also, and from henceforth ye know Him and have seen Him" (John 14:7).

Philip voiced their astonishment in the words: "Lord, shew us the Father and it sufficeth us." Now this man wanted a revelation of the Father, and he came to the only being on earth that had it; for it is written, "No man knoweth the Father but the Son, and he to whomsoever the Son will reveal him."

The words of Jesus in answer to this pertinent query must be classified as the very best answer that could be made. Otherwise we limit the infallibility of Jesus. Listen: "Have I been so long time with you, and yet hast thou not known me, Philip? He that hath seen me hath seen the Father. How sayest thou, then, shew us the Father?"

Look at this tremendous claim: The son here disclaims any separate identity between Himself and the Father. These **two** are **one.** One, as to vision with the eye: "He that seeth me seeth the Father." One as to expression: "The words that I speak unto thee I speak not from myself." One, as to miraculous demonstration: "The Father that dwelleth in me, He doeth the works."

Are we ready for the breathtaking conclusion? Listen: It wasn't the man Jesus that turned the water into wine. It was the Deity dwelling inside the flesh that did it. It was the Creator who drew the curtain of flesh aside and looked at the insipid water and it blushed into wine. It wasn't the man Jesus who called Lazarus out of the grave, it was God who spoke through His human lips and said, "Lazarus, come forth." Jesus' claim in the above words logically involves this conclusion regarding all His mighty works.

One who received a clear revelation of this mystery through its proclamation, wrote:

"If you're looking for the Father,
You will find Him in the Son.
Much concerned about the Spirit,
Don't you know these Three are One?"

"He's the resting place for sinners,
He is God in form of man.
God, our Saviour, wrought redemption's
wondrous plan."

That song writer expressed the only legitimate deduction that can be drawn from Jesus' astounding words. The sign-Son of God, disowns, disavows and disclaims any of the glory. He takes the place of the humblest: "I, of mine own self, can do nothing. The Father that dwelleth in me, He doeth the works." Paul's explanation is: "To wit that God was in Christ reconciling the world unto Himself. Not imputing their trespasses unto them." William Phillips Hall says, "The Apostles taught that there was no Creator, Redeemer, High Priest, or King, but the One that dwelt in Jesus and expressed Himself through Him." This is true; for "God, who at sundry times and in divers manners, spake unto the fathers through the prophets hath in these last days spoken unto us through His Son" (Heb. 1:1-2). The marginal reading is: "Spoke out of a Son."

It is a point of supreme significance that Jesus invariably appealed to the fact that "The Father dwelt in Him" as the final and complete proof of His Deity. "Say ye of him, whom the Father hath sanctified and sent into the world, thou blasphemest; because I said, I am the Son of God" (John 10:36).

When the Trinitarian brethren say, that Jesus was God's equal in nature, eternality, and deity, we must all substantially agree. Otherwise Jesus' claims would be absurd: "Your father Abraham rejoiced to see my day, and he saw it and was glad." The Jews mocked at this claim and said, "Thou art not yet fifty years old and hast thou seen Abraham?" But Jesus solemnly answered: "Verily, verily I say unto you, before Abraham was, I AM." Scofield, in his Bible notes, says, "Jesus claimed the Jehovistic 'I AM'. Now the origin of the name that was translated 'I AM' is found in God's words to Moses out of the burning bush, when Moses inquired about His Name: 'Tell them that the I AM hath sent thee.' Christ's claim to be the 'I AM' is made in many places in the New Testament; the pronoun 'HE' is absent in the Greek in John 8:24; 8:55-58; 10:33; 18-4-6."

Jesus asserted His absolute identity with the Father. (See Matt. 28:19; Mark 14:62; John 10:30.) That the Jews so understood Him is shown by verses 31 and 32.

Jesus claims omnipotence (Matt. 28:18; Luke 7:14; John 5:21-23; 5:19); Mastery over nature and creative power (Luke 9:16-17; John 2:9; 10:28); Omnipresence (Matt. 18:20; John 3:13); Omniscience (John 11:11-14); When Jesus was fifty miles away (Mark 11:6-8).

There is not a single Scripture that asserts that Jesus existed eternally as a Son. He is called "The Word," "God's Wisdom," "Back in the Beginning," but never God's Son. See John 1:1; Prov. 8:22-31. So when it is claimed that Jesus' Sonship existed eternally, in any other sense than in the predetermined purpose of God, the claim is invalid from a scriptural standpoint, and it is outside the claims that Christ made for Himself.

It is true that Jesus did claim eternality of being, but it was not an identity of being separate from God. He asserts that His existence was inseparable from the One True God. He asserted that back in the beginning He was in "The bosom of the Father." It is written in Zechariah that He was "God's fellow." Micah said that the Babe of Bethlehem was "From everlasting." Isaiah says He was "The Everlasting Father," or "The Father of Eternity," and no scriptural proof can be found that any being beside God or distinct and separate from God in individuality could be called "The Everlasting Father" or "The Mighty God."

The one true God declares that "He is ONE LORD." But the erroneous doctrines of men have made Him three. The tenets of the first Christian church, expressed by James, the Bishop of the church at Jerusalem, "You believe that God is one," was fundamental to fellowship or membership in that church and was based on the great commandment to Israel about their doctrine of Jehovah: "Hear, O Israel, the Jehovah, our Elohim, is ONE Elohim." That same God asks, "Is there any other Elohim beside me; Yea, I know not any." 1 Tim. 3:16 says, "God or Elohim, was manifested in flesh." And John 1:14 says, "The Word, which was Elohim, came in the flesh." What theology of carnal minded men can ever translate into the language the terrific, infinite involvement of Christ's statement: "Except ye believe that 'I AM' ye shall die in your sins"?

Finally Jesus claimed the chief prerogative of Elohim: He claimed human worship and, indeed received it. Instead of rebuking Thomas for worshipping Him, He commended him for believing that He was Elohim: "Thomas, you believed because you see, but happy are they that have not seen, yet have believed."

Again, when the disciples of Jesus came back after the first missionary tour, saying, "Lord, the very demons are subject unto us in Thy name," Jesus replied, "I was standing by when Satan fell like lightning from heaven." These amazing claims of Jesus do not startle us any more since we got a clear revelation that He was the eternal God in the form of a Son. God (Elohim), Himself, gave the sign: "Behold, a virgin shall conceive and bring forth a Son and ye shall call His Name Emmanuel, which being interpreted is God (Elohim) with us." We truly need the wisdom from above to interpret Him as "The Lord of the Glory." Paul said if the princes of this world had known Him, they never would have crucified the LORD OF GLORY. This omnipotent, eternal Jesus confronts humanity, seeking to find Elohim, and declares, "Except ye believe that I AM HE, ye shall die in your sins." May He graciously help us to see and believe it.

THE NAME ABOVE EVERY NAME

"What is His name and what is His Son's name, if thou canst tell?" The above quotation taken from Proverbs 30:4, embraces the great issue that has swept the religious world for twenty-seven years past. No great truth has been more vehemently contested by the religious leaders of our day. History repeated itself; for exactly as in the case of the Apostles, preaching in the name of Jesus was banned on the threat of death. "Did not we straitly threaten you not to preach or to teach in this name? And, behold, ye have filled Jerusalem with your doctrine and intend to bring this man's blood upon us" (Acts 5:28). "And they called them and commanded them not to speak at all nor teach in the name of Jesus" (Acts 4:18). "By what power or by what name have ye done this?" (Acts 4:7). So palpable is the fact that the Name of Jesus was the great issue the religious leaders denounced here, that one of the modern champions of the opponents of the so-called new issue, Dr. Scofield, has Acts Fourth Chapter divided in sections: "The First Persecution" and "Preaching in the Name of Jesus Forbidden." (See Scofield Bible.)

We have often marvelled that our precious brethren who have been baptized with the Holy Spirit as the early Apostles were, should continue in succession of these inveterate persecutors of the Apostles, and do it for the very same reason: namely, because we, like the Apostles, practice and preach in the Name of Jesus. The great Apostle Paul commanded, "And whatsoever ye do in word or deed, do all in the name of the Lord Jesus." He, himself, taught the Ephesian converts about the real meaning of the great commission as in Matt. 28:19, and it is written: "When they heard this, they were baptized in the name of the Lord Jesus." To offset the irrefutable fact of the Apostles doing everything in the name of Jesus, including Christian baptism, our opponents have put forth the argument that in the four notable cases of baptism in or into the name of Jesus, who is both Lord and Christ, namely, Acts 2:38; 8-16; 10:48;19:5, the writer of the Acts simply meant that they were baptized into the "Name of the Father and of the Son and of the Holy Ghost," by the authority of the name of Jesus. How silly such a position is! If this were so, which, thank God is not the case, the history of the early church is a mass of contradictory and confused statements. Jesus commanded the disciples to baptize their converts into "The Name," and Acts 5:41 reads, "Rejoicing that they were counted worthy to suffer reproach for " THE NAME" (Revised Version). James calls the name of Jesus, "That worthy name," and Paul calls it, "The name which is above every other name that is named." Peter declares, "That there is none other name given under heaven among men whereby we must be saved." Philip preached to the Samaritans and his theme was, "The Kingdom of God and the name of Jesus Christ." And so we could continue ad infinitum.

Every Greek and Hebrew authority knows that the name of God is not and never was, **"Father, Son and Holy Spirit."** It is declared by God to Moses out of the burning bush, which was a type of Christ, to be a name which is the equivalent of four Hebrew letters, corresponding to the letters YHWH. This is called the ineffable name, the lost name, the terrible name. Yahweh is the name Rotherham used, and it is declared to be the exact duplicate in Hebrew of Jesus in Greek. We don't like to turn the exponents of the Trinitarian theory's guns against their own intrenched position, but surely we are justified, if one single soul could be enlightened on this, the greatest truth of the Gospel. Matthew 28:19 is the only place in the Bible where "Father, Son and Holy Ghost," are connected with a name. "There is absolutely no support whatever to be found in the New Testament, that either by the original disciples or by the church of the Apostolic Age, the words 'I baptize thee in the name of the Father and of the Son and of the Holy Spirit,' were ever used in Christian baptism."—William Phillips Hall. "No trace is to be found of the employment of these words, 'The name of the Father and of the Son, and of the Holy Ghost,' by the Apostolic church."—Meyer, in Lange's Commentary. "There is not the slightest doubt that the baptisms in the Acts were in or into the name of Jesus only, but that does not necessarily mean that Jesus never spoke Matthew 28:19."—Prof. J. A. Faulkner, D. D. "The Teaching of the Twelve Apostles" is the oldest book outside the New Testament. In the ninth chapter and the fifth verse of this book, we read, "Let no man partake of your Eucharist, except those baptized into the name of the Lord."

Again, if the phrase, "Father, Son and Holy Spirit," is the name of God, then Paul was in error when he declared that Jesus obtained "The more excellent name" than the angels. (Heb. 1:5). And, also, in calling the name of Jesus "The greatest name that is named" (Eph. 1:21). The writer's dear friend, William Phillips Hall, from whose pen, now laid down forever, he has many wonderful and affectionate letters, states in the preface of his book, "A Remarkable Biblical Discovery—The Name of God," that Dr. Gaebelien asked him to dig up fresh truth on the Name of God, as that was a subject the church was comparatively ignorant on, and that he studied and made research for twenty years with the result that he was convinced that the Great Commission in Matt. 28:19 was fulfilled by the Apostolic practice of baptizing their converts into the name of the Lord Jesus Christ. That the name of the Father, Son and Holy Spirit is Lord Jesus Christ. This great discovery was confirmed by the scholarship of Christendom. But, it never altered their practice in baptism, and although Brother Hall stated and proved that the phrase, "Father, Son and Holy Spirit," was never used as a baptismal formula in the early Christian church, and they assented to it, they still held tenaciously to the dogma of the Trinity and kept on doing what they all acknowledge the Apostles never did. What marvellous inconsistencies are wrought by the demi-god called TRADITION!

The greatest of all those great events which are scheduled for a positive fulfillment in these last days is that of the perfect church. The church restored. It is inconceivable that the church of the last days should have a baptismal formula in opposition to that of the early church which was indwelt by the Holy Spirit. And it must be evident to all who are concerned about this vital matter that the Lord —the Head of the church—Jesus Christ, is not going to permit such a flagrant violation of His own command, as that with which we are faced today.

As we have before said, the revelation of this truth is spreading over the Christian world, and is being accepted by the humble in the spirit of joy and gladness. It is a beacon light to all the world that God hath set His hand a second and last time to redeem His people. Are the Pentecostal saints, who years ago suffered so much because of their faith in the Holy Spirit's revelation of the truth, now going to ignore and oppose so clear a revelation of His Word? The formula of water baptism used in many so-called Pentecostal and Apostolic faith churches, is the exact formula used by that church which God in His unerring Word calls, "The Great Harlot, The Great Whore!" God Almighty, forbid that this latter day Apostolic church, called by His name, and baptized with His Holy Spirit, with the gifts in operation, should have a single thing in common with the Great Whore that sitteth on many waters. She is full of the names of blasphemy and is drunk on the blood of the martyrs of Jesus.

No doubt the Pope of Rome and the iniquitous system he represents and heads, will figure large in the last days. Many Bible students believe that he is the "False Prophet." Jesus said, "I am come in My Father's Name and ye won't receive me; when another shall come in his own name, him ye will receive."

It is extremely dangerous in these last days, when apostasy abounds on every hand, to deny the necessity of the name of the LORD JESUS CHRIST. A church, denomination, organization or assembly which refuses to take the name of the Lord-Jesus-Christ in Christian baptism could never have a place in His Bride. Why, such a statement? Because the Bride always does gladly take up the name of her bridegroom, and she is glad to let her own name be swallowed up in his.

The zeal for the truth is eating us up! In the interests of harmony and oneness in all the church of God, regardless of what past practices have been, we make our plea, for a return to the Apostolic Pattern in all things. The Word of God is the authority of the true church. Even His name is subordinate to His Word. "He has exalted His Word above all His Name." It is dangerous to close the heart against the name of the Godhead—the Lord Jesus Christ, which is declared to be the greatest name in heaven, in earth or under the earth. (Phil. 2:8-10.) The name of God and His dignity and honor are inseparable. They always did and always will go together. Some have even gone so far as to baptize converts in the formula of Matt. 28:19 and anoint sick people and pray for them in the name of Jesus Christ. The Apostles did everything in the name of the Lord Jesus Christ. The time is coming when all tongues shall confess and every knee shall bow in the name of Jesus, to the glory of God, the Father.

The last great crisis is now upon us. God is moving for the complete restoration of His Holy Church. He never duplicates Himself. What He commanded in the beginning of the church is true at the end of the church age. Now He is about to shake everything that can be shaken, that the unshakable might remain. Back to the authority of Jesus Christ and honor the revelation of the Holy Spirit. Amen!

THE PERSONALITY OF GOD

The only passage in the New Testament that mentions God's person is Heb. 1:3. This passage declares that Jesus was the exact representation of God in visible form. The American Revised renders this passage, "The express image, of His substance." Weymouth translates, "He brightly reflects God's glory and is the exact representation of His being."

The thought brought out here is one of blessed illumination. However, we cannot take it in, unless we will extricate our minds from the hurly burly of heated argumentation about the "Mystery of God" which Paul says, is confessedly great: 1 Tim. 3:16. No one but an abnormally radical zealous advocate of the present truth would insist that Jesus was Deity from His head to His feet. Some throw away their brief by such statements: "Mary was the mother of God Almighty"; or, "The Blood of Calvary was the blood of God." There is a truth embraced in such statements; but that truth is nullified by wrong terminology. There is no scripture to prove that the flesh of Jesus was not the same as ours, only, in the stated fact that He was sinless. Indeed, the Scriptures state emphatically that, "The Lord took on flesh and blood like the children." (See Heb. 2:14.) This passage is a signal proof that the Father, God, became incarnate in a CHILD in order to save HIS CHILDREN. So the sinless humanity of Jesus and His absolute Deity are sustained.

Such Scriptures as, "Express image of His substance; God was manifest in the flesh; In Him dwelleth all the fulness of the Godhead bodily; God was in Christ reconciling the world unto Himself; The Word was made flesh—or, 'came in the flesh'; The Father which dwelleth in me, He doeth the works," with many others that will come to the devout reader's mind, abundantly prove that the real mystery which Paul defines as, "The mystery of God even Christ" (Col. 2:2), and which he exhorts us to fellowship, is, that the Eternal Spirit, who had no visible form, took possession of the body of Jesus, spoke out of it, worked through it, gave it His name and nature, took it up the hill of Calvary, offered it on the altar of sacrifice, as the Lamb of God, and thus ended the sacrificial system. Took it up on high and deified it—"For in Him dwelleth all the fulness of the Godhead bodily."

Now the Greek word rendered "Express image" is **characteer"** —not "character." It is that which the written character makes. The impress made upon the wax table used in writing among the ancient, or the indentations made upon the papyrus by the stylus, or the impress made by dropping the die or seal upon the soft wax. It was the emptiness which let in the fulness of the seal or stamp. Were there as much as a rose-leaf of thickness between the seal and the impress, it could not be an exact characteer—not an express image, everywhere and everyway prepared to fit the fulness of the seal. Its fulness drops into the characteer's emptiness; as the fulness of the key fits into the empty spaces of the lock, so Christ in HIS mortal condition perpetually gave place to the fulness of the Father. The Son, because He was a perfect Son, disowned, disclaimed, disavowed: "I of mine own self, can do nothing." There it is! And the reason is obvious. "He learned obedience by the things which He suffered." He just renounced all independent thought and action, and God, the key, turned at will inside Christ, the lock.

Thus does God say of Him in His utter self-abandonment: "Who is blind like my servant, or deaf as my messenger that I sent? Who is blind as he that is perfect, and deaf as the Lord's servant? Seeing many things but thou observest them not; opening the ears but he heareth not. The Lord is well pleased for His righteousness' sake."

There is an illuminating word in Luke 6:40, "The disciple is not above his master; but everyone shall be perfected as his master" (Marginal reading). Jesus was truly our example. He was the "SIGN SON." "The Lord Himself shall give you a sign: Behold a virgin shall conceive and bear a Son, and ye shall call His name IMMANUEL." However, that sign or example was never intended by God to be slavishly copied or imitated in the flesh. "Ye are not in the flesh, but in the Spirit." The Holy Spirit comes within us to make good what Christ did for us. This is surely what the Apostle Paul must have meant in that arresting statement, "Though we have known Christ after the flesh, from henceforth knew we him no more" (2 Cor. 5:16). The Holy Spirit translates the life of Jesus out of the flesh into the Spirit. He takes Jesus out of a mere unit in human history and makes Him a living fact in human experience.

Christ came to demonstrate how God could live in flesh, dominate it, conquer it, subdue it, live in it continuously and uninterruptedly only for the glory of God. To do that, God had to get Himself into a real man, not a painted image. Jesus was assailed with every conceivable form of temptation, individually and collectively, that could assail mankind. A peculiar form of this temptation was in Gethsemane's agony. A subtle snare to the Christian worker is in making the **"will of God"** subservient to the **"work of God."** Most of the great men throughout the church's history have made this fatal mistake. As God breaks out in new and more wondrous ways, Christian workers can only be saved from rejecting His new methods and truth, by sacrificing the work of God on the altar of the will of God.

Gethsemane the place, midnight the hour. He began to be exceeding sorrowful, even unto death. He sweat, as it were great drops of blood falling down to the ground. From such conditions, death was very imminent, and He had not yet come to the cross—the very thing He came into the world for: to work out expiation for the sin of the world. Hence His prayer, "Father, if thou be willing, remove this cup (the cup of His premature death, before He had come to the time and place for the offering) from me." Since prayer to be saved from death was heard, it could not have been the death on the cross He was praying to be delivered from. He prayed to Him that was able to save Him from death, and was heard in that He feared. Oh, what depths of consecration was called for in the human nature of Christ! The Hexapla of Mystery is worded by Paul in Hebrews: "Though He were a Son, yet learned he obedience by the things which he suffered, and being. made perfect He became the author of eternal salvation unto all them that obey Him" (Heb. 5:8-9).

The sons of God are in preparation for unveiling. They are predestined "to be conformed to the **image of a son** that he might be the first-born among many Brethren." Did you ever hear of the Gobelin Tapestry? Of course you did. It is the legacy of royalty. Its manufacture is a secret of the French handed down from one generation to another. The workman sits at the loom, his feet on the treadle, his hands both engaged, but his eyes are fixed on an image or pattern before him. All the threads of various colors are woven into the picture, that is, they all work together to make one result, and flashing of the shuttle and the dazzling movements of the thread continue until the picture is complete.

A spiritual analogy would be something like this: The weaver is the Holy Ghost, the pattern on the wall is the Son of God, the flying loom and dazzling threads are "All things working together for our good," the finished product is what Christ presents to Himself.

Years ago we were conducted through a Royal Pottery in England, called Minions. Oh, the spiritual parables that thronged us while viewing the earth, the moistened earth, the clay on the wheel, the vessels in the fire, the artists' work in decoration, the gilding, the enamel bath, and then, the oven again. When we went into ecstacies over some beautiful work, we were told that the most perfect pieces were never shown. Artists commanding fabulous wages, day by day, worked in seclusion at their own plans, designed for the Royal courts of Europe, and were never exposed to the gaze of the public. Pieces commanding 50,000 to 100,000 pounds each were removed to the exclusive studios of the Royal artists to be finished there. Now, can we stand the drilling and polishing for real sonship? Do we wish to bear His "Express Image"? No wonder the Psalmist cried out, "Let the beauty of our God be upon us."

This article, though off the regular path, is after all on the Lordship of Jesus Christ. You can believe the message in the letter. You can manifest wonderful zeal in defending it, but you never really crown Jesus Lord at all unless you crown Him Lord of all. Let the doctrine of His absolute Lordship jump out of theology into our experiences. Let us adorn this doctrine of God, our Saviour, in all things. The great truth that Jesus is Lord of all is demonstrable in our lives. He complains about some people, "Why call ye me Lord, Lord, and do not the things which I say?" He that willeth to do His will he shall know the doctrine. He will make Him Lord of his life as well as his theology. Amen.

Printed in U. S. A.

THE

BIRTH OF THE SPIRIT

IN THE DAYS OF THE APOSTLES

BY ELD G. T. HAYWOOD

CHRIST TEMPLE
BOOK STORE

430 West Fall Creek Parkway
Indianapolis, Indiana, U.S.A.

FOREWORD

Because of the great controversy over what is the Birth of the Spirit we hereby present in this book the facts upon this subject as they are found in the Word of God.

We trust that no one will misunderstand the writings herein and lay the book aside before giving it a thorough examination with your Bible in hand to see whether these things are so. If we follow the book of Acts of the Apostles there can be but one conclusion as to what constituted The Birth of the Spirit in the Days of the Apostles.

What men need today is truth. Ye shall know the Truth and the Truth shall make you free. Let no one disregard these things but consider them in the fear of God. If our experiences do not measure up to the Word of God it is up to us to lay aside everything and seek God till we find Him.

May the Holy Spirit of God rest upon all who read these pages, and grant that they may all be filled with the knowledge of His Will in all spiritual understanding.

Author.

CHAPTER I

THE BIRTH OF THE SPIRIT IN THE DAY OF THE APOSTLES

From the beginning of the Reformation even down to the days in which we now live, the cry of the hearts of the people of God has been incessantly, "Back to Pentecost." Every advance truth that forged its way to the front, throwing light on the "path of the just," has always met with a storm of opposition from those who are supposed to be seeking for a closer walk with God.

The Jews were set in their doctrines that the Lord Himself found it a difficult proposition to lead them into the way of life for which they had sought so long. "No man also having drunk old wine straightway desireth the new; for he saith the old is better" (Luke 5:39), is the manner in which He summed up the situation in His day. They were so imbided in their traditional doctrine that they laid aside, and rejected the commandments of God and made "the word of God of none effect" through their traditions which had been delivered unto them. (Mar. 7:5-13.) Even so it is today. We have been so absorbed in our ancestral views concerning the new birth that the Holy Spirit's work in bringing the people to the kowledge of the truth seems to be a difficult task.

Very few will agree with us on this subject at the first, but if they will lay aside the doctrine of men, and for a moment remove their thoughts from the abnormal state of the present day Christianity, they will find

—1—

no trouble in grasping the truth as it is now revealed to many of the children of God in these closing days of the Gospel dispensation.

It is our purpose to take up the subject from a Bible point of view to see whether there is an experience in the New Testament scriptures, called the birth of the Spirit, aside from the baptism of the Holy Ghost, according to the second chapter of the Acts of the Apostles. If we cleave to the Word of God we cannot fail. Neither should we be afraid to declare what the Lord has revealed to us on this matter.

The Rest

The first scripture that we wish to bring to notice is that of Matt. 11:28. "Come unto Me all ye that labour and are heavy laden, and I will give you rest," is one of the most favored texts used in inviting the lost sinner to seek the way of Salvation. No one has ever been known to interpret the "rest" that Jesus offers here to be anything short of the new birth, or full salvation. With this we must all agree, and that that "rest" comes in being born again. But the question arises, what has that to do with the baptism of the Holy Ghost?

In turning to Isa. 28:11, 12 we find these words "For with stammering lips and another tongue will he speak to this people. To whom he said, This is the rest wherewith ye may cause the weary to rest." It was on the day of Pentecost that God spake unto the people "with stammering lips and another tongue." (Acts 2:4.) From these scriptures it can be plainly seen that the "rest" and the baptism of the Holy Ghost are one and the same thing. Those who have really experienced the full baptism of the Holy Ghost and walked uncompromisingly before God can truly testify to these things, that they have in truth "found rest for their souls."

Born of Water and the Spirit

To Nicodemus Jesus said, "Verily, verily, I say unto you, except a man be born of water and the Spirit, he cannot enter into the kingdom of God." Nicodemus was a Jew and a Pharisee. His morals were perfect; he was a master of Israel. To him, to be born a Jew was a great favor of God, but his pride was humbled, and he was filled with astonishment when Jesus said unto him, "Ye must be born again." To be born into the kingdom of the Jews was one thing, but to enter into the kingdom of God was another. In reply to his question, "How can a man be born when he is old?" Jesus answers, "Except a man be born of water and the Spirit, he cannot enter into the kingdom of God." In these words He set about to explain to him what He meant by being born again. Not that it was any different from the salvation that was offered, or to be offered, to the Gentile, but the illustration of a birth would best convey it to the minds of those who boasted in the fact that they were a people of God through being born a Jew.

In fact, it was another way of saying, "He that believeth and is baptized, shall be saved." The statement was most astonishing to that stalwart Pharisee, but

Jesus, knowing his thoughts, proceeded to further explain the manner of this new birth, by saying, "The wind bloweth where it listeth, and thou hearest the sound thereof, but cannot tell whence it cometh, and whither it goes:" So is everyone that is born of the Spirit. The fact that on the day of Pentecost there came a "sound" from heaven as of a rushing, mighty "wind," undisputedly links the baptism of the Holy Ghost with the experience of "everyone that is born of the Spirit."

St. John is the only writer in the New Testament who likens salvation unto a birth. St. Peter only mentions it slightly in one place. St. Paul, the apostle to the Gentiles, never used such a term in his writings to those whom he had brought "out of darkness into light." But instead, he used the word "baptize" or its equivalent, more than any other writer. While Jesus spake to Nicodemus concerning being "born of water and the Spirit," yet there is no record in the Acts of the Apostles that will indicate that his instructions were ever carried out, except by being baptized in water and the Holy Ghost. Not one place in the book of Acts can we find the words "born of water and the Spirit," or "born again," but we can find the words relating to "baptism" twenty-seven times. If to be "born of water and the Spirit" is not the baptism of "water and the Spirit," where is there any record of anyone ever being "born again?"

One dear brother, in his efforts to show that a man is born again without the baptism of the Holy Spirit stated that all the Jews had to be baptized for the remission of their sins before they could be born again, and that that was the reason Peter told them to "Repent and be baptized for the remission of their sins," but if we take our brother's word in this matter, it will strengthen the fact that the birth of the Spirit is the baptism of the Holy Ghost, because what they were to receive after being "baptized in the name of Jesus for the remission of sins" was "the gift of the Holy Ghost." (See Acts 2:38.)

Synonymous Terms

Scripture will interpret scripture if we seek to rightly divide the word of truth. To be born of "water and the Spirit," and "believe and is baptized" (John 3:5 and Mar. 16:16), are proven to be synonymous terms expressing the one and self-same thing, by reading, or comparing the words of Jesus in John 10:9. All three of these expressions are spoken by the same Person. In the first mentioned scripture He says that if a man is not born of water and the Spirit he cannot enter into the Kingdom of God, while in the second, He says that he that believeth and is baptized shall be saved. But in the third, He combines the thoughts of the first and second by saying, "I am the door, by ME if any man *enter in* he *shall be saved.* A man that *enters in* it is certain that he *shall be saved;* and no man shall be saved unless he enters in.

The Household of Cornelius

We take to record the household of Cornelius as a proof that the birth of the Spirit, or full salvation, in the days of the Apostles, was the baptism of water and the Holy Ghost. Cornelius was not saved! (Acts 11:14.) He was a devout man and feared God with all his house, but he was not "born again." And as Peter began to tell him words whereby he should be saved, the Holy Ghost fell upon them and they spake with tongues and magnified God. And Peter later declared that the Spirit fell upon them as it did upon the Jews "at the beginning." (Acts 10:44, 46; 11:15.) Then answered Peter, "Can any man forbid water that these should not be baptized who have received the Holy Ghost as well as we? And he commanded them to be baptized in the name of the Lord."

It was God's plan that they be "born of water and the Spirit," but because of the doubts in the minds of the six men, that were with Peter, as to the Gentiles being accepted, God, being sovereign, baptized them before they were baptized in water, in order to convince the Jews of their acceptance. The Apostle, recognizing this to be a fact, remembered the words of the Lord, how that He said, "John truly baptized with water; but ye shall be baptized with the Holy Ghost," and immediately commanded them to be baptized in water in the name of the Lord. From the foregoing facts it can be clearly seen that it is utterly impossible for one to conceive the idea that the birth of the Spirit is separate and distinct from the baptism of the Holy Ghost.

Was the Church at Rome Born of the Spirit?

While no one will deny that the church at Rome was born of the Spirit, yet there is not a word in the whole book that states the manner in which they received it apart from the record in the sixth chapter, where it says, "Know ye not, that so many of us as are (margin) baptized into Jesus Christ were baptized into His death? Therefore, we are buried with Him by baptism into death: that like as Christ was raised from the dead by the glory of the Father, even so we also should walk in the newness of life (which is the new birth)." (Rom. 6:3, 4.)

In Christ Jesus, the Church

That they were in Christ Jesus is plainly stated in the eighth chapter. There is no way for a man to be in the Church, apart from being in Christ Jesus, for the Church is His body. (Eph. 1:22, 23; Rom. 12:5.) The body is Christ (I Cor. 12:12, 13, 27.) And the only way to get into the body is "by one Spirit are we all baptized into one body." The Galatians were of the same body, and in writing to them the Apostle declares, "As many of you as have been baptized into Christ (the body) have put on Christ." (Gal. 3:26.) In other words, "as many as have *not* been baptized into Christ, have *not* put on Christ." And with this we must all agree, that no man can enter into Christ without being "born again."

The Church and the Kingdom of God

A strong point to consider is that the church which is the body of Christ, and the Kingdom of God are synonymous. A man must be born of water and Spirit, in order to enter into the Kingdom of God, and he must be baptized into Christ in order to put on Christ. Upon

first reading this it may sound somewhat foreign to
some, but if it will be prayerfully considered, I am sure
that all will agree that these things are so. The Church
is the body of believers baptized in the Holy Ghost. The
Kingdom of God is in righteousness and peace, and joy
in the Holy Ghost. (Rom. 14:17.) When the Pharisee
desired to know when the Kingdom of God should come
Jesus answered, "the Kingdom of God is within (margin, among you) you," that is, in their midst. (Luke
17:20, 21.) It was Christ who was "among" or in the
midst of them, but they could not see it (John 3:3),
because it came "not with observation." To enter into
the Kingdom of God one must be born of water and the
Spirit, or, to enter in Christ, the Church, one must be
baptized in water and the Holy Spirit.

What the Bible Teaches

In reading the Bible carefully it will be seen that its
principal mission is to restore man to his Maker, and
that this can only be done by the "washing of regeneration and the renewing of the Holy Ghost." (Titus
3:5). The foregoing scripture, or expression, is merely
another way of expressing the thoughts conveyed in
John 3:5; Mar. 16:1; John 10:9; Acts 2:38; Gal. 3:27.

No man who really reads the Bible will ever say that
a man can be born of God without being baptized with
the Holy Ghost. The Methodist, Baptist, Presbyterian,
Christian, Episcopalian, Adventist and all others know
that the Bible teaches this beyond dispute. If you confront them about the baptism of the Holy Ghost they

will not hesitate to tell you that they have it, and that they received it when they were born of the Spirit. Furthermore, they will tell you that a man could not be born of the Spirit without being baptized with the Holy Ghost. And that is just what the Bible teaches.

The question may arise, "What is the difference between the view we take and that of these denominations above mentioned?" Let us say right here that there is as much difference between our views as there is between a millionaire and a pauper. The pauper talks about wealth, but the millionaire possesses it. The other denominations talk about the baptism of the Holy Ghost, but we believe in possessing it as they did at Pentecost. If everyone who called themselves Christians possessed the baptism of the Holy Spirit as they did in the days of the Apostles there would be no argument at all over the matter of the birth of the Spirit.

A Misconstrued Explanation

Recently we heard a strange interpretation given to verses 12 and 13 of the first chapter of St. John in a feeble effort to prove that a man is born of God before he receives the Holy Ghost. The twelfth verse says that "as many as received Him, to them gave He power to become sons of God." Our contention (Jude 3) was that the "power to become sons of God" was the baptism of the Holy Ghost, and this we proved by referring to Acts 1:8. But to avert a sudden collapse of this argument the expounder attempted to prove his statement by putting special stress on the word, "Which were born . . . of God" The fact that the word "were" was in the past tense seemed to give him a strong point in his favor, that they were born of God before they received power to become sons of God. If they had to be given power to become sons of God after they were born, what were they before they got the power to become sons of God. "O, consistency thou art a jewel."

The words, "Which were born," have no reference to their state before receiving the baptism of the Holy Ghost, and for one to attempt such an explanation is to misconstrue the scriptures. But instead, it was to show that those who had been given power to become sons of God were not made so by being born "of blood," or "the will of the flesh," or the "will of man," but that they became sons of God by being born of God (the Spirit).

Begotten and Born

Everyone with ordinary understanding knows that there is a difference between "begettal" and "birth." The begettal is from the father side while conception and birth is from the mother side. (Matt. 1:1-16, also note verses 16, 20, 25.) In those scriptures it will be seen that the father "begat" the child, while the mother "conceive" and "born." A child of God is first "begotten" by the Word (I Cor. 4:15) of the Gospel before he can be born of the Spirit. The disciples were "begotten" unto a lively hope by the resurrection, but

—10—

they were "born of the Spirit" on the day of Pentecost (I Pet. 1:3.)

No child can ever be born until it is first begotten, but there are many who have been begotten, but were never born into the world. So it is in the Spirit. Many may have been begotten by the word but have never been born of the Spirit. There are multitudes who are in that state today. They have been begotten, but the church has had no "strength" to bring them forth. (Isa. 37:3; 52.1.) In the fifty-second chapter of Isaiah the church is exhorted to awake and put on her "strength," because of the lack of "strength," many had come into her "uncircumcised and unclean." But when she would put on her "strength" (see Isa. 28:5, 6; Gal. 3:27; Rom. 14:17; Neh. 8:10) no more would there come into her the "uncircumcised and the unclean." No congregation can bring the people to the "birth of the Spirit" except it is itself a congregation of Spirit-baptized believers. And when such a congregation enters into soul-travail she will surely bring forth, for God with send forth the Spirit of His Son into their hearts, crying "Abba," (interpreted "Father" Rom. 8:15; Gal. 4:6.) Thus was the birth of the Spirit manifested in the days of the Apostles.

Circumcision of the Heart

"Circumcision of the heart" is not a different experience from the new birth, but rather another way of conveying the same thought. That to be born of water and Spirit, and circumcision of the heart are one and the same experience can be seen by reading Col. 2:11, 13, where the Apostle unmistakably connects it with baptism of water and Spirit by saying, "Buried with Him by baptism; wherein ye are risen with Him through the faith of the operation of God. * * * And you * * * hath He quickened together with Him, having forgiven in all your trespasses." They were "buried" in water, and "quickened by the Spirit." (Rom. 8:11.)

Are the Unborn Lost?

The one question that is so often asked is, "are all those people who thought they were born of the Spirit, and were not, lost?" No, not by any means. They shall be given eternal life in the resurrection if they walked in all the light that was given them while they lived. God is a just Judge, and there is no unrighteousness in Him. But those who refuse to walk in the light shall be overtaken with darkness. (John 13:35, 36; see also John 15:22-24.)

It is often asked whether Wesley, Luther, Whitefield and other mighty men of God were baptized in the Holy Ghost according to the Acts of the Apostles. That is more than we can say. They may have been, and they may not. They lived up to the light of their day. We must live up to the light of our day. Their light will not do for us today, neither could they have walked in the light that we now embrace. The evening time has come, and the true light now shineth. If we compromise, God will raise up another people who will carry His word.

Many other words could be written upon this subject, but time and space will not permit. Yet if any man will follow these lines with an open heart and Bible in hand, he will be made to see that the birth of the Spirit, in the days of the Apostles, was a baptism of water and the Holy Ghost. If it were so then, why is it not so today? When, where and by whom was the change authorized? We await the answer.

CHAPTER II

THE GIFT vs. GIFTS OF THE SPIRIT

The Birth of the Spirit

That to be born of the Spirit is to be baptized with the Holy Ghost, is the conclusion drawn from the word of God by every close student of the Holy Scriptures. No church, no creed, whatever their differences may be on other passages of the Scriptures, holds a contrary view of this matter. The Word of God emphatically proves this to be true.

What We Must Do

Jesus told Nicodemus that he "must" be born of water and the Spirit. When the multitude cried, "What 'shall' we do?" Peter's answer was to "repent and be baptized every one of you in the name of Jesus Christ (in water) * * * and ye shall receive the gift of the Holy Spirit." Saul cried out to Jesus, "What wilt Thou have me to do?" but Jesus told him to go on to Damascus and it would be told him what he "must" do. The thing that he was told that he "must" do was to be baptized and filled with the Holy Spirit. (See Acts 9:6, 17, 18; 22:16.) At Philippi, when the keeper of the prison said, "Sirs, what must I do to be saved?" the Apostles' answer was, "Believe in the Lord, Jesus

Christ," which implied baptism as in all other cases before it. (Acts 16:14, 15, 30th to 34th verses.)

I am sure that almost all will agree that no one could honestly deny or misconstrue these facts. To show that other writers or commentators saw this fact that the new birth implied the baptism of the Holy Spirit, in the days of the Apostles, we hereby quote what Mr. Adam Clarke, the famous Bible commentator, had to say on the subject:

"When John came baptizing with water, he gave the Jews the plainest intimations that this would not suffice; that it was only typical of that baptism of the Holy Ghost under the similitude of fire, which they "must" all receive from Jesus Christ (See Matt. 3:11.) Therefore, our Lord asserts that a man "must" be *born of water and the Spirit, i.e.,* of the Holy Ghost. ... I would not merely say to thee (reader), *read* what it is to be *born of the Spirit:* but pray, O pray, to God incessantly, till He gives thee to *feel* what is implied in it! Remember, it is Jesus *only* who baptizeth with the Holy Ghost. (See chapter 1:33 John.) He who receives not this baptism has neither right no title to the Kingdom of God; nor can he with any propriety be termed a Christian, because that which essentially distinguished the Christian dispensation from that of the Jews was, that its author *baptized* all his followers *with the Holy Ghost.*

The above quotation is what that eminent servant of God draws from the Word of God concerning the "birth of the Spirit." Not only is this his view of what the Bible teaches, but many, many others also.

But with many of today, although they acknowledge that the birth of the Spirit and the baptism of the Spirit are synonymous, yet they disagree on the point as to whether speaking in other tongues accompanies the "birth of the Spirit." As long as we were taught that the birth of the Spirit was one thing, and the baptism of the Spirit was another, practically all of those who received this miraculous experience as it is recorded in the second chapter of Acts, stood firm and proclaimed far and wide that, according to the apostolic record, all who were baptized with the Holy Spirit spoke with other languages as the Spirit gave them utterance. Wherever this was preached all who received the baptism of the Spirit spake with other languages as they did at Pentecost.

As time rolled on the illumination of the Holy Spirit began to reveal to the church more truth. (John 14:26, 16:12-15.) And many of those who saw the light began at once to walk therein. (John 12:35, 36.) While others faltered, and began to draw back. Because of this some have attempted to prove that the "birth of the Spirit" and the "baptism of the Spirit" are two different experiences, while others hold that the two are synonymous, but that all who receive it do not speak with tongues. It is the latter view that we especially wish to dwell upon.

The Controversy

The argument used is strengthened by this passage of scripture, "Do all speak with tongues?" (I Cor. 12:30.) We do not take this up for mere argument's sake, strife nor controversy, but that by this we may arrive at just what the word of God teaches on this matter. If we are wrong, it is our desire to be set right by the Word. The time is too short for us to seek honor, or applause. The church of God is at stake. If we err, many souls will be required at our hands. There is but one thing upon which we can rely to judge between us in this matter, and that is the infallible Word of God, "which liveth and abideth forever."

There Is a Difference

In the first place, the Bible teaches that there is a difference between the "gift" of the Holy Spirit, and the "gifts" of the Holy Spirit. The second chapter of Acts records the reception of the "gift (singular) of the Holy Ghost," while the twelfth chapter of I Corinthians deals with the operation of the "gifts (plural) of the Holy Ghost." If we consider this, the rest will be clearly understood. The speaking with other tongues as the Spirit gives utterance accompanied the "gift" of the Holy Ghost; but the "divers kind of tongues" is one of the "gifts" of the Holy Spirit, which He divides severally has He wills.

At Caesarea the Apostle knew that the Gentiles had received the "gift of the Holy Ghost" (not one of the gifts), "For they heard them speak with tongues, and magnify God." (Acts 10:45, 46.) When Peter rehearsed the incident that transpired at the house of Cornelius, he declared that God gave them the "like gift" as He did unto them at Jerusalem on the day of Pentecost.

—17—

The Gift of God a Sacrifice

That we might note that there is a distinction between "gift" of the Holy Ghost and the "gifts" of the Holy Ghost, we will refer you to the original Greek wording of the same. We do not do this to make a display of knowledge, but since some have resorted to this method to strengthen their points, or overthrow the truth, we feel that we have an equal liberty to use the same methods. We do not profess to be a Greek student, but we desire to use a little Greek at this point, as we believe it will help some. In the New Testament there are fourteen places where the word "gift" is used in reference to the Holy Spirit, directly or indirectly (note the following places: John 4:10; Acts 2:38, 8:20, 10:45, 11:17; Rom. 5:15, 16, 17, 18; II Cor. 9:15; Eph. 2:8, 3:7, 4:7; Heb. 6:4); and the word in each instance is taken from the word *doron,* which means, a sacrifice, while the word used for "gifts" is *charisma,* which means a spiritual endowment, that is, a religious qualification, or a miraculous faculty.

By this one can we clearly see that the "gift" of the Holy Ghost refers to the life which was *sacrificed* and given unto us. The "gift" of the Holy Spirit is the life of Christ Himself. The gift (doron) which God has given us is eternal life. But the gifts are spiritual endowment, religious qualifications, or miraculous faculties, given for the edifying of the Church. (I Cor. 12:1-11.) In Eph. 4:8, the original word for "gifts" is doma, which means *presents.* In Heb. 2:4, the original word used for "gifts" is *merismo,* which means *distribution.* In none of these latter cases is the same word used as that which is used with reference to the Holy Spirit, thereby making a clear distinction between the "gift" (doron) of the Holy Ghost and the "gifts" (charisma, doma) of the Holy Ghost.

A More Simple Explanation

We trust that none of the children of God will stumble over these Greek words, for it is written to meet the oppositions of the learned ones. But we have a more simple manner of conveying the truth of this matter to those who love the Word of God.

"To speak as the Spirit gives utterance" is the thing that accompanies the "gift" of the Holy Ghost but the gift of "divers kinds of tongues" is distributed among the members of the body as the Spirit wills. (I Cor. 12:11; Heb. 2:4.) Though every man "speaks as the Spirit gives utterance" when he receives the "gift" of the Holy Ghost (which is the manifestation of the Spirit, I Cor. 12:7), yet all are not given the gift of "divers kinds of tongues." It is this gift of "divers kinds of tongues" that the Apostle refers to when he says, "Do all speak with tongues?" By reading the entire chapter, it will be seen that he is dealing with all the gifts and not with speaking in tongues only.

The Gift of Tongues

It was this gift that was most particularly dealt with in the fourteenth chapter of his first epistle to the Corinthians. Those having the gift of tongues, and not knowing how to control it, were causing much trouble in the church at that time and his instructions to those was "to keep silent in the church, and speak to himself and to God," if there was no interpreter present. If they were all "speaking as the Spirit gave utterance," would there be any confusion there? The Spirit of God is not the author of confusion (ver. 33). If they were "speaking as the Spirit gives utterance" would the Apostle give orders for the Spirit not to speak, or for the people not to let the Spirit speak through them? Would he be so foolish as to dictate to the Spirit of God in such a manner, and then at the same time tell the saints "quench not the Spirit," and "grieve not the Holy Spirit?" God forbid. There must be a distinction between "gifts or divers kinds of tongues" and "speaking as the Spirit gives utterance."

Concerning the gift of tongues, the Apostle says, "If I pray in an unknown tongue MY spirit (not the Holy Spirit) prayeth" (ver. 14.) If it is his spirit praying in an unknown tongue, then there must be a difference between his Spirit operating the "gift of tongues" and the "Holy Spirit giving utterance." Hence, when he saith, "do all speak with tongues?" he has no reference to the Spirit's utterance when one receives the gift of the Holy Ghost, but, to the "gift of tongues" which is among the gifts that are given to the members of the Church as He wills.

Tongues Are For a Sign

Tongues were a sign on the day of Pentecost that the Comforter had come. They were a sign to the saints at Damascus that Paul was one of them. They were a sign to Peter and the six Jews that God had accepted the Gentiles, and that they had received the Holy Ghost. They were a sign to Paul at Ephesus that the disciples had the real thing and were sealed to the day of their redemption. They were a sign that the Corinthians were baptized into the body. They were a sign that Isaiah's prophecy was true. They were signs to Apostolic Fathers that a man received the Holy Ghost. They are a sign that modern Christendom has not received the Holy Ghost. They are a sign that the time of refreshing has come from the presence of the Lord (Isa. 28:11, 12; Acts 3:19-21), and Jesus is soon to come. And we cannot believe that a man has received the Holy Ghost until we see the signs as were manifested in Apostolic days, therefore tongues are for a sign.

The Terms Begotten and Born

In order to help those who seem to be a little confused over the meaning of the begotten, and born, we wish to give the following explanation:

Some of our young brethren have been trying to stir up the Greek language to prove that begotten and born mean the same thing. But it is not necessary to do that when we can go to the dictionary and find the following: Beget, or (begotten)—To procreate as a father, or sire. Born—Brought forth (by the mother).

Because the same Greek word, gennao is used in the original for both words, it does not necessarily imply that the words are the same in meaning. The word gennao, literally, means to bear, beget, be born, bring forth, conceive, be delivered of, gender, make, spring. And its translation depends upon what the sentence refers to in which it is used.

To ignore natural things in our search for spiritual or heavenly things, is a gross error on the part of the ministry today. Jesus said to Nicodemus, "If I have told you earthly things, and ye believe not, how shall ye believe if I tell you heavenly things?" And the Apostle Paul says, "For the invisible (spiritual) things of Him from the creation of the world are clearly seen, being understood by the things that are made, even His eternal power and God-head; so that they are without excuse." (John 3:12; Rom. 1:20.) Look at the earthly things, things that are made and see if there is not a difference between begotten and born.

CHAPTER III

BAPTISM FROM APOSTOLIC POINT OF VIEW

Baptism in water is a command of God. It is said, by many, to be an ordinance, that is, "an outward sign of inward purity." But such an expression cannot be found in the Word of God. Christ never made such a statement in all His ministry.

Jesus says, "He that believeth and is baptized shall be saved." Again, "Except a man be born of water and the Spirit, he cannot enter into the kingdom of God." The Apostle Peter said, "Repent and be baptized for the remission of sins." Ananias said to Brother Saul, at the direction of Jesus Christ, "Arise, and be baptized, and wash away thy sins, calling on the name of the Lord." (Mar. 16:16; John 3:5; Acts 2:38; Acts 22:16.)

The Apostle Paul said elsewhere, "He saved us by the washing (baptism) of regeneration, and renewing of the Holy Ghost." Again, "Christ also loved the church, and gave Himself for it; that He might sanctify and cleanse it by the washing (baptism) of water by the word." (See Tit. 3:5; Eph. 5:26, and Acts 19:1-5.) It has been taught that the "washing of water by the word" means a "washing in the word," but this is misleading, for it plainly says "washing of water" and not a "washing in the word." Our bodies (Heb. 10:22) are to be washed in water according to the word, and that is, according to the words of Jesus by both precept (Mar. 16:16; John 3:5), and example (Matt. 3:15, 16).

It is commonly stated that baptism does not save us. But the Word of God says, "Repent and be baptized in the name of Jesus for the remission of sins." Many years afterwards Peter confirmed his instructions given on the day of Pentecost when he wrote, "In the days of Noah * * * eight souls were saved by water. The like figure whereunto even baptism doth now also *save us*." Then, lest some should think that he meant the water baptism saves them by removing the bodily defilement, he adds "not the putting away of the filth of the flesh," but, deeper than that "the answer of a good conscience toward God." The strength in baptism as a saving medium comes "by the resurrection of Jesus Christ from the dead." (I Pet. 3:20, 21.)

The Blood and the Name

Water alone does not save us. "Not by water only but by water and blood." The blood and the name of an individual are inseparable. John Smith's son is a "Smith" no matter what other name you may give him, because he has Smith's blood in him. By this I want to show that the Blood and Name are inseparable. You cannot honestly bear the name of Smith unless you have Smith's blood in you; neither can you deny that you are a Smith as long as you have Smith's blood in your veins. The Blood and the Name of Jesus are inseparable. To be *saved* by water baptism, it must be administered in the name of Jesus, for there is "no other name under heaven given among men, whereby we must be *saved*." The life of the Blood of Christ is connected with baptism when it is administered in His Name. It is not by water only, but by water and blood, and the blood is in His name. (See Acts 5:28.)

It is for this reason that we find these various scriptures all relating to the same thing: "He that believeth and is baptized shall be saved." "Repent and be baptized * * * in the NAME of Jesus, for the remission of sins." "When they believed * * * concerning * * * the NAME of Jesus, they were baptized." (Acts 8:12.) "Through His NAME whosoever believeth in Him shall receive remission of sins." (Acts 10:36, 43, 47, 48.) "Believe on the Lord Jesus Christ, and thou shalt be saved, and thy house." (Acts 16:30-33.) (Belief in the name of Jesus was always followed by being baptized in His name. See Mar. 16:15, 16; Acts 16:14, 15, 31, 33; Acts 18:8; Acts 19:4, 5.)

This is God's plan. It proved successful in the days of the Apostles, why should it not be so now. Have we become instructors of the Almighty, that we should "correct" the "errors" of apostolic days by substituting our modern methods in the place of those given by the Holy Ghost sent down from heaven? Has God changed His plan of salvation? If so, when? and where?

For Jew and Gentile

Was baptism for the remission of sins given for Jews only? The Lord Jesus said "Go ye into all the world, and preach the Gospel to EVERY creature (Jew and Gentile). He (Jew or Gentile) that believeth and is BAPTIZED shall be saved." As many (Jew or Gentile) as received Him (they that *received* His word were baptized in His name, Acts 2:38, 41), to them gave He power (the Holy Ghost, Acts 1:8) to become the sons of God, even to them that believed on His (Jesus) name." (John 1:12.)

—25—

The truth is being confirmed wherever it is preached. The Gospel of old is just the same today. The traditions of men have made the word of God of none effect, but every vine that our Heavenly Father has not planted shall be rooted up. (Matt. 15:1-13.) God grant that the minister be not afraid to trust His word. Our fear toward God has been taught by the precepts of men, but we now behold a better day dawning. The Church is hearing the cry, "Awake, awake; put on thy strength, O Zion; put on thy beautiful garments, O Jerusalem, the holy city; for henceforth there shall no more come into thee the uncircumcized and the unclean. Shake thyself from the dust; arise, and sit down, O Jerusalem; loose thyself from the bands of thy neck, O captive daughter of Zion * * * Therefore My people shall know My NAME; therefore they shall know in that day that I am He that doth speak; behold, it is I. * * * The Lord has made bare His holy arm (Isa. 53:1) in the eyes of all the nations; and all the ends of the earth shall see the SALVATION of our God. (Isa. 52:1-10.)

CHAPTER IV

ONE WAY FOR ALL NATIONS

There has been considerable said about the "gospel to the Jew," and the "gospel to the Gentiles," signifying that there is one way for the Jew and another for the Gentile to enter in and be saved. This is even now being taught.

The Gospel of Christ is the good news of the death, burial and resurrection of Christ Jesus our Lord. It is evident that this is the Gospel, and the only true Gospel. The Apostle declared that if any man bring any other Gospel than that which He had preached, let him be accursed. There has been but one Christ Jesus that died, who was buried, and rose again the third day according to the scriptures. (I Cor. 15:1-8.) It is evident from the foregoing fact that there is but one Gospel for both Jew and Gentile.

Since the truth of water baptism has come to light, that is, its proper purpose, place and manner of administration, the question arises as to whether the command of Peter in Acts 2:38 is for the Jews only, or was it intended for the Gentiles also. So in fact it is not really a question as to whether there are two gospels, but whether there are two ways of entering into the possession of the grace of God brought unto us through the preaching of the Gospel.

One Way to God

That there is but one way to enter in is clearly stated in the words of our Lord Jesus Christ, "I am the WAY," "I am the DOOR," "No man can come unto the Father but by ME," "By ME if any man enters in he shall be saved." (John 10:7, 9; 14:6.) And again He said, "Other sheep I have, which are not of this fold (referring to the Gentiles); them also I must bring, * * * and there shall be ONE fold, and ONE shepherd." From this it can be seen that there is but one fold for both Jew and Gentile, and consequently, ONE door, or way of entrance.

The fold is the Spirit-filled life, called by our Lord "The Kingdom of God." (John 3:3, 5; Rom. 14:17.) To this Jesus declared that He is the Door; and not only the Door, but the Shepherd that enters in by the door. (John 10:2.) Moreover, He says, "Except a man be born of water and the Spirit, he cannot *enter into* the Kingdom of God." And again, "By Me if any man *enters in,* he shall be saved." Are there then two ways of *entering in?* No. Then it is evident that to enter through Christ is to be "born of water and the Spirit."

Synonymous Terms

There cannot be two ways to be saved. Jesus says, "By ME if any man enters in he *shall be saved.*" And again, "He that believeth, and is baptized, *shall be saved.*" (Com. John 10:9 and Mark 16:16.) By honest

—28—

observation of these scriptures we are bound to admit that to be "born of water and the Spirit," to enter by "ME (Jesus Christ)" to "enter by the Door," and to "believe and be baptized" means exactly the same thing. There is but one fold and one door, and both Jew and Gentile must enter alike, for with God there is no respect of persons. To Nicodemus the way of salvation was termed a birth "of water and the Spirit," because he being a Jew, a Pharisee, felt himself eiligible to receive the things of God by reason of the fact that he was born into the family of God's people according to the flesh. His "flesh" birth was not sufficient, therefore, he must be born again," but "of water and the Spirit."

On the day of Pentecost the way of entrance was presented to both Jew and Gentile (proselytes, Acts 2:10) alike, "Repent and be baptized, every one of you in the name of Jesus Christ for the remission of sins, and you shall receive the gift of the Holy Ghost." And as the Gospel of repentance and remission of sins in Jesus' name was preached and presented, "beginning at Jerusalem," so was it to be preached "among all nations." (Luke 24:46, 47.) Moreover He said, "Go ye into ALL the world and preach the Gospel to EVERY creature (Jew and Gentile). He that believeth (Jew or Gentile) and is BAPTIZED (Jew or Gentile) shall be saved." Could there be anything plainer than this to show that there is no difference in the method by which God saves the Jews and the way by which He saves the Gentiles?

Gospel of Uncircumcision

In reference to the terms, "gospel of the circumcision," and the "gospel of the uncircumcision," it will be clearly seen that it has no reference to water baptism in any respect. But rather to the question as to whether Gentile Christians had a right to enter into the fellowship of the Jewish Christians without being circumcized in the flesh. (See Acts 11:1-8; 15:1-31.) There seemed to be no end to the trouble. More than "fourteen years after" the Jews continued to trouble the Gentiles (uncircumcision) over this question, and later on Paul writes the Galatians his experience with the Apostles at Jerusalem. (Read Gal. 2:1-14.)

When the Apostles at Jerusalem saw that God, who had wrought mightily through Peter towards the circumcision (Jews), wrought as effectually through Paul toward the uncircumcision (Gentiles), then they gave Paul and Barnabas the right hand of fellowship, that they should preach the gospel to the uncircumcision, while they preach the gospel to the circumcision. Not that they were to preach a different gospel, or manner of entering in, but one to a people circumcised and the other to a people uncircumcised. Hence, Paul was given the "gospel of (to) the Uncircumcision," and Peter the "gospel of (or, to) the Circumcision."

Seeing it is one of God, which shall justify the circumcision (Jews) BY faith, and the uncircumcision (Gentile) THROUGH faith (Rom. 3:30), does not in any wise signify that it is a different gospel, but rather shows the wisdom of God in bringing the Jews to Christ through the Law BY faith (Gal. 3:23-25), and of the Gentiles by Grace THROUGH faith (Eph. 2:8). The Book of Galatians, instead of revealing two different gospels, shows the difference between Works and Faith, Flesh and Spirit, Law and Grace, and Jew and Church of God.

CHAPTER V

A GOSPEL MESSAGE OF HOPE

This sermon was delivered by Eld. G. T. Haywood at the Apostolic Faith Assembly, Indianapolis, Ind., during a Sunday morning service in April, 1922.

We wish to call your attention to the third chapter of Romans, beginning at verse 1, "What advantage then hath the Jew? or what profit is there of circumcision? Much every way: chiefly, because that unto them were committed the oracles of God." That is, the first opportunity to know God. The law of the ten commandments was given to them. God had committed unto their trust the oracles of God, and gave them that they might bring the light of God to the world. And although they failed their God, yet His purpose went forward. Even though some did not believe, "shall their unbelief make the faith of God without effect?" Man's unbelief does not change God's word, nor stop Him from working out His purpose.

The word of God is true whether the people believe it or not. God will bring Salvation near. It makes no difference what you say, or what I may say, "God hath said." Our God can work while we are sleeping. And when we are folded away like a garment in our graves, God will still be working. If one man or one people fails God, He will take up another and move on. God brought Israel out and made them a great people, through a man who was only a shepherd of the plains of Midian and not a warrior, but could speak words of wisdom by the spirit of God—words which even to this day have astonished the world. God sent His Word from heaven unto this people, and walked in the midst of them with mighty signs and wonders showing His mighty arm. And yet they failed God through their unbelief.

The Lord had no people He could trust. So He declared He would "take a people who are not a people and make them a people of God." He did this to prove that He does not have to depend on any nation or individual. God Himself never failed and could not fail. Even the prophets He ordained became weak along the line and were filled with fear, or took honor to themselves. "The priest and the prophet have erred through strong drink, they are swallowed up of wine, they are out of the way through strong drink; they err in vision, they stumble in judgement." (Isa. 28:7.)

What if man does not believe the Gospel as it is laid down in the Book? The Gospel is true regardless of his unbelief. I believe in the Blood of JESUS CHRIST, and that without shedding of blood there is no remission of sins. But the question is: how shall I get the remission? One may say, "I will just believe." But to "believe" means more than to just say "I believe," Matt. 26:28 says.

If any people start out with the power of God in their midst and become full of pride and lose their spirituality, God will put them aside and take up another. And if the latter fails, He will set them aside and take up still another. I am satisfied that God does not depend upon any of us to carry His work through, but we are compelled to depend upon Him for without Him we can do nothing.

"For this is My blood of the New Testament, which is shed for many for the remission of sins." Jesus was the greatest preacher the world has ever known, and turned the preaching of the Gospel over to Peter as though He said, "You are next, Peter. You shall begin where I leave off." And that preacher in Acts 2:38 said: "Repent, and be baptized, every one of you, in the name of Jesus Christ, for the *remission of sins* and ye shall receive the gift of the Holy Ghost." That is the way the Holy Spirit gave it out on the day of Pentecost. In those days the people were always baptized in the name of Jesus Christ for the remission of sins that they might receive the Holy Spirit, which was God's witness to their faith.

What is the Holy Ghost? He is a witness to your having received remission of sins. That is what the Apostle said: "There are three that bear witness in the earth, the Spirit, the water and the blood." He did not say one was any greater than the other. All three of them are required to make one witness. Many people look at water alone, but the proper thing to do is to see the name in which it is administered. Take away the blood, and you have nothing but faith. Take away the water and you make Jesus a liar. The Bible, in the first epistle of John, tells us plainly that "this is He which came by water and blood; not by water only, but by water and blood." And that, "it is the Spirit that beareth witness." I do take notice of this much: there was so much authority in the command of JESUS to baptize, that nearly all the churches (with a few exceptions) try in some way to administer it, if it only be the dipping the finger in the water. But if it is worth doing at all, it is worth doing rightly. However, a man's failure to believe does not change the Word of God. You can scarcely join a church in the city without some mode of baptism. There are about as many ways as there are human minds, and all for the lack of following the mind of the Spirit.

The reason some people do not live holy is because they have not been taught it and have been brought up wrongly. But you start a man or woman believing the Word of God, and you can bring them out on the Word. Our experiences are so varied that it does not pay to attempt to tell others about it, for they will try to get our experience instead of what is written in the Book. I do not want anybody to be able to rise and say the Word of God is not true. There has always been somebody filled with the Spirit, ever since the day of Pentecost. God has never left Himself without witness. No doubt some did not know just what they had. Luther had it. Wesley, Finney and Fox had it; and they had a hard, severe trial in their days.

We want God to be justified. We have not a thing to boast of this day. There is false holiness and true holiness. The true, is the Holy Ghost in you; and the false, is human efforts without God; self-righteousness. If we acknowledge our own failures God will give us His power to overcome day by day. God does not get behind a man with a whip and drive him to heaven, but He fixes it up so you "will" follow Him because you love Him.

Who is it that never did sin? Paul shows the whole human family had sinned, and if all sinned, all were condemned. But God had mercy. We could not help but sin. We were born that way. But God said, "You must be born again." And no new-born child walks perfectly at once. First they crawl, then they totter and fall. But they do not keep falling. By this I mean that a man or woman who is filled with the Holy Ghost and starts out to walk with Jesus Christ, may stumble and fall at first, but don't get discouraged if the devil tries to trip you up. God will help you. He is able to keep you from falling, says Jude. I am talking about those who have it in their hearts to live for Christ. Do not let any failure daunt your courage. You know God is able to carry you through. Many have found it to be so.

If God brings judgment upon a sinner for his wrong doing, some will charge Him with injustice. But how can God then judge the world? God said He would give us a light for our path, and put His angels around us, and give us a pattern in Jesus, and place His Spirit within us. Brother, I would be ashamed to tell God I could not live right with all that help! And then folks will try to tell you, "You can't make it, Brother!" So we are going to commend the righteousness of God, by acknowledging—"O Lord, we are all failures."

It is the grace of God that is able to sustain and uphold any man or woman who desires to be kept by the Power of God. There are people who desire to boast of themselves and never have had a change of heart. And some even go so far as to say, "I am all right. I am good enough. I don't need that Holy Ghost." I don't care if you did not steal, drink, or commit adultry—it is in your *heart* anyhow! Everybody needs the power of God. Good works never did save anybody. It takes the "power of God unto salvation." I am not telling a moral man to get worse in order to get saved. No! I am telling him there is no condition so bad but that God has grace to save us from it.

You cannot make men righteous by legislation. "Ye must be born again." God says to the church "preach the word" and make a fertile spot in the terrible desert of sin, that men may see the water of life along the side of the road. No law can make you live right. God Almighty tried it Himself with the children of Israel, and the Word says, "What the law could not do, Christ did." (Rom. 8:3.) But do you know when a man becomes saved he will keep the spirit of the law? There is no law against attending to your own business, paying all your debts, and no law against praying—yet! Do right, and bless God, and pray without ceasing. No law is against doing that which is just and good. (Gal. 5:22, 23.)

Many homes have been torn asunder. Sorrow and mouring drapes the human heart because of sin. I dislike to hear some people talk because of their disgraceful utterances. But let God get into their hearts and then note the change. Everybody without Christ is guilty. Had God Alimighty demanded justice, every living person would have been dead, and brought before the judgment bar to give an account of their misspent lives. The only thing that is going to save a man is the power of God. I am talking about genuine salvation, too! You can go any place and hear everything else but the Gospel of salvation. But men shall be saved. That is our whole service—to "save men." The church was ordained for that purpose.

God sums up the whole human family and declares that it is "full of wounds, bruises and putrefying sores." To tell a man he should not steal, or covet, or commit adultery is not enough. Tell him how to get saved so he will not do those things. The power of God can save anybody that will believe. The god of carnality has certainly got some folks fast. But O, I am so glad I am saved! Saved by the power of God! It is wonderful to be God's free man, delivered from the power of the pride of life, the lusts of the eye, and the lusts of the flesh. It does not make any difference whether a man is old or young, rich or poor, black or white or brown, just so he *believes*. If you have never been to school to learn a letter, you can "believe." I am satisfied that you do not have to have eyes to believe. You do not have to be able to speak to "believe." You may have both hands cut off, but still you can "believe." If you cannot hear, somebody will write, or make signs and you can "believe." You do not have to weigh so many hundred pounds or write letters, or understand the Bible to get saved. All God said was to "believe." Why, Jesus paid it all! The people that are saved to-day are people that "believed" the Gospel. And you do not believe God if you do not obey Him! I will prove it to you, too. "Show me your faith without your works, and I will show you my faith (without saying a word) by my works!" It is not merely *saying* "I be-lieve;" it is *proving* your belief. If you actually believe then you know what Jesus was talking about when He said "He that believeth and is baptized shall be saved," and prove it by your actions. Jesus declared that "ex-cept a man be born of water and the Spirit he cannot enter into the Kingdom of God." (John 3:5-7.) If you do not obey, then you do not believe.

God has fixed the matter so you need make no mis-take about it, either. Too many jump over the fifth verse of the third chapter of John's Gospel. Moreover, Jesus stated emphatically that He "testified of that which He had seen; and spake that which He did know" (John 3:11), and this is what He spoke: "I know that if a man be not born of water and the Spirit, he cannot enter into the Kingdom of God." If you have never been baptized in the name of JESUS CHRIST, you have never been immersed properly. This is the only name under heaven given among men whereby they must be saved. If you repent deeply enough in your heart, and be baptized in the name of Jesus Christ, I will guarantee that you shall receive the baptism of the Holy Ghost as you "come up out of the water."* If people do not believe God's Word they never get His best. Even if you do not understand, you must believe, before you can "see" the Glory of God.

*At the end of this sermon seven persons accepted the word, came forward immediately for baptism. Four of them received the Holy Ghost while coming out of the water, and another soon after changing clothes.

(THE END)

INDEX

CHAPTER I

THE BIRTH OF THE SPIRIT IN THE DAYS OF THE APOSTLES

Page

CHAPTER II

THE GIFT vs. GIFTS OF THE SPIRIT

CHAPTER III

BAPTISM FROM APOSTOLIC POINT OF VIEW

CHAPTER IV

ONE WAY FOR ALL NATIONS

CHAPTER V

A GOSPEL MESSAGE OF HOPE

Divine Names and Titles
of Jehovah

By Elder G. T. Haywood

CHRIST TEMPLE
BOOK STORE
430 West Fall Creek Parkway
Indianapolis, Indiana 46208

THE NAMES OF JEHOVAH GOD COMPREHEND IN JESUS

Divine Names and Titles

I. ELOHIM occurs 2,700 times in the Old Testament. Its first occurrence connects it with creation and gives it its essential meaning as the Creator. It shows forth His relation to mankind as His creatures. Notice 2 Chron. 18:31, where Elohim (God) is contrasted with His name Jehovah; to Jehosaphat. He was JEHOVAH, his Covenant God, while to the Syrians He stood only in the relation of Creator (Elohim) to His creatures, because He had made no covenant with them as a nation at any time. Elohim is God, the living God, the power of creation. (John 1:1-3; Col: 1:15-17; Rev. 3:4-11). He first assumes a creature form, though spiritual in nature (Gen. 12:7; 32:24-30; Isa. 6:1, 5) afterwards, the human form for the purpose of redeeming mankind. (John 1:14; Heb. 2:9, 14, 16, 17; Phil. 2:7; Rom. 8:3). That Elohim, in His creature form spiritually, who appeared to the Patriarchs and Prophets is the same who appeared in a human form 1,900 years ago to Israel can be clearly seen by reading the following scriptures: Gen. 17:13; Ex. 6:2, 3, with John 8:56-58; Isa. 6:1, 2, 5, 9, 10, with John 12:39, 40, 41, 44, 45.

II. JEHOVAH. While Elohim is God as the Creator of all things Jehovah is the same God in covenant relation to those whom he has created. Jehovah means the Eternal, the Immutable One. He who WAS, and IS, IS TO COME. The Divine definition is given in Gen. 21-33, where Abraham called on the name of JEHOVAH, the everlasting God. He is especially, therefore, the God of those who are redeemed and are thus now "in Christ." Like Thomas, we can truly say, "My Lord and my God."

Jehovah is indicated (in A.V.) by small capital letters, "Lord"; and "God" when it occurs in combination with Adonai, in which case Lord God—Adonai Jehovah.

The name Jehovah is combined with ten other words which form what are known as "the Jehovah Titles."

They are as follows in the order in which they occur in the Hebrew Canon:

1. **Jehovah-Jireh**—Jehovah will see, or Provide. (Gen. 22:14).

2. **Jehovah-Ropheka** — Jehovah that healeth thee. (Ex. 15:26.)

3. **Jehovah-Nissi** — Jehovah my banner. (Ex. 17:15.)

—4—

4. Jehovah-Mekaddishkem—Jehovah that doth sanctify you. (Ex. 3:13.)

5. Jehovah-Shalom — Jehovah (send) peace (Judge 6:24.)

6. Jehovah-Zebaoth—Jehovah of host. (I Sam. 1-3, and frequently.)

7. Jehovah-Zidkenu — Jehovah our righteousness. (Jer. 23:6.)

8. Jehovah-Shammah—Jehovah is there. (Ezek. 48:35.)

9. Jehovah-'Eylon—Jehovah most high. (Psa. 7:17.)

10. Jehovah-Roi—Jehovah my shepherd. (Psa. 23:1.)

III. JAH is Jehovah in a special sense and relation. Jehovah as having BECOME our Salvation. The word JAH occurs forty-nine times in the original Hebrew version of the Old Testament, but is translated "Lord" in every place but one (Psa. 68:4.) Its first occurrence in the original is in Ex. 15:2, He Who Is, and WAS, and IS TO COME.

IV. EL is essentially THE ALMIGHTY, though the word is never so rendered. El is Elohim in all His strength and power. It is rendered or translated "Gid" as Elohim is, but EL is God the Omnipotent. ELOHIM is God the CREATOR putting His omnipotence into operation. It is sometimes transliterated in the proper names, Imanu-EL, Beth-EL, etc., where it is translated as explained in the margin.

V. ELOAH is Elohim who is to be worshipped, Eloah is God in connection with His WILL rather than HIS power. The first occurrence associates this name with worship. (Duet. 32:15, 17.) Hence it is the title used whenever the contrast (latent or expressed) is with false gods or idols. Eloah is essentially "the living God" in contrast to inanimate idols.

VI. ELYON first occurs in Gen. 14:18 with EL, and is rendered "the most high (God)." It is EL and Elohim, not as the powerful Creator, but as "the possessor of heaven and earth." Hence the name is associated with Christ as the Son of "the Highest." (Luke 1:32; Matt. 28:18.) It is ELYON as possessor of the earth, Who divides the nations "their inheritance." In Psa. 82:18, He is "over all the earth." The title occurs thirty-six times in the Old Testament, but translated "God." ELYON is the dispenser of God's blessings in the earth; the blessings proceeding from a Priest Who is King upon His throne (compare Gen. 14:18-22 with Zech. 6:13; 14:9). Melchizedek abideth a priest forever; without beginning of life or ending of days. Now Christ also abideth a Priest forever. A priest is a mediator between God and man. Melchizedek and Christ are both said to abide a priest forever, and there is but one Mediator between God and man! Who is Melchizedek? (Heb. 7:1, 2, 3, 8, 15, 16, 17, 24, 25; I Tim. 2:5.)

VII. SHADDAI is in every instance translated "Almighty," and is indicated by small capital letter (ALMIGHTY). It is God (EL), not as a source of strength, but of GRACE; NOT AS CREATOR, but as Giver. Shaddai is the All-bountiful. This title does not refer to His CREATIVE power, but to His power to SUPPLY all the needs of His people. Its first occurrence is in Gen. 17:1, and is used to show Abraham that He who called him out to walk alone before Him could SUPPLY all his needs. Even so it is in 2 Cor. 6:18 where we are called to "come out" in separation from the world. It is always used in connection with El (God).

VIII. ADON is one of three titles. (ADON, ADONAL and ADONIM) all generally translated "Lord;" but each has its own peculiar usage and association. They all denote HEADSHIP in various aspects. They have to do with God as "overlord."

(1) ADON is the Lord as Ruler in the earth. It is always translated "Lord" in the authorized version of the Bible, and printed in small letters.

(2) ADONI is the Lord in His high relation of the earth; and as carrying out His purposes of blessing in the earth. In this respect it is always equivalent to Jehovah. Indeed, it was from an early date so used, by associating the vowel points of the word JEHOVAH with ADON, thus converting ADON into ADONAI.

(3) ADONIM is the plural of ADON and never used of man. ADONIM carries with it all that ADON does, but in a greater and higher degree; and more especially as OWNER and PROPRIE-TOR. An ADON may rule others who do not belong to him. Hence (without the article) it is often used of men. But ADONIM is the Lord Who RULES His own.

Now having given the names and titles of the great God of Heaven in their original terms, and the purpose and meanings of the use of each separately, which one of these do we find not incorporated in the Name of JESUS? The Pslamist declared, "Thou hast magnified thy WORD above all Thy name." In the beginning was the WORD and the WORD was with God, and the WORD was God. And the WORD became flesh." His

—8—

Name shall be called JESUS. And He has been given a name that is above every name, both in Heaven and in earth. (See Psa. 138:2; John 1:1-14; Isa. 9:6; Matt. 1:21-23; Eph. 1:21-23; Phil. 2:9.)

Thus were the names of Israel's God known in the days of old. Every one of them signifying a different relationship of the great Divine to mankind. Whenever He was approached carefulness was needed, lest haply they would "take the name of the Lord in vain." Whenever the name of the Lord was even written, the person doing so was obliged to wash himself clean, and put on a clean linen garment, and be free from every defilement. "Whosoever named the name of the Lord" had to "depart from iniquity."

To keep all these names and titles in memory and to pronounce them correctly was undoubtedly a very, very difficult task. Just think what a proposition it would be for a man to call all those titles in an effort to comprehend the fullness of the divine attributes! All these things were hard, but God has provided some better things for us.

It was the purpose of God to make Himself known to His people from the beginning. His name was to be declared among the brethren. The secret of all ages was to be afterwards revealed. In Psalms of David it is declared, "Thou hast magnified Thy word above all Thy name." (Psa. 138:2.)

When Jacob wrestled with the Angel he sought to obtain the secret name, but was prohibited. The Angel in the burning bush was hearing the secret name, and when Moses sought to obtain the secret name, all he received was "I am that I AM." The Children of Israel were led by the angel of the Lord and Jehovah said, "Beware of him * * * for My name is in him." (Ex. 23:21.) To Manoah the Jehovah Angel replied, "Why asketh thou after my NAME, seeing it is secret (margin, Wonderful) ?" (Judges 13:18.) The prophet Isaiah declared that His NAME shall be called WONDERFUL. (Isa. 9:6.) From these scriptures it can be clearly seen that Jehovah had a name to be revealed which was to be "above all His names."

There is not a shadow of a doubt but that the Angel that appeared to the Virgin in Nazareth was the Jehovah Angel of old who bore that "wonderful" name. It was there that He had finished His journey over the hills of time and deposited that secret name in the bosom of her who was "highly favoured of God." Mary pondered these things in her heart and told no one the message of the

Angel that she should bring forth a son and that his name should be called JESUS.

The Word was God from the beginning (Jno. 1:1-4) and when the Word became flesh, it was given a name that "is above every name," for He there and then "magnified His Word" above all His name. His name shall be called JESUS. What a wonderful word! All the titles that Jehovah ever bore are comprehended in this one name JESUS. The name of Jesus bears in it all that God's other name ever bore. Jesus is Elohim, the creator (Col. 1:16), Jehovah and Shaddai (Rev. 1:8), Eloah (Heb. 1:6), Elyon, the Most High (John 3:31; Eph. 4:6), in fact, all the attributes of God as are revealed by His names are all found in Jesus. Thus in all things He is given pre-eminence, and a name that is above every name. On the Isle of Patmos He declares that He is the Lord which is, which was, and which is to come, the ALMIGHTY, * * * the First and the Last. If He who appeared on the Isle of Patmos is the ALMIGHTY (Shaddai) (Rev. 1:8; Ex. 6:3), then the Almighty's new name is JESUS, and He has magnified His Word above all His name. (John 1:1-14; Rev. 3:12.)

THE ONE SPIRIT

That there is but one Holy, Eternal Spirit of God, the Father, and Christ is clearly set forth in the word of God. Our traditional theology has gotten this truth badly confused. In a close searching of the word we will see that the apostles were in nowise divided over this matter, but all recognized that the Spirit of the Father, the Spirit, and the Holy Spirit, and the Spirit of His Son, were different expressions of the one and self-same Spirit.

A man in Chicago is reported to have said that he could tell when the Spirit of the Father spoke through him, and when the Son spake, and when the Holy Spirit spake. This is very erroneous. Let us look at the Scriptures. Jesus said: "For I have not spoken of Myself; but the Father which sent Me, He gave Me a commandment, what I should say, and what I should speak therefore, even as the Father said unto Me, so I speak." (John 12:49, 50.) Again: "I speak not of Myself but the Father that dwelleth in Me." "And the word which ye hear is not Mine, but the Father's which sent Me." (John 14:10, 24.) Here we see that the words spoken by Jesus were spoken by the Spirit of the Father "that dwelleth in Him." This evidently identifies the Spirit of the Father, and Spirit of the Son to be the Self-same Spirit.

The Spirit of the Father

In Matt. 10:18-20, Jesus tells the disciples that they shall be brought before governors and kings for His sake, but when they were delivered up take no thought as to how or what they should speak, for it would be given them at the same hour what they should speak. "For," he said, "it is not ye that speak, but the Spirit of your FATHER which speaketh in you." Now, this did not take place until after the Holy Ghost had fallen on the day of Pentecost for they were not delivered up to "governors and kings for His sake" until after that time. In Acts, 4th chapter, when the first persecution set in, we find Peter "filled with the Holy Ghost," speaking the words of God with boldness (verses 8 and 31). In Acts 6:5 and 10, we find Stephen full of the Holy Ghost, so much so, that the enemy was "not ably to resist the wisdom and the Spirit by which he spake." This proves conclusively that the "Spirit of the FATHER" spoken of by Jesus is none other than the Holy Ghost.

It has been said by some that where the word SPIRIT is used without the attribute "Holy," it referred to God, and not the Holy Ghost. Let the WORD judge in this case also. In Matthew 3:16, the writer says: "The Spirit of GOD" descended like a dove upon Jesus. St. Luke, in recording the same incident, says: "The Holy Ghost descended in a bodily shape like a dove." (Luke 3:22.) St. John in relating the phenomena says: "John bare record, saying, I saw the Spirit descending * * * like a dove." (John 1:32; Mark 1:10.) Here we have three different writers (inspired writers) in recording the same miracle using three different terms for the self-same Spirit. This should be evidence enough, but we will go farther.

The "distinction" between the Spirit of Christ, the Spirit of God, and the Holy Ghost can be readily dissolved by the word of God, for His word is "like a fire." (Jer. 23:29.) That the Spirit of God and the Holy Ghost are the same Spirit can be proven by reading Matt. 3:16 and Luke 3:22. But to convince one that the Holy Ghost and the Spirit of Christ are the same One Spirit, we need only to take the words of the Apostle Peter, who declares that the "Spirit of Christ" testified through the prophets in one place, and that they spake as they were moved by the "Holy Ghost" in another. (See 1 Peter 1:10, 11; 2 Peter 1:21.) We conclude that "two things equal to the same thing are equal to each other." "There is

—14—

one Spirit," and "The Lord is that Spirit"; there is but "one Lord" and the Lord, He is God. (Eph. 4:4, 5; 2 Cor. 3:7; Psa. 100:3.)

The Seven Spirits of God

It has been asked by many what is meant by the "seven Spirits of God" if there is but one Spirit. This expression is found in Rev. 4:5 and 5:6. In one place it says the seven lamps are the "seven Spirits of God," and in the other place it says the seven eyes of the Lamb are the "seven Spirits of God." The seven lamps are evidently the illuminations of the Holy Spirit throughout the churches, that is, throughout the church age. The fourth and fifth chapters of Revelation are visions of the preparation for judgment. But the judgment will be rendered to the people according to the "illumination of the Spirit" in the dispensation in which they lived. Seven lamps—seven Spirits—"The Holy Ghost in His sevenfold operation as the light-and-life Giver." This is the explanation of Jameson, Faussett and Brown, commentators, but I believe the former is the true interpretation of the mystery. However, it is the One and self-same Spirit.

JESUS IS BOTH

In Rev. 22:6, it declares that the "Lord God of the holy prophets sent His angel to show unto His servants things which must shortly be done," but in the 16th verse JESUS says in plain words, that cannot be misunderstood: "I JESUS have sent Mine angel to testify unto these things in the churches." This sets forth clearly that Jesus Christ is BOTH.

That Jesus Christ is BOTH the God of Abraham, and the promised SEED of Abraham, may be seen from the following scriptures: In Gal. 3:16 we find that Christ is the seed of Abraham; but in comparing Rev. 1:8, where Jesus declares Himself to be the Almighty with Ex. 6:2, 3, where God declares that Abraham knew Him, not by His Name JEHOVAH, but by the name of God ALMIGHTY; then compare this with John 8:56-58, we have conclusive evidence that Jesus Christ is BOTH.

In the fourth chapter of Revelation we read of "One sitting on the throne," and that the four beasts and the four and twenty elders fall down before "Him that sat on the throne," and cast down their crowns, saying, "Thou art worthy, O Lord, to receive glory, and honor, and power, for

Thou hast created all things and for Thy pleasure they are and were created." That this refers to Jesus Christ, in His glory, everyone will admit (Col. 1:16), but in the fifth chapter of Revelation we find a "Lamb, as it had been slain," which cometh forth and takes the Book out of the right hand of "Him that sat upon the throne." That this Lamb is Jesus none will attempt to deny. Then combining the record in the 22nd chapter of Revelation, we find that the Throne of God and the Lamb is one throne, and it further declares that "His servants shall SERVE HIM (not 'them'), and they shall see HIS face" (not "their" faces); and "HIS Name shall be in their foreheads," (not "their" names). From this it can be clearly seen that Jesus Christ is BOTH the Lord God and the Lamb.

THE MYSTERY OF THE REVELATION

The Mystery of Revelations is liken unto the blossoming of a rose. While a rose is confined in the bud, every petal is perfect; but though we try ever so earnestly to pick it open before its time, we are forced to admit that all of our efforts are in vain. And the final result is that the petals are torn and the rose as a whole is marred beyond recognition.

But if we leave it until its appointed time it will gently unfold itself in all its beauty, every petal in its place and the air will be filled with its fragrance. Oftentimes a rosebud may be clipped from the bush before it is fully developed. The only way for it to be properly unfolded is to place it in a glass of water, then it will unfold itself.

Thus it is with the Mystery of the Godhead. It has been folded away in God's infinite wisdom, awaiting the day appointed, when "in the dispensation of the fulness of times" all things were to be gathered in Christ, both which are in heaven and in earth. (Eph. 1:10.) Men have endeavored to solve this mystery centuries ago, but the more they "picked" at it, the more obscure and mysterious it became; so they were compelled to cease from any further intrusion, shake their heads and utter with a gasp of dismay, "Things too wonderful for me; it is a MYSTERY."

Now that the "fulness of times" has come, the hidden mystery is now being revealed in Christ. The Rose of Sharon has gently unfolded, and we are beginning to see the "King in His Beauty." What a fragrance fills the air! JESUS, JESUS, BLESSED JESUS! The Mystery of the FATHER, SON and HOLY GHOST is fully comprehended in Christ Jesus. As Father, He was the Creator, Begetter of all things. (John 1:1-3; Col. 1:16-18.) As Son, He was our example in the days of His flesh, from His baptism in the Jordan up to His ascension on the resurrection morning. (Matt. 3:15-17; John 20:17.) As Holy Ghost He comes within and abides forever. (John 14:16-18; Matt. 28:18-20.)

The FINEST of the WHEAT

by
Elder G. T. Haywood

Published by
CHRIST TEMPLE BOOK STORE
430 W. FALL CREEK PKWY.
INDIANAPOLIS, INDIANA 46208

INDEX

CHAPTER I.

FORWARD.

The need of the hour is the unfolding of the truths of God unto his people. Wisdom and knowledge are the stability of the times. The spirit of research is the spirit of the age. Those who read the word of God are anxious to know just what the things or record mean. In many places there are no instructors, and when men of corrupt minds pass their way they are soon carried away with divers and strange doctrines.

In these pages we are endeavoring to give forth wholesome instructions in the word of God that will enable one to increase his confidence in guidance of the Holy Spirit. All of the articles contained in this book have been published heretofore at various intervals in The Voice In The Wilderness, and have been of great help to those who have read them. Our prayer is that they will open up the understanding of the reader to things that hitherto have been vailed in mystery. It is God's will that his people should be fed on the finest of the wheat.

AUTHOR.

CHAPTER I.

THE FINEST OF THE WHEAT.

Oh, that my people had hearkened unto me, and Israel had walked in my ways! I should have soon subdued their enemies, and turned their hand against their adversaries. The haters of the Lord should have submitted themselves unto him; but their time should have endured forever. He should have fed them also with the finest of the wheat; and with honey out of the rock should I have satisfied them. Psa. 81:13-16.

But my people, saith the Lord, would none of my counsel; for they hated knowledge and did not choose the fear of the Lord. Therefore hath the glory of God been hidden from their eyes. Evil hath come into the land and destruction wasteth at noonday. The people to whom God gave the light of salvation, to restore the altar of the Lord that has been thrown down for centuries, are drifting with the tide of worldly ambition and missing the mark of the high calling.

When the Spirit was poured out a few years ago all hearts were rejoicing in Jesus. Time after time the Holy Spirit, in exalting Jesus, would in turn prophesy through tongues and interpretation, or a voice more solemn than the natural voice of the speaker, and foretold of these days we now behold. Little heed was given to those messages because of the counterfeits that entered therein; but if you were to review some of them that are hidden away somewhere you would be startled to note the accuracy of the fulfillment of the same. We do not say that all of them were truly inspired, but there were some direct from God.

However that may be, we are facing the crisis foretold. Some have stumbled and fell; and some have been snared and taken; while others through fear have failed to go on with God. Yet there are a few who are contending for the faith that was once delivered unto the saints. Multitudes, multitudes, are in the valley of decision! But I have made my choice forever! I will follow the lowly Nazarene through the Jordan, through the Wilderness, through the Garden, through the Judgment Hall, through Calvary's rugged brow, and on and on until I sit down with Him in the throne of His glory. My soul is satisfied at bearing His reproach, the fellowship of His suffering, being made conformable unto His death.

Had we maintained an "ear to hear what the Spirit saith," and walked in the ways of the Lord, what wonders might our God have performed; and what a sweeping victory would have been wrought in "subduing" our enemies! Failing to understand God's way and purpose many have cleaved to the traditions of the past, and like the golden wedge, the shekels of silver, and the Babylonish garment (Joshua 7:10-21), they have caused internal conflicts amid God's people, and our enemies have smitten us on every side. They boast themselves, and make wide their mouths, gloating over the "failure" of the apostolic faith movement, but out of the midst of the camp comes a shout, "Rejoice not against me, O mine enemy: when I fall, I shall rise; when I sit in darkness, the Lord shall be a light unto me." (Mic. 7:8.) Our only hope of victory is the destruction of Achan (troubler) and his for-

bidden treasures (traditions). See Josh. 7:22-25;
Mat. 15:1-13 and Gal. 5:12. Every vine that our
heavenly Father hath not planted must be rooted
up. Achan must be stoned.

The traditions of men have hidden God's truths
from his people. Tradition obstructed the view of
the entrance into the Kingdom of God. This door
of entrance was most beautifully exemplified at the
river Jordan when our Shepherd entered in before
us through "water and Spirit," leaving us an example, saying, "Thus it becometh us to fulfill all
righteousness." The righteousness of the Law can
only be fulfilled in us through Christ by the new
birth and that is by being born of water and the
Spirit. See Mat. 3:13-17; Rom. 8:3, 4; 6:3-5; John
3:5; 10:2, 7, 9. The baptism of Jesus in the Jordan
is never used by modern theologians as an example
of the new birth, but instead it is used to bolster
up the Romanish idea of "three persons" (corporeal
beings) in the Godhead. And all who are filled with
such teachings are blinded to the deeper things of
God, denying the only Lord that bought them. Acts
20:28; 2 Pet. 2:1.

Now that we have been delivered from the errors
of the past through being properly baptized into
Christ (John 3:5; Acts 2:38; Rom. 6:3-5; Gal. 3:27)
we have come into a rich store-house of wisdom and
knowledge of heavenly things, for in him "are hid
all the treasures of wisdom and knowledge." Col.
2:2, 3. Our souls are being "fed with the finest of
the wheat." Daily there cometh down from heaven
to us "our daily bread." The beauties of the revelation of "the Father and Son" in Christ; the New
Birth of water and Spirit; the Seven Parables and
Seven Candlesticks; the closing of the dispensation;

the Revelation of the Ages; the Federation of the Nations, and many others heretofore hidden mysteries of God, truly have become "hidden manna" to our hearts.

But that is not all. He has also promised us "honey out of the rock." All these promises are ours. The test of our loyalty to Christ has come. The trials are hard and many, yet there is a sweetness in it all. Through Christ our Rock we can glory in tribulations. There is a calm and sweetness in Christ in these moments that could never be experienced in any other way. Through suffering we alone can behold his glory. Let us then be true and faithful; press the battle to the gate; love your enemies, hate the devil; through Job's patience learn to wait. Weeping may endure for a night, but joy cometh in the morning.

CHAPTER II.

___

THAT ROCK WAS CHRIST.

The land of Palestine is a very mountainous country, and also a land of many rocks, which, in the days of old, made part of the strength of the country; for in the times of danger the inhabitants retired to them, where they found a refuge against any sudden irruption of the enemy.

When the Benjaminites were overcome, and almost exterminated by the Israelites of the other tribes, they secured themselves in the rock Rimmon, and there they hid themselves for four months. Judges 20:47. In that rock was their salvation. After Samson had smitten the Philistines "hip and thigh with a great slaughter" he went down and dwelt in the top of the rock, Etam. Judges 15:8.

It was into the rocks that David often hid himself when he was persecuted by Saul. At Engedi he entered into the cave of rock which was of so vast extent that he was able to hide himself and 3,000 men, and although Saul entered into it, while they were concealed therein, yet he did not discover them (I Sam. 24:1, etc.)

From the security and deliverance of their people so often through the rocky regions of their coveted land the Israelites began to apply the metaphor to the God of their fathers, Abraham, Isaac and Jacob. Nothing could have been more appropriate than esteeming Him as the Rock of their salvation. In Him they had found a refuge from the hands of their enemies. He was their Rock, His work was

(and is) perfect: * * * a God of truth * * * just
and right is He. (Duet. 32:4.)

In rehearsing the wonderful work wrought
through the mighty hand of their God, Moses inquires, "How should one chase a thousand, and two
put ten thousand to flight, except their Rock had
not sold them, and the Lord had shut them up? For
their rock is not as our Rock, even our enemies
themselves being judges." (Duet. 32:15, 18, 30,
31). Moses had not forgotten the God of his fathers, who in the time of the most decisive moment of
his life, said, "My presence shall go with thee, and
I will give thee rest * * * Behold there is a place
by me, and thou shalt stand upon a rock; and it shall
come to pass, while my glory passeth by, that I will
put thee in the clift of the rock, and will cover
thee with my hand while I pass by." Ex. 33:12-23.
It was while in the clift of the rock that the Lord
proclaimed and revealed the meaning of His name,
(Ex. 34:1, etc.) and renewed the tables of stone
which had been broken in the hands of Moses.

David's faith in the Rock of Israel was firm.
He trusted in Him alone saying, "Who is a Rock,
save our God? God is my strength and power."
Unto thee will I cry, O Lord, my rock. From the
end of the earth will I cry unto thee, when my heart
is overwhelmed: LEAD ME TO THE ROCK THAT
IS HIGHER THAN I. He brought me up also out of
an horrible pit, out of the miry clay, and set my
feet upon a rock. What a blessed thing it is to be
made to stand upon a rock!

"In the Lord, Jehovah, is the rock of Ages"
(margin Isa. 26:4). He is the hope of His people.
When fainting and thirsty in the "waste howling
wilderness" Moses smote a rock and "water gushed

out," and they all did eat and drink and were satisfied, and "that Rock was Christ." I Cor. 10:1-4. In
his flesh as a man he was the "shadow of a Great
Rock in a weary land," but spiritually, "that Rock
was Christ." It is on this Rock that the Church of
God is built (Matt. 16:18), and the gates of hell
shall not prevail against it. Though rain descends,
the floods come, the winds blow and beat upon it,
it shall never fall for it is founded upon a rock. If
we put our trust in Him, we shall be like Mount
Zion which shall never be moved. He that believeth
in Him shall have the life of the Rock of Ages.

CHAPTER III.

THE ALLEGORY IN THE BOOK OF JOB.

That there was once a man whose name was Job there can be no doubt, from the fact that God classes him with Noah and Daniel (Ezek. 14:14), while James refers to his patience in connection with the "prophets" and "the Lord" (Jas. 5:10, 11). But in the record of his life is concealed a most wonderful allegory of the fall and rise of the human family.

Abraham, Sarah, Hagar, Ishmael and Isaac were real persons, yet in reading Galatians 4:22-31 we find that the Apostle Paul in speaking of the casting out of Hagar and Ishmael says that those things "are an allegory." (Verse 24). An allegory is "the description of one thing under the image of another."

Job, in his prosperity, was like man "hedged" about in Eden. Satan, the accuser of the brethren, intended to make man curse God, by depriving him of his blessings in Eden. But though man was put out of the garden, yet he endeavored to worship God through sacrifices and offerings. (Gen. 4:1, etc.)

To offset the spirit of worship Satan caused the world to be filled with sin and violence. There was none good, no, not one. The human family was full of "wounds, and bruises, and putrifying sores"; the whole head was sick and the whole heart was faint. From the sole of the foot even to the head, there was no soundness in it." Isa: 1:5, 6.

The three friends of Job are the conscience, the Law and the Prophets. As these three men's council was unprofitable so far as helping Job out of his condition, even so the conscience, law and prophets were unable to deliver man from his miserable, loathsome state.

The cry of Job, in his misery, for a "daysman" (mediator) who could "lay his hand upon both" himself and God (Job 9:33), and his yearning cry, "Oh, that I knew where I might find him" most wonderfully portrays the craving of the human heart for the Saviour, who could lay his hand upon both man and God. The Conscience accused him, (Rom. 2:14, 15); the Law condemned him (2 Cor. 3:9), and the Prophets reproved him (Isa. 29:21; 59:1-15), but none of these three could show man the way out of his miserable, wretched condition.,

The sudden appearance of Elihu upon the scene and his silencing of the arguments of Eliphaz, Bildad, and Zophar is like Christ coming "suddenly" to this earth (Mal. 3:1; Lu. 2:1-14; Mat. 3:13-17) as a "daysman" or Mediator between God and man. As Elihu was "in God's stead" (Job 32:6) and "also formed out of clay" and exhorted Job to be not "afraid" (verse 7), even so Christ "in God's stead," was made like unto sinful "flesh" in order that man be not "terrified" at his presence. His words, "neither shall my hand be heavy upon you," conceals the words of Jesus, "My yoke is easy, and my burden is light." As Elihu was the end of the arguments of Job's three friends, even so was Christ the end of the accusation, condemnation, and reproof of the Conscience, Law and Prophets. At the transfiguration Peter, Moses, and Elias were silenced, and they saw "no man" but Jesus only.

The departure of Elihu is as mysterious as his appearance. In the closing of his remarks he exhorts

Job to "stand still, and consider the wondrous works of God." Jesus showed man (sinful man) the "wondrous works of God," and as Elihu's presence was swallowed up by the presence of God coming and speaking out of the "whirlwind," so it was on the day of pentecost, that the testimony of Christ was confirmed by the "rushing mighty wind" (Acts 2:14; Matt. 10:20), God speaking in the Holy Ghost. (See Job, 32nd Chapter to 37th, Elihu's testimony. Chapter 38th to 41st, God's testimony.)

When man was deprived of the happiness of Eden, he lost all that he had. Like Job, it seemed he could say, "The Lord gave, and the Lord hath taken away, blessed be the name of the Lord." He was stripped of everything but yet he offered homage unto God. In the "latter end" of his life God blessed Job more than he did at the beginning. So shall it be with man, the latter days of our human existence will be glorious and far exceed anything that mortal eye has ever beheld. For it is written, eye hath not seen nor ear heard what God has prepared for them that love him. (1 Cor. 2:9, 10.)

It was through faith and patience that Job passed through the terrible ordeal and obtained the multiplied blessing in the end. His undaunted courage and confidence sustained him. He endured as seeing Him who is invisible. The hope of a resurrection gave him strength to press his claim. Though in the beginning he reasons, "If a man dies shall he live again?" and, again, "As a cloud is consumed and vanisheth away, so he that goeth down to the grave shall come up no more," yet toward the last he caught a distant vision of his Lord and cried, "I know that my Redeemer liveth, and that He shall stand at the latter day upon the earth. And though after my skin worms destroy this body, yet in my flesh I shall see God."

Thus, we who are called unto suffering, that we might obtain a better resurrection, must not be "slothful, but followers of them who through faith and patience inherit the promises." Though our conscience has accused us, the law has condemned us, and the prophets have reproved us, thank God, that there is a "daysman" between us; one that has laid his hand on both God and man, the Man Christ Jesus, our Lord.

CHAPTER IV.

GOD'S MASTERPIECE.

Man is a threefold creature, consisting of Spirit, soul, and body. All that is visible is the body. Man is the masterpiece of God's workmanship, and is "wonderfully and fearfully" made. Nothing like him has ever been brought into being.

The body was formed from the dust of the ground. God breathed into his nostrils the breath (spirit) of life, and he became a living soul. The union of the Spirit and the body apparently produced the soul. (Gen 2:7.)

The soul is never separated from the body. It is the seat of affections. It is the subconscious realm of human activity. On it is impressed the desires, or affections gathered by the spirit through the mental realm, and afterwards carried into actions by the body. The soul is to the body what the records are to the phonograph. (See Rom. 1:20.) Whatever is imprinted on the soul will be acted out unconsciously by the body.

When the spirit of man begins to reach out after evil things, evil impressions are stamped upon the soul, thus resulting in evil deeds, wicked works and practices. The Psalmist says man is "estranged from the womb; they go astray as soon as they are born, speaking lies." Psa. 58:3. The soul is often spoken of as the "heart". (Gen. 6:5; Psa. 51:10; 84:2.)

The preaching of the gospel stirs one's spirit to seek after righteousness. Though the spirit may be inclined towards righteousness, yet it cannot do the things they desire to do on the account of the soul being, as it were, filled with evil engravings of past affections. Hence there is a struggle between the spirit and the body, because the body is inclined to fulfill deeds recorded on the soul, while the spirit endeavors to perform the works of righteousness. (Rom. 7:9-24.) This is genuine conviction unto godly sorrow, working repentence unto salvation.

There is nothing that can remove those evil records engraved upon the soul, or heart, but faith in the blood of Jesus, the Bishop of our souls. The true cry of a penitent spirit is, "O wretched man that I am! who shall deliver me from the body of this death?" "Create in me a clean heart, O God; and renew a right spirit within me!" "What must I do to be saved?" When a soul reaches that state he should be taught full faith and obedience in the command of God, "Repent and be baptized in the name of Jesus Christ for the remission of sins, and ye shall receive the gift of the Holy Spirit," and God will confirm His word.

When the soul is cleansed the Holy Spirit comes in to help the spirit to place new records on the soul, that the body might perform the will of God, walking in the newness of life. Through the Holy Spirit He will "put My laws in their minds (spirit), and write them upon their hearts" (soul). See John 14:26; 16:13; Heb. 8:10. The mind is the realm of the spirit's activity, while the heart is the seat of the soul's affections. Thus by having new records on the soul it becomes as easy for a man to walk and live righteous as it was for him to live wickedly in his former life. Many are cleansed and filled with the Spirit, but fail to get God's truth hidden, or engraved in their hearts. Psa. 119:11; Hos. 4:6. They need the TRUTH, and not tradition! John 8:32; 17:17.

The modern purchasing plan beautifully illustrates the purpose of spirit, soul, and body, and their final disposition. Whenever an article is purchased the salesman writes out the price, date, and description of the article on two bills at one writing,—an original and a duplicate bill. When the goods are delivered the duplicate goes with the article purchased, while the original is signed and returned to the Company that gave it. Should any question arise over the goods they are returned with the duplicate, which is immediately compared with the original, and judgment is rendered according to the records of the two bills. Thus it is with the spirit, soul and body.

The body is the article of purchase. The spirit and the soul are the two bills,—original and duplicate, respectively. The records of bodily action originate with the spirit, and are duplicated on the soul. When the body is delivered up to death and the grave, the deeds of the body are still imprinted on the soul. The soul and body enter the grave together. (Job 33:18, 22, 28, 30; Psa. 16:10, and Acts 2:27, 31. Psa. 49:14, 15.) But the spirit returns to the God that gave it. (Ecc. 3:21; 12:7; Lu. 23:14, and Acts 2:31; Acts 7:59, 60.) The dead know not anything that is transpiring in this life after their departure, but they do know what is transpiring in the realm wherein they are confined. The spirit of the wicked is tormented by remorse, being conscious of his future destiny. His soul is harassed while sleeping, like a man with wicked, horrible, tormenting dreams, but unable to awake. And when he awakes on the morning of the second resurrection

(Rev. 20:10-15), he will awake expecting relief, but will find that his punishment has in reality just begur. (See Luke 16:22-31.)

As for the righteous their spirit departs to be with Christ in Paradise (Phil. 1:23), while the soul is at rest sweetly sleeping in Christ like "one who has folded the drapery of his couch about him and laid down to pleasant dreams." And in the resurrection morning he "shall be satisfied when he awakes with His likeness." His spirit and soul will be united in "a glorious body" and shall enter into that realm of life eternal, where there shall be no death, no night, no sleep, no sorrow to break in on the feast of unending joy in the presence of the Lord. (See Psa. 17:15; Isa. 26:19; Dan. 12:1-3; 1 Cor. 15:49-55; 1 Thes. 4:13-17.

CHAPTER V.

THE GLORY OF THE SON OF MAN.

The manifestation of the sons of God is evidently near at hand. The whole creation groaneth and travaileth in pain together until now for that grand and glorious event. It must come! It shall come! It will come and will not tarry!

For a number of years we have been touching upon this subject and many hearts have been made to rejoice when they beheld what the future held in store for them that love him. (I Cor. 2:9, 10). And like the Psalmist of old we are made to cry, "Glorious things are spoken of thee, O city of God!" Psa. 87:3. The Bride of the Lamb, the Spirit-filled saints are the City of God. And to her shall be given power to rule over nations.

To teach that these despised followers of the Lowly Nazarene, who are rejected, scoffed and ridiculed, will become rulers of the nations may seem a thing incredible to many, but with God all things are possible. Joseph was hated by his brethren. He was cast into a pit. He was taken out and sold into Egypt. In Egypt he was thrown in jail, but when the time had come he arose from the prison and ascended to the throne. Daniel declares, "The kingdom and dominion, and the greatness of the kingdom under the whole heaven, shall be given to the people of the saints of the Most High." (Dan. 7:27). And in verse 22 he says, "And judgment was given to the saints of the Most High; and the TIME CAME when the saints POSSESSED the Kingdom."

The Son of Man.

The vision which Daniel saw of one like the Son of Man coming to the Ancient of days and receiving a kingdom, has always been a conundrum to many. To most people the "Son of Man" referred to is Jesus Christ personally, but this view can clearly be proven erroneous by comparing the vision (Verses 13, 14) with the interpretation given by "one that stood by" (Verses 18, 22, 27). He here declares in plain words that the one like the "Son of Man" is the "Saints of the Most High."

The saints of the Most High are one in Christ, and are one body. "For as the body is one, and has many members, and all the members of that one body being many are one body; so also is CHRIST." (1 Cor. 12:12, 13). All who are baptized by that "one Spirit" and living a clean, holy life (2 Cor. 6:14-18) are members of that one body. The Spirit that thrills and vibrates the bodies of the baptized saints of today, is the same that made up the "one body" in the days of old. And this is that body that Daniel saw in his vision of the "Son of man." The Ancient of Days is Christ in His ancient and eternal Glory. (Compare Dan. 7:9 with Rev. 1:13-15). The "Son of man" is the body of spirit-filled saints. Jesus Christ is "our" Lord, and we are "His Christ (anointed)," and the "Kingdoms of this world are (to) become the kingdoms of OUR Lord, and HIS Christ, or anointed ones." (Rev. 11:15).

The Great Question?

But when and how shall these things be, is the thing that awaits solution. As to when shall it be, the Prophet states that he "beheld until thrones were cast down." In this we obtain a faint idea as to "when shall these things be." During the past world conflict there were evidently more "thrones cast down" than ever was known. Since that time "uneasy lies the head that wears the crown." Wars and rumor of wars have been precedent in the past few years in confirmation of the fact that "the time is at hand."

The great war has left the European nations in a desolate, restless, and suffering condition. Famine is rife, everywhere, and thousands are dying for lack of medical attention. In Austria, it was said that many thousands were dying because there are no physicians to administer unto them. What an opportunity is this for the people of God who know of the power of God to heal! What a mighty awakening it would be if only a company of spirit-filled people was to march through this afflicted world and heal them in the name of Jesus! If ever there was a time for God to manifest His sons to the world it is now.

The conditions are growing from bad to worse. Medical science is proving a failure. The Christian world is beginning to realize that there is a possibility of the health of the people being restored by the prayer of faith. In certain nominal churches, the Episcopal Churches of the middle Northwest, especially, have begun "weekly healing missions." Then comes Sadhu Sundar Singh, the apostle of India, preaching healing by the prayer of faith. He says, "I have come to help Christianize America." With faith revived to the old apostolic standard, and a world crying for God, how easily would it be for God to raise up his people in authority over this generation by the manifestation of His power through his people.

Is not this the event spoken of by the great apostle Paul, for which he declares that "the whole creation groaneth and travaileth in pain together until now?" Has not the whole world been in pain and sorrow like the pains of travail, during and since the world war? The very scripture (Rom. 8:18) which precedes the above quotation has even been used by the secular press to console the torn and bleeding soldiers at the front and the wounded hearts at the fireside. It was used in connection with a painting which portrayed a wounded soldier being directed by an angel to the rays of light above him, saying, "For I reckon that the sufferings of this present time (referring to the war) are not worthy to be compared with the glory that shall be revealed in us." How significant is this incident! What can the "glory" be but the "manifestation of the sons of God!" While the world is groaning without, we who have the first fruits of the Spirit "groan within ourselves, waiting for the adoption; to-wit, the REDEMPTION of our bodies."

The Day of Redemption is surely near. All creation bears witness to this glorious event. Note what St. Luke says of this day. (Chap. 21:25-28.) Can we find time for strife, envy, prejudice, bigotry and worldly honour at such a time as this? Now is the time for God to be glorified in His saints. WATCH and PRAY. Greater things than we have ever witnessed are near at hand. The power that now lies apparently dormant may revive and burst forth at any moment. The Church is rapidly coming to "the unity of the faith, and of the knowledge of the SON of God, unto a perfect man, unto the measure of the stature of the fulness of Christ." (Eph. 4:13.) The works that Christ did, in the days of His flesh, must be done by the Church (John 14:12), and even greater. The people spoken of by the prophet Joel are about to appear. (Joel 2:1-11.) St. Paul speaks of it as the time when God "shall come to be glorified in His saints." 2 Thes. 1:7-10. Surely the hour is come that "the Son of man be glorified, and God is glorified in him. If God be glorified in him, God shall also glorify him in himself, and shall straightway glorify him." (John 13:31, 32). When Judas was manifested God became glorified in Christ. When the antichrist is manifested God will be glorified in Christ, the church, which is His body. Be ready. We are all members of His body and the glory which He had shall be given us, that He might be glorified. (John 17:22).

CHAPTER VI.

HE THAT OVERCOMETH.

The promises of God are to those that overcome. He that overcometh shall inherit all things. He that fails to overcome shall suffer loss. To the entire period of the Church there are seven promises given to the overcomers. These are found in Rev. 2:7, 11, 17, 26-28; Rev. 3:5, 12, 21.

He that overcometh the spirit that existed in the Ephesian period of the Church shall be given "to eat of the tree of life, which is in the midst of the Paradise of God." To retain one's "first love" is the secret of life. The beloved apostle John had evidently reached that place. He was the most lovable of all the twelve. In his gospel and epistles there is more said about love than in all the books of the New Testament. And there is more said about eternal life in his gospel than in all other writings together. It was he of whom Jesus said, "If I will that he tarry till I come, what is that to thee?" John 21:22. By this the disciple understood that he was not to die. All other disciples met death by martyrdom, but John passed through all those things because he had evidently been "given to eat of the tree of life that was in the midst of the Paradise of God." By some it was said that he died in a ripe old age, while others report that he was translated; by some there is an old tradition circulated that John is yet alive somewhere on earth. However that may be, translated, or yet remaining, it is evident that he did not leave his "first love." God grant that we all retain our "first love" and eat of the tree of life.

To the overcomers of the spirit of the Smyrnian age,—the spirit of persecution, tribulation, poverty and suffering,—shall be given a "crown of life," and they "shall not be hurt of the second death." The "crown of life" is the gift of life eternal that shall be given to the martyrs in the resurrection. They that enter into life eternal shall escape the lake of fire (Matt. 25:41-46) which is the second death. (Rev. 20:14, 21:8.) Those who "suffer" here with Christ have promise of "reigning with him" (2 Tim. 2:12) and that reign is a "reign in life" (Rom. 5:17), therefore he that faileth not in the hours of suffering and tribulation, but overcometh, shall be given a crown of life, thereby being delivered from the "hurt of the second death." He that seeketh to save his life shall lose it; but he that loseth his life shall preserve it unto life eternal.

To overcome these things we must not shrink from hard trials and persecutions. He that endureth to the end shall be saved. Do not faint in these trying hours. But call to remembrance the former days, in which, after you were illuminated, you endured a great fight of afflictions. Cast not away therefore your confidence which hath a great recompence of reward. * * * Now the just SHALL live by faith; but if any man draw back, my soul shall have no pleasure in him. By God's grace we shall overcome!

The spirit in the church of Pergamos was that of instituting the doctrines of men, at the instigation of Satan who had succeeded in obtaining a "seat" in the church. Instead of the people being fed upon the true word of God they were made to eat things sacrificed to idols and to commit spiritual fornication.

That spirit is abroad in the world today. But he that overcomes these things shall be given to eat of "hidden manna," and shall be given a white stone in which is a new Name written, which no man knoweth saving he that receiveth it. That "hidden manna" is the "true bread from heaven," Jesus Christ. (John 6:41, 48, 49, 50, 51, 58.) In Christ is "hidden" all the treasures of wisdom and knowledge. The mystery of God is "hidden from the wise and prudent" but is revealed unto babes (Lu. 10:21, 22.) To feast on the revelation of Jesus Christ is truly "hidden manna" to our souls. The "white stone" is the same that Daniel saw "cut out without hands," but the name written in that stone was unknown in other ages to the sons of men, but in these last days the knowledge of these mysteries is coming forth. That new name is "Jesus," but no one knoweth it save he that receiveth it, and this is he that "overcometh." (See Mat. 11:14, but all did not receive it.) Tho this revelation of Christ Jesus is offered to all, but all will not receive, hence, no man knoweth that this "New Name" is JESUS saving he that will receive it. To the rest it is veiled in mystery, but to him that overcometh shall all these things be made known. The doctrine of Balaam was the spirit of preaching in order to obtain riches and honor. Balaam was not so eager to speak the Words of God as he was to gain honor and promotion from Balak. (Num. 24:15-17.) Because of many failings to overcome that spirit of "honor seeking" they are not able to believe the revelations on the Name of Jesus. (See John 5:44.)

The Thyatirian spirit is the increasing of the spirit of the preceding period. The woman Jezebel (Roman Catholicism) takes up the doctrines inaugurated

by those of the Pergamos period, and for the love
of riches and honor, has seduced the religious world
to "eat things (traditions, not the Word, Matt. 4:4)
sacrificed to idols (many gods), and to commit (spiritual) fornication" by worshipping other gods beside the only true and living God who is manifested
in the Person of Jesus Christ. (Deut. 31:16; Rev.
17:1-5.) The spirit of "that woman Jezebel" is to
rule over nations. She has committed fornication
(compromised) with the kings of the earth in order
to seduce them to come under her rulership. Many,
seeing the prestige that she is gaining with the nations of the earth, are being seduced to follow in
her pernicious ways. But her agreement with the
kings will not stand. (Rev. 17:12-18.) In one hour
her destruction shall come, and she and her children
(followers) shall be cast into a (hot) bed of Great
Tribulation. (See Rev. 2:20-24; 18:1 to 19:2.) Her
false rule shall come suddenly to an end. But to
those that OVERCOME that spirit in these days
shall be given "power over nations, and shall rule
them with a rod of iron." For the greatness of the
kingdom under the whole heaven, shall be given to
the people of the saints of the Most High. (Dan.
7:27) and they shall rule them with a rod of iron.
Moreover He saith, "And I will give him the morning star." That morning star is the Star and Sceptre of Jacob. (Num. 24:17.) The Star of Jacob and
Sceptre of Israel is beyond a doubt, Jesus Christ our
Saviour, who distinctly declares, "I am the root and
offspring of David and the bright and MORNING
STAR." (Rev. 21:16.) Therefore, to him that overcometh shall be given the life, power, and authority
that was manifested in Jesus Christ in the days of
his flesh, or in the "morning" of the gospel dispensa-

tion. The truth of these things have come in the "evening" time, as it is written, "but it shall come to pass, that at evening time it shall be light."

The spirit of the Sardis period was the spirit of false conception. They had a name that they lived, but were dead. This spirit appeared at the time of the reformation. Many who followed Luther and the reformers held fast to what knowledge they had and refused to return to paganism, although they did not have the spirit of life in them. They stood on negative faith alone. Because of their firm stand God honored them, and exhorted them to hold fast to what they had received and heard, but to deepen their repentence. Even though they did not have the fullness of the Spirit yet because they walked in all the light that they had, He who had the seven Spirits (fullness) of God, declares "they shall walk with me in white," and counts them acceptable, saying, "for they are worthy."

Today we encounter the same spirit everywhere. Many are professing to have that which they have not, yet they endeavor to keep themselves pure and spotless before God. He that is able to overcome this Spirit shall be filled with the fullness of the Spirit, or "clothed in white raiment." (Compare these scriptures, Rev. 19:8; Jer. 23:6; 1 Cor. 1:30; Rom. 13:14; Gal. 3:27.) Those who died without the knowledge of God's Holy Spirit shall be "counted worthy," but those who now live and will walk in the light shall be "made worthy" by being "clothed in white raiment" (the Spirit).

The promises to the overcomers of the Church of Philadelphia are deep and wonderful. The prevalent spirit was that of brotherly love. It is the spirit of true holiness, both negative and positive; that is,

within and without as well. Before such there is set
an open door. The secrets of the Lord are with
them that fear Him. No man can shut the door
that God has opened to His Philadelphian saints.
Their strength is small. They must rely on Jesus'
Name alone, for in the Lord Jehovah is everlasting
strength. Their victory is through having faith in
His WORD, therefore He says, "and hast kept the
WORD of my patience, and hast not denied MY
NAME." Thank God the "door is open" and there
are many who have not denied His Name! Our enemies shall be put to shame. (Com. Isa. 66:5 and
Rev. 3:8, 9.)

Furthermore, He has promised to keep them who
have kept his word, from the hour of temptation,
which shall come upon all the world, to try them
that dwell upon the earth. Waves of that hour of
temptation have already swept over the face of the
earth. Terrible plagues have tempted many to re-
sort to the "arms of flesh" for deliverance, but all
those who put their trust in the NAME OF JESUS
have found his promise true. There are yet other
plagues to follow, but the Name of the Lord is a
strong tower, the righteous run into it and are safe.
His coming is near at hand, for this time He says,
"Behold, I come quickly: hold that (Name) fast
which thou hast, that no man take thy crown."

Him that overcometh He will "make a pillar" in
the temple of God. Peter, James, and John were
"pillars" in the house of God. (Gal. 2:9.) They
kept the word of His patience, and denied not His
Name. (Acts 4:8-20; 5:27-32.) The house of God
today needs "pillars" in the midst of her. Whosoever overcometh the false teachings of them of the

synagogue of Satan shall be made a firm support (pillar) in the temple of God. And "he shall go no more out," for he shall find in Christ all that he needs.

Moreover Jesus says, "I will write upon him My New NAME." What is his new Name? Before this can be determined it will first be necessary to find out his old name. In Chapter 1:8 He declares that He is the LORD which is, and which was, and which is to come, the ALMIGHTY. Further on he declares "I am the First and the Last." The Almighty is the name of the God of Abraham. Ex. 3:13-16; 6:2, 3. That Jesus is the God of Abraham is proven by the following passage: John 8:56-58. If the one in the midst of the candlesticks was Jehovah, the Almighty, the Lord of Host, the Holy One of Israel, the Redeemer, the First and the Last (See Isa. 43:3; 44:6), then His "New Name" is JESUS, the greatest name in heaven or in the earth!

"The name of my God." By this he does not mean that he is going to write upon the overcomer three names. The Name of God is revealed to the overcomer only. Even now while I write these lines the Spirit says all who read these words will not understand. There is but one God. The God that Jesus worshipped in the days of his flesh as (a son) is the same God that we worship since we have become "sons of God." His God and our God is one and the same. (John 20:17.) To the world this is a great mystery (1 Tim. 3:16), but to him that overcometh is this mystery revealed. In Rev. 21:6 Jesus says, "He that overcometh shall inherit all things; and I WILL BE HIS GOD, and he shall be MY son." Now that he has made known to us our God, we know his

God also. (John 14:7-9.) The name of our God is JESUS, and his GOD and our GOD is the same. This is only for them that overcome.

"The name of the City of my God" is the name of the New Jerusalem which cometh down from God out of heaven. By turning to Rev. 21:9, 19 we find that the New Jerusalem is the Bride, the Lamb's wife. That the Lamb is Jesus our heavenly **Bridegroom** no one will deny. The Lamb's wife must evidently bear the name of her husband. Her Maker is her husband (Isa. 54:5) and JESUS is his name. In all things he must have pre-eminence. The name of our God, the name of the City of our God, and His New Name is JESUS!

To the overcomers of the spirit of the Laodicean Period of the Church is given the privilege of sitting with Christ in His throne. The lukewarm spirit of this church is identical with the present spirit prevalent throughout the religious world. The nominal christian profess to be neither "saint, nor sinner". Neither hot, nor cold. They are not condemned, no matter what they do. God has "spued them out of his mouth". They claim to be "rich, and increased with goods", but knoweth not that they are wretched, miserable, poor, blind and naked". To overcome his spirit, one must buy gold (faith) tried in the fire, (1 Pet. 1:7) ; white raiment (Rev. 19:8), and be anointed with eyesalve (Acts 10:38) so that they might see. The faith of the Son of God, the raiment of righteousness, and the anointing of the eyes of our understanding are things greatly needed in order to overcome this lukewarm, sickening, adulterous age. The Lord will come in and sup with such and grant them to sit with him in his throne. And this is the victory that overcometh the world, even our faith. See Rev. 3:14-22.

CHAPTER VII.

THE CITIES OF ISRAEL AND THE COMING OF THE LORD

"Ye shall not have gone over the cities of Israel, till the Son of man be come."—Matt. 10:23.

When our Lord gave the twelve their commission before His crucifixion He commanded them, saying, "Go ye not into the way of the Gentiles, and into any city of the Samaritans enter ye not: but go rather to the lost sheep of the house of Israel." At that time they were forbidden to go unto the Gentiles. They were sent to their own people first.

This commission to Israel (Matt. 10:1-15) was what might be termed the "pre-Calvary" commission; that is, a commission that was fulfilled before the crucifixion. See Mar. 6:7-13; Lu. 9:1-16. But in Matthew 10:16-23, etc., is the "postcalvary" commission; that is, it was to be fulfilled during the gospel age, which began on the day of pentecost.

In the first commission they were instructed not to go unto the Gentiles (ver. 5), but in the second they were to be "brought before governors and kings for my sake, for a testimony against them and the Gentiles." To make this clear, it is a well known fact that the disciples were not "delivered up to councils," or "scourged in synagogues" until after the Holy Ghost had come. Neither was the "Spirit of the Father" in them until the day of pentecost.

It is in this last commission that He says, "Ye shall not have gone over the cities of Israel, till the Son of Man be come." **This statement has always**

been a mystery to Bible students and ministers.
It is generally believed that the gospel has not only
been preached to all Israel, but also throughout the
whole world (Ro. 10:18; Mar. 16:15, 16, 20), and
yet the "Son of man" has not yet come. Some have
believed this to refer to the destruction of Jerusalem under Titus, the Roman general, in the year
seventy, while others have interpreted it to mean
the coming of the Comforter, or the Holy Ghost by
using the following scriptures, "The Father * * *
will give you another Comforter, * * * I will not
leave you comfortless: I WILL COME UNTO YOU."
John 14:16-18.

While it is true that the Holy Ghost is "Christ in
you, the hope of glory," yet that is not the interpretation of the mysterious passage. The coming
of the "Son of man" undoubtedly refers to his personal, bodily appearance at the end of the gospel
age. It could not have been fulfilled in the days of
the apostles because at that time there were no

Cities of Israel.

For that reason alone the words of that prophecy
could not have been fulfilled. What was formerly
the kingdom of Israel was at that time a Roman
province under the governorship of Pilate. The sins
of Israel had deprived her of her kingdom. This
was also proved by their own admission, "We have
no king but Caesar." John 19:15.

Further proof that all Israel acknowledged that
they had no Kingdom may be found by noting the
words of the Disciples prior to the ascension, "Lord,
wilt Thou all this time RESTORE the KINGDOM
to Israel?" In reply to this, Jesus did not say that
the Kingdom is spiritual, nor did He say that it

would not be restored, but, instead He said, "It is not for you to know the TIMES, or SEASONS" in which it is to be RESTORED. (Acts 1:5-8.)

Today we are witnessing the restoration of the Kingdom of Israel on every side. The great World war was Jehovah's arm wresting Jerusalem from the hands of the Ottoman Empire. The Times of the Gentiles being fulfilled, the Times and seasons for the Restoring of the Kingdom to Israel is at hand. The land of Palestine is rapidly becoming a Jewish State to be ruled exclusively by the Jews. From every nation they are returning by thousands, and the "cities of Judah shall be built, and Jerusalem shall be inhabited." (Isa. 44:26; Amos 9:11-15; Hosea 3:4, 5.)

As soon as the Kingdom of Israel is completely restored, her temple shall be rebuilt. Already it is reported that they have offered millions of dollars for the site of their former Temple which is now occupied by a Mohammedan Mosque, the Mosque of Omar. The eyes of the world are upon Jerusalem and the ancient glory of Israel. The fig tree is putting forth her leaves, proclaiming in silent tones "the summer is nigh at hand."

Now that the kingdom is being restored, her cities shall be built. Israel of today has never heard "the gospel." That which has been proclaimed by the various denominations since the Reformation is not "the gospel." But the Gospel must be preached throughout the cities of Israel. Hundreds of missionaries are now being called to Palestine. The time is surely at hand. The gospel of the kingdom must be preached in all the world before the end comes. It began in Palestine and must end in Palestine. The first shall be last.

By this it is clearly seen that the coming of the Lord is very, very near at hand. Soon there shall be a great revival in Palestine, and the preachers of this gospel will "not have gone over the cities of Israel till the Son of Man be come." O that God would awaken the people to the knowledge of this great truth! The coming of the Lord is nearer than when we first believed. It is high time that we lay aside envy, strife, malice, and evil speaking, and seek the face of the Lord. Zeph. 2:1-3. Surely the love of many has grown cold and they have despised the name of the Lord. It is at this time that Jesus says we shall be hated of all men for His NAME'S sake. See Matt. 24:9; Lu. 21:17; Mar. 13:13; Matt. 10:22, 23; and Isa. 66:5 shows that it will take place about the time of the Lord's appearing, and consoles those who are hated for His name's sake by saying, "He shall appear to your joy, and they (who hate you and cast you out) shall be ashamed."

My friend, are you being hated for His name's sake, or are you among those who are hating and casting out their brothers for "His name's sake?" Where are the people who are being hated for His name's sake? Is it not those who are being baptized in the name of JESUS? Was not the name of Jesus hated in the beginning of the gospel age, and was it not prophesied to be so in the end? Then why not consider what we do, lest haply we be found to be fighting against God. Does a feeling of resentment arise in your heart when you hear any one declare that Jesus is God? Or when one speaks of baptizing in Jesus' name? Then there must be something wrong. Because (the mystery of) in-

iquity aboundeth, the love of many shall wax cold.
Matt. 24:12; 2 Thess. 2:7.

The mystery of iniquity is the spirit of anti-Christ.
The MAN (not spirit, or system) of sin, the Son of
Perdition, who is to be revealed is commonly called,
or generally acknowledged by all Bible students to be
the anti-Christ. 2 Thess. 2:3, 4. But in reading the
foregoing reference, it will be noticed that he is
against "all that is called God," yet we do not think,
or mention him as anti-God, but anti-Christ. Why
is this if Christ is not God? The only person that
the Bible declares

Shall Be Called God

is Jesus Christ our Savior and Redeemer. In Isaiah
9:6 we have this familiar quotation, "Unto us a child
is born, unto us a son is given, * * *and his name
shall be CALLED * * * the Mighty GOD." And
again in chapter 54:5 he says, "Thy Maker is thine
(the church's) husband; and thy Redeemer * * *
the GOD of the whole earth he shall be CALLED."
Again in another place the prophet declares, "A
virgin shall conceive, and bear a son and they shall
CALL his name Immanuel," which is interpreted
"GOD with us." Isa. 7:14; Matt. 1:22, 23. In these
scriptures it can be clearly seen that Jesus is the
person that shall be called GOD. This is exactly
what the Man of Sin, the Son of Perdition, shall do.
He shall make war with the Lamb through his
agents, but the Lamb shall overcome them, for he is
King of kings, and Lord of lords. Rev. 17:13, 14;
1 Tim. 6:14-16.

Those who oppose Jesus being called God are partaking of the spirit of anti-Christ. Many are doing

this ignorantly, but these are they upon whom
God will have mercy. But those who are doing it
because of prejudice, hatred, personal ambition,
honor of one another, or because of the fear of los-
ing friends or money, are in danger of being left in
darkness. Read John 12:35-46.

The Deity of Christ.

The teaching of the deity of Christ is nothing
other than the efforts of men to bring forth this
same truth, namely, that Christ is God. To deny
that Christ is God robs him of all his glory. He is
both God and man. He is both Jehovah and the
Anointed (Lord and Christ). He is both Father
and Son. He is both High Priest and the sacrifice.
He is both in Heaven and on earth. He is both
Creator and first-born of every creature (Col. 1:15,
16). He is both the Shepherd of the sheep and the
Lamb of God. All these expressions are various
ways of showing forth the divinity and the humanity
of Christ. God was in Christ reconciling the world
unto himself. 2 Cor. 5:19.

In the fortieth chapter of Isaiah, verses 3 to 18,
is foretold the message and mission of John the
Baptist. With him all flesh was grass. With God
there was no difference. He was able to raise up
stones to be the children of Abraham. Matt. 3:1-9.
Israel as a people was to be set aside, for God had
chosen Zion for His habitation; a people filled with
the Spirit. And today Mt. Zion, heavenly Jersua-
lem, is the Bride, the Spirit-filled church. The
Church, Zion, which was with Israel, has been taken
from them and placed among the Gentiles until the
time of the Gentiles be fulfilled. Gal. 4:22-27; Heb.
12:22.

For almost 1,900 years Israel has been blinded in part, waiting for the fullness of the Gentiles to come in. Rom. 11:25. Even to this day when the Law of Moses is read the vail is over their hearts so that they can not see the end of those things. (2 Cor. 3:7-16.) Christ is the end of the Law, but Israel has not known it. (Rom. 10:4.) The vail that Moses put over his face (Ex. 34:33) was only a type of God vailing His glory (face, Ex. 33:18, 20) with a vail of flesh. (Heb. 10:20.) It is this vail,, or mystery, that has hidden Jehovah from His people. He came to His own (the Jews) and they received Him not. He was in the world, and the world knew Him not. John 1:1-14.

The Mystery of God.

The mystery of God vailed in flesh presenting the three-fold relationship of Father, Son and Holy Ghost was the thing that blinded Israel. Even to this day they have believed that the Christian Testament taught there were three Gods, and for this cause they could not accept their doctrine, because the "first and great" Commandment says, "Hear, O Israel, the Lord thy God is ONE." Deut. 6:4. The Christian churches have taught that there are three "persons" in the Godhead, drawing their conclusion from the mysterious expression "Father, Son and Holy Ghost." The term "three persons" is erroneous, and unscriptural. The personal, visible form of God was Jesus Christ, and today the Christ with us and in us is "that Holy Spirit." These three are one, and not three. I John 5:7. John 14:7 to 10, and 16 to 18, reveals Father, Son and Holy Ghost all in one person, Christ. This agrees with the teachings of the Great Apostle to the Gentiles, also. Col.

1:19; 2:9; 1 Tim. 3:16; 2 Cor. 5:19. But no one can know this but he to whom it is revealed. Matt. 11:27; Lu. 10:22.

It is to Zion that these things are being revealed. For "in this mountain (Mt. Zion) will God destroy the covering cast over all people, and the vail that is spread over all nations. He will swallow up death in victory; and the Lord God will wipe away tears from off all faces; and the rebuke of his people (Israel) shall be taken away from off all the earth: for the mouth of the Lord hath spoken it. And it shall be said in that day (by Israel), Lo, this is our God; we have waited for Him, and He will will save us: this is the Lord (JEHOVAH); we have waited for him, we will be glad and rejoice in his salvation." Isa. 25:6-9.

It is Zion, the church, that must carry the good news to Israel, for it is written, "Out of Zion, the perfection of beauty, God hath shined." "Our God shall came, and shall not keep silence." Psa. 50:1-7. And again, "And so all Israel shall be saved: as it is written, There shall come out of Zion the Deliverer, and shall turn away ungodliness from Jacob." Rom. 11:26.

The revelation of Jesus as the MIGHTY GOD of Jacob is given to Zion in order that she might carry the glad tidings to Israel. O church of God, we have good news this day. We do not well if we keep it from Israel. Through their unbelief we have obtained mercy, and why not now permit them through our mercy to obtain mercy? Rom. 11:30, 31. "O Zion, that bringeth good tidings, get thee up into the high mountain; O Jerusalem, that bringeth good tidings, lift up thy voice with strength; lift it up, be not afraid; say unto the cities of Judah, Behold your God." Isa. 40:9, 10. And I say unto you, ye shall not have gone over the cities of Israel, till the Son of man be come.

Everything is pointing to that eventful hour. When God removes this covering from the face of all people He declares that He will "swallow up death in victory." Isa. 25:7, 8. Are we nearing that great climax? The apostle Paul tells us that when God returns His favor to Israel it will mean "life from the dead" (resurrection). This is also seen in 1 Cor. 15:50-54, where he unfolds the great mystery of the resurrection. Here we are told that when this corruptible shall have put on incorruption, and this mortal shall have put on immortality, THEN shall be brought to pass the saying that is written, "Death is swallowed up in victory."

The end is near! For thus saith the Lord, "And when these things begin to come to pass, then look up, and lift up your heads: for your redemption draweth nigh." Now is the time for God's people to rally around the name of Jesus! The name of the Lord is a strong tower; the righteous run into it and are safe. As it is written, A man shall be as an hiding place from the wind, and a covert from the tempest; as rivers of water in a dry place, as the shadow of a great rock in the weary land. Isa. 32:2.

CHAPTER VIII.

THE HIDING PLACE FROM THE WIND.

It is blessed to know where we are in these peril-
ous times. One night there was a woman in one of
our meetings who left the church for home, when
pains seized her head, and in a few days there was
a crepe on the door of her house. It is not a light
thing to sit in a meeting seeing the glory of God,
hearing the gospel and then walk out without yield-
ing to God.

A Man As An Hiding Place.

In the thirty-second chapter of the book of Isaiah,
we find this remarkable statement, "A man shall be
as an hiding place from the wind, and a covert from
the tempest; as rivers of water in a dry place, as
the shadow of a great rock in a weary land." It is
claimed in this passage that "a man" shall fill these
positions. The "wind" spoken of here is not the at-
mosphere which shakes the trees, but we read in
the seventh chapter of the book of Daniel, that "the
four winds strove upon the great sea,"—the conflicts among the nations of Babylon, Medo-Persia,
Greece and Rome being here spoken of as the "striving of winds upon the great sea (many waters.)"
Also in the book of Revelation, the seventh chapter,
we are told that "four angels stood on the four cor-
ners of the earth, holding the four winds of the
earth."

This Scripture in Isaiah tells you that a "man"
is going to rise up and become a hiding place large

enough to protect you from the "wind." Also, he will become a "covert" from the tempest. In another place it says that we should "sanctify the LORD of Hosts himself; and let him be our fear, and let him be our dread. And he shall be for a "sanctuary"—Isa. 8:13, 14. That is, God shall be a "sanctuary" in that He shall become a special abiding place wherein His presence shall continually dwell with them that put their trust in Him. You well know that no mortal man can hide you from the coming tests. But there is a "Man" who is destined to fulfill this prophesy, and that is the "man Christ Jesus." By this I mean, the God-Man: He who was manifested in the flesh more than 1900 years ago.—1 Tim. 3:16.

You had better be sure you have found your hiding place from the destructions, sorrows, and woes which are coming upon the earth! Yea, there is "a tempest of hail" coming!

A few years ago, the whole world was caught suddenly by the terrible plague of influenza, and in it mothers, fathers and children were swept away. Crepes upon the door abounded on every side. The people died by the thousands. But God said, "I will deliver you in the hour of temptation."—Rev. 3:10. The man that knows the Name of Jesus Christ is safe. "The Name of the Lord is a strong tower into which the righteous runneth and is safe." He does not lose any time, either, but RUNS into it. It is a mysterious abiding place; and although you cannot see it, yet it is there.

Why did so many die when the influenza plague came? Because they were frightened—killed themselves by fear. Many of the remedies that were resorted to for healing only hastened their death.

Judgment is in the land, and because of its awakening influence on the people many throughout the world are shouting the victory in the name of the Lord. Medical science is unable to cope with the new diseases breaking out upon the inhabitants. The florists are still making wreathes and bouquets. But I have found a Friend, indeed! His medicine is always on hand, and it is not some sort of bitters or dry powders, but it is joy and a "merry heart which doeth good like a medicine."—Prov. 17:22.

Happy Resting Place!

God fills our hearts with joy! When you get happy your whole being becomes filled with light. Praises to the Lord drives away gloom and sickness. When Christ comes into your life, He makes you a new man or woman. When the demons are raging, and when your friends have turned their backs upon you, you can still give glory to God. If you love the Lord, you cannot go back on Him. What profit is there in drawing back from God, the Lord? He cannot deny Himself, and though we prove untrue, yet He abideth faithful.

God meant every word that He spake, and for that cause I believe that the real life of Christ is able to quicken any mortal today. The question that confronts us, no matter where we came from, "Do you know where you are going?" I have no fear concerning the future since I have become acquainted with the Lord of life, whom to know is life eternal. —John 17:3. I love God, and He loves me—and He knows that I love him! You cannot separate us. My life is in a bundle with my Lord's. Whenever a man strikes me, he strikes Jesus, too. That person who kicks and opposes holy living or the speaking in tongues, is mocking the Christ that authorized the same. There are some people who speak as though they knew more than God, and as much as say, "Had I been God I would not have done this or that thing." But those who love Him will obey Him. They will stand up for Him, and follow Him all the way. He stood by us when the forces of hell were endeavoring to overcome us. I believe in living for Him who died for me! He took my place in sorrow, suffering and death that He might give me His life and joy. He bore all my pains and gave me His health. I am determined to stand up boldly for Jesus.

It is written, "Whosoever will may receive of Him, freely." Will you let God have His way in your life? It is to your interest to know

How To Get Into That Man

who shall be an "hiding place from the wind," who, when He walked on earth centuries ago, declared, "The Father dwelleth in me." "He was in the Father and the Father in Him." And He further said that "in my Father's house are many mansions." To confirm this, He promised: "I am going away to prepare a place for you." Many people look upon the literal side of this saying, but there is the spiritual phase also, and if you fail to see it, "only believe." Jesus Christ, the Man, was nothing more, nor less than "the Father's house," even the temporary dwelling place and the tabernacle of God. He went "away" from this natural, visible, form of a man, and made a way for us to come into the spiritual body of Christ.

I am "in Christ," now. I know where I dwell. You cannot overthrow a man who gets inside of Christ and knows where he is. But you might daunt one that is not sure of his dwelling place. You cannot overthrow the name of JESUS, in which we make our refuge. Though some may ridicule our experience in salvation yet we must abide in Christ and finish our sojourn here below with joy. That man or that woman who has heard the voice of God,— settle it today in your heart to go through with Jesus. I never shall regret the day when God's Spirit moved on me to accept the Gospel.

When the children of Israel came out of Egypt, the blood was shed down in the land of Ham; but remember they did not escape Pharaoh until they had crossed the water. Christ was crucified near 1900 years ago, but you cannot escape according to God's word until you cross the waters of baptism in Jesus' Name. (See John 3:5; Acts 2:38; Mark 16: 16.) I will guarantee you that if your heart is honest and you really repent with a determination to ever after live for God, when you are immersed in the Name of Jesus Christ for the remission of sins, heaven will open unto you immediately and the voice of God shall be heard in you. Every ambassador of a country will say what the Government that sent him authorized him to say; and the ambassador of God will tell you what God has commanded Him to say.

How does a man get in Christ? In the third chapter of Galatians, the Apostle Paul said, twenty-sixth verse,—"For ye are all the children of God by faith in Christ Jesus." Note that this says "by faith," and not by the keeping of days, months, new moons, or the Sabbath. And the next verse goes on to say, "For as many of you as have been BAPTIZED INTO CHRIST have put on Christ." You do not get into Christ by shaking hands, or joining some system, nor by feeling sorry that your mother is dead. You must be baptized into that "Man" who shall be a hiding place. The method which God has laid down for us to get into Christ is through immersion in water in Jesus' Name and the baptism of the Holy Spirit. Note that Romans 6:1-2 states "so many of us as are (margin) baptized into Jesus Christ, WERE baptized into His death." But how am I to be baptized "into His death?" Whenever a man acknowledges that he is a sinner before God and sees himself doomed to destruction, and then accepts Christ as his sacrifice, recognizing himself dead indeed, he is ready to be "buried with Him by baptism into His death." And the latter having been done, the converted one is to be quickened by the life (the Holy Ghost) which is in Christ Jesus, for the Scriptures saith, "In Him is life," and "life more abundant."

Nothing less than God's own plan will satisfy, or avail. You know that the Word of God is true. There is no other book than the Bible that shows you the true way to God and heaven. The old Bible is the book of books! It declares that if you are baptized into the body of Christ, He will protect you from the storm which is coming. He shall be unto you as the "shadow of a great rock in a weary land." For they who trust in the Lord shall never be confounded!

CHAPTER IX.

GOD WHO CAN NOT LIE.

"God is not a man that he should lie, neither the son of man that he should repent."—Nu. 23:19.

This was spoken by a prophet going forth to do the wrong thing; but God took hold of his mouth and made him speak the word of prophecy. The Bible further declares that "the Strength of Israel also will not lie nor repent." If God has ever made a promise to you, He gives you this guarantee that He will never repent, nor turn back from doing the thing which He hath spoken.

In the book of Malachi it is written: "For I am the LORD, I change not; therefore ye sons of Jacob are not consumed." Mal. 3:6. The sons of Jacob had so miserably failed God that in justice they really should have been consumed. But God could not lie, for He had promised to preserve Israel in order to bring forth the "Seed." The reason why we are living today is because God made a promise. And that promise was "And I will put enmity between thee and the woman, and between thy seed and her seed; it shall bruise thy head, and thou shalt bruise his heel." Gen. 3:15. After God has given you the opportunity in your life to let the serpent be bruised, and you reject it, then God can say He has kept His promise, and will send judgment unto that soul which has sinned, and it must die. "The soul that sinneth, it shall die." Ezek. 18:20. And it is declared that "All have sinned, and come short of the glory of God." Rom. 3:23; Ps. 14:1-3. The only man on earth that never did sin is the Man Who was more than a man, and that is the "Man Christ Jesus." 1 Tim. 2:5. A terrible condemnation hangs over every human being. But there is a Man Who took our disfavor that we might have His fellowship. A sinless Man took the place of a sinful world. All had sinned and come short of the glory of God. The best of men God declared to be "vanity" and "nothing, and less than nothing." Yet that same God can turn around and say we are His peculiar treasure.

All had sinned because all were unbelievers. But Christ came that we might "believe," and turn from our "nothingness" to be called a "holy people," a "city not forsaken," and obtain life eternal! Isa. 62:12. One man sinned and caused us all to be condemned to death. Another man died and caused us all to have the hope of life. 2 Tim. 1:1.

The thought I want you to bear in mind is that "God can not lie." Titus 1:2. It is stated in the Book of God that "the glory of the LORD shall be revealed, and all flesh shall see it together; for the mouth of the LORD hath spoken it." Isa. 40:5. Whether they can stand it or not, all flesh must see the glory of the LORD. Wicked men must see it. Righteous men have the reward of seeing it. And why? "For the mouth of the LORD hath spoken it." Men who have committed suicide must see it! God will not lie! We all must appear at the judgment seat of Christ (2 Cor. 5:10), whether old or young, rich or poor. Rom. 14:10. The sea must give up the dead which are in it; death and hell are forced to deliver up the dead which are in them, and small and great must stand before God. The

Voice will either say, "Come, ye blessed," or "Depart from me, ye cursed."

Men may idle away their time and walk the streets thinking themselves to be somewhat, trampling the mercy of God underfoot, but ALL must appear before the judgment bar of heaven. For—"The Strength of Israel will not lie, nor repent!" 1 Sam. 15:29. He who is the "Victory" (margin) of Israel will not lie, does not have to lie, and can not lie! He will let every man be a liar that the Scriptures may be unbroken!

I do not want to find a spot of wickedness in my life. I want to have everything clean and above board, and to be found walking before the Lord with a perfect heart. My past shall never meet me again, by the grace of God. He hath set my soul free from sins and I shall see that no transgressions shall accumulate to meet me at the judgment bar of the Most High. For the "LORD of Hosts is my sanctuary," as it is written in the book of Isaiah the Prophet. Yea, I dwell on high and He dwelleth in me! Our God dares anybody to talk about His "anointed" after He has set them in the right way, and made them to walk the world in white. (What we are to do now is to hold to God's unchangeable hand.) God will not lie, and, therefore, I am determined not to lie. God blessed me and I shall bless Him! He saved me from sore troubles and I shall save Him from any more trouble with me. Jesus did not call me out of the world and lie to me; neither did He accuse me of being proud or puffed up; but He told me, "Thou art mine." "I will never leave thee, nor forsake thee." "When thou passest through the waters, I will be with thee, and through the rivers, they shall not overflow thee; when thou walkest through the fire, thou shalt not be burned; neither shall the flame kindle upon thee." Isa. 43:1-2. And OUR GOD CAN NOT LIE!

When the skeptics shall say, "Well, how do you know you are going to make it to the City?" we can answer, "God can not lie!" A multitude may arise against you, but nothing can stop a soul that has faith in God. I have nothing else to live for but the Lord. I could not live without Jesus. I would rather be dead than not to have Christ in my life. True it is that "God will take care of you, o'er all the way, through every day!" You need not grumble, nor murmur; just put your trust in the Lord. When your foodstuffs are short—put your confidence in God. You do not live by gold and silver, but by the word of God. Yea, "Man shall not live by bread alone (and he surely will be 'alone' if he walks with God), but by every word that proceedeth out of the mouth of God." Matt. 4:4. You are welcome to all the world has in it, but give me JESUS! What will it profit a man, if he shall gain the whole world, and lose his own soul. Mark. 8:36. I had rather be a child of God than a prince, a king, a president, or a millionaire banker's scn! He is more to me than gold and silver. The lame man at the Gate Beautiful received healing for his feet, but my soul has been healed! He leaped up and walked on his feet, but my soul within me is leaping for joy in God!

If God Almighty can not lie and the "Word of our God shall stand forever (Isa. 40:8), then what hope has the man or woman who knows the Word of God, but will not obey it? The day is coming in which there shall be upon the bridles and bells of the horses —"HOLINESS UNTO THE LORD." Zech. 14:20.

Again He hath commanded us to be "holy for He is holy." And God is He who can not lie. Holiness means having the Holy Spirit within you, making you holy. Then you can walk before the Lord God in both "righteousness and true Holiness all the days of your life." Eph. 4:24; Luke 1:75.

Everybody loves to be loved. Even God loves to be loved. There is something in His great, eternal bosom which loves to hear us say, "Lord, I love you." God will so fill your heart with love that you will love everybody. And "everybody ought to love Jesus." True holiness means something; for God declares that without it no man shall see the Lord. Hebrews 12:14. Now since God hath thus said through His Word, you may as well be persuaded that it is truth, for "it is impossible for God to lie." Heb. 6:18. I believe in a clean life and a clean heart. God is against the soul that desires unrighteousness. He warned the sons of men that He would be a "swift witness against the sorcerers, and against the adulterers, and against false swearers, and against those that oppress the hireling in his wages, the widow, and the fatherless, and that turn aside the stranger from his right, and fear not me, saith the LORD of hosts." Mal. 3:5.

Do what God commands. For He knows what He is talking about. There is one way to be saved. Said Jesus, "I am the way, and the Door, by which if any man enters in he shall be saved." That Doorway is the birth of water and the Spirit. And God can not lie. A man may argue that any person can be saved only by "faith," or "believing." I agree with that, but faith in what? I say, "Faith in the Word of God." That Word which was made flesh and said, "Ye must be born again, of water and the Spirit, in order to enter into the Kingdom of God." John 3:3, 5; Mark 16:15, 16; Acts 2:38. Faith without works is dead, being alone. If Christ told us we must be baptized and receive the Spirit of life from God, then if we say we believe we must be doers of the word, and not hearers only, deceiving our own selves. Every man will be held responsible for that degree of light which he has received. And concerning all these things, it still remaineth true that GOD WILL NOT LIE.

CHAPTER X.

POWER TO SAVE.

There are many things in the Word of God over which men are stumbling and walking in darkness. When they meet people who are supposed to know and enquire of them concerning the meaning of the scriptures, they get no satisfactory answer and therefore decide that there is nothing to it. But we are glad to know that there is power in Jesus Christ, and that there is a God in heaven that revealeth the deep and secret things. Nothing but the power of God can save a man. It actually saves and delivers from the powers of sin and Satan. Many imagine they have been delivered when they really do not know what deliverance is. Some are brought up in a good family, and because they are trained well they think that they are all right. But salvation is of God, and not of training. When God does it you know it, and something else is added to it,—namely, "boldness" to tell about it. People have their own manner and method of expressing what God has done for their soul; but however crude that may be, God gets the glory out of it.

There are thousands of people today who think when you go back to dust that that is the end of you. They do not know God and the power of the gospel of Jesus Christ. No exterior work of man can save his soul. It takes the gospel of Christ, preached in the power of the Holy Ghost sent down from heaven, and not taught to a man from an intellectual point of view. The Lord from heaven never attempted to preach the Gospel until He was anointed with the Holy Spirit at the Jordan. Immediately He hid Himself away for forty days, and afterward came up to the city where He had been brought up, and standing up in the synagogue, said, "The Spirit of the Lord is upon me, because He hath anointed me to preach the gospel to the poor; he hath sent me to heal the broken-hearted, to preach deliverance to the captives, and recovering of sight to the blind, to set at liberty them that are bruised; to preach the acceptable year of the Lord." Luke 4:18-19. O, the millions of despondent and broken-hearted, who are lying along the wayside today, not knowing what to do, because of having tried everything, and found them all a failure! But, thank God there is a Gospel preached in the Holy Ghost which will do the work and will bind up the broken hearts. Every man and woman has a soul which must meet God and pass through that long lane of eternity. Yet great and wise people who are looked upon as somewhat, will not stop to consider this thing. Hear old Brother Job say, "Man that is born of a woman is of a few days, and full of trouble. He cometh forth like a flower, and is cut down," Job 14:1-2. It is high time to awake and consider. Many are going on and on in sin when their very hair is blossoming with age.

I do not care in the least about intelligence if it does not assist me to find more of God. I desire to have my heart right in His sight. I want to keep a conscience void of offense toward God and men. I hope to meet Jesus just beyond the veil and go with Him all the rest of the way through the ages to come. Jesus wept with them that wept, and He bore their infirmities, and had compassion on their sick, and we must be like Him. I am glad to know that though we walk through the valley of the shadow of death yet if Christ be in us we need fear no evil. Thus saith the Lord, "Fear not: for I have redeemed thee, I have called thee by thy name; thou art mine. When thou passest through the waters I will be with thee; and through the rivers they shall not overflow thee: when thou walkest through the fire, thou shalt not be burned, neither shall the flame kindle upon thee." Real salvation is what the people need today. Society is not salvation. There is no kind of system known that can take sin out of the human heart. It requires Christ in the Holy Ghost to save a man in this present evil world. I pray constantly that, not only those seeking God, but those already filled with the Spirit of the Lord will stand up and prove to the world that there is power in the gospel of Christ.

People are not mean and in sin because they want to be, but because the devil has them bound and they cannot help it. The most foolish man, who is worse than the worst fool, is that man who is not wise enough to save himself from this untoward generation. We are anxious about the salvation of others. It is for the benefit of the sinners that services unto the Lord are constantly held to show them the way of life, and the Power of God to Save.

CHAPTER XI.

THE WOMAN AND THE MANCHILD.

What does all this commotion concerning the woman and the man-child mean? Why is there so much being said about this subject? Who has really struck the keynote of this mysterious vision? What could in reality be the interpretation of the Apocalyptic Seer of the desolate Isle of Patmos? Mysterious things always invite speculation and multitudes of hypothetical expositions.

There are many phases of the progress of the church to which this symbolical wonder has been made applicable by the various writers and teachers upon this prophetic vision of the Apocalypse. The interpretations have been almost as numerous as the interpreters.

It is not my intention to present the final conclusion of all these views, but to see if there can not be a harmonizing of them. By way of application it can be used to designate any stage of the Church (the ecclesia) from the call of Abraham until the setting up of "the Kingdom that shall not be destroyed." Many of the illustrations used in this attempt are beautiful, but there is something lacking when we come to look the subject squarely in the face.

From what we can observe the Woman is the Church during God's final dealings with the Jewish nation. They were the Church first (Acts 7:38), and shall be the Church last (Matt. 20:16). The Church today at the close of the Gentile age is no

doubt bringing forth a "perfect Man" who shall come
forth in the power of the Spirit.   See Eph. 4:13.
These are the overcomers of the Laodicean age who
"shall sit with me in my throne," Rev. 3:21.   But
those who fail shall pass on into the "time of Jacob's
trouble."   During that time the Church, which is no
longer Gentile, but Israelitish, comes to the knowledge of Christ, evidently through the preaching of
the "two witnesses" (Rev. 11:3-12), and becomes
"clothed with the Sun," that is, the glory of the gospel of Christ.   The Law, symbolized by the "moon
under her feet," loses its force.   She rises above it.
Her crown of glory is that the twelve apostles were
her own people according to the flesh.

Though she has come to the acknowledging of
Jesus as her Messiah, yet she has not come to the
full knowledge of the truth as a whole, hence she is
in travail to bring forth a "Man-Child" who was to
"rule all nations with a rod of iron."   The Law, during the reign of Christ on earth, shall go out from
Mt. Zion.   (Isa. 2:3.)   If the Man-Child is to rule
the nations, he must rule in Mt. Zion, for there is
the place from whence shall come the law.   To confirm the foregoing statement we find "the 144,000"
Israelites on Mt. Zion with the Lamb after the Man-
Child is caught up to the throne.   See Rev. 14:1.
The women here represent the Church in its consummation.   The Man-Child is the 144,000 overcomers
out of the Israelitish Church.   The Woman, the Jewish nation (Rom. 11:26), flees into a place God has
prepared for her.   The remnant of her seed with
whom the dragon makes war, are those who were
remnants, or left by the church during the close of
the Gentile period (Rev. 12:17), and also those who
failed to overcome with the 144,000 and became de-

filed through Babylon, the great, and her daughters. Rev. 17:1-3.

Even though that be so, yet we must not overlook the fact that we must be overcomers today if we desire to take part with that "perfect man" to which the church is destined to arrive during the Gentile period of the Church. There are many blessed truths coming forth on this subject and some are seemingly ready to reject them. Let us stand still and see the salvation of our Lord. An honest heart need have no fear. There is no fear in love. If our love is set on Him, He will deliver us. Psa. 91:14, etc.

CHAPTER XII.

THE MINISTRY OF ANGELS.

Destruction, sorrows, crimes, and death are filling the earth with tear-stained faces. The most horrifying accidents are prominently recorded on the front pages of the daily papers. These are surely "the beginning of sorrows."

In the midst of these things many of the saints of God are being made to suffer the same afflictions that are in the world. The wicked one is no respecter of persons. He will destroy whosoever he wills. It appears at times that he takes delight in destroying the children of God while going "thru the land seeking whom he may devour." But for the people of God there is a way of escape. Lu. 21:36; 1 Cor. 10:13.

We are told by the prophet Daniel that in the time of the end there would be a time of trouble, such as there never was since there was a nation, "And at that time shall Michael stand up, the great prince (archangel, Jude 9), which standeth for the children of thy people." It is very evident that the "time of trouble" is upon us, and the people of God need to know their source of protection.

To him that dwelleth in the secret place of the Most High God has promised to "give his angels charge over thee, to keep thee in all thy ways. They shall bear thee up in their hands, lest thou dash thy foot against a stone." Psa. 91. There is our place of refuge. The secret place of the Most High. There it is that he "will give his angels charge over" us.

The angels shall be our guardians, our watchers, and our keepers. For the "angel of the Lord encampeth round about them that fear him, and delivereth them." Ps. 34:7. O taste and see that the Lord is good: blessed is the man that trusteth in him. We must commit our ways unto the Lord and he will redeem our lives from death.

It is for this cause that we who have come unto Mount Zion have also "come unto an innumerable company of angels." Heb. 12:22. They fight the battles of the people of God. Michael, the captain of the Lord's host, leads a great company of angels to wage war against our adversary. Rev. 12:7-9. In the days of Joshua when he crossed the Jordan into Canaan he met the "captain of the Lord's host" standing over against him with his sword drawn in his hand. Josh. 5:13. He had come to the rescue of the people of God. They did not have to fight the people of Jericho, but the invisible host of angels, at the command of the "captain of the host of the Lord" evidently lent their force against the bulwarks of the city and the "walls of Jericho fell down." For a proof that angels have power to remove stones we only need to turn to the record of the resurrection morning, "for the angel of the Lord descended from heaven, and came and rolled back the stone from the door, and sat upon it." Mat. 28:2.

When Jesus came into the world he came to show us our privilege as sons of God. In his conflict with Satan in the wilderness, after His baptism in Jordan, "behold, angels came and ministered unto him." Mat. 4:11. And again, at the close of his ministry, on that memorial night beneath the olive trees of Gethsemane, the night of sorrow, and agonizing prayer, "there appeared an angel unto him from heaven, strengthening him." At the moment of His most severe trial He rebuked Peter's attempt to protect Him with a sword, saying "Thinkest thou that I cannot pray to my Father and he shall presently give me more than twelve legions of angels?" Mat. 26:53. What a privilege we have if we only knew it! If Jesus could pray to the Father and immediately have seventy-two thousand angels at his command, why cannot we? He said, "He that believeth on me, the works that I do shall he do also." Brother, call unto God for angels and he will send them. We need them in these days. Be not afraid; it is your God-given privilege.

In his letter to the Hebrews the apostle Paul declares that angels are "ministering spirits, sent forth to minister for them that shall be heirs of salvation." Are you an heir of God? Have you received the spirit of adoption, whereby we cry, Abba, Father? If so, then you are an heir of God, and a joint-heir with Christ, and have a perfect right to the protection and ministry of angels.

Neither should this thing be thought impossible in our day. It was an angel that delivered Peter from the hands of Herod. It was an angel of the Lord that delivered the apostles in the first persecution. It was an angel that spake to Philip in Samaria and sent him into the desert. (Acts 8:26.) And it was an angel that talked with the aged seer of Patmos. And He who sent his angels in those days is just the same today. His love is never failing. He will keep that which is committed into his hands against that day.

Wherever we go we have the right to ask God to let angels accompany us on our journey to protect us from danger. Even in heaven doth our angels al-

ways behold our Father's face, standing in readiness
to come to our rescue at his command. Matt. 18:10.
They will watch you while you sleep. They will
stand guard at the doors of your home when dangers
are threatening. They will follow you on your journey whether by rail or by motor. They will warn
you of approaching danger so that no evil will be-
fall thee. What need have we to fear when God has
made such a provision for His children? Oh, that
men would praise the Lord for His goodness, and
for His wonderful works unto the children of men.
There is no God like Him. His works are truly wonderful. Wherever I go I always ask my heavenly
Father to send His angels with me. And over the
many, many thousands of miles that I have been
permitted to travel by steam, electricity, or gasoline,
He has seen to it that I arrived safely at my many
destinations, and brought me safely home again.

We need not be afraid to ask for them, for the
host of angels are without number. God will send
as many as you will need. The multitude that John
saw on the Isle of Patmos were ten thousand times
ten thousand, and thousands of thousands. Ten
thousand times ten thousand are equal to one hundred million! And besides that there are "thousands of thousands." Ministers, evangelists, missionaries, ask God for angels to help you in the
battle against Satan and the powers of darkness.
They will come and help you to break the powers
of heaviness in your meetings. When you pray,
BELIEVE that they are there and the victory is
won. If you will preach the gospel and tell the story
of the sufferings of Christ the angels will be there.
It is these things that "the angels desired to look
into." 1 Pet. 1:10-12. And every sinner that re-

penteth and turns to God causes there to be great
joy in the presence of the angels of God. For every
new-born soul will talk about the wonderful things
wrought in his life thru the death and suffering of
Jesus Christ our Lord, which things angels desired
to look into.

The angels that appeared unto Abraham on the
plains of Mamre; and delivered Lot from Sodom;
that spake to Moses on the back sides of the desert;
that appeared to Joshua at Jericho; that brought
the message to Gideon; that spake to the wife of
Manoah; that endeavoured to save Balaam from error; that brought the answer to Daniel and locked
the lions' mouths; that spake to Elizabeth and Mary;
that delivered the apostles from prison; that smote
Herod for his wickedness; and comforted John on
the lonely Isle of Patmos, they are just the same today. They will come to us for the asking. For he
that spared not his own Son, but delivered him up
for us all, how shall he not with him also freely
give us all things?

THE END.

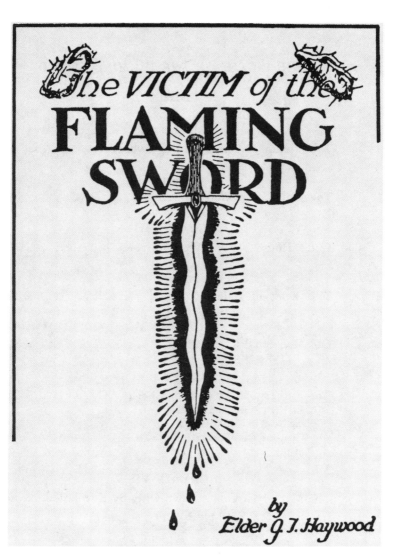

The VICTIM of the FLAMING SWORD

by
Elder G. T. Haywood

Published by
CHRIST TEMPLE BOOK STORE
430 W. FALL CREEK PKWY.
INDIANAPOLIS, INDIANA 46208

THE VICTIM OF THE FLAMING SWORD

INDEX

FOREWORD

To the reader of these pages it is our purpose to give a glimpse of the greatness, and the majesty of our Lord Jesus Christ.

We have all read of the flaming sword in the hand of the cherubims placed in the Garden of Eden to keep the way of the tree of life. But there are very few who have considered the fact that that sword must need be passed before we could have a right to the tree of life.

That we have life through Christ Jesus is beyond a shadow of a doubt. This being true He must evidently have come up against that flaming sword in His endeavor to make it possible that we might "have life, and that more abundantly".

In the first chapter we have endeavored to give a picture of our Lord coming forth as The Victim of the Flaming Sword, rising in power after all other sacrifices failed. Follow the scriptures closely and the beauty of this book will be unfolded to you.

The following chapters have to do with His Deity, and the answering of perplexing questions concerning the same. God bless all who read and understand the things contained herein.

These articles have been collected from our many writings published heretofore in The Voice of the Wilderness, and other publications.

The cover design and illustrations on pages 4, 38 and 48 were drawn by Mr. W. E. Scott.

AUTHOR.

3

THE EXPULSION

CHAPTER I.

THE VICTIM OF THE FLAMING SWORD

The fall of man was a tragedy that has been keenly felt by all humanity from Eden to Calvary, and from Calvary till now. We have read of the fatal calamity and have been made to mourn and weep over our lamentable downfall. But in spite of all this the fact still remains the same, that the sin of our forefather Adam thrust us out from the paradise of God.

Although coats of skin were brought forth to cover the nakedness of the transgressor, and the blood of an innocent creature had been shed, temporarily staying the hand of Justice, yet the words "the day that thou eatest thereof thou shalt surely die" stood steadfast, still unchanged.

The enmity between the serpent's seed and the seed of the woman, the bruising of his heel, the multiplying of her sorrows and conception; the cursing of the ground, the sorrow of eating the products of the earth all the days of his life, the thorns, the thistles, and the eating of bread by the sweat of his face until he should return to the ground, were severe inflictions of punishment upon the first violators of God's unalterable law. There is no doubt but that they felt the keenest remorse and shame but to be sent forth from out the garden lest he should partake of the tree of life and live forever, was doubtless received with surprise.

5

Apparently the anger and indignation of God was increased, for it is further stated, "So he DROVE out the man; and He placed at the east of the Garden of Eden Cherubims, and a FLAMING SWORD which turned every way, to keep the way of the tree of life." Man by his wisdom was never to lay hold on the tree of life. The sentence of death was passed upon all, and the rights to the tree of life had been forfeited. Whoever attempted to regain it must come against the Flaming Sword.

From the time of the expulsion from Eden till the Exodus from the land of Egypt the way of the tree of life had been kept from Adam's posterity. No man had ever been able to pass the flaming sword. Death reigned from Adam to Moses, even over them who had not sinned after the similitude of Adam's transgression. Hope had almost vanished. The old patriarch declared that there was hope for a tree, but a man dieth, and wasteth away: yea man given up the ghost, and where is he? And again, If a man dies, shall he live again? No man could by any means redeem his brother, nor give to God a ransom for him; that he should still live forever, and not see corruption. (Job 14:8, 10, 14; Psa. 49:7-9.) No man could approach the tree of life.

There was a temporary restraint through the offering of the sacrifices of bullocks, goats, lambs, doves and pigeons. It appears that in order to redeem his forfeited position mankind sought the aid of these innocent creatures, and as they approached the tree of life these sacrifices fell victim to the flaming sword. One after another fell bleeding upon the altar, breathing its final breath, and died. None of them were revived from the dead to prove that they had succeeded in passing the sword and regained the way of the tree of life.

So great was the slaughter of the bulls, goats, and lambs that God himself grew weary of its continuance, and said: "To what purpose is the multitude of your sacrifices unto Me? I am full of burnt offerings of rams, and the fat of fed beast; and I delight not in the blood of bullocks, or of lambs, or of he goats." (Isa. 1:11.) "For my Sword shall be bathed (Revised Ver. 'hath drunk its fill') in heaven: Behold it shall come down upon Idumea (Edom), and upon the people of my curse. The Sword of the Lord is filled with blood, it is made fat with the fat of the kidneys of rams; for the Lord hath a sacrifice in Bozrah, and a great slaughter in the land of Edom." Isa. 34:5, 6.

From the foregoing scriptures we see that the Sword was filled with the blood of the sacrifices. To God it was "enough." He had a better sacrifice "in Bozrah," and it was to be a "great slaughter in the land of Edom" (Idumea). Edom was the name given to the descendants of Esau. Esau and Jacob were two great types. In Esau we see the type of God's people after the flesh (Israel), while in Jacob we see the type of the Church who is God's people after the Spirit. And as Jacob supplanted Esau, even so has the Church supplanted the Israelites. It is for this reason that God said, "Jacob have I loved, but Esau have I hated." Rom. 9:13; Gen. 25:21-26.

When He said that He had a sacrifice in Bozrah, and that His sword would come down upon the land of Edom, it was then that He pointed out where His flaming Sword would mete out justice. The Prophet foreseeing, cried out later. "Who is this that cometh

from Edom, with dyed garments from Bozrah? this
that is glorious in his apparel, traveling in the greatness of his strength?" The Spirit of Christ within him
(1 Pet. 1:10, 11), answered, "I that speak in righteousness, mighty to save." Isa. 63:1. The word Bozrah
signifies sheepfold. It was in the midst of Israel that
His garments were to be dyed in blood. See John 10.

David in his day, foreseeing the sufferings of Christ
as the sacrifice, records in the 22nd Psalm, verse 1,
the very words of Jesus upon His cross. In verse 20, He
says, "Deliver My soul from the Sword; my darling
from the power of the dog" (the Gentiles). Through
this we can see that the Sword is connected with
Calvary. For a long time the Sword seemed to have
been in silence, but because there was one coming to
redeem the forfeited possession, we hear Justice
crying through the Prophet Zechariah, "Awake, O
Sword, against my shepherd, against the man that is
my fellow, saith the Lord of hosts; smite the shepherd
and the sheep shall be scattered." Zech. 13:7. See
Matt. 26:31.

After many weary years of waiting One came who
was to be a commander and a leader of the people
(Isa. 55:4). He came to show the way to the tree of
life. His words, "I am come that they might have Life,
and that they might have it more abundantly," cast a
ray of hope across the path of the people who sat in
darkness and in the shadow of death. He came to restore the way to the tree of life.

To accomplish this He must pass the Flaming
Sword in the hand of the cherubim that was placed
at the east of the Garden of Eden. When His hour
arrived He was not discouraged. He faced it like a

man of war. The conflict was terrific. The Sword pierced His brow and blood came streaming down His face. His body was lacerated. His hands were torn and bleeding, the Sword wounds entered His feet and His side, but onward yet He pressed.

In the midst of His suffering He gave the thief an assurance that He would regain the entrance into paradise. He, too, was paying the penalty, "Thou shalt surely die." The tree of life was in the midst of paradise. And to him He says, "Verily I say unto thee, today shalt thou be with Me in paradise."

In the heat of the struggle He cried, "I thirst," and as darkness settled upon Him the lamentable cry, "My God, my God, why hast thou forsaken me," brought the terrible conflict to an end. And when He cried with a loud voice, "It is finished," He gave up the ghost and entered into paradise. Thus he braved the flaming sword and gained for us a right to the tree of life in the midst of the paradise of God. (Rev. 2:7, 22:14.) Whether we live or die, that life is for us and He shall raise us up in the last day. (John 6:54; Rev. 2:10.)

CHAPTER II.

THE ONLY TRUE GOD.

With reverence and adoration we bow our knees unto Jesus Christ the "Victim of the Flaming Sword" to give to our God the glory due His name. And we now make mention that His name is exalted above every name that is in heaven and in earth. Hence, the demons of hell are enraged, the religious world is astonished, and the tents of the fearful pilgrims are being violently shaken by the rushing mighty wind that is moving through the land proclaiming the NAME of the Lord. He who was slain is worthy.

We have beheld the Lamb of God. We have honored the Prince of Peace. We have rejoiced in the Rock of our Salvation, and have walked in the Light of Life. We have seen that Christ was our Shepherd as well as the door to the fold. He is the root and Offspring of David, as well as his son and his Lord. We have claimed Him as our High Priest in heaven, and the offering that was slain for our sins. He is the Temple of God and the Shew-bread, the vail, the altar, and the Lamb. He was Servant and Master at the same time. We have found Him to be the foundation of the Church, and the Chief Corner Stone thereof. He is a Destroying Storm, and covert as well from the Tempest. Considering all these things, it is no wonder that the people cried, "What manner of man is this?" "Who art Thou? Whom maketh Thou thyself?"

The Ungodly Parallel.

These questions in the minds of many, are yet unsolved in spite of all the institutions of learning filled with science, philosophy, and human wisdom. To many Jesus was a prophet, mighty in words and deeds. Some have hailed Him to be a great reformer. Mohammedans declare that He was a great prophet and nothing more. By many, Confucius, Mohammed, Buddha, Bahah, and any of the prophets are as equally as much divine as the Holy One of Israel. Theosophy asserts that the Divine spirit has manifested itself at various times thru different great religious leaders such as Confucius, Buddha, Moses, Mohammed, and that the time is ripe for the divine spirit to manifest itself again through some other "great personage." This is purely the spirit of anti-Christ. The next "great personage" will be none other than the son of the perdition, who will exalt himself above all that is called God or that is worshipped. John 17:12. 2 Thess. 2:3, 4.

Thousands are being swept away in this error, deceiving and being deceived, because they have not "known the Holy Scriptures." (1 Tim. 4:1; 2 Tim. 3:13-17.) The divinity of Jesus Christ, with the majority, has merely been a speculation and not a revelation from God. The vision of all has become as the words of a book that is sealed, which men deliver to one that is learned, saying, "Read this I pray thee," and he saith, "I cannot, for it is sealed." (Is. 29:11.) They have only seen our Savior as a man. They have judged Him after the flesh, as the Son of God, and not being able to go beyond this, thereby laying themselves liable to the deceptions of the spirit of anti-Christ that are abroad in the land.

God as Well as Son of God.

That Jesus Christ is the son of God, is acknowledged by all Christendom, and we believe that with all our heart. There is no argument there with us at all. But the thing that sets the religious world in a commotion is this revelation that Jesus Christ is God, the only true God that we can ever see. To whom be honor and glory forever and ever. Amen. Those who have been doctrinated with the "three person God" idea are bewildered. Their theory is crumbling under the mighty sledge hammer of God's word. Jer. 23:29.

There is but one God and He has been manifested in a three-fold manner. And this three-fold manifestation was not intended to establish a "three person" God idea, but instead, it was to reveal to mankind that there was a true and living God who loved them with an everlasting love. For four thousand years God had been waiting to visit and redeem his people. He appeared unto them in various forms, and spoke unto the fathers by the prophets in divers manners and declared the character of His name to them, saying, "I am that I AM: the Lord, God of your fathers, the God of Abraham, the God of Isaac, and the God of Jacob, * * * this is My name forever." The Lord, thy God is one Lord. "And again, "Ye are my witnesses," saith the Lord, "and my servant whom I have chosen; that ye may know and believe that I am He: before me there was no God FORMED, neither shall be after me. I, even I am the Lord; and besides me there is no Saviour." (Exod. 3:14, 15. Isa. 43:10, 11.)

The Spirit of God declared through the mouth of Isaiah that the king of Israel, the Redeemer, the Lord of Hosts, is the First, and the Last, and besides him there is no God. "Thus saith the Lord that created the heavens; GOD Himself that formed the earth and made it; He hath established it; He created it not in vain. He formed it to be inhabited: I am the Lord; and there is none else." Thus did God declare Himself to His people of Israel, but they were children that could not understand, for they had forsaken the Lord, and provoked the Holy One of Israel, and had every one gone away backward. They had forgotten his signs and wonders which he wrought in the days of old, but yet he loved them more and more and could not give up His treasure. He remembered His promise to Abraham and his covenant that He made in Chaldea, therefore he withheld his judgments and prepared to visit and redeem his people.

Mystery of Incarnation.

His visitation was to be shrouded in mystery, that they which see not might see; and they which see might be made blind. To some it was given to know the mysteries of the kingdom and to others it was not. But to those who had an ear to hear what the Spirit saith, the prophet gave an intimation as to the form of His coming, "Unto us a Child is born, unto us a Son is given, and the government shall be upon His shoulders; and His NAME shall be called Wonderful, Counsellor, THE MIGHTY GOD, THE EVERLASTING FATHER, the Prince of Peace." And again He saith, "Hear ye now, O, house of David; * * * Behold, a virgin shall conceive and bear a son, and shall call His name Immanuel." And in another place He saith, "Say unto the city of Judah, Behold your God! Behold the Lord will come with a strong hand, and His arm shall rule for Him: (and that they might know him, he adds) he shall feed His flock like a SHEPHERD; he shall gather the lambs in His arms, and carry them in His bosom." (Isa. 9:6, 7:13, 14; 40:9-11; John 10:14.)

When the fullness of time was come, a messenger from heaven came down and saluted the Virgin in Nazareth, and declared that the Holy Ghost would come upon her, and that she should bring forth a son and shall call his name Jesus, for He should save His people from their sins. And this was done, says St. Matthew, that it might be fulfilled which was spoken of the Lord by the prophet, "Behold, a Virgin shall be with child and shall bring forth a son, and they shall call his name IMMANUEL, which being interpreted is , GOD WITH US." The time came when the child was born. And the heavens bowed down and the Lord God of heaven and earth took on the form of man and became a pattern for us who should afterward follow in His steps.

How to Become Sons of God.

At the river Jordan he showed us how to fulfill the righteousness of God, saying, "Thus it becometh as to fulfill all righteousness," and when he came forth out of the water, the spirit of God descended in the bodily form of a dove and abode on him. And a voice came from heaven saying, "This is my Beloved Son in whom I am well pleased." It was thus that he demonstrated the manner in which we should come to be sons of God, and that, by being brought forth of the water and Spirit. Many failing to see this have attempted to use this blessed scene to establish the doctrine of a "three person" God, but there is no refuge there, for only one Person was visible and that was Jesus. The Spirit assumed the form of a dove (not man) that John might know Him who was to baptize with the Holy Ghost and with Fire. See John 1:31-34. The voice that came from heaven was also a witness to establish the fact that Jesus Christ was more than a prophet and greater than an ordinary man.

The Lord of Hosts.

The prophet Malachi in speaking of John the Baptist, said, "Behold, I send my messenger, and he shall prepare the way before ME, and the Lord whom ye seek, shall suddenly come to His temple, even the MESSENGER of the Covenant, whom ye delight in. Behold, He shall come, saith the LORD OF HOSTS. In this passage two messengers are mentioned. The first referred to John (Matt. 11:10), but the second MESSENGER of the Covenant is the LORD Himself. These words were spoken by the LORD OF HOSTS, and He says that John was to prepare the way before HIM. But who is the LORD OF HOSTS? Let Isaiah answer. "In the year that King Uzziah died I saw also the Lord sitting on His throne, high and lifted up * * * And above it stood the seraphims: * * * And cried one to another saying, Holy, holy, holy, is the LORD OF HOSTS: the whole earth is full of His glory. * * * Then said I "Woe is me! for I am undone: * * * for mine eyes have seen the King, the LORD OF HOSTS." (Isa. 6 chapter.) St. John, in speaking of this vision, declares that Isaiah saw the glory of Jesus, and spake of Him. (See St. John 12:39-41.)

The mystery of Christ is this, "How could the Mighty God, Creator of the heaven and earth, who fills the immensity of space, become confined to the limits of the body of a Virgin and assume the form of man?" It is beyond human conception. It was astonishing to the hosts of heaven. The angels desired to look into the eternal purpose of God, but they, too, were forbidden. The prophets were confounded at their own utterances, and inquired and searched diligently * * * what manner of time the Spirit of Christ in them did signify, when it testified beforehand the sufferings of Christ and the glory that should follow. Even the Eternal Spirit cried with amazement, saying, "Listen, O isles, unto me; and hearken ye people from afar; the Lord hath called me from the womb; from the bowels of my mother hath he made mention of my name." These words spoken by Isaiah the prophet (Isa. 49:1-6) met their fulfillment in Christ. Elizabeth speaking by the Spirit hails Mary as the Mother of her Lord, and His name was mentioned while He was yet in the "bowels of His mother," saying, "and thou shalt call His name JESUS: for He shall save His people from their sins." (Matt. 1:21.) A light to lighten the gentiles and the glory of my people Israel. (Compare Isa. 49:6, and Luke 2:32.) With man this is impossible, but with God all things are possible. "And the zeal of the Lord of Hosts hath performed it." These words spake the prophet when he said, "Unto us a child is born, unto us a son is given, * * * and His name shall be called * * * the Mighty God, The Everlasting Father, * * * the Zeal of the Lord of hosts shall perform this." Isa 9:6, 7.

The Father Revealed.

As He walked among the sons of men, as one of them, he became partaker of all his temptations, afflictions and sorrows. He wept with them that wept. He suffered with those that suffered. And in all their afflictions and griefs, He was touched with the feelings of their infirmities, and bore with them their burdens and heavy oppressions. He prayed, as a man, to the heavens and obtained answers to confirm and strengthen those that were with Him. He often made mention of his "Father in heaven," but no one durst question His statements. His works were so filled with wonder that his identity was near to disclosure. And many would marvel and wonder as to "what manner of man is this?" At times they thought they knew and understood him, then again they were lost in amazement. The disciples were confident that they knew him, but on the last night of his sojourn on earth he astonished them by saying, "If you had known me, you would have known my Father also: and from henceforth ye know Him and have seen him." These words stirred up the curiosity of Philip so that he could refrain no longer, and he said, "Lord, show us the Father and it sufficeth us." But Jesus answered, "Have I (the Everlasting Father) been so long a time with you and yet thou hast not known me, Philip? He that hath seen me, hath seen the Father: and how saith thou then, Show us the Father?" (John 14:1-11.) What could be clearer than these words? Jesus is the Father as well as the Son. And no man knoweth the Son but the Father and neither knoweth any man the Father, save the Son and he to whom the Son will reveal him. (Matt. 11:27.) This passage finds

its fulfillment in Matt. 16:16, 17 and John 14:7-11. The
Divine reveals the human side of God and the human
reveals the divine.

The life of Christ in the flesh was the example of
a son of God. And of all that he suffered, He bore it as
man. But on the resurrection morning he came forth
with power and proclaimed "All power is given unto
me in heaven and in earth." Thomas, who was with
them in the upper chamber the night of His passion,
and heard him reveal the Father to Philip, acknowledged Him to be the Almighty by exclaiming when
he saw His resurrection glory, "My Lord and My
God!" Peter said that Jesus had been made both Lord
and Christ. All power in heaven and earth had been
transferred from the invisible God and centered in
Jesus Christ, "God manifest in the flesh." And now
we see according to the Apostle Paul that it was Jesus
who created the heaven and earth, thus proving beyond a doubt, that Jesus Christ, the Mighty God, the
Everlasting Father, spoken of by Isaiah, is the one and
only true God that we ever will see or can see. (Col.
1:15, 16.)

Revelation of Jesus Christ.

While John the beloved was on the isle of Patmos,
it was there that he received the revelation of Jesus
Christ, which God gave him. And as he began to
prepare his message to the Churches, meditating over
this glorious vision, he burst forth with rapturous
strains, "Behold, He cometh with clouds; and every
eye shall see him; and they also which pierced him; and
all the kindred of the earth shall wail because of him.
Even so. Amen. I am Alpha and Omega, the beginning

and the ending, saith the Lord which is, which was, and which is to come, the Almighty." And he said he heard a great voice as of a trumpet, saying, "I am Alpha and Omega, the First and the Last." And when he turned he saw one in the midst of the candlesticks "like unto the son of man" (Jesus Christ), and when he saw him he fell at his feet as dead. And he laid his right hand upon him, saying, "Fear not; I am the First and the Last." These are the words of God concerning himself, spoken by the prophet Isaiah (Isa. 41:4; 44:6; 48:12.) and here we find Jesus applying the same words to himself. And in order that the Seer might not be mistaken in this revelation He adds, "I am He that liveth, and WAS DEAD; and behold, I AM alive forevermore. Amen! and have the keys of hell and death." (Rev. 1:1-18.)

In Rev. 21:6, 7, Jesus says, "I am Alpha and Omega * * * He that overcometh shall inherit all things; and I WILL BE HIS GOD, and he shall be MY SON." Truly this is wonderful!

The Record of St. John.

It was after this revelation that he wrote the gospel bearing his name, and no wonder he could sit down and unfold the mystery of the incarnation. Listen, what boldness he uses in opening this secret of all ages! "In the beginning was the Word and the Word was with God, and the Word was God. The same was in the beginning with God. All things were made by Him, and without Him was not anything made that is made. In Him was life, and the life was the light of men. The light shineth in darkness and the darkness comprehended it not. There was a man sent from God whose

name was John. The same came for a witness, to
bear witness of the light that all men through him
might believe. He was not that light, but was sent to
bear witness of that light. That was the true light
which lighteth every man that cometh into the world.
He was in the world, and the world was made by Him,
and the world knew Him not. He came unto His own
and His own received Him not. But as many as
received Him, to them gave He power to become the
sons of God, even to them that believe on HIS NAME."
Let us repeat these words, "even to them that believe
on HIS NAME." On whose name? Reading the context we find no one mentioned but God and John. His
theme is God. It must be God's Name! And we understand, beyond a doubt, that the only name whereby we
have become sons of God is by believing on the name
of Jesus. (Acts 2:38; 4:12; 8:12; 16:31.)

In explaining the mystery of the incarnation he
says, "And the word was made flesh and dwelt
among us, * * * full of grace and truth." That there
should be no doubt as to the divinity of Jesus, and
that no attempt to be made to make God and the
Son of God separate persons, the Apostle places in
parenthesis these words (and we beheld His |God's|
glory, the glory as of the only begotten of the Father).
Without controversy great is the mystery of godliness:
God was manifest in the flesh, justified in the Spirit,
seen of angels, preached unto the gentiles, believed
on in the world, received up into glory. This is the
TRUE GOD, and Eternal life. (1 Tim. 3:16. I John
5:20.)

CHAPTER III.

GOD'S HOUSE FROM EPHRATAH

In reading the 7th Chapter of 2nd Samuel, we will find a record how that David, after the Lord had given him rest round about from all of his enemies, felt within his heart a keen desire to build a house for God to dwell in. In the midst of his prosperity he could not forget his God. "See now I dwell in a house of cedar, but the Ark of God dwelleth within curtains," and with these words upon his lips he swore unto himself that he would not come in the tabernacle of his house, nor go up into his bed, nor give sleep to his eyes, nor slumber to his eyelids, until he had found out a place for the Lord, an habitation for the Mighty God of Jacob. (Ps. 132.)

God seeing the earnestness of his heart, said unto Nathan the prophet, "Go and tell my servant David, thus saith the Lord, shalt thou build for me an house to dwell in? Whereas I have not dwelt in any house since the time that I brought up the children of Israel out of Egypt even until this day, but have walked in a tent and in a tabernacle." And, furthermore, He reminded him of the fact that He had made no mention to any of the tribes of Israel that He desired a house to dwell in; and yet David had the welfare of his Lord in his heart, and desired to find a place for Him to dwell in. This thing so pleased God that He sent His word to David by His servant the prophet, saying: "Also the Lord telleth thee that HE WILL MAKE THEE AN HOUSE."

21

He did not say that He would make a house for
David, but rather that He would make David's body
His house. For David had a house of cedar already,
and needed not that another house should be built
for himself. In the 132d Psalm the writer declares,
"Lo, we have heard of it (this house of God) at
Ephratah; we found it in the field of the wood."

Ephratah.

In Genesis 35:19 we find that Ephratah is Bethlehem; and again, in 1 Samuel 17:12 we find that
David, whom God declared He would make His house
was the son of that Ephrathite of Bethlehem, Judah.
And it was there that God found him "in the field
of the wood" and took him "from the sheepcote,
from following the sheep," to be ruler over His people,
Israel. In the 11th verse of the above-mentioned
Psalm, we read these words: "The Lord hath sworn
in truth unto David and will not turn from it. Of
the fruit of thy body WILL I SET UPON THY
THRONE." Here it is plainly declared that JEHO-
VAH will, HIMSELF, set upon the Throne of David
in person, and in that day shall Zion be chosen for
an habitation; "I will abundantly bless her provision; I will satisfy her poor with bread. I will also
clothe her priests with salvation, and her saints
shall shout aloud for joy."

Since God's house was to come out of Ephratah,
which is Bethlehem, we now turn our attention to
the words of the prophet Micah: "But thou, Beth-
lehem-Ephratah, though thou be little among the
thousands of Judah, yet out of thee shall he come
forth unto me that is to be ruler in Israel; whose
goings forth have been from of old, from everlasting,

(Marg. the days of eternity)." Micah 5:2. That this prophecy points directly to the birth of Jesus Christ in Bethlehem is clearly proven in the 2d Chapter of St. Matthew's, when Herod desired to know where the Christ should be born and the priests and scribes of the people said unto him, "In Bethlehem of Judea: for thus it is written by the prophets, And thou, Bethlehem in the Land of Judah, art not the least among the princes of Judah, for out of thee shall come a Governor that shall rule my people Israel." Matt. 2:1-6. That Christ Jesus was of the loins of David, God's word affirms; for both Joseph and Mary were of the house and lineage of David and were therefore compelled to go up out of Nazareth into Judea unto the City of David, which is called Bethlehem, to be taxed; and it was while there that Christ was born. This alone is sufficient to convince any one that Jesus, the Christ, is GOD.

"Now, all this was done, that it might be fulfilled which was spoken of the Lord by the prophet, saying, Behold a virgin shall be with child and shall bring forth a son, and they shall call his name Emmanuel, which, being interpreted, is GOD WITH US." (Matt. 1:22-23.) And when we behold the body of our Lord Jesus Christ we look upon the habitation of the Mighty GOD of Jacob, for GOD was in (the body of) Christ, reconciling the world unto Himself.

The House of Bread

The word "Bethlehem" literally means "The House of Bread," and God declared that when He had taken up His abode in His new tabernacle, "I will abundantly bless her provision: and will satisfy her poor with bread." (Ps. 132:15.) And after Jesus had fed the

5,000 with five loaves and two small fishes, He declared unto the multitude, the next day, "I am the Bread of Life," and again, "I am the Living Bread which came down from Heaven: if any man eat of this bread he shall live forever." (Jno. 6:48-51.) Truly God has given unto us, in these last days, to eat of that Living Bread. He that cometh to Him shall never hunger; he that believeth in Him shall never thirst. Lord, evermore give us of this Bread! "Man shall not live by bread (natural) alone, but by every WORD that proceedeth out of the mouth of God." "And the WORD was made flesh, and dwelt among us." "And the Bread that I will give is my flesh, which I will give for the life of the world." When Jesus spake these words many were offended and said, "This is a hard saying: who can hear it?" and from that time many of His disciples went back and walked no more with Him. Then said Jesus unto the twelve, "Will ye also go away?" Then Simon Peter answered Him, "Lord, to whom shall we go? Thou hast the words of Eternal Life." These words of that dear old Saint of God should dwell deep within every heart, "LORD, TO WHOM SHALL WE GO? THOU HAST THE WORDS OF ETERNAL LIFE."

May the love of God fill every heart that reads these precious words, and cause them to lay aside their bitterness, wrath and strife, and seek to behold the Glory of God in the face of Jesus Christ, our Lord. If you do not catch the thought of this little message at first, read it again and again, and I am sure that God will cause this great Truth to unfold unto you and cause your heart to overflow with joy.

CHAPTER IV.

THE KING OF SALEM.

When Abraham left his father's house and started forth unto a land that he was afterwards to receive for an inheritance, little did he realize the many experiences that he was to pass through during his journey to the land of promise. Neither did he know of all the ways in which God Almighty had intended to lead him, for it is written, "By faith Abraham, when he was called to go out into a place which he should after receive for an inheritance, obeyed; and he went out, not knowing whither he went." Heb. 11:8. It was this thing that pleased God.

Upon his arrival in Canaan he builded an altar and there he called upon the name of the Lord. From thence he went down into Egypt because "the famine was grievous in the land," and there he encountered a great difficulty through fear of his wife being taken from him, but God delivered him from the land of Egypt, and he came forth very rich.

The strife between his herdsmen and those of Lot came unexpectedly upon him. The dispute was no little matter to settle. Somebody must give in. Abraham was master. The great man humbled himself and took the lowest place, saying, "Let there be no strife, I pray thee, between me and thee, and between my herdsmen and thy herdsmen; for we are brethren." Lot chose the better part, while Abraham submitted himself to the lesser part with a silent, but contented amen. Submission is a stepping stone to advancement. Humility is the path to honor and exaltation. The lesser is blessed by the better.

A blessing awaited Abraham. This was God's way to bring it about. Lot pitched his tent toward Sodom. In order that He might bless Abraham, God stirred up four kings against the kings of Sodom, Gomorrah, Admah, Zeboiim and Zoar, and overcame them, taking Lot and all his goods among the captives of Sodom. And when Abraham heard of it he armed his trained servants and went forth in the name of God Almighty, smote the enemy and brought back all the goods, and his brother Lot, his goods, the women and all the people.

On his return from the slaughter of the kings, Abraham is met first by the king of Sodom, who comes for the purpose of offering him worldly possessions, but Melchizedek, king of Salem, priest of the Most High God, in the meantime, intervenes and brings forth bread and wine, and blessed him with a blessing that far exceeded the blessings of any earthly king. And to him Abraham gave a tenth of all that he possessed. So great was that blessing that Abraham spurned the offers Bera and kept his vow which he had made to the Most High God. Gen. 14:17-24.

How great this man must have been! Greater than Enoch! Greater than Noah!! Greater than Shem!!! How great this man (if it be lawful to call him a man) must have been, to whom the patriarch Abraham gave the tenth of the spoils. Greater even than Abraham, to the extent that he blessed him that had the promises. And without contradiction the less is blessed by the better. Heb. 7:1, etc. Was he of the descent of the sons of men? That has long been the question that has confronted the students of divinity in almost every age.

By some he is said to be the king of an earthly city called Salem, a city of the Jebusites, but this is merely supposition, and most of the Biblical students consider it as such, ending their statement with a (?) question mark. There are others who have ventured to claim this Melchizedek to have been Shem, but this could not be true and yet be in harmony with the Scriptures. Shem had both father and mother; beginning of life and ending of days. Gen. 5:32; 11:10, 11. Melchizedek was "without father, without mother, without descent, having neither beginning of days, nor end of life." Heb. 7:3. This can not be said of Shem.

There are many that reckon him with the ancient Egyptian record of "hykos" or "shepherd king," who was supposed to have invaded Egypt and built the great Pyramid, and then departed as peaceably as they came. To one who has studied the structure of this great "stone witness" in the land of Egypt, that in a measure might be true, but who was this "shepherd king," is the question that is before us. In the construction of this pyramid is revealed some most astonishing facts. (See "A Miracle In Stone," by J. A. Seiss.) In its descending and ascending passages, its grand gallery, anti-chamber, king's chamber, queen's chamber, etc., is portrayed a most wonderful plan of the ages, and who could know such things at so early an age but God. No mortal could have known it. But let us return to the word of God for our proof and conclusion.

Melchizedek was, or rather, is a priest of God and "abideth a priest, continually." His priesthood is an everlasting priesthood, and even today "it is witnessed that he **liveth.**" A high priest is a mediator between God and man. And since Melchizedek has an endless priesthood, and yet liveth, who, then, is "this that cometh up from Edom, with dyed garments from Bozrah?" Who is this that now cometh forth after the order of Melchizedek, made not after the law of carnal commandments, but the power of an endless life?"

That this is Christ Jesus every one must admit. The word declares that Jesus is the only mediator between God and men. 1 Tim. 2:5. And no man can come to God but by Him. John 14:6. From this it is impossible for us to have two Mediators. If Melchizedek abideth a priest continually, and Christ being come an high priest continually, then it is evident that Christ and Melchizedek are one, for there is but "one mediator between God and men, the man Christ Jesus."

The apostle tells us that he had "many things to say, and hard to be uttered" concerning Melchizedek, seeing that the saints were dull of hearing. Heb. 5:10, 11. From this we see that the depth of the personage of Melchizedek was withheld, because the people were not ready to receive them. In chapter 7 he ventured to give a little further account of him by comparing him with Abraham, and giving the interpretation of his name. Here he declares him to be King of righteousness (note capital K), after that King of Salem, which is King of peace. Who is the King of righteousness save our Lord Jesus Christ? Jer. 23:5, 6; Zech. 14:9; I Cor. 1:30. Who is the King of Peace, but Christ Jesus our Lord? Judges 6:24; Isa. 9:6, 7; Lu. 2:14; Eph. 2:14, 17.

To eliminate the thoughts of Melchizedek being of human lineage, he further states "without father,

without mother, without descent, having neither beginning of days, nor end of life." What could be
clearer? And finally he openly declares, and yet
treading softly, "made like unto the Son of God."
That Christ and Melchzedek are one may also be
seen through the words of Jesus himself: "Your father
Abraham rejoice to see my day: and he saw it and
was glad." And when the Jews said, "Thou art not
yet fifty years old, and hast thou seen Abraham?"
Jesus answers, "Verily, verily, I say unto you, Before
Abraham was I am." When did Abraham see his day
and was made glad, or blessed, was it not when
Melchizedek met him?

Moreover, as Melchizedek administers Bread and
wine to Abraham (the first communion service) even
so does Christ administer Bread and Wine to the new
generation of the seed of Abraham. From the fact
that Melchizedek still lives and abides a priest of
God, and that Christ still lives and abides a priest
forever, it is my honest conviction that Melchizedek
was Christ before His incarnation, but since his incarnation he has become a High Priest who is touched
with the feelings of our infirmities, having been
tempted in all points like as we are, yet without sin.
It became him to become liken unto us that he might
be a faithful High Priest that He might have compassion on the ignorant, and them that are out of the
way; for that He himself also is compassed with infirmities. He knoweth our feeble frame and remembers
that we are but dust. There is no weakness, no sin,
no failure so great but that our merciful high priest
can reach our case.

The blessings that Melchizedek bestowed upon
Abraham are bestowed upon us, the seed of Abra-

ham (Gal. 3:26-28), through Christ Jesus. It was
after that Melchizedek had given Abraham the bread
and wine that he blessed him, so Christ, after he had
prepared the bread and wine (His body and blood),
that he led the disciples out as far as Bethany and
blessed them. See Mat. 26:26-28; Lu. 24:50. It was
through His broken body and His shed blood on
Calvary that made peace between God and man
Christ is the King of Salem! Christ is the King of
PEACE!

CHAPTER V.

OUR GOD SHALL COME.

Our God shall come and not keep silence; a fire shall devour before him, and it shall be very tempestuous round about him. For yet a little while he that shall come will come and will not tarry.

In the beginning God created the heavens and the earth. (Gen. 1:1.) The Word was with God and the Word was God. The same was in the beginning with God. All things were made by Him and without Him was not anything made that is made. He was in the world and the world was made by Him and the world knew Him not.

He came to his own (people, the Jews) and his own received Him not. He declared Himself to be their God, but they could not understand. The works He did, no other man on earth hath ever done. He healed their sick and raised the dead and walked upon the sea, till questions rose in every heart, "What manner of man is this?"

The prophet declared that the "Child Born" was to be the "Everlasting Father"; the "Son" (of God) given was the "Mighty God." (Isa. 9:6.) There is no difference. He that was in the world "as" the only begotten of the Father, is the same who laid the foundation of the earth in the beginning. The prophet declared it before He came. (Isa. 44:24; 40:9, 10, 11, 22; Psa. 104:2, 5.) The Spirit spake of it through the Psalmist and confirmed it through the apostle Paul. (Psa. 102:25-27 with Heb. 1:10-12.)

He came to visit His people, but began with Moses in Horeb. (Gen. 50:24, 25; Ex. 3:8.) His presence was with them all along the way, but no man had seen His shape. (John 1:18; 5:37.) Moses desired to see His face (His glory) but was not granted the privilege. (Ex. 33:18-23.) He was given a glimpse of His future manifestation (1 Tim. 3:16), but some day we shall behold His glory (John 17:24), for we shall see His face. (Rev. 22:4.)

Long, weary years passed by as the prophets sat on the shores of time scanning the distant horizon, while in their anxious bosoms arose the querulous sign, "O, when shall our Lord God come?" The sacrifices of the temple were polluted. The priests had erred in judgment, and the joy and mirth of the feasts had gone. The holy House had been shamefully desecrated and the glory of the temple had waned. Their "idols had spoken vanity," and the diviners had seen a lie and told false dreams. Their attempt to comfort them was in vain, therefore they went their way as a flock and were troubled, troubled because there was no shepherd. (Zech. 10:2.)

To give comfort and hope to his people, the Lord sent word of rejoicing, saying, Comfort ye, comfort ye, my people * * * speak comfortably to Jerusalem * * * prepare ye the way of the Lord, make straight in the desert a highway for our God. And the glory of the Lord shall be revealed, and all flesh shall see it together. * * * O Zion, that bringeth good tidings, * * * O Jerusalem, that bringeth good tidings, lift up thy voice with strength * * * be not afraid: say unto the cities of Judah, Behold your God! Behold, the Lord

GOD shall come with a strong hand * * * He shall feed His flock like a SHEPHERD. (Isa. 40:1-11.)

When the fulness of time was come, a Virgin brought forth a Son whose name was Immanuel (God with us). The hope of Israel had come. He came to visit and redeem his people. He fed "His flock like a Shepherd," and declared, "I am the Good Shepherd." He came unto His own, and His own received Him not. They smote the SHEPHERD of Israel. He bowed His head and died. He arose and ascended into heaven and He will come again. Not in the glory "as of the only begotten of the Father," but in all the glory of the Father, the Great God our Saviour. Titus 2:13.

Slain and Glorified From the Foundation of the World.

In the garden of Eden God slew a lamb to make a coat of skins. He had to shed blood for the transgression of Adam. Now this did not take away sin but only covered it until the true Lamb should come that (taketh away the sin of the world). In this manner God was beginning to fulfill his purpose and plan before the foundation of the world, that man should be holy and without blame before him in love. (Eph. 1:4.)

God foresaw the fall of mankind and therefore (predestinated us unto the adoption of children by Jesus Christ to himself, according to the good pleasure of his will. (Eph. 1:5.)) God predestinated the destination set before man, that he should either be saved or damned.

In this connection note the word of the Lord in Isaiah 46:10, saying (Remember the former things of old; for I am God, and there is none else; I am God, and there is none like me, DECLARING THE END FROM THE BEGINNING, and from ancient times the things that are not yet done, saying, "My counsel shall stand, and I will do all my pleasure; calling a ravenous bird from the East, the man that executeth my counsel from a far country: yea, I have spoken it, I will also bring it to pass; I have purposed it, I will also do it.")

God laid his plan out and saw it all before it took place. Now you can begin to see how "the Lamb was slain from the foundation of the world," in the heart and foreknowledge of God; also how he has chosen us according to this plan which he ordained to come to pass in these last days, whereby we should be saved. Amen. Before the foundation of the world God planned to save us through the method of the cross of Calvary, but which is now made manifest in these last times for us. Jesus once said, "Glorify thou me with the glory which I had with thee before the world was." John 17:5. Since this glory was to follow the sufferings of Christ, was the Lamb of God slain twice? No. This glory for which Jesus prayed was ordained before the foundation of the world through the foreknowledge of God in the beginning even as was also the slaying of the Lamb.

CHAPTER VI.

THE FATHERHOOD OF GOD IN CHRIST.
High Priests and His Sons

The High Priest of the Old Testament was chosen of God. No man took that office unto himself. But when God desired to establish a typical priesthood it was to be patterned after the heavenly priesthood. (Heb. 8:4, 5.) And in His choice for that divine office He chose Aaron and his sons and appointed it to them for "a perpetual statute." Thus the office of the High Priest became hereditary. (Ex. 28:1, 2, 3, 40-43; 29:9, 29, 30.)

No one was admitted into the priesthood but the sons or descendants of Aaron. The High Priest was always the father of those who entered into the priesthood and gained admittance into the sanctuary. (See Eli's family degraded from the office. 1 Sam. 2:27-36.)

Now that Christ has become the High Priest, the priesthood also has been changed. For he is a "priest forever (everlasting) after the order of Melchizedek." The priesthood no longer remains in the house of Aaron, but has been bestowed upon the house of God, whose house are we—the heavenly family. We are the "royal priesthood" (1 Pet. 2:9) that minister in the true tabernacle, and are made unto our God kings and priests (Rev. 5:8).

The fact that we are the "royal priesthood" and Christ is the High Priest, proves conclusively that Christ Jesus is our Father. For the High Priest was

always the father of those who partook of the priesthood. Moreover, Christ is a Priest forever (everlasting), hence He is our "Everlasting Father," as so saith
Isaiah the prophet. (Isa. 9:6.)

There is but "one God and Father of all, who is
above all" (Eph. 4:6), and speaking of Christ, John
bore witness that He was the one who was "above
all," showing clearly that He who was "from above
(and) is above all" is the "one God and Father of
all, who is above all, and through all, and in you all",
(John 3:31.)

Our High Priest and Father has entered into that
four square city alone, while we, His sons minister
in His sanctuary, the Spirit-filled body of Christ. He
entered by the door into the sanctuary at the River
Jordan, when He was baptized in water and Spirit.
After the Resurrection He went into the Holy of Holies,
or heaven itself. On the day of Pentecost He came out
in the person of the Holy Spirit and gave us "power
to become the sons of God" that we might minister in
the true sanctuary. (Acts 1:8; John 1:12.)

It was on the Isle of Patmos that John saw Christ
clothed in His Priestly costume. It was there that
Christ declared himself to be the Alpha and Omega,
the First and the Last. (Comp. Isa. 44:6, with Rev.
1:8, 11, 17, 18.) Therefore He could easily say: "He
that overcometh shall inherit all things; and I will be
his GOD, and he shall be MY son," because the High
Priest was the Father of all that partook of the priesthood. (Rev. 21:7.)

For what other purpose did God so arrange the
typical Priesthood after this manner if it were not
to reveal the fact that the Fatherhood of God was

THE SWORD OF THE LORD IS FULL OF BLOOD
See page 6

to be found in Christ Jesus, the High Priest of the Royal Priesthood? All things written in the Law, Psalms and Prophets were concerning Him. Luke 24.

The Head of Christ Is God.

There are only two great factors in the plan of the world's redemption, and these are The Lord and His Church. The most important factors in the great drama of Creation were Man and Woman. The formation of man out of the dust of the ground and making him a living soul to afterwards enter into a " deep sleep" so that from his side is taken substance with which God "builded" (Margin) the woman, was typical of the "Second Adam" entering into a "deep sleep" on Calvary where from His side flowed a substance (blood and water) with which He "builds" His church. See Gen. 2:21, 22; John 20:34, Matt. 16:18.

The Lord Jesus Christ is the head of the church, which is his body. Eph. 1:22, 23. The body is Christ. For as the body is one and hath many members, and all members of that one body, being many, are one body: SO ALSO IS CHRIST. 1 Cor. 12:12, 13. And we, the members, are "by one Spirit baptized into one body" (and the body IS CHRIST). The way we get into this Christ, the Church, is by baptism. "For as many of you as have been baptised into CHRIST have put on Christ." Gal 3:27; John 3:5; Mar. 16:16.

Unless we recognize the body of Christ on the earth we will fall into the great error that is coming upon the whole breadth of the land. When they shall say, "Lo here, and lo there is Christ," we who acknowledge that we are in CHRIST will never be deceived by any person arising and saying, "I am Christ." Mat. 24:5; 23, 24, 25, 26.

Christ in Person, Spirit and Mystery.

Christ in person is our Lord Jesus Christ. Christ in mystery, is the Church. Eph. 3:3, 4; Col. 1:26; 4:3. Christ in Spirit is the Holy Ghost. Heb. 11:24, 26; 1 Cor. 10:1-4; 1 Pet. 1:10, 11, with 2 Pet. 1:20, 21. These are thoughts that need much consideration in these days to preserve God's people from error. Because of the lack of knoweldge on these things many are being made to believe that there is no "personal coming" of the Lord Jesus Christ.

It is the Christ in person whom we are expecting to come again. Acts 1:11; 1 Cor. 1:7; Phil. 3:20; Col. 3:4; 1 Thes. 2:19; 3:13; 4:15-16; 2 Thes. 2:1; Ti. 2:13; 1 Pet. 1:7; 2 Pet. 1:16-18.

Christ in you the hope of glory we recognize to be the Holy Ghost, which is the Spirit of Truth. Jesus said that in the day when the Holy Ghost came "ye shall know that I am in my Father, ye in me, and I IN YOU." John 14:6, 16, 17, 18, 20; Col. 1:27.

But Christ the Church is the body of baptized believers, that is, Spirit-filled, according to John 3:5; Mark 16: 16-18; Acts 2:4; Rom. 6:3, 4; 1 Cor. 12:12, 13; Gal. 3:27.

Christ, the Church.

The head of every man is Christ. Jesus Christ is the head, or leader, of every man. He is the perfect example, worthy to be followed. Christ, the Church, is the head of every man. No individual, or company of individuals is superior to Christ, the Church. As the head of every woman is the man, even so is Jesus the head of the Church. Col. 1:18. Since the Church is Christ (Col. 2:17) it can be clearly seen that Jesus, who is the head of Christ (the Church) is God. Therefore, "The head of every man is Christ; and the head of every woman is the man; and the Head (Jesus) of Christ (the Church) is GOD." 1 Cor. 11:3. Note Mat. 1:21-23. They shall call His name Immanuel, which being interpreted is, GOD with us.

When the Last Enemy Is Destroyed

That God is doing wonders in these last days is a thing that is most generally acknowledged by the whole religious world, no matter what their various beliefs may be. Even the ungodly of this world admit that the time of marvelous revelation of things unknown heretofore has come.

Not only are things being revealed to the scientific world, but also to the Church of God in which many of us are playing a particular part. We are told that "in Christ are hid all the treasures of wisdom and knowledge" (Col. 2:2, 3). Men, by scientific research, are revealing to the world things that have been hidden for thousands of years, but God, through the Eternal Spirit, is making known to us the mysteries concerning Jesus Christ "which was kept secret since the world began."

Many things have been written in the past concerning our illustrious Saviour, but not since the beloved apostle received his mysterious visions on the Isle of Patmos, has so great a flood of revelations of

Jesus Christ been given to the sons of men as are being revealed by the Spirit of God in these closing days of the Gospel. Surely there has been set before us an "open door" which no man can shut. (Rev. 3:7, 11.)

There are many who have written upon the subject of the Son "delivering up the kingdom of God," but there has always been something lacking. We had settled it in our hearts by the "things which were written in the law of Moses, and in the prophets, and in the Psalms" that Jesus was the God of Israel, but this expression in I Cor. 15:24-28 was not as clear to us as we desired it to be.

The perplexity began to lift when we noticed in Dan. 7:14 that the dominion of the Son was to be "an everlasting dominion, which shall not pass away, and * * * shall not be destroyed." Also in Psalms and Hebrews it is said concerning the Son's dominion, "Thy throne, O God, is forever and ever." (Psa. 45:6, 7; Heb. 1:8.) The passages just mentioned apparently stood in open contradiction to that of first Corinthians. One says his kingdom shall be "everlasting," "forever and ever," while the other says it shall come to an end and be "delivered up to God." Because of this apparent contradiction the best Bible Commentators have declared I Cor. 15:24 to be one of the most difficult passages in the Word of God. Their conclusion is that it is his "mediatorial" position that He assumed for the suffering of death that shall come to end, which position he must hold until "the last enemy is destroyed" which is death (ver. 26). The seed of the woman (the Son of Man) must bruise the Serpent's head. This will not be fully accomplished until the Judgment of the Great White Throne, at which time death and the devil shall be cast into the lake of fire. Rev. 20:10, 14.

When the "last enemy is destroyed" the Sonship that God assumed will come to its end. The full work of redemption will have been completed. It is after death is destroyed that God will be all and in all. Then turning to Rev. 21:4 we read that when "there shall be no more death" and God himself shall be with men and shall be their God we hear the voice of Jesus saying, "Behold I make all things new. Write for these words are true and faithful. It is done. I AM Alpha and Omega, the beginning and the end. I will give unto him that is athirst of the fountain of the water of life freely. He that overcometh shall inherit all things; and I WILL BE his GOD, and he SHALL be My Son." (Compare Rev. 1:10-18 and 21:6,7. The Son in this manner only will deliver up the Kingdom to God, for he was God (John 1:1) is now (John 1:14; Tim. 3:16), and forever shall be. The Lord which is, which was, and which is to come, the ALMIGHTY. (Rev. 1:8.)

On the Right Hand of God.

As there are many who are anxious to be enlightened, or to get an explanation of the scriptures concerning Jesus being "on the right hand" of God, since this present great message has come forth, we hereby set forth the meaning of the "right hand" according to the word.

When Rachel brought forth her last son, Jacob, his

father, called him Benjamin, that is, "Son of my Right Hand." Benjamin was Jacob's "favorite" son, and became the head warrior tribe (Gen. 49:27) and he was the most "favored" among his brethren by Pharoah. (Gen. 45:22.)

Of the two sons of Joseph, Ephraim received the "right hand" blessing, Jacob guiding his hand wittingly, and when it displeased Joseph and prompted him to remove his right hand to the head of Manasseh, Jacob refused and said, * * * "truly his younger brother shall be greater than he," * * * and he set Ephraim before Manasseh, power and authority being given unto him. Gen. 48:13-20.

It was at the Red Sea that God's "right hand" was made "glorious in power," and being favored God in this trying hour the children of Israel recognized themselves as being on the right hand of the Most High. Power and authority had been given unto them, and as a nation they were destined to show forth, in a measure, the future glory of the Coming Kingdom of Christ. (Ex. 15:6.)

In the Law it was understood that he who received the Right Hand blessing was eligible to exercise all authority over the possessions to which he has fallen heir. All things are given into his hands. In all cases it was the "first-born" who became his father's right hand child, with the exceptions of the cases of Ephraim and Manasseh, Esau and Jacob, Joseph and Benjamin, and such like wherein God endeavored to show the transferring of his favor from the Jews (the first) to the Gentiles (the last).

When David was in trouble, he cried, "Will the Lord cast off forever and will he be favorable no more?

Is his mercy clean gone forever? Doth his promise fail forevermore?" Then he said, "This is my infirmity: I will remember the years of the 'right hand' of the Most High." Psa. 77:7-11. Here it can be plainly seen that the "right hand" of God is the "favor" of God. He would remember the years when he was favored of God; when he was in power and authority, and all his enemies had been subdued unto him. So it is with Christ.

He was God in the "likeness of men"; the Lord and Master in the "form of a servant;" The Everlasting Father "as a son"; the Eternal Spirit "manifest in flesh"; Divinity robed in "humanity"; the High and Lofty One in "humility"; and in his humiliation His judgment was taken away. He was misjudged. They judged him to be a man, speaking blasphemy against the Most High. Though they judged him cursed of God, yet He said, "Ye shall see the Son of man (this human form) sitting on the RIGHT HAND OF POWER, and coming in the clouds of heaven." (Mark 14:62). On the resurrection morning he arose from the earth as Almighty God, favored with "all power given unto Him both in heaven and in earth." Matt. 28:18.

It is this truth that sent conviction to the hearts of Israel on the day of Pentecost, "Therefore being by the right hand of God exalted * * * God has made this Jesus * * * both Lord and Christ." Acts 2:32-36. When Stephen saw Jesus "standing in the favor of God," in defense of whom the Jews had put to death, it was more than his enemies could bear, and they dragged him out of the city and stoned him to death. Acts 7:55-59.

To say that Christ is on the right hand of God does not mean that there is another human form like unto that of Jesus seated in heaven, but instead, it showed that the humanity of Jesus Christ (Son of Man) had been highly favored by God against whom he was accused of speaking blasphemy. What a rebuke! What a sting! Jesus of Nazareth, the blasphemer, the desecrater of the Sabbath, sitting on the right hand of God! Could it be possible? These are the things that confronted the Jews after the resurrection, and those who testified to the truth of these things only enflamed the Jews with bitter hatred. Acts 7:55-60.

In reading the following scriptures, you will find that Jesus did not use the term "right hand of God" but instead, "the right hand of POWER." Matt. 26:64; Mark 14:62; Luke 22:69. Moreover, it will be noticed that He also uses the term "Son of Man" (humanity), instead of "Son of God." He was the Eternal Spirit's right hand Man. (Jehovah's fellow. Zech. 13:7).

CHAPTER VII.

THE MYSTERY OF GOD ONLY KNOWN BY REVELATION.

All things are delivered to me of my Father; and NO MAN knoweth who the SON IS, but the Father, and who the FATHER is, but the Son, and he to whom the Son will reveal Him. Luke 10:22.

According to these words of Jesus no man can know who the Father, nor the Son, is, except it be revealed. The Jews declared that they knew God, the Father, but Jesus said they did not. (John 8:19, 54, 55.) Even to this day they claim to know God, but Jesus said He alone can reveal the Father. Is Jesus, therefore, revealing the Father to those who rejected Him?

The Mohammedans claim to know God, the Father, even in the same sense in which the Jews know Him. Can it be said that Jesus is revealing the Father to those ungodly Moslems who look upon his sacrificial death with unspeakable hatred?

Modern theological institutes, seminaries, and colleges, the majority of which are destitute of the Spirit of God, claim the same knowledge of God that the Jews maintain. Is Jesus revealing this mystery to them contrary to His own words that these things are hidden from the "wise and prudent," but are revealed unto babes?

Almost any one that is able to read at all can take up the Bible and see, what is apparently, "three

46

THE VICTORIOUS VICTIM OF THE FLAMING SWORD

47

persons," the common view held by Catholic and all other denominations, but is Jesus revealing this to them? I tell you "Nay." God has taken the wise in their own craftiness. For it is written, "I will destroy the wisdom of the wise, and will bring to nothing the understanding of the prudent." Isa. 29:11-14; Mat. 11:25.

That Jesus Christ is the MIGHTY GOD was declared by the Prophet Isaiah (Isa. 9:6); acknowledged by the Apostle Thomas and accepted by Christ (John 20:28, 29); revealed by the Spirit (Rev. 1:1); and spoken by the glorified Christ himself, saying, "I am Alpha and Omega * * * the Frst and the Last * * * I am he that liveth and was dead; and behold, I am alive for evermore. Amen." (Rev. 1:8-18.) "I am Alpha and Omega, the beginning and the end. I will give unto him that is athirst of the fountain of the water of life freely. He that overcometh shall inherit all things; and I will be his GOD, and he shall be my son." (Rev. 21:6, 7.)

To acknowledge Jesus Christ as the only true God does no more detract from His Sonship than does acknowledging Him as our High Priest detract from His sacrificial office as a Lamb slain for our many sins. It is the "veil of flesh" assumed by the Mighty God that is causing men to stumble at the word. In the flesh he was the Son of man and Son of God. As a man he walked, wept, prayed, suffered and died. As God He raised Himself from the dead (John 2:19-21) and shined forth in the radiance of eternal glory. "Yea, though we have known Christ after the flesh yet, now know we him no more." (2 Cor. 5:16.) When He came in the flesh He was beheld in the Glory as the Son (John 1:14), but when He comes again He will come in the glory of the Father. (Matt. 16:27 with Matt. 25:31.) Compare Isaiah 6:1-9 with John 12:39-41, also verses 44 and 45.

Our Lord and His Christ.

And the seventh Angel sounded; and there were great voices in heaven, saying, "The kingdoms of this world are become the kingdoms of our Lord and His Christ; and he shall reign for ever and ever." Rev. 11:15.

These sayings are faithful and true. They are the true sayings of God. And he said unto me, Write: for these words are true and faithful. Rev. 19:9; 2:15; 22:6. But since the revelation of Jesus Christ has come and has proven Him to be "our Lord," who then is "his Christ?"

That Jesus Christ is LORD must be acknowledged by all, whether in heaven, or in earth (Phil. 2:10, 11.). To say that there is more than "one Lord" is to flatly contradict the Word of God which saith, "Hear, O Israel: The Lord our God is ONE LORD." Deut. 6:4; Mar. 12:29; Eph. 4:5. Jesus has been proven to be "Lord of all," and in his own time he will show who is that blessed and only Potentate, King of kings, and LORD of lords." 1 Tim. 6:14, 15.

The earth is the Lord's and the fullness thereof. All things were made by him and for him, and without him was not anything made that was made. He (Jesus) was in the world, and the world was made by him, and the world knew him not. (Psa. 24:1; John

1:1, 2, 10; Col. 1:16, 17.) The God that created the
heavens and earth (Gen. 1:1), is our Lord Jesus, who
made them all by himself. (Isa. 44:24.) Jesus Christ
our Lord is LORD of all creation. He created it for his
glory and his own pleasure, but Satan has usurped the
authority and made himself the god and prince of this
world. (See Rev. 4:11; and 2 Cor. 4:4; John 14:30.)
The world is now being ruled by Satan and his people,
but thank God, the kingdoms of this world shall soon
become the kingdom of our LORD and his Christ, or
anointed.

Since Jesus is our Lord, we, then, are his anointed.
The church, anointed with the Holy Ghost, is the body
of Christ. (1 Cor. 12:12-14.) As God called all the
children of Israel in Egypt His son, saying, When
Israel was a child, then I loved him, and called my
SON out of Egypt (Hos. 11:1), even so does he call the
body of baptized believers "his Christ, or anointed."
We shall reign here with him, if we suffer here with
him. We are his sons (Rev. 21:7), being overcomers.
It is Christ Jesus who has anointed us (Mat. 3:11; John
15:26; 16:7), and he that hath anointed us is GOD.
(2 Cor. 1:21, 22.)

The kingdom of this world shall become the
kingdom of our Lord Jesus Christ and his saints, the
body of Christ. By reading Dan. 7:18, 22, 27, these
words will be verified. "For the greatness of the
kingdom under the whole heaven, shall be given to
the people of the saints of the Most High, whose
kingdom is an everlasting kingdom, and all dominions
shall serve him." Dan. 7:27. If you will notice this
passage closely you will see that the "people of the
saints of the most High" are spoken of as "him"
(singularly); that is, as all nations and kingdoms must

"serve" Israel (Isa. 60-12), even so must they "serve" our Lord and his Christ. This is not that we are "his Christ" separately, or individually, but collectively as one body.

And they sang a new song, saying, Thou art worthy to take the book, and to open the seals thereof; for thou wast slain, and hast redeemed us to God by thy blood out of every kindred, and tongue, and people, and nation. An hast made us unto our God kings and priests, and we SHALL REIGN ON EARTH! The fact that it is said we shall "reign on earth" confirms the words that the Church, which is the body of Christ, shall have part in his dominion, for the kingdoms of this world shall become the kingdom of "our Lord and His Christ."

Dangers of Denying the Father.

There are many honest souls who are anxious to obey the Voice of God and be baptized in the name of Jesus Christ, but they are intimidated by persons misconstruing the scripture which says, "He is antichrist, that denieth the Father and the Son." John 2:22.

There is no one who knows the word of God, and has been baptized in Jesus' name, that denies the Father and the Son. They acknowledge the Father and Son in Christ Jesus. To acknowledge the Father and the Son does not necessarily mean to believe in "three persons in the Godhead."

The Fatherhood of God is found only in the Son, who was God manifested in the flesh. The following portion of this article will be sufficient to convince any Godfearing person that they cannot deny the Father by being baptized in Jesus' name.

Whosoever denieth the Son, the same hath not the Father; but he that acknowledgeth the Son hath the Father ALSO. 1 John 2:23.

We desire to call the attention of the reader to the above quotation for prayerful consideration. While reading the above passage the words, "the Father also" drew my particular attention. And I believe it will help many to see God's purpose in these last days.

The thought before us is, that he that denieth the Son (Jesus Christ) the same has denied the Father ALSO. Why is this; is it not because Jesus and the Father are one? John 10:30. There is no scripture that says, "He that denieth the Father, the same hath not the son," but, to the contrary, all scriptures seem to be to the opposite. By this I mean that all scriptures identifies the Father in the Son. God was in Christ reconciling the world unto himself. 2 Cor. 5:19. God was manifest in the flesh. 1 Tim. 3:16. Therefore, when one turns from Christ he turns from God.

He that believeth not on the Son, the same believeth not on the Father; but he that believeth on the Son, believeth on the Father ALSO. Compare John 12:44; 14:1. The Jews believed that God would take their sins away (Jer. 31:31-34), but they did not believe Jesus had anything to do with it; and Jesus said, "If ye believe not that I am he, ye shall die in your sins." John 8:24.

He that knoweth not the Son, the same knoweth not the Father, but he that knoweth the Son, knoweth the Father ALSO. See John 8:19; 14:7. To know Christ is to know God the Father, for the mystery of God, the Father, is Christ. Col. 2:2, 9.

He that seeth not the Son, the same seeth not the Father; but he that seeth the Son, seeth the Father ALSO. John 12:45; 14:9.

He that loveth not the Son, the same loveth not the Father; but he that loveth the Son loveth the Father also. John 15:23, 24. To love God one must love Jesus. For Jesus and God are one and inseparable. If the Father and Son were two separate persons then we could love one and hate the other (as the Jews sought to do.) If you do not love Jesus you cannot love God, but you cannot love Jesus without loving God, for Jesus is God (manifest in the flesh, in a visible form).

If the above scriptures are true (and no one could honestly say they are not), why does not the same hold with the NAME used in baptism? Let us look at it from a scriptural standpoint.

He that baptizeth not in the name of the Son (Jesus), the same baptizeth not in the name of the Father; but he that baptizeth (or is baptized) in the name of the Son (Jesus), baptizeth (or, is baptized) in the name of the Father ALSO.

By the scriptures this is clearly proven, from the fact that the Commission given, as recorded by St. Matthew, to baptize in the name of the Father, and of the Son, and of the Holy Ghost (Mat. 28:18, 19); but on the day of Pentecost, and thereafter, according to the Book of Acts, all the disciples baptized in the name of Jesus (the Son) proving that they recognized it to be the name of the Father ALSO. See Acts 2:38, 8:12-16; 9:18 with Acts 22:16; Acts 10:47, 48; Acts 19:5.

All who are baptized in the name of Jesus **are** baptized in the name of the Father ALSO, but those who have not been baptized in the name of Jesus, have never been baptized in the name of the Father. The only way to fulfill the command of Jesus in Mat. 28:19 is to do as the Holy Ghost authorized on the day of Pentecost and carried out by the Apostles according to the Books of Acts.

The only way that a person can really "deny the Father" is to fail to acknowledge that Jesus is the true and only living God. I John. 5:20; Jude 25. When you are baptized in Jesus' name you thereby acknowledge that the Father, Son and Holy Ghost "are one" (1 John 5:7) and that in Christ Jesus dwelleth all the fullness of the Godhead in a bodily form. Cor. 2:9. Be not faithless, but believe. John 12:44, 45; 20:26-28.

CHAPTER VIII.

TRINITARIANISM.

"Wherefore the Lord said, Forasmuch as this people draw near me with their mouth and with their lips do honor me, but have removed their heart far from me AND THEIR FEAR TOWARD ME IS TAUGHT BY THE PRECEPTS OF MEN: therefore, behold I will proceed to do a marvelous work among this people, even a marvelous work and a wonder: for the wisdom of their wise men shall perish and the understanding of their prudent men shall be hid." Isa. 29: 13-14.

Today these Scriptures are again meeting their fulfillment even as it was at the close of the Jewish dispensation. Tradition has so filled the religious world that little regard is given to the WORD of GOD; for many honor God with their lips, but their heart is far from Him. They are willing at any time to uphold their traditions, at the expense of the WORD of GOD; and when one begins to speak against the "Trinitarian Doctrine," (God in three persons) great fear seems to come upon the people that such teaching is dishonoring God, and many even prophesying judgment to come upon those who think it a light against such tradition. They think it a light thing to ignore water baptism, in the Name of JESUS; the One Person God, and the Holy Ghost New Birth, which are clearly set forth in the Scriptures. They don't mind saying that water is nonessential. They don't mnid saying that Jesus is the Second Person in the "Trinity" when

Jesus, Himself, declares, "I AM THE FIRST and I AM THE LAST." Truly their fear towards Him is taught by the precepts of men!

Touching the Doctrine of the Trinity, the Apostles knew of no such thing; they knew nothing about three Spirits; they had no knowledge of three separate Persons in the Godhead; they had not been informed that the Holy Ghost, the Spirit of God, and the Spirit of Christ were the Spirits of three separate Persons. They knew of but One GOD, One Spirit and One LORD. They knew that God was a Spirit (John 4:24) and that the Lord was that Spirit (2 Cor. 3:17), and that Jesus Christ was that Lord. Com. Matt. 3:16; Luke 3:22; 1 Pet. 1:10-11; 2 Pet. 1:20-21.

The word "Trinity" is not found in the Bible from Genesis to Revelation. The term "Three Persons in the Godhead" has no place there. The phrase, "God the Father, God the Son and God the Holy Ghost," is unscriptural. Tradition has coined these terms, and thrust them forth into the religious world and hath obscured the glorious vision of the Mighty God, the Everlasting Father, in the Person of Jesus Christ.

In the second chapter of Colossians, the Apostle Paul directs his words to "them of Laodicea," and as many as have not seen His face in the flesh.

According to the Church Age, the Laodicean period is the present age, in which we are now living. This being true, his admonitions in this chapter should have a great bearing upon the minds and hearts of God's people at this time, for it is to them that he makes known his heart's desire that they might be comforted, knit together in love, and unto all riches of full assurance of understanding to the acknowledgement of the mystery of God, and of the Father, and of Christ, and further warns them against philosophy, vain deceit, tradition of men and the rudiments of the world. From this it appears that God gave unto him a foreknowledge of errors that were to come upon the world touching the Person of the Godhead; therefore, in mentioning of Christ, he declares that in Him dwelleth all the fullness of the Godhead bodily; and further adds, "And ye are complete in Him, which is the head over all principality and power."

God, foreseeing the fear that would come upon the people in proclaiming Jesus to be our God, prophesied beforehand, saying, "O Zion, that bringeth good tidings, get thee up into the high mountains; O Jerusalem, that bringeth good tidings, lift up thy voice with strength, lift it up and BE NOT AFRAID; say unto the cities of Judah, BEHOLD YOUR GOD! Behold, the Lord God will come with strong hand, and His arm shall rule for Him: behold his reward is with Him, and His work before Him. He shall feed His flock like a SHEPHERD." That this Shepherd is Jesus Christ, no one can deny. (John 10:14.) Yet, in the face of these words, many are afraid to proclaim that Jesus Christ is our God. Isa. 40:9-11.

We hereby quote a clipping of an article entitled, "Holy Trinity Feast." The writer says, "The Feast of the Holy Trinity was observed in many Catholic and some Protestant churches throughout the city, yesterday, with special services, in which particular attention was paid to the doctrine of the Trinity. This Feast Day is considered the **foundation** of all Feast Days, and the day of celebrating a mystery **which is not to be understood through human reason.**" He further states that there is no doubt the mystery cannot be understood. But who shall we believe, man or God? The WORD OF GOD declares that the Spirit will search all things, yea the deep things of God. He will teach us all things, and in this is included the mystery of God, and of the Father, and of Christ.

So long as man will endeavor to solve this mystery, apart from Christ Jesus, it will always be to him a mystery; but Christ is the true solution of all perplexing problems, for in Him are hid all the treasures of wisdom and knowledge. In Him dwelleth all the fullness of the Godhead in a bodily form. When the Disciples desired to see the Father, apart from Christ, He pointed them unto His own body, standing in their midst; and when He further made mention of the Comforter, the Holy Ghost, He again said, "You know Him; for He dwelleth with you and shall be in you." (John 14:9, 16, 17.) In this chapter, alone, is the mystery revealed.

In our spirit, we have always known but one God; but in our theology we have recognized three. If the Father, Son and Holy Ghost are three separate Persons, Spirits and Personalities, we have on our hands three separate, distinct Gods. But if Father, Son and Holy Spirit bear God's relationship to mankind, then it can be clearly seen that there is but One God: and that God is manifested in the Person of the Lord Jesus Christ; for God hath declared, "Thus saith the Lord, the King of Israel, and his Redeemer, the Lord of Hosts; I am the first, and I am the last; and beside me there is no God." (Isa. 44:6.) Jesus, the King of Israel, the Redeemer, declared, "I am Alpha and Omega, the first and the last. . . . Fear not; I am the first and the last; I am He that liveth and was dead, and behold, I am alive forevermore. Amen." (Rev. 1:11, 17, 18.) And in another place He says, "I am Alpha and Omega, the beginning and the end . . . he that overcometh shall inherit all things: and I will be his GOD and he shall be my son." (Rev. 21:6-7.) Here Jesus plainly declares Himself to be God. Compare this with 2 Cor. 6:16-18.

God help us to gird up the loins of our minds, be sober, and hope to the end for the grace that is to be brought unto us at the Revelation of Jesus Christ! Truly the time for this fulfillment is almost at hand. The glory of God is filling our vision; our eye has become single, and our body is being filled with light. We see no man save "JESUS ONLY." And we now, with open face, beholding as in a glass the glory of the Lord are changed into the same image from glory to glory, even as by the Spirit of the Lord. For God, Who commanded the light to shine out of darkness, hath shone in our hearts to give the light of the knowledge of the glory of God in the face of Jesus Christ. (2 Cor. 3:18, 4:6.)

CHAPTER IX.

THE REVIEW OF SOME ARTICLES

Since there are many who have taken it upon themselves to combat the revelation of Jesus Christ as the Mighty God, and have set forth their views in print for circulation, we hereby make a review of some points contained in them for the consideration of all scripture-loving children of God. Not for argument sake, God forbid, but for the sake of those who desire to know the truth regarding this great message that is confronting the religious world today.

In one publication the editor has set forth an article, entitled "The Tri-unity of God," the beginning of which an unscriptural quotation is used as a basis. It is evident that if the article starts wrong it will end up in the same manner. The following is the quotation from the Book of Ecclesiasticus (not Ecclesiastes), one of the books of the "Apocrypha"; "Seek not out things that are too hard for thee, neither search the things that are above thy strength. But what is commanded thee, think thereupon with reverence; for it is not needful for thee to see with thine eyes the things that are in secret." The writer further says: "With this injunction before us we are inclined to refrain from prying into the secret things that belong to God, and from meddling with that which God in His wisdom has seen fit to conceal from us."

Here is where we differ. In the first place he uses

an unscriptural quotation written many years before the birth of Christ, but since that time the Spirit of God has been poured out upon us and has given us an understanding. We hereby quote a passage of Scripture that will totally offset the entire premise of the article: "But the Comforter, the Holy Ghost, whom the Father will send in .my name, he shall teach you ALL THINGS"; Howbeit, when he, the Spirit of TRUTH, is come, he will guide you into all truth. * * * He will show you things to come. * * * He shall receive of mine, and shall shew it unto you. All things that the Father hath are mine; therefore, I said that he shall take of mine and shall SHEW it UNTO YOU." These are the words of Jesus himself. We further take the words of the great Apostle Paul: "But as it is written, eye hath not seen, nor ear heard, neither hath it entered into the heart of man, the things which God hath prepared for them that love Him. But God hath REVEALED them unto us by His Spirit; for the Spirit SEARCHES ALL THINGS, yea, the DEEP things of God." Brethren, which are we to believe? As for me, give me the Bible.

If the Spirit has come, according to the Word of God, his duty is to "reveal," "search," "teach" and "guide" us into all truth. Why then should we let Satan fill us with fear when the Holy Spirit begins his great work of revelation of the mysteries that have been hid for ages? If God has not revealed it to you, why should it be thought that He is not revealing his secrets to others? If it is the Spirit's work to search into the DEEP THINGS of God, who can hinder him? Our duty is to trust God and follow on.

The article further states that the term "Trinity"

appeared for the first time in the writing of Theophilus at the close of the second century. This proves itself that it was not known in apostolic times. It was about this time that the "tares began to appear with the wheat." All the apostles were dead (while men slept), and it was then that the enemy sowed the tares; but it was in the third century that it really was established. It evidently was not of God, for its very introduction and continuance have brought a great "degree of strife" in the religious world, and after its formation the Church went into the most miserable darkness that ever came upon any people.

As to the present message "leading us into all sorts of extravagant and erroneous teaching concerning the person of Christ," Jesus declares of the Holy Spirit: "He shall glorify me." "He shall testify of me." (John 15:26; 16:14.) What could these words mean other than that the Spirit would exalt "the person of Christ"? What honor, what glory is there that is too "extravagant" for the "person" of Christ? Or what could be more "extravagant" than the words of Thomas when he cried, "MY LORD and MY GOD!" as he beheld the "person of Christ"? What about Peter's "extravagant" words when he said, "God (the Spirit, John 4:24) has made this Jesus (personal) both LORD and Christ"? What would be more "extravagant" than to identify the "person of Christ" with the Holy One of Israel who said, 'I am the first, and I am the last; and beside me there is no God." (Stop and look up these scriptures: Isa. 43:3, 14, 15; 44:6-8; 45:11; 47:4; 48:12, 17; Psa. 16:10, 11 and Acts 2:27, 31.) What could be more "extravagant" than to say, "He (his person) was in the world and the world was made by Him"? Or what could be more "extravagant" than these words of the

Apostle Paul, "For by him all things were created, that are in heaven, and that are in earth, visible and invisible, whether they be thrones, or dominions, or principalities, or powers; all things were created by him, and for him: And he is before all things, and by him all things consist. And he is the head of the body, the church: who is the beginning, the firstborn from the dead; that in all things he might have pre-eminence." (Col. 1:16-18.)

Look in the Book of Revelations and see the "extravagance" concerning the "person of Christ." Behold, He declares in His own words, "I am Alpha and Omega, the beginning and the ending, saith the Lord, which is, which was, and which is to come, THE ALMIGHTY" (that is the name He bore when Abraham rejoiced to see His day and was made glad, see John 8:56-58, Ex. 6:3). And when John turned to see the "person" that spoke, behold! it was the "person" of the Son of Man, and He said, "Fear not; I am the FIRST AND THE LAST; I am he that liveth, was DEAD: and, behold! I am alive for evermore, Amen." Listen to these "extravagant" words: "I am Alpha and Omega, the beginning and the end. * * * He that overcometh shall inherit all things; and I WILL BE HIS GOD, and he shall be MY Son." (Rev. 1:8-18, and 21:6-7.) After considering these scriptures and many others, too numerous to mention, how could any man that has the love of Christ in his heart honestly accuse a brother or sister of being too "extravagant" in their teaching concerning the person of Christ? Oh, beloved, come and magnify the Lord with me, and let us exalt His name together!

After taking the original word "Elohim" to prove

that there are three persons in the Godhead (because the word is a plural noun), and setting forth in blackface type, throughout the paragraph on this subject, "Gods, Gods, Gods, Gods," the writer then further down states that we must be careful lest we drift into "Tritheism—the doctrine of three gods—to which Trinitarianism is said to come so dangerously near." Now this is very inconsistent, for if "Elohim" means Gods and proves that there are three separate persons in the Godhead, what have we but "tritheism" before us? The word "Elohim" embraces a plurality of the "attributes" of the Holy Spirit, rather than a plurality of "persons," and this is clearly shown forth in Gen. 3:22, where man, after being in the image of God, in holiness, wisdom, knowledge and authority, is said to "become as one of us," knowing good and evil. The knowledge of good and evil was an attribute of the Spirit, and when man came into possession of it he was said to "become as one of us." This verse alone proves that the plural pronoun is in reference to attributes and not persons. If the Godhead consists of three separate persons, personalities, or bodies, why is it that man, who is made in His image, does not consist of three separate persons, personalities, or bodies? Beloved, let us stop and consider these things. Beware of tradition of men, philosophy and vain deceit, for in Christ dwelleth all the fullness of the Godhead bodily. (Col. 2:10-11.)

Further, our brother asserts: "We cannot hope to penetrate the 'inaccessible' mystery of the Godhead in its trinity of persons or distinctions. We exclaim with Isaiah: 'Verily, thou art a God that hideth thyself, O God of Israel, the Savior.' Nor is it necessary that we should." We are told that the Spirit would "penetrate," investigate, or search all things; yea, the deep things of God. (I believe the word of God.) But as to God hiding himself, let us look at the word and see from whom He "hideth" himself. In Luke 10:21-22, we find that the mystery of the Father and the Son is "hidden" from the wise and prudent. (See Luke 19:41-44.) In John 12:35-36, it is clearly set forth that God of Israel, the Saviour, hid himself from those who would not "walk" in the light while they had the light." Is there any wonder then that so many are groping in darkness today, opposing the revelation of Jesus as the Mighty God of Israel, the Saviour?

"We are confronted with such a difficulty in the use of the word "persons." Hence we need new words," says our brother. But why not use the scriptural terms, "manifestation," God in "three manifestations," instead of God in "three persons"? (See John 1:31; 1 Cor. 12:7; 1 Tim. 3:16.) These were the terms used by

Sabellius.

The doctrine of Sabellius was more scripturally based than that of the Athanasian Creed." So great was his (Athanasius) influence in the propagation of the trinitarian doctrine as sanctioned by the Nicean Council, that the Church (Catholic) honored him as the "Great," and as the "Father of Orthodoxy." It also should not be overlooked that it was after the doctrine of the Trinitarians had become the orthodox faith of the Church that the Church went into papal darkness. After reading the articles carefully, one is no nearer the solution of the mystery than when begun. To say, "The threeness is in the oneness, and the oneness is in the threeness" is like starting out and ending where you started from without getting anywhere. The only solution of the mystery is that "In Him (Christ Jesus) dwelleth all the fullness of the Godhead bodily."

The Son.

At present there is a great controversy about the Sonship of Christ, and some are being made to believe that to behold Jesus Christ as the "Mighty God," the "Everlasting Father," is to deny the Son. Some say we are denying the Son, and others say we are denying the Father. Now which is it?

To believe that Jesus Christ is the Son of God means more than a confession of the lips. How many are there today who acknowledge with their mouth that Jesus is the Son of God, but yet have not let Him come into their life. Are they born of God? I tell you, NAY! To believe that Jesus is the Son of God must be made manifest by letting His life come into you, that you may live the life of the Son. The devils confessed with their voice that Jesus was the Son of God, but they did not manifest the life of the Son. As for those who see in Jesus that He is God, their proof that they believe in the Sonship of Christ is from the fact that they are following in His steps, endeavoring to fashion their lives after the pattern. Christ, "as a Son." (Heb. 3:6.)

Separate Identity Theory.

There are some who desire to prove the "separate identity" of the Father and Son, but this is wholly out of the mind and will of God, according to the words of Jesus Christ and the apostles. Nowhere in the New Testament did Jesus attempt to establish or teach a separate identity, but rather to the contrary.

The Prophets Witness.

In going back to the prophets as a foundation, we will find many passages that will completely overthrow the "separate identity" theory. David declared, "Our God shall come." (Psa. 50:1-6.) And JEHOVAH swore unto David, "Of the fruit of thy body will I set upon thy throne." (Psa. 132:11.) There is no separation there, for Jesus was the one to sit on David's throne.

Solomon in prophecy asks, "Who hath ascended into heaven, or descended? Who hath gathered the winds in his fist? Who hath bound the waters in a garment? Who hath established the ends of the earth? What is His name, and what is His Son's name, if thou canst tell?" And Jesus answers "No man hath ascended up to heaven, but He that came down from heaven, even the Son of Man which is in heaven." (Prov. 30:4; John 3:13.) Is there a separate identity here?

Isaiah declared that the "child" born, the "Son" given was to be called "the Mighty God, the Everlasting Father." Is there a separate identity there? Read Isa. 40:1-11, compare it with Matt. 3:1-11 and

John 10:1, etc. Is there a separate identity there be-
tween God, the Shepherd and Jesus the Shepherd?
Read from Isaiah 40th chapter carefully over to the
54th chapter, and notice how often the Lord of Hosts,
the Redeemer, the King of Israel, the Holy One of
Israel is mentioned as God the Saviour, the First and
Last. You will find no separate identity there. In
Isaiah 54:5, the Bridegroom, the Husband of the
Bride, the Church, is the LORD OF HOSTS, the
REDEEMER, the HOLY ONE of Israel, and further
declares, "The GOD OF THE WHOLE EARTH
SHALL HE BE CALLED." There is no separate
identity there.

Look at Daniel's vision of the Ancient of Days
and the Son of Man coming in the clouds of heaven,
and then turn to Rev. 1:8-18 and notice the Son of
Man with hair like the ANCIENT OF DAYS. You
say the ANCIENT OF DAYS is God, and the SON
OF MAN is Jesus; but compare Isa. 44:6-7 with Rev.
1:17-18, and you will find it impossible to show a
separation of identity there.

Listen to Zechariah in speaking of the JEHOVAH
"which stretcheth forth the heavens, and layeth the
foundation of the earth. * * * I will pour upon the
house of David * * * the spirit of grace and supplica-
tions: And they SHALL LOOK UPON ME WHOM
THEY HAVE PIERCED, and they shall mourn for
HIM, as one mourneth for his only son. (Zech. 12:1,
10.) In this we find "ME" and "HIM" referring to the
one and selfsame person.

Jesus' Testimony.

That Jesus did not intend to establish a separate identity between himself as Father and Son is clearly shown by the following: "I am not alone, but I and the Father that SENT me." "He that SENT me is with me." "He that seeth me seeth Him that SENT me." "He that believeth on me, believeth not on me, but on Him that SENT me." (See John 8:16, 29; 12:44, 45.)

"Ye neither know me, nor my Father: if ye had known me, ye should have known my Father also." "I and my Father are one." (Here is where the Jews understood Him to mean that he was the Father and took up stones to stone Him.) "If you had known me, ye should have known the Father also: from henceforth ye know him and hath seen him." "He that hath seen me hath seen the Father: how sayeth thou then, Show us the Father? Believeth thou not that I am in the Father, and the Father in me?" These are the words of Jesus himself. Can it be said that there is a separate identity of the Father and Son here? "Destroy this temple and in three days I WILL RAISE IT." "Him GOD RAISED UP THE THIRD DAY." (John 2:19, and Acts 10:40.) There is undoubtedly no separate identity here.

Peter's Testimony.

On the day of Pentecost Peter declared Jesus to be "both" the LORD and the ANOINTED of the LORD, saying, "God hath made this Jesus, who ye have crucified, 'both' Lord and Christ." In other words, "The Spirit (John 4:24) has proven this Jesus,

* * * to be both JEHOVAH and His Anointed." It was this revelation, no doubt, that caused Peter to proclaim baptism in the "name of JESUS CHRIST" as identical to the commission to "baptize in the name of the Father, and of the Son, and of the Holy Ghost." For the Father, Son and Holy Ghost were one and the self-same person, for in Christ Jesus dwelleth all the fullness of the Godhead bodily. (Col. 2:9.)

To say that the "Word was a part of God" is unscriptural, for the Bible says, "THE WORD WAS GOD," and not a "part of God." "And the WORD was made flesh" and called "Immanuel, which being interpreted is, GOD WITH US." There is no argument with us at all as to the SONSHIP of Christ being manifested in the days of His flesh, but now are we sons of God, and His life as a Son is made manifest in our mortal flesh. Though we have known Christ after the flesh, says the Apostle Paul, yet now henceforth know we him no more. (II Cor. 5:16.)

What Think Ye of Christ?

Another article published, entitled "What Think Ye of Christ? Whose Son is He?" carries the wrong impression to the people of that passage of Scripture. Let us notice that it does not say, "What think ye of Jesus of Nazareth?" but of "Christ." All the Jews believed in Christ and looked for Him to come (Luke 2:15; John 1:25, 41; 4:25, 29; 7:26, 27, 31, 41, 42; 10:24; 12:34), but the question among them was whether JESUS was the CHRIST. Many believed He was, while others said "Nay!" It was for this reason that Jesus asked the Pharisees their opinion of the CHRIST, and whose Son (after the flesh) is He. And when they said "David's Son," it was here that He astonished them by proving that the Christ was both David's LORD and SON. And if the Spirit said that the Christ was both David's SON and LORD, why should they reject Him. That shut their mouths from that time forth. They saw only one side of the office of the Christ. Thus it is today, many see only the one side of the office of Christ, and are fighting like one "mad" since Christ is being revealed as BOTH FATHER and SON, crying "antichrist," when in fact their own attitude in opposing the exaltation of Christ Jesus is more the spirit of antichrist than those they are accusing.

In conclusion, let us notice that only through the acknowledgment first that Jesus Christ is the Son of God will any man be able to get the revelation that He is God himself. No man that denies his Sonship will ever call Him God. The Jews deny His Sonship. Do they call him God? No! The Mohammedans deny His Sonship. Do they call Him God? No! The Unitarians deny His Sonship or divinity. Do they call Him God? No! But we acknowledge His Sonship by the manifestation of His life in us and now through the Spirit's revelation behold in Him the Mighty God of Jacob, the Everlasting Father, the coming Prince of Peace.

THE END

TITLES in THIS SERIES

9. RUSSELL KELSO CARTER ON "FAITH HEALING." R. Kelso Carter, *THE ATONEMENT FOR SIN AND SICKNESS* (Boston, 1884) *"FAITH HEALING" REVIEWED AFTER TWENTY YEARS* (Boston, 1897)

10. Daniels, W. H., *DR. CULLIS AND HIS WORK* (Boston, [1885])

11. HOLINESS TRACTS DEFENDING THE MINISTRY OF WOMEN. Luther Lee, *"WOMAN'S RIGHT TO PREACH THE GOSPEL; A SERMON, AT THE ORDINATION OF REV. MISS ANTOINETTE L. BROWN, AT SOUTH BUTLER, WAYNE COUNTY, N. Y., SEPT. 15, 1853"* (Syracuse, 1853) *bound with* B. T. Roberts, *ORDAINING WOMEN* (Rochester, 1891) *bound with* Catherine (Mumford) Booth, *"FEMALE MINISTRY; OR, WOMAN'S RIGHT TO PREACH THE GOSPEL . . ."* (London, n. d.) *bound with* Fannie (McDowell) Hunter, *WOMEN PREACHERS* (Dallas, 1905)

12. LATE NINETEENTH CENTURY REVIVALIST TEACHINGS ON THE HOLY SPIRIT. D. L. Moody, *SECRET POWER OR THE SECRET OF SUCCESS IN CHRISTIAN LIFE AND WORK* (New York, [1881]) *bound with* J. Wilbur Chapman, *RECEIVED YE THE HOLY GHOST?* (New York, [1894]) *bound with* R. A. Torrey, *THE BAPTISM WITH THE HOLY SPIRIT* (New York, 1895 & 1897)

13. SEVEN "JESUS ONLY" TRACTS. Andrew D. Urshan, *THE DOCTRINE OF THE NEW BIRTH, OR, THE PERFECT WAY TO ETERNAL LIFE* (Cochrane, Wis., 1921) *bound with* Andrew Urshan, *THE ALMIGHTY GOD IN THE LORD JESUS CHRIST* (Los Angeles, 1919) *bound with* Frank J. Ewart, *THE REVELATION OF JESUS CHRIST* (St. Louis, n. d.) *bound with* G. T. Haywood, *THE BIRTH OF THE SPIRIT IN THE DAYS OF THE APOSTLES* (Indianapolis, n. d.) *DIVINE NAMES AND TITLES OF JEHOVAH* (Indianapolis, n. d.) *THE FINEST OF THE WHEAT* (Indianapolis, n. d.) *THE VICTIM OF THE FLAMING SWORD* (Indianapolis, n. d.)

14. THREE EARLY PENTECOSTAL TRACTS. D. Wesley Myland, *THE LATTER RAIN COVENANT AND PENTECOSTAL POWER* (Chicago, 1910) *bound with* G. F. Taylor, *THE SPIRIT AND THE BRIDE* (n. p., [1907?]) *bound with* B. F. Laurence, *THE APOSTOLIC FAITH RESTORED* (St. Louis, 1916)

15. Fairchild, James H., *OBERLIN: THE COLONY AND THE COLLEGE, 1833-1883* (Oberlin, 1883)

16. Figgis, John B., *KESWICK FROM WITHIN* (London, [1914])

17. Finney, Charles G., *Lectures to Professing Christians* (New York, 1837)

18. Fleisch, Paul, *Die Moderne Gemeinschaftsbewegung in Deutschland* (Leipzig, 1912)

19. Six Tracts by W. B. Godbey. *Spiritual Gifts and Graces* (Cincinnati, [1895]) *The Return of Jesus* (Cincinnati, [1899?]) *Work of the Holy Spirit* (Louisville, [1902]) *Church—Bride—Kingdom* (Cincinnati, [1905]) *Divine Healing* (Greensboro, [1909]) *Tongue Movement, Satanic* (Zarephath, N. J., 1918)

20. Gordon, Earnest B., *Adoniram Judson Gordon* (New York, [1896])

21. Hills, A. M., *Holiness and Power for the Church and the Ministry* (Cincinnati, [1897])

22. Horner, Ralph C., *From the Altar to the Upper Room* (Toronto, [1891])

23. McDonald, William and John E. Searles, *The Life of Rev. John S. Inskip* (Boston, [1885])

24. LaBerge, Agnes N. O., *What God Hath Wrought* (Chicago, n. d.)

25. Lee, Luther, *Autobiography of the Rev. Luther Lee* (New York, 1882)

26. McLean, A. and J. W. Easton, *Penuel; or, Face to Face with God* (New York, 1869)

27. McPherson, Aimee Semple, *This Is That: Personal Experiences Sermons and Writings* (Los Angeles, [1919])

28. Mahan, Asa, *Out of Darkness into Light* (London, 1877)

29. The Life and Teaching of Carrie Judd Montgomery Carrie Judd Montgomery, *"Under His Wings": The Story of My Life* (Oakland, [1936]) Carrie F. Judd, *The Prayer of Faith* (New York, 1880)

30. The Devotional Writings of Phoebe Palmer Phoebe Palmer, *The Way of Holiness* (52nd ed., New York, 1867) *Faith and Its Effects* (27th ed., New York, n. d., orig. pub. 1854)

31. Wheatley, Richard, *THE LIFE AND LETTERS OF MRS. PHOEBE PALMER* (New York, 1881)

32. Palmer, Phoebe, ed., *PIONEER EXPERIENCES* (New York, 1868)

33. Palmer, Phoebe, *THE PROMISE OF THE FATHER* (Boston, 1859)

34. Pardington, G. P., *TWENTY-FIVE WONDERFUL YEARS, 1889-1914: A POPULAR SKETCH OF THE CHRISTIAN AND MISSIONARY ALLIANCE* (New York, [1914])

35. Parham, Sarah E., *THE LIFE OF CHARLES F. PARHAM, FOUNDER OF THE APOSTOLIC FAITH MOVEMENT* (Joplin, [1930])

36. THE SERMONS OF CHARLES F. PARHAM. Charles F. Parham, *A VOICE CRYING IN THE WILDERNESS* (4th ed., Baxter Springs, Kan., 1944, orig. pub. 1902) *THE EVERLASTING GOSPEL* (n.p., n.d., orig. pub. 1911)

37. Pierson, Arthur Tappan, *FORWARD MOVEMENTS OF THE LAST HALF CENTURY* (New York, 1905)

38. *PROCEEDINGS OF HOLINESS CONFERENCES, HELD AT CINCINNATI, NOVEMBER 26TH, 1877, AND AT NEW YORK, DECEMBER 17TH, 1877* (Philadelphia, 1878)

39. *RECORD OF THE CONVENTION FOR THE PROMOTION OF SCRIPTURAL HOLINESS HELD AT BRIGHTON, MAY 29TH, TO JUNE 7TH, 1875* (Brighton, [1896?])

40. Rees, Seth Cook, *MIRACLES IN THE SLUMS* (Chicago, [1905?])

41. Roberts, B. T., *WHY ANOTHER SECT* (Rochester, 1879)

42. Shaw, S. B., ed., *ECHOES OF THE GENERAL HOLINESS ASSEMBLY* (Chicago, [1901])

43. THE DEVOTIONAL WRITINGS OF ROBERT PEARSALL SMITH AND HANNAH WHITALL SMITH. [R]obert [P]earsall [S]mith, *HOLINESS THROUGH FAITH: LIGHT ON THE WAY OF HOLINESS* (New York, [1870]) [H]annah [W]hitall [S]mith, *THE CHRISTIAN'S SECRET OF A HAPPY LIFE*, (Boston and Chicago, [1885])

44. [S]mith, [H]annah [W]hitall, *THE UNSELFISHNESS OF GOD AND HOW I DISCOVERED IT* (New York, [1903])

45. Steele, Daniel, *A SUBSTITUTE FOR HOLINESS; OR, ANTINOMIANISM REVIVED* (Chicago and Boston, [1899])

46. Tomlinson, A. J., *THE LAST GREAT CONFLICT* (Cleveland, 1913)

47. Upham, Thomas C., *THE LIFE OF FAITH* (Boston, 1845)

48. Washburn, Josephine M., *HISTORY AND REMINISCENCES OF THE HOLINESS CHURCH WORK IN SOUTHERN CALIFORNIA AND ARIZONA* (South Pasadena, [1912?])